Women and Labour in Late Colonial India

The Bengal Jute Industry

Samita Sen's history of labouring women in Calcutta in the nineteenth and early twentieth centuries considers how social constructions of gender shaped their lives. She demonstrates how – in contrast to the experience of their male counterparts – the long-term trends in the Indian economy devalued women's labour, establishing patterns of urban migration and changing gender equations within the family. She relates these trends to the spread of dowry giving, enforced widowhood and child marriage.

The book provides insight into the trials and tribulations of poor urban women who were often perceived as prostitutes and social pariahs by the middle classes and upper echelons of society. Even trade unions refused to address their problems seriously and women remained on the margins of organised political protest. Eventually, over the course of the period, women workers in the jute industry declined from 25 per cent to two per cent of the workforce.

The study makes a significant contribution to the understanding of Indian social and economic history and to notions of gender construction.

SAMITA SEN is a lecturer in the Department of History, Calcutta University

Cambridge Studies in Indian History and Society 3

Cambridge Studies in Indian History and Society will publish monographs on the history and anthropology of modern India. In addition to its primary scholarly focus, the series will also include work of an interdisciplinary nature which will contribute to contemporary social and cultural debates about Indian history and society. In this way, the series will further the general development of historical and anthropological knowledge and attract a wider readership than that concerned with India alone.

1 C. A. Bayly, *Empire and Information: Intelligence Gathering and Social Communication in India, 1780–1880*   0 521 57085 9 (hardback) 0 521 663601 (paperback)

2 Ian Copland, *The Princes of India in the Endgame of Empire, 1917–1947*   0 521 57179 0

Women and Labour in Late Colonial India

The Bengal Jute Industry

Samita Sen

CAMBRIDGE
UNIVERSITY PRESS

PUBLISHED BY THE PRESS SYNDICATE OF THE UNIVERSITY OF CAMBRIDGE
The Pitt Building, Trumpington Street, Cambridge CB2 1RP

CAMBRIDGE UNIVERSITY PRESS
The Edinburgh Building, Cambridge CB2 2RU, UK http://www.cup.cam.ac.uk
40 West 20th Street, New York, NY 10011–4211, USA http: //www.cup.org
10 Stamford Road, Oakleigh, Melbourne 3166, Australia

First published 1999

Printed in the United Kingdom at the University Press, Cambridge

Typeset in Plantin 10/12 [CE]

A catalogue record for this book is available from the British Library

Library of Congress cataloging in publication data
Sen, Samita.
Women and labour in late colonial India: the Bengal jute industry / Samita Sen.
     p.   cm. – (Cambridge studies in Indian history and society: 3)
Includes bibliographical references and index.
ISBN 0 521 45363 1
1. Women – Employment – India – Bengal.
2. Women – India – Bengal – Social conditions.
3. Women – India – Bengal – Economic conditions.
4. Jute industry – India – Bengal.
I. Title.   II. Series.
HD6190.B46S457   1999
331.4′0954′14 – dc21   98–38080   CIP

ISBN 0521 45363 1 hardback

Contents

Tables

Acknowledgements

An early version of this book was submitted for the fellowship competition (1990) at Trinity College, Cambridge. It has since been rewritten for submission as a Ph.D dissertation (1992) to Cambridge University. In this rather protracted process, the support of many friends and colleagues has been invaluable.

My supervisor, Dr R. S. Chandavarkar, has been the prop and mainstay of this project. His own writings on Bombay textile workers have inspired many of the ideas in this book. I doubt these are sufficiently acknowledged in the footnotes. His help extended from encouragement to write and think to a general supervision of my well-being in Cambridge.

Professor T. Raychaudhuri, supervising my work at Oxford, provided many critical insights. Dr Rosalind O'Hanlon read drafts at various stages and offered advice and encouragement. Dr Hilary Standing and Dr Gordon Johnson examined my Ph.D thesis. They gave many valuable suggestions. My teachers in Calcutta University have always taken an interest. I thank Professor Rajat K. Ray for his continuing support of my work. But for Dr Tapati Guha Thakurta's and Dr Hari Vasudevan's initial guidance, this research might well have been impossible. Dr Ranajit Dasgupta has been extremely generous with his time and material.

This book has been enriched by comments and suggestion from many others. I would like to thank my father, Sandip, and my brother, Suhit. They also painstakingly edited various drafts. Dr Joya Chatterjee, Dr Vivek Dhareshwar and Dr Hari Vasudevan helped to give final shape to a recalcitrant manuscript.

Friends in *Sachetana* provided the initial inspiration for this study. Joyanti, my mother, first induced me to think about 'women'. Professor Nirmala Banerjee's investigations into women's work in Bengal was my starting point. Dr Ratnabali Chatterjee's research on the history of prostitution helped clarify many of my arguments. Professor Jasodhara Bagchi, Bela Bandopadhyay, Rajashri Dasgupta,

Madhusree Dutta and Sutapa Neogi supported this work in uncountable ways.

My fellow 'jute researchers' provide sustained companionship. My work has been enlivened by discussions and, more particularly, arguments with Subho Basu, Arjan de Haan and Parimal Ghosh.

This book, and its author, enjoyed many homes. In Cambridge and in Delhi, Joya, Prakash and Kartik have always shared theirs. In Delhi, Sarbajeet, Subha and Mia have patiently put up with my eccentric demands. In London, Sunip and Ragini, Indira, Shyamal and Rohini, Sunrita, Vipul and Ishan extended the warmest hospitality. Many friends shared the pleasures and pains of this writing. I use this occasion to remember Ali Alavi, Arijit Banerjee, Sudeshna Banerjee, Dwaipayan Bhattacharya, Charu Chakrabarty, Lakshmi Daniel, Damayanti Dutta, Sugato Ghose, Nandini Gooptu, Rama Goyal, Sharmistha Pal, Sucharita Roy, Jayasree Roychoudhury, Somak Raychaudhury and Ajay Skaria.

I thank Laura Cordy for her unfailing assistance with the mysteries of the word processor. Srila Baptista gave invaluable help with the bibliography and the map.

I wish to thank the staff of West Bengal State Archives, National Library, Secretariat Library, the office of the Deputy Inspector General of Police, Commercial Library, Bengal Chamber of Commerce Library, Bangiya Sahitya Parishad and Chaitanya Library in Calcutta, Joykrishna Library in Uttarpara, the Bally Library, National Archives of India and the Nehru Memorial Museum and Library in Delhi, Bihar State Archives in Patna, the India Office Library and Records in London, and the Cambridge University Library. Dr Lionel Carter at the Centre of South Asian Studies (Cambridge) and Ms Joan Auld of the Dundee University Library gave invaluable assistance, especially with voluminous private papers. Mr Shakti Roy, Librarian, Ananda Bazar Patrika, gave me permission to delve into their old files. He also made it possible to reproduce the photograph appearing on the cover.

I would also like to thank those who have patiently answered my many queries: Ms Shanti Pasricha, Mr R. Dasgupta, Sri Satyajit Choudhuri, Mr P. S. Thapa of Thomas Duff & Co., Mr D. Gupta of the National Jute Mills, Mr P. Dasgupta and Mr S. Dhara of Fort Gloster Jute Mill, Mr H. Hazra of the Howrah Mills, Mr Surya Sen, Mr C. N. Chakravarty and Mr Sarit Ray of the Indian Jute Mills Association, Mr P. Dasgupta and Mr S. Sengupta of the Bengal Chamber of Commerce and Ms Subha Dasgupta of the Calcutta Nursing College.

The women workers of Nuddea Jute Mill, Kankinara Jute Mill, Gourepur Jute Mill, Fort Gloster Jute Mill, Howrah Jute Mill and

Titagarh Jute Mills indulged my many unreasonable demands on their time. To them I owe many of the fundamental insights that inform this book. I especially thank Sulekha Das of Nuddea Jute Mill who took me around the Naihati-Kankinara mill areas.

Kakoli Sinha and Subhayan Ganguly, who have assisted my research, have my very special gratitude.

The research and the writing of this book were aided by financial grants from various sources. I wish to thank Oxford University, the Manjusree Birla Trust, the State Bank of India and the Cambridge Commonwealth Fund, Cambridge, for their assistance. I thank, especially, the Master and Fellows of Trinity College (Cambridge) for their generosity during my time as a graduate student and then as a fellow.

I thank Professor Amiya Bagchi and Dr Nirmal Chandra for their assistance in making this project possible. I remember with gratitude Dr Anil Seal's help and support during my stay in Trinity. Professor Goutam Chattopadhyay and Dr Manju Chattopadhyay have always given of their time, experience and affection.

To fully thank my mother, Joyanti, and my brothers, Suhit and Seshadri, would take too long. My father and I shared this interest in labour which was his particular field of expertise first as a 'personnel man' and later as a 'labour lawyer'. I dedicate this book to his memory.

Acronyms and abbreviations

BCCI	Bengal Chamber of Commerce and Industry
BCMU	Bengal Chatkal Mazdoor Union
BJWU	Bengal Jute Workers Union
BP	Benthall Papers
BPI	Bolshevik Party of India
BSA	Bihar State Archives, Patna
CID	Criminal Investigation Department
Comm. Comm.	Commerce Department Commerce Branch
CPI	Communist Party of India
CSAS	Centre for South Asian Studies, Cambridge
DIG	Deputy Inspector General of Police
DUL	Dundee University Library
EPW	*Economic and Political Weekly*
FA	Report on the Working of the Factories Act in Bengal
HPC	Home Political Confidential
IB	Intelligence Bureau
IESHR	*Indian Economic and Social History Review*
IFC	Indian Factory Commission, 1891
IFLC	Indian Factory Labour Commission, Morison, 1908
IJMA	Indian Jute Mills Association
IJMAR	*Report of the Indian Jute Mills Association*
IOL	Indian Office Library and Records, London
JAMWI	*Journal of the Association of Medical Women of India*
Judl.	Judicial Department
LEC	Labour Enquiry Commission, Calcutta, 1896
LIC	Labour Investigation Committee, An Enquiry into Conditions of Labour in the Jute Mill Industry in India, Calcutta, 1946
MRD	Manager's Report to the Directors
NA	National Archives of India, Delhi

RCLI	*Report of the Royal Commission on Labour in India*, London, 1931
TDP	Thomas Duff & Co. Papers
UP	Uttar Pradesh (formerly United Provinces)
WBSA	West Bengal State Archives, Calcutta

Glossary

Months:

Vaishakh	April–May
Jaistha	May–June
Ashar	June–July
Sravana	July–August
Bhadra	August–September
Aswin	September–October
Kartik	October–November
Agrahayan	November–December
Poush	December–January
Magh	January–February
Phalgun	February–March
Chaitra	March–April
abarjana	garbage
abru	veil
aghani	main winter rice crop in Bihar
akhara	gymnasium; society for physical culture; Baishnab centre
andar	women's quarters in the house
anna	one-sixteenth of the rupee
anna	cooked rice
antahpur	inner apartments of the house
anturgha	delivery room
arkathis	recruiting agents for tea gardens
atta	coarse flour
ayurveda	herbal medicine
baboo (also babu)	Bengali clerk in European managed business
badli	temporary worker

badmash	rogue
bahinji	respectful form of address for sister
bairagi (also vairagi)	a Baishnab; a caste; a mendicant
bairer	outside
baper bari	married woman's natal home
barababu	Head Clerk
basti (also bustee)	slum
bazar	market
beshya	a prostitute
bhadoi	autumn crop
bhadralok	lit. gentleman, respectable men of the middle class
bhadramahila	lit. gentlewoman, respectable women of the middle class
bhaga	job-sharing
bhita	home
bibaha	marriage
bidhaba	widow
bidhabasrama	shelter home for widows
bighas	one-third of an acre
bihao	marriage
biri	tobacco wrapped in tobacco leaf, like a cigarette
bishakta	poisonous
burqa	cloak with veil covering entire body
chapati	hand-made bread
charka	spinning wheel
chaudhuri	recruiter; supervisor
chawls	slums
cheerah	flattened rice
chhotolok	lower classes; manual worker
chullahs	open oven
churi	marriage
coolie (also cooly)	worker
dai	midwife
dalal	agent
dayabhaga	Bengal school of Hindu law of inheritance
dhenki	manual rice-pounder
dhopanis	laundresses
durwans	gatekeeper, security man, armed retainers

garbhadan (also gauna)	consummation ceremony
ghari	clock
ghats	river front
ghee (also ghi)	clarified butter
gherao	surround in protest
goonda	ruffian
griha	home
gurkha	ethnic group from Nepal; security guards
hartal	strike
hasuli	heavy bangle, usually of silver
hat	local market
haathi	elephant
Holi	spring festival of colours
itar	lower classes (derogatory)
izzat	honour
jalacharaniya	castes who can serve brahmins water
jamadar	sweeper or guard
jandrel	aggressive and assertive
jangi	militant
jhara	token issued to women workers to leave the mill for nursing
jharoonis	sweepers
jhum	slash and burn cultivation
kabuli	pathan moneylender
kal	machine
kaliyuga	the last age of sin before doom according to Hindu mythology
kaprawallis	hawkers of cloth
khabo	eat
khatbo	work
khichuri	simple preparation of rice and lentils
khoraki	subsistence allowance
khoyee	fluffed rice
kshata	sore
kukri	sharp knife
kulakalanka	disgrace of the exogamous kin group
kulin	highest grade among brahmins
kutcha	mud huts
lakhs	hundred thousand
Lakshmi	Hindu goddess of wealth; ideal housewife

laraku	militant
lathi	stick
ma (also maiji, mairam, mataji)	mother
madrasis (also madrassis)	lit. of Madras, used for people south of Orissa
magh (also magi)	lit. woman (derogatory)
mahajan	moneylender
maro	attack
mattha	butter milk
maunds	unit of weight varying from about 15 to 45 kilograms
meheraru	woman; wife
melas	fairs
mistri	workman
mooree	puffed rice
moorkhe	fluffed rice with jaggery
mota	Shia marriage
nika	second or subsequent marriages for Muslim women
paithoo	marriage
palkhi	palanquin
panchayat	self-governing institution
panibharin	women who fetch water for wages
panwallis	betel-leaf sellers
parakiya	extra-marital sexual relationship
pat	widow remarriage
pies	lowest denomination in Indian currency (Re. 0.08)
pucca	built of brick
pujas	worship; festival
punkha	fan
purdah	lit. curtain; custom of secluding women
rabi	spring crop
rarh	widow; prostitute
sadar	district headquarters
sadi	marriage
sagai	remarriage; engagement
sahib	boss; generally referring to British in colonial India
samasya	problem
samsar	household

sanga (also sangat)	marriage; widow remarriage
sardar (also sirdar)	lit. headman, chief; jobber in jute mills
sati (also suttee)	lit. chaste wife; the practice of immolating widows on the funeral pyre of their dead husband
seer	0.75 of a kilogram, approximately
shakti	power
sowatin	co-wife
streedhan	marriage portion of daughter, usually in form of ornaments
sugrihini	ideal housewife
sumata	ideal mother
swadeshibabu	middle-class nationalist or Congress activist
thana	police station
vaisya	commercial caste; prostitute
varna	caste
verandah	balcony
zamindars	landlord

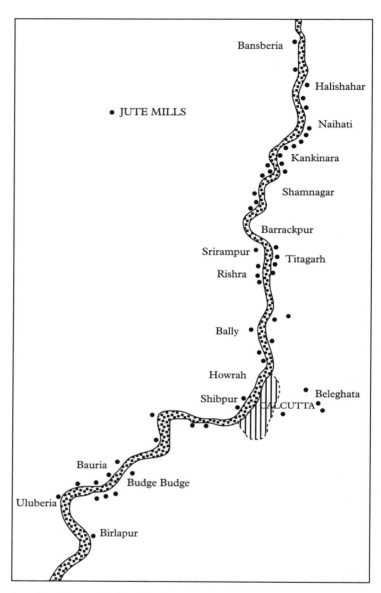

Location of jute mills along river Hooghly

Introduction

Bhikari Paswan was a worker and a trade-union activist in Victoria Jute Mills at Telinipara. He became involved in a spate of inter-union clashes and, in October 1993, he was arrested. He died while in police custody. Bhikari's father, Lakshmi Chand, sued the police. His case hinged on the evidence given by Bhikari's wife, Lalti. Subsequently, in July 1995, when the case was being heard by a Division Bench of Calcutta High Court, the Officer-in-charge of Bhadreswar Thana cast doubts on the prosecution's case by deposing that Lalti was not Bhikari's wife. In the protracted hearings it emerged that Lalti had been married to Jagu Paswan of Naihati and had not obtained a divorce. She lived with Bhikari, but was not his 'wife'. Her evidence as a witness, crucial as it was to the case, was undermined by the legal uncertainty of her marital status.

Lalti herself did not work in any mill. She became the central figure in the most controversial industrial dispute in recent years because of her disputed status as the 'wife' of a mill worker allegedly killed by the police. In the hands of political parties who espoused the cause of Bhikari Paswan, she became both a symbol of working-class resistance and the quintessential victim of managerial, state and police brutality. In either case, her 'class' position devolved from marriage (or cohabitation) and her dependence on Bhikari's earnings for her own and her children's livelihood. The police responded by undermining this equation. They questioned the 'marriage' from which the worker's 'wife' derived her formal legal rights *vis-à-vis* the state and the mill management. By doing so, they brought Lalti's identity as a woman (and wife) into clearer play. If Lalti was to be able to depose in court or assert her rights to redressal, she could only do so as Bhikari's wife and dependant. Lalti's legal and economic rights were premised, in that case, on her rights as a 'wife'. Her dilemma was clearly different from that of the worker, man or woman, who sought the help of unions or courts to win compensation. Thus, her situation underlined the problems of subsuming women into 'class' by virtue of marriage and motherhood. Her case is discussed here in such length because it brings to the fore the importance of examining the interplay of gender and class which is the purpose of this research. This book is about the many dilemmas of women like Lalti and of other women who, though they worked with men in the jute mills of Bengal, found their experience of being 'working class' different from that of their male colleagues. It is a history of labouring women in Calcutta and its nearby mill towns between 1890 and 1940 which was the heyday of the jute industry. The period of this research predates Lalti Paswan; but that only shows the hardiness of the issue. The way in which social constructions of gender constituted Bengal's working classes has had long-term and enduring implications.

In order to examine these implications, this study steps beyond the immediate world of working class women. In any case, to understand how social constructions of gender shaped the lives and work of women wage labourers, wider social anxieties about women's role and position in the home have to be taken into account. The concerns about women's domestic and familial identity included, for instance, the middle classes in the cities. During the late nineteenth and early twentieth centuries, new constructions of gender relations were made explicit in course of the debates over women's emancipation, widow remarriage, and the physical and social seclusion of women. These wider constructions of gender relations sometimes extended from and at other times intruded upon the organisation of women's work in the countryside. By the late nineteenth century, changes in the agrarian economy had led increasing numbers of poor women to work outside the home to augment household resources. At the same time, many intermediate groups in rural society were adopting new practices of women's seclusion. Poorer women were seen to work more and better-off women were seen to work less: in both cases, there were changes in rural women's self-identity and the attitudes towards their work and status.

The rural context is, without doubt, critical to any examination of the constitution of the jute working-class. So far, the 'rural' connection of the workers has been invoked to understand every aspect of working-class life and behaviour. In popular and academic parlance, the figure of the industrial worker as the semi-rural semi-urban peasant-proletariat has abided for almost a century.[1] Mill owners explained the impermanency and the inefficiencies of workers in these terms. Indeed, they argued against welfare measures for these very reasons. The colonial state too, ironically enough, sought to thus understand workers' mili-

---

[1] This was first formulated by the Commission of 1908. *Report of the Indian Factory Labour Commission* (henceforth *IFLC*), London, 1909.

tancy or the lack of it. The village connection explained at times a greater and at other times a lesser commitment of the worker to the city and the factory job. Until recently, social scientists have held, with equal plausibility, diametrically opposed views about its implication for collective action. It is sometimes argued that the resilience of 'rural' ties of kin, caste and community divided workers, fractured their solidarity and vitiated the growth of a 'working-class' consciousness. The contrary view holds that networks (of kin, caste and community) carried over from rural society provided a physical, material and ideological basis for political collectivities in the urban context and promoted cohesive action.[2]

And yet, the most significant consequence of the 'rural' connection has rarely been considered: men jute workers, factorised wage labourers, lived and worked in the city while the women and children worked in the village in petty commodity production, services or retail; the household was spatially fragmented; the members of the household were engaged, simultaneously, in different production regimes; and the working-class household and its strategies of survival straddled the village and the city. Given the close interaction of agriculture and industry (and by implication the rural and urban economies) in shaping the milieu of organised industry, in structuring the labour market and in determining workers' household arrangements, any attempt artificially to sustain distinctions between agriculture/industry and rural/urban can only be misleading. In fact, it is only by questioning such distinctions that we can fully appreciate the wider processes of labour within which industry operated. The 'rural' linkage was far from being extrinsic to the industrial situation. To begin with, the industrial working class was reproduced, generationally and socially, through the intensification of women's and children's labour in the rural economy. The jute mill owners, like other urban employers, depended upon a steady and continued supply of workers from the countryside. These workers were

---

[2] Ranajit Dasgupta, 'Material Conditions and Behavioural Aspects of Calcutta Working Class 1875–1899', *Occasional Paper No. 22*, Centre for Studies in Social Sciences, Calcutta, 1979; Dipesh Chakrabarty and Ranajit Dasgupta, 'Some Aspects of Labour History of Bengal in the Nineteenth Century: Two Views', *Occasional Paper No. 40*, Centre for Studies in Social Sciences, Calcutta, 1981; Dipesh Chakrabarty, *Rethinking Working Class History, Bengal 1890–1940*, Princeton, 1989; A. K. Bagchi, 'The Ambiguity of Progress: Indian Society in Transition', *Social Scientist*, 13, 3, 1985, pp. 3–14 and 'Working Class Consciousness', *Economic and Political Weekly*, 28 July 1990, pp. PE54–60. A notable exception is Chandavarkar's attempt to break down the boundaries between 'urban' and 'rural', and 'workplace' and 'neighbourhood', in the context of the Bombay textile industry. R. S. Chandavarkar, *The Origins of Industrial Capitalism in India: Business Strategies and the Working Classes in Bombay, 1900–1940*, Cambridge, 1994.

usually men who left their female kin to work in the rural economy. A persuasive case for examining the close interrelationship between shifting gender equations in the countryside and the constitution of the urban working class can thus be made.

So far, however, these issues of gender have not evoked any response from Indian labour historians who have sustained their arguments about 'class' by narrowly focusing on 'organised' industrial workers. Since industrial workers are primarily men and usually 'single' migrants, it has been assumed that 'working-class women' have no specific relevance to 'class'. It has not even been asked why or how the industrial working class became overwhelmingly male. As a result, the more fundamental issue of how gender was, in fact, crucial to the very constitution of labour processes – not only in organised industry but in other arenas of economic activity – remains unaddressed. This study takes these questions as a starting point, but by pursuing diverse interrelated themes it also seeks to draw attention to the need for a more multi-dimensional approach to the study of labour.

At the most elementary level, the jute industry's increasingly male workforce offers an interesting case of women's 'exclusion'. Initially, the jute industry, like other textile industries of India, employed a low proportion of women. This proportion declined over time. At the turn of the century, women constituted about 20 per cent of total workers, the highest recorded proportion. For most of the period between 1890 and 1940, women were about 12 to 17 per cent of the workforce (Table 1). While the industry began to draw on an increasingly wider variety of castes, communities and regions, they drew more and more on men. As wages and working conditions improved through the collective political struggle of the jute workers, unionised male workers also contributed to a more rigid exclusion of women.

The manner of this 'exclusion' begs a host of other questions about the material and social reproduction of the working class. Some of these questions are difficult to treat within a rigid framework of mutually antagonistic but internally cohesive 'classes'. To start with, the very gendering of organised industrial labour cannot be understood without

Sources to Table 1:
1. *Report of the Committee of the Indian Jute Mills Association*, Half-Yearly Report, December 1897.   2. *Social and Economic Status of Women Workers in India*, Labour Bureau, Ministry of Labour, Government of India, 1953, p. 14.   3. *Report on an Enquiry into Conditions of Labour in the Jute Mill Industry in India*, S. R. Deshpande, Delhi, 1946.   4. *Census of India*, 1901, Vol. VI, Pt. 1; *Census of India*, 1911, Vol. V, Pt. 1.

Table 1. *Average daily number of persons employed in jute mills of Bengal,*
1897–1950

sl.	Date	No. of factories	Men	Women	Children	Total	% of women
1	1897		72440	17905	12104	102449	17. 4
4	1901		64420	13489			20. 9
4	1911		161239	35263			17. 9
3	1912	61	145389	31329	23007	199725	15. 6
3	1913	64	158261	34010	24106	216377	15. 7
3	1914	69	167858	36800	25969	230627	15. 9
3	1915	70	181445	40674	26606	248725	16. 3
3	1916	70	191036	42145	27606	260787	16. 1
3	1917	71	192667	41395	27320	261382	15. 8
3	1918	72	199977	43278	27709	270964	15. 9
3	1919	72	201009	43112	28628	272749	15. 8
3	1920	73	207255	44545	28521	280321	15. 8
3	1921	77	207908	44705	29235	281848	15. 8
3	1922	80	239660	49257	28265	317184	15. 5
3	1923	83	242652	51495	28400	322547	15. 9
3	1924	85	252107	54801	27823	336731	16. 2
3	1925	83	256312	55511	26474	338297	16. 4
3	1926	86	253935	52827	20785	327547	16. 1
3	1927	85	253691	52935	19249	325865	16. 2
3	1928	86	260342	53678	17879	331899	16. 1
3	1929	90	267717	54670	17278	339665	16. 0
3	1930	91	264417	52114	11646	328177	15. 8
3	1931	93	222573	42254	3462	268289	15. 7
3	1932	94	212505	40294	1515	254314	15. 8
3	1933	92	208246	37337	1134	246717	15. 1
3	1934	93	213894	36932	915	251741	14. 6
3	1935	95	225372	37749	278	263399	14. 3
3	1936	94	233481	38261	4	271746	14. 0
3	1937	96	249737	37997	9	287743	13. 2
3	1938	97	242342	36683	9	279034	13. 1
3	1939	101	243496	37699	34	281229	13. 4
3	1940	101	248046	36640	34	284720	12. 8
3	1941	101	251388	35255	38	286681	12. 2
3	1942	101	252799	35083	32	287920	12. 1
3	1943	101	245125	34759	35	279919	12. 4
3	1944	101	231121	36005	67	267193	13. 4
2	1945			40963		303319	13. 5
2	1946			43165		313133	13. 8
2	1947			41872		319302	13. 0
2	1948			41966		329429	12. 7
2	1949			41576		322159	12. 9
2	1950			37531		303364	12. 4

reference to relations of conflict and interaction between and among various groups – workers, entrepreneurs, the state and its officials. Moreover, the relations of gender and generation that obtained within the working class created the specific conditions for its continued male character. Generally speaking, the organisation of work according to gender and age was naturalised by the deployment of familial ideology. As a result, the hierarchical nature of these arrangements often remain obscured. Yet, the way these impinged on the process of household decision-making had crucial consequences for the distribution of labour and its rewards. Also, equally significantly, if the working class was divided by gender and generational interests, they did not face a monolithic alliance between the state and the entrepreneurial class. The state had diverse interests which were further fragmented by competitive claims from capitalist entrepreneurs who, in turn, were riven by internal competition.

To take the issue of entrepreneurial behaviour: a re-evaluation of jute 'capitalism' is long overdue. R. S. Chandavarkar's recent analysis of the Bombay cotton textile industry indicates that many of the conundrums of Indian labour historiography follow from a mistaken presumption of capitalist unity and the capitalists' ability to establish control over factor markets. He argues that individual entrepreneurs were rarely in a position to maximise efficiency by long-term rational calculations.[3] Jute entrepreneurs, in particular, have been ascribed remarkable influence over the state and an ability to unify their individual interests. It has often been argued that the Indian Jute Mills Association was able to exert both monopolistic and monopsonistic pressures on the market. Led by expatriate Scottish businessmen, the Association is supposed to have achieved an effective racial alliance with the colonial state. In fact, jute entrepreneurs were riven by internal competition and IJMA failed as often as it succeeded in uniting mill owners. Also, the central and provincial governments were faced with conflicting claims. They were not always willing to and sometimes did not co-operate.

Jute entrepreneurs, while attributed unities and influences they did not possess, have been charged with failures in business strategies and practices. Doubtless, they were tardy with technological innovation and investments for modernisation. But one needs to be cautious. The jute entrepreneur or his managers were not really endowed with an infallible foresight beyond a host of pressing problems. Certain immediate indices of more or less satisfactory efficiency had to be met in the proximate future. Once so met, the challenge of the distant future tended to be

[3] Chandavarkar, *The Origins of Industrial Capitalism in India*.

more dimly perceived, if at all. Hindsight may reveal flaws in or failures of foresight. Nor is it unnatural for investors remotely situated from the scene of industrial activity to push 'to take the cash in hand [a]nd waive the rest'. Moreover, jute entrepreneurs operated with disorganised factor markets and a fluctuating international market. They were not engaged in a quest for efficiency in the very long term. Instead, they adopted their own particular labour strategies: they accepted a ready, if relatively casual, labour force; they refused to pay for training and settling an 'efficient' workforce; and they expected their labour force to be manipulable, deployable at will and for such short or long-term periods as suited them.

Thus, jute mill owners drew their labour from 'single' migrants. These migrant men were not 'proletarianised' in the classic sense, since they retained a rural base – some land or just a homestead in which the 'family' lived and worked. It was this rural base, moreover, which provided the 'single' migrants with a buffer against uncertainty in the urban labour market and, as a result, conferred on them the additional flexibility which the employers desired. Such migrants were usually men because they had control over migration decisions in the household and could opt for the higher cash wages of the city. Proletarianisation in these circumstances was unnecessary, as was the individualisation of labour. Men retained control over the household's migration decision because labour was not 'free' from family authority. It was the male head of the household, moreover, who used his familial authority to retain his flexibility in the urban labour market by commanding more intensive work from women for increasingly lower allocation of resources. As a result, women's migration followed a different pattern. They left their villages when their rural resources were exhausted – either accompanying their displaced families or alone, having been denied access to household resources because of widowhood, barrenness or inchastity. Such women were less prone to periodically visit the village 'home'. Even if conventional wisdom has exaggerated their abrogation of the 'rural connection', there must have been steep hurdles to the deserted or deserting wife's return to the village. Certainly, most women migrants had less rural or household resources to draw on by way of insurance. As a result, they were more often 'proletarianised' in the conventional sense than the men – a disadvantage in the insecure urban labour maket. Thus did gender play a constitutive role in the making of the jute working class.

Women's disadvantage in the urban market extended to the factory shopfloor. By ignoring the issues of job segregation and the gender division of labour, Indian labour historians have for long sustained the notion of the 'factory' as an arena where increasingly homeogenised capital and labour are in conflict only with each other. Thus, the workplace itself is not usually seen as a source of differences and disunities among workers. Dipesh Chakrabarty, who has recently intervened most effectively against a purely 'class'-oriented approach to the study of Indian labour, argued that the technological backwardness of jute entrepreneurs conferred an unusual degree of deskilled homogeneity to jute labour. And yet, he argues, jute labour did not become a 'working class' because the pre-capitalist 'conditions and culture' obtaining in the larger society outside the workplace (and, by implication, brought over from the rural society) hierarchised and divided the workers more effectively than the workplace united. He steps, as it were, outside the relations of the workplace to understand 'communal' conflicts within the working classes. In his reading, communal divisions follow from 'pre-capitalist' hierarchies and remain relatively unaffected by industrial employment.[4] Such an argument could be extended to understand inequalities of gender in the jute mills and their neighbourhoods. Unequal gender relations were, of course, 'pre-capitalist' and were both prior to and obtaining outside the jute mill. Manifestly, jute entrepreneurs drew on existing ideologies of gender to sustain hierarchies of skills and wages. However, as this study will seek to show, gender relations are also 'capitalist'. While industrial employers did draw on existing and wider perceptions of gender, their own policies and strategies also served to modify, reinforce or even enhance gender inequalities and differences. Industrial employers created new and different myths about skill and segmentation which served to reinscribe gender hierarchies on the workforce. In the jute mills, the employers fostered personalised and informal channels of recruitment which tended to entrench gender-ghettos. They employed women in low-skilled and low-paid jobs on the grounds that their earnings were 'supplementary' to the men's and argued in favour of longer working hours for women on the grounds that their extra earnings would benefit their household. When employers wished to reduce their workforce they drew on domesticity and motherhood to delegitimise women's factory employment and thereby enhanced women's social marginalisation.

The employers succeeded in thus segmenting and stratifying their workforce no doubt because they were able to harness widely shared gender perceptions which, in turn, contributed to the effectiveness of employers' strategies, as also to their consequences. The state, the middle classes and male workers shared and sometimes even contested

[4] Chakrabarty, *Rethinking Working Class History*.

these perceptions of gender. The gendering of the organised industrial workforce can, therefore, only be appreciated in the context of a wider social phenomenon. In the last two decades, feminists have interrogated conventional notions of 'class' and noted broad similarities in the organisation of women's work across classes and cultures. Their interventions raise some critical questions about the role of gender in class formation. In nineteenth-century Bengal, gender was, in fact, emerging as a key to class identity. Increasingly, a variety of elite discourses marked out specific articulations of gender relations as the crucial mark of status. The organisation of marriage, motherhood and domesticity and the way these were defined for women became crucial, not only to the reproduction of class identity but also to the quotidian maintenance of class barriers.

These processes were discernible in the urban environment of Calcutta and the mill towns. For example, the attribution of migrant status exclusively to the poor and to industrial workers was more an ideological disposition than a sociological description. The term was used to indicate the 'foreignness' of labourers and to underline their alien language, culture and lifestyle. Increasingly, the separation of the native and the migrant became overlaid with distinctions of high and low culture, moral purity and laxity, order and lawlessness. A specific characterisation of gender relations was central to such distinctions. In this discourse, the upper castes upheld the sanctity of marriage, the chaste, modest and secluded demeanour of elite women. In contrast, the poor lived in 'temporary' marriages, experiencing frequent divorces and desertions. They suffered the public appearance of their women in menial and manual occupations.

Elite discourses on femininity elaborated an ideology of 'domesticity' which was intensely preoccupied with the nature of women's work. Was domesticity to subsume or to delegitimise women's productive labour? The first was possible in the case of physically segregated or household-based work. The second usually applied to women's 'visible' work in the streets and mills of the cities. The idealisation of domesticity raised questions about how women's work was to be valued. Increasingly, domestic tasks, subsumed within definitions of femininity, were stripped of their labour content and denuded of their economic value for the household. The physical and social invisibility of elite women's work underwrote the denigration of women's remunerated work. The effectiveness of the ideology of domesticity as a mark of status lay not in preventing poor women from working, but in promoting the claims of middle-class women to the highly valued domain of exclusive housewifery and childcare.

What sustained the 'domestication' of elite women in the nineteenth century? There were in fact some significant similarities in the way the new articulation of domesticity affected women across classes. It is often forgotten that the urban middle classes also had a 'rural link'. A vast majority of men in clerical and service employment left their wives and children in the village. These women, like the wives of migrant workers, suffered relative devaluation of their contribution to the household. In the absence of the men, wives in poor and middle-class rural households had to take a greater role in decision-making. In the case of the middle-class wives, this involved supervisory responsibilities which became part of their extended housework. In the case of the wives of migrant workers, however, greater responsibilities also meant more intensified labour for poorer returns. Thus, poor women's visibility in active labour increased significantly in high-migration areas. In all cases, the men earned the cash that paid the rent and ensured access to credit. The middle-class women had fewer independent means of access to earnings – either as wages or in productive resources. Those among them who came to the city lost their earlier direct access to consumption goods – especially food – and their new 'domestic' activities became dependent on men's cash earnings. In the case of all these women, domesticity subsumed significant portions of their labour. Consequently, their productive role was marginalised and their labour devalued.

To appreciate this idealised 'domesticity' in any meaningful way, one needs to open up the nature and meaning of 'work' itself. Feminist researchers investigating women's work in the household, in food production and processing and in the informal sector, have directed our attention to how 'work' is often made invisible. Calcutta and the mill towns had fewer women and even fewer were deemed as 'employed'. In 1901, only 20 per cent of the female population as against 80 per cent of the male population were registered in various occupations.[5] This was a direct consequence of the intermittent nature of women's work. Women's entry into the wage labour market was often driven by household exigencies. For instance, married women undertook extra-familial paid work when male earnings were inadequate or inconstant. For many women this meant that they worked almost all their lives. Their work, however, was regarded as 'supplementary' by their employers and their families. As a result, women were inherently and essentially handicapped in the labour market at their very point of entry. They were forced into inferior and casual jobs like petty trading, domestic service and into small industries.

[5] *Census of India*, 1901, VI, Calcutta, p. 83.

Among the various industries registered under the Factories Act, jute alone employed any substantial number of women. Other major industrial employers of women were small seasonal units where hours of work were longer, pay lower and employment more casual. In 1921, in the seasonal cotton ginning, cleaning and pressing mills women constituted about 40 per cent of the workforce, in bone mills they were 31.5 per cent of the total workforce, while in rice mills they constituted 36 per cent of the workforce. The largest concentration of women in rice mills was in establishments employing less than fifty workers, which meant these mills were outside the purview of factory legislation. The building trade employed women as day labourers. Many were employed in the preparation of food.[6] Registering authorities often lumped the various casual and seasonal occupations of women under blanket categories of 'indefinite', 'non-productive' or 'general labour'. In Calcutta, in 1881, the highest number of women were reported in 'indefinite and non-productive' occupations, the only category in which women outnumbered men. The sting came in the tail – much the largest number of women appeared in a column headed 'none stated'.[7]

Women's marginality in the urban labour market – in terms of the numbers employed or of the inferior jobs in which they were concentrated – has been one of the most abiding features of capitalist societies. This aspect of capitalism has escaped most Indian labour historians who have assumed the centrality of the factory system in the process of industrialisation. The narrow focus on organised factory labour has limited the story of class formation to men, because they were the ones who actually worked in factories. Women, merely because they constituted a smaller proportion in 'modern' industries and in the city populations, have been written out of the history of the working class. The specific interests of women workers are either subsumed within the collectivity of the working class, or they are ignored altogether. The difficulties of understanding women's specific situations from within this orthodox 'class' perspective constitutes the most compelling justification for its reassessment.

This book uses both the terms 'gender' and 'class' frequently. It does so in a generally descriptive sense. Both these have been subjected to specific criticisms. For several decades, the use of 'class' to denote Indian social groups was carefully avoided, since their correspondence with conventional Marxist definitions of the term was bitterly disputed. Indeed, it seemed that 'class' could, properly speaking, only exist in advanced capitalist societies. Equally, the universalistic claims of

[6] Ibid. Also see *Census of India*, 1921, V, 2, pp. 374–6.
[7] *Report of the Census of the Town and Suburbs of Calcutta*, H. Beverley, Calcutta, 1881.

'gender' analysis have been challenged. The radical feminists' timeless sweep of 'patriarchy' often fails to explain the specific expressions of even gender relations. In the 1970s, Marxist-Feminists used the notion of 'reproduction' as a complement to 'production' to great effect. They thus influenced many new understandings of class formation. But their 'dual systems' theory sets up a binary relationship between gender and class, obscuring their complex interaction. The need remains, besides, to trace the specificities of historical experiences which cannot be captured within such limiting analytical frameworks.

A growing corpus of Indian feminist literature is attempting a historically and culturally nuanced treatment of 'gender'. In the context of the nineteenth-century social reform movement, historians have examined constructions of gender by colonial administrators and by elite Indian men. The economic and legal interventions in the colonial period have been shown to have had significant impact on gender relations. Research on women's role in the labour market and the terms on which they participate in wage labour has been immensely valuable in advancing our understanding of the nature and pattern of women's work in nineteenth- and twentieth-century Bengal. Scholars have also attempted to recover the indigenous discourse on gender, exploring the contestatory voice of women. Historical research in this direction has dealt, necessarily, with literate middle-class women who have left behind their own writings.

The working classes have rarely spoken on their own behalf in historical records. At particular historical moments, however, they have found numerous and heterogeneous spokespersons. Historians have depended on these – the state, the capitalists, the well-intentioned middle-class philanthropists and trade unions – to write working-class histories. In the case of women, the moments are more fragmentary, the spokespersons fewer, their voices more remote and judgemental. This study cannot claim to 'recover' working-class women's own voices. It can only try to question the assumptions and judgements of the earlier writers and to tell a new story about the jute mill women. These limitations have sometimes directed the themes addressed and the questions raised. Thus, considerable importance has been accorded to the policies of the colonial state and jute mill owners. Legislative intervention – from the Indian Factories (Amendment) Act of 1891 which first intervened in women's working conditions to the Bengal Maternity Benefit Act of 1939 – provides a framework to study shifts in these policies.

A concern about the impact of urbanisation in the period after the First World War produced a variety of literature, some of which has

provided inavaluable source material for this research. Many contemporary observers – notably some European women – recorded their
impressions of industrial employment of women. A number of doctors
from the Women's Medical Service in India conducted surveys and
compiled data on health and maternity conditions among the urban
poor. They have provided a wealth of information on subjects that are
not often detailed in official sources.

Academic interest in the gendering of labour in India is still relatively
recent. Moreover, an investigation into women's employment is expected, not surprisingly, to choose areas and industries where women
predominated. It may seem, at first sight, paradoxical to select the jute
industry for such an investigation. But it is precisely because the jute
industry employed fewer women (and now employs hardly any) that it
offers the scope to investigate both women who undertook industrial
employment and those who were 'excluded'.

Jute, the golden fibre, called *paat* in Bengali, was the one single
commodity that dominated the economic life of Bengal from the mid-
nineteenth to the mid-twentieth centuries. It straddled the agricultural,
the mercantile and the manufacturing sectors. Peasants in eastern and
central Bengal cultivated jute in their small holdings using family labour.
The sandy loam, optimal rainfall, the hot and humid climate and access
to many rivulets made this riverine tract ideal for growing jute. Bengali
peasant households developed great skill in handling the tricky process
of 'retting' on which depended the quality of the fibre. Bengal practically
monopolised the world's production of raw jute. From the field to the
factories and docks, jute passed through many hands in a large and
varied network of traders and dealers who bought, processed, baled,
sold and exported raw jute.[8]

Meanwhile, Bengal's own factories and mills became major consu-
mers of raw jute. By the early twentieth century, more than half of the 9
million bales of raw jute produced were processed, spun, woven and
manufactured into bags in Bengal.[9] By the 1930s there were more than
100 factories within 25 miles north and south of Calcutta.

The factory production of jute and its importance as packaging for
the world's expanding commodity trade brought it into prominence in
the nineteenth century. Jute had, however, been known in Bengal for
many centuries. Two castes, the Kapalis and the Jogis, grew, spun and

[8] Hem Chunder Kerr, *Report on the Cultivation of and Trade in Jute in Bengal: The Bengal
Jute Commission, 1873*, Calcutta, 1877. Also see Omkar Goswami, *Industry, Trade and
Peasant Society: The Jute Economy of Eastern India, 1900–1947*, Delhi, 1991.
[9] *Imperial Gazetteer*, Bengal, VII, Oxford, 1908, p. 269; D. H. Buchanan, *The Development
of Capitalist Enterprise in India*, New York, 1934, p. 239.

wove jute. As in many other low-paid and low-status jobs Hindu widows of even the higher castes were allowed to engage in this poorly rewarded occupation. The coarse yarn was used for cordage and for making paper. A few handlooms produced matting, bedding, rough garments, and even bags for handling sugar, coffee and grain. The growing international demand for packaging material, however, led to an unprecedented extension in jute cultivation and manufacture. From 1795 Bengal began to export raw jute and jute cloth, mainly to south-east Asia.[10] Around this time manufacturers of flax and hemp bags in Dundee began to toy with the idea of mechanical manufacture of jute cloth and bags. The fibre proved too weak and brittle. The Dundee manufacturers made a breakthrough in 1835 when they applied whale oil to sufficiently strengthen and soften the fibre. Mechanical spinning started and power weaving followed immediately. The real impetus for the growth of the industry came with the outbreak of the Crimean War when the supply of Russian hemp became uncertain. Jute was now substituted for hemp. The shift required no significant replacement of existing machinery and with a little additional investment the packaging industry in Dundee continued to prosper. Scottish jute mills also derived an enormous cost advantage from the easy and almost exclusive access to colonised Bengal's raw jute. The hessian and the gunny sack were to hold the field for the next hundred years.

Twenty years after the first successful foray in machine spinning of jute, George Auckland, a retired tea planter from Ceylon, decided that the mountain need not go to Muhammad; if all the world's jute grew in Bengal, it should be possible to manufacture jute cloth and bags in Bengal, and more cheaply than in Dundee. In 1855 he built a shed in Rishra, a few miles north of Calcutta in Serampore. Rishra was a ferry ride across the river Hooghly from Barrackpore, where a thriving township had grown around the British military cantonment. Auckland opened his first factory intending to bleach jute for export to Dundee. The scheme failed and he turned his attention to machine spinning. He collaborated with a Bengali financial agent, Byam Sundar Sen, who provided some of the capital. Auckland imported all the machinery and an expert mill overseer from Dundee. Later he added a few handframe looms to his factory. This first jute mill did not do too well. Following many vicissitudes it was taken over by Champdany Company as their new branch Wellington Mill. After these first faltering steps, the Bengal industry soon made great strides. The mills bought raw jute cheaper and paid workers lower wages. The machinery had to be imported from

[10] *Imperial Gazetteer*, Bengal, VII pp. 266–70.

Europe but power-driven spinning and weaving was simple and Indian workmen learnt the skills easily and quickly. In a few years the Calcutta jute mills outrivalled their Dundee counterparts. Four years after Auckland's first efforts at machine spinning, the Borneo Jute Company was floated at Baranagar. This was followed by two mills in 1862, India Jute Mills at Serampore in 1866 and five more mills in 1872–3. These mills 'simply coined money' till the mid-1870s. Borneo Jute Company declared dividends at 10–25 per cent till 1875. Their prosperity attracted other investors and ten more mills were established in 1874–5.[11]

These first twenty mills were scattered on either side of the river Hooghly north and south of Calcutta. There were, however, four main clusters. The first mill came in Rishra and others followed closely around Serampore on the west bank of the river. Further to the south, a group of mills came up in Howrah. On the east bank of the river, groups of mills were situated from Shyamnagar in the north to Sealdah, within Calcutta proper, along the newly laid railway track. In the southern suburbs of Calcutta, a group of mills came up near the docks and jetties of Khidirpur and Garden Reach. Further south along the east bank came Budge-Budge Jute Mills and later Birla Jute Mill. Thus the bulk of the industry was not located within the municipal limits of the city unlike the Bombay cotton industry. Rather, the mills were concentrated in a narrow strip of land within commuting distance of Calcutta comprising in effect the suburban fringe of this vast city. In the early years most of these mills were carefully situated in or near already thriving commercial and urbanised satellites. A few mills chose isolated sites which later developed into 'mill towns'.

For the first two decades of its existence, the Bengal jute industry served the domestic and the south-east Asian markets. It gained the first major advantage over Dundee in the late 1870s when the Calcutta mills secured the burlap orders for the Australian wool trade. Soon they cut into the New Zealand and US markets for cornsacks, branbags, woolpacks and burlap wheat bags. In the 1880s, the industry entered a new phase of growth. Older mills were extending their production capacity and many new mills were being set up. The loomage more than trebled between 1873 and 1879, and by 1899, trebled once again. This entailed a massive increase in employment of labour. While in 1881 the industry employed about 28,000 workers, in the next three decades its employment doubled every ten years.[12] Elsewhere in Bengal, the coal and tea

---

[11] D. R. Wallace, *The Romance of Jute*, 2nd edn., London, 1928. Also see *Handbook and Directory of the Jute Industry*, Indian Jute Mills Association, Calcutta, 1967 and WBSA, Registration Department, July 1890.
[12] Wallace, *The Romance of Jute*, pp. 95–6.

industries were also growing apace.[13] There was a suddenly accelerated demand for labour in Bengal, more particularly in the Calcutta region where the jute industry was competing for labour with the expanding port and a variety of other small industries and services. Since cheap and plentiful labour was one of the main advantages they enjoyed over the Dundee industry, the Calcutta mills became increasingly concerned with the issue of labour supply.[14]

The early jute entrepreneurs established their mills in thriving commercial centres near the Calcutta port and with ready access to local labour. But the area around Calcutta was the most prosperous in the province and could not meet the escalating demand for labour. Meanwhile, in the 1880s, growing impoverishment in northern Bihar and eastern UP drove large numbers of men to Calcutta. For the next century, the mills had no problem in securing a sufficient number of workers.

Chapter 1 investigates the migration of labour to the jute mill belt of Bengal and, particularly, its implications for the employment of women. The Bengali women in the mills – primarily widows and deserted or deserting wives – were quickly overwhelmed by the migrant men. Bihari and UP women did not come to the mills in large enough numbers to preserve the gender composition of the workforce. There was a greater proportion of women among those who came from northern Andhra Pradesh than among those who came from Bihar and UP, but in absolute terms the Andhra women were a small minority. The women who did migrate to the city, alone or with their families, did so when rural resources were exhausted. They rarely retained a rural base to protect them against the uncertainties of the urban labour market. Consequently, their labour was less desirable from the mill owners' point of view.

The jute mills were both unable and unwilling to intervene in male migration or to assist women's migration. It was convenient for mill owners to employ long-distance male migrants. These men's 'rural connection' gave the employers additional flexibility. Bengal jute mills were, in addition, particularly fortunate in that they lay at the centre of

---

[13] Employment in the collieries nearly doubled between 1891 and 1901 and went up by a further 175 per cent between 1901 and 1911. The employment in Bengal's tea gardens nearly trebled between 1881 and 1891 and went up by an additional 270 per cent in the next decade.

[14] The Dundee industry attempted to influence the Government of India against the Calcutta mill owners' 'exploitation of workers'. However, the Dundee Chamber of Commerce lacked the lobbying power of Manchester and Lancashire and very little was done about their complaints. *Dundee Advertiser*, 1894–5; *Annual Report of the Indian Jute Manufacturers' Association* (henceforth *IJMAR*), 1895; Wallace, *The Romance of Jute*, pp. 54–9.

the major streams of migrations from northern and central India. Thus mill owners did not incur any of the costs of inducing migration that troubled tea planters. Their labour demands, in conjunction with other large-scale employers like planters, were certainly unprecedented. They 'pulled' large numbers of men from north, east and central India; but they were not large enough. From the 1880s migrants crowded Calcutta's labour market. By the beginning of the twentieth century the Calcutta labour market was satiated, and every increase in demand was outstripped by growing numbers of migrants. The jute mill owners, now operating in a labour surplus market, were able to hold the threat of retrenchment over the workers. Since workers found it more difficult to resist wage reductions and higher workloads, mill owners sought to tide over short-term market crises by manipulating labour.

Women were disadvantaged in entering the labour market by the perceptions of their familial roles. Their participation in wage labour was subordinated to the needs of the household. These influenced the terms on which they undertook wage labour, and the conditions in which they migrated from the village to the city.

Chapter 2 explores the migration strategy of the peasant household and its impact on women's work. The declining income from land, labour and crafts impelled larger numbers of women to participate in general and field labour. But their economic contribution to the family was increasingly devalued. First, their work was defined as 'domestic' and, therefore, 'unproductive'. Second, as labour was cheapened in nineteenth- and twentieth-century Bengal, the difference between men's and women's earnings sharpened. The men earned cash wages in the city while women worked in the rural economy for lower returns. This devaluation of women's work is the key to some of the most significant social changes in early twentieth-century Bengal: the spread of dowry, the increasing restrictions on widow remarriage, the diffusion of *purdah* and child marriage.

The pattern of migration and the organisation of women's work in the rural economy described in the first two chapters provide the basis in the third chapter for a closer examination of women's work in the jute mills. The mills veered increasingly towards a concentration of women in a few lower-paid departments of the mill. At different times different arguments about women's lack of 'skill' and their 'family' responsibilities were used to justify the relegation of women to lower-paid jobs or to reduce the employment of women. Mill owners drew these arguments from prevailing ideologies of gender which associated manual and repetitive tasks with 'feminine' domestic skills and the wielding of machinery with a peculiarly 'masculine' skill. Mill managers also deployed notions of domesticity according to their labour requirements. Thus, when they wished to employ women they emphasised the importance of their contribution to the household budget; when they wished to reduce labour, they found it easier to retrench women, rather than men, on the grounds that women's earnings were 'supplementary' and that their primary task lay in housewifery and childcare. In general, managers advanced these arguments to explain women's lower wages and the poorer conditions provided for them in the mills. During the crisis of the 1930s, mill owners formulated concrete policies to increase their direct control over women's activities and to systematically replace women by men. Together, these various policies led to women's marginalisation in the industry.

The gendering of the workforce affected social and cultural attitudes to women's work and negatively affected the status of urban women. The poor conditions of women's work and the lower wages they were paid affirmed the ideology of domesticity and seclusion and further devalued women's contribution towards family sustenance.

The child-bearing and rearing practices of poor women received enormous public attention in the 1920s and 1930s. The state and the mill owners, prodded by the International Labour Organisation, discovered the 'problem' of the woman factory worker's 'motherhood'. Their policies in this regard are discussed in Chapter 4. While the state made some attempt to address the larger issue of high rates of infant and maternal mortality, the mill owners were focused on the notion of 'mothercraft' that had already gained popularity in England. In defining motherhood as a skill that had to be learnt, such a notion placed the responsibility of high mortality rates on poor women – women who were too ignorant to be good mothers, whose work in factories endangered the lives of their unborn children, and midwives who, by their barbarous methods, caused death and disease. The mill owners, supported by the Government of Bengal, adopted welfare clinics and 'baby shows' as a cheaper and more convenient alternative to maternity benefits and other welfare measures.

From the very beginning, women's induction into the industrial workforce had raised Indian and British reformist hackles. Poor women's sexual and mothering roles were considered to be threatened by their employment in factories. In the 1920s, rapid urbanisation heightened these fears. Government officials and the urban middle classes became increasingly anxious about the possibility of social dislocation in poor neighbourhoods of the large cities. There was a growing concern with the fate of the working-class 'family'. A proliferating public discourse focused on disease, crime and prostitution in working-class areas. In official and Bengali middle-class literature, the poor came to be char-acterised as sexually promiscuous. Such characterisations drew on the contrast between the brahmanical norm of sacramental marriage and the openly prevalent low-caste practices of divorce, second or temporary marriages and widow remarriages.

Chapter 5 shows how the colonial officialdom lumped together diverse sexual and marital arrangements of the urban poor as 'temporary marriage' and held them up as immoral practices peculiar to Calcutta's working classes. But the state's attempt to legislate against these immoral practices did not fare well. It attempted to accord selective brahmanical norms of marriage the force of new colonial law and to impose these on the lower-caste poor. Since, however, the new laws ignored the specificities of lower-caste marital practices, they failed in their objectives. Usually women did find themselves at the unequal end of marriages, 'temporary' or otherwise. By the new laws, however, women in 'temporary' marriages found themselves denied legal standing as 'wives'. This only deepened the vulnerability of their situation because they could be deprived of family resources, maintenance for themselves and their children more easily. At the same time, ironically enough, the 'husbands' also found themselves unable to legally ensure their exclusive control over these women's labour and sexuality.

The concluding chapter attempts to draw together the wide-ranging issues which constitute the interplay of gender and class. It argues that even though women workers in the jute industry were numerically and socially marginalised, these women did not fulfil expectations of femi-nine docility. Their participation in working-class politics was vigorous though unorganised. The jute trade unions paid them less attention that they did the men workers, but unions had to induct middle-class women to mobilise women workers whose participation was crucial to the success of strikes. But none of the many trade unions in the jute mills ever seriously addressed women workers' specific problems. Some of the middle-class women activists assumed positions of leadership, but even they rarely raised gender-specific issues. Women workers remained at the margins of organised working-class protest. In political demands their interests were subsumed within male or general working-class interests.

Women workers themselves rarely perceived a stark opposition between wage work and their family roles. Their family responsibilities usually included and overlapped with their role as workers. An elitist definition of womanhood, which celebrated the exclusively domestic, never applied to these women. However, such elitist perceptions did also accord primacy to poor women's family roles and they affected, through state and entrepreneurial policies, poor women's position in the workplace. Working women had to negotiate and contest these perceptions and they had to resist both class and sexual oppression. As a result, their protest gained a remarkably militant edge. They became reputed for their militancy in strikes and in violent confrontation with managers and the police. Their participation in strikes, however, often derived from criteria of self-worth and notions of honour that were not part of the organised structure of elite-led trade union politics.

1   Migration, recruitment and labour control

The exclusion of women from modern factory industries is no doubt related to their low proportion in the population of the cities and towns in which the factories and mills were situated. Both these – women's exclusion from industry and their absence from the city – were the products of a gender-specific pattern of migration which started in the late eighteenth century, gathered momentum in the late nineteenth century and still continues, though to a much lesser extent. Men travelled long distances to cities and towns where they spent long periods of their working lives. They occasionally visited the villages where they left their wives and children to procure a subsistence from a range of occupations. This pattern of migration obtained in many industrial centres of South Asia. The Bengal jute industry was no exception in this regard. It meant that Calcutta and its industrial suburb were continuously augmented by fresh male migration and that the proportion of women available for industrial employment was consequently low. Such an explanation of women's exclusion from the jute industry, however, raises more questions than it answers. To begin with, the proportion of women in the adult population of Calcutta and the mill towns was higher than their proportion in the jute mills. So there remains, still, a question of relative 'exclusion'. The problem could be and was sometimes inverted: given the culture of segregation and seclusion, as in the purdah system which operated so stringently in Bengal, why at all did women enter jute mills where they had to work alongside men and under male supervision. And there is no doubt that initially women did work in jute mills, if in dwindling proportions over time. There were, always, a few Bengali women, primarily widows and deserted wives. There were also women who came with families or alone from Bihar, the United Provinces, northern Andhra Pradesh and the Central Provinces. Was it merely that these women were so desperate, their survival so precarious that they were forced into this undesirable occupation? Or could it be argued that women were unable to compete successfully with men for the coveted jute mills jobs?

On first sight, it appears that jute mill management should have favoured women's employment. They paid the women and children they employed less than the men. Many of the really large Managing Agencies like Thomas Duff had bases in Dundee in Scotland. There women, who were paid less than the men, were employed in large numbers across the shopfloor. Many managers and supervisors in the Calcutta jute industry were Scotsmen trained in Dundee. The Calcutta mills could not have been unaware of the cost advantages of employing women. Yet, all those concerned – managing agents, managers, supervisors, colonial officials, the indigenous elite and jute mill workers – deemed women unsuitable for the Calcutta jute mills. Why was this so?

Historically, capitalists have shown a preference for women's labour in three different ways. First, as in China and Japan, women's wages were so low as to offset the higher cost of recruiting them. There the cotton textile industry was able to draw on a large pool of young unmarried women. They harnessed cultural values of chastity and female subservience to exercise an extraordinary degree of control over their workforce. Second, women have been valued, as in the tea plantations of Assam, for their reproductive functions – to stabilise the labour force and ensure that it is self-reproducing. Third, all the world over capitalists have used and reinforced the notion of women's wages being 'supplementary' to the main earnings of the male head of the household to pay women less and ensure the flexibility of their workforce.

The first option was not available to Bengal's jute mill owners: there was no pool of young single women since the ages of marriage and childbearing were very low. But why were the mills not interested in a self-reproducing labour force? And why were they not interested in women's cheaper labour? These questions will have to be examined in light of the specific historical circumstances that shaped labour-force formation in Calcutta and its industrial environment.

The early jute mills – location and labour supply

The early jute entrepreneurs selected the sites for their new mills with some care. Their mills had to be near enough to Calcutta to obtain access to its infrastructural facilities but they also needed to be able to draw quickly on a large number of workers.

Jute mills near Calcutta were able to gain from the transport systems whch converged upon the city. There were, first, the railways: the East Indian Railway, the North West Railway and the Bengal–Nagpur Railway. The Eastern Bengal State Railway operating from Sealdah ran parallel to the river and traversed what was to become by the turn of the century the great heartland of the jute industry.[1] This became especially significant after the 1890s when the railways brought men from villages of United Provinces, Bihar, Orissa and the Central Provinces. In addition to the railways, rivers, canals and roads carried raw jute from eastern and central Bengal to Calcutta and the mill towns. And the Khidirpur docks were the route through which manufactured jute goods found their way to markets in Europe, Australia and America. Three-eighths of the outward trade from Calcutta port comprised raw and manufactured jute.[2]

When Auckland selected Serampore as the site for the first jute mill in 1855, he had been attracted by William Carey's experiments with a paper mill.[3] In addition, it was not only close to and had easy access to Calcutta, but was also one of the chief centres for the jute handloom manufacture (Dhaniakhali, Sheoraphuli, Baidyabati and Bhadreswar). The yarn was prepared by men and women wove the cloth.[4] This inverted the practice in the Bengal cotton handloom industry in which women were forbidden by ritual taboo to touch the loom: they could only spin.

The Hooghly district, in which Serampore was situated, had been for long a centre of commerce and manufacturing.[5] In the late nineteenth century, almost 40 per cent of its population were engaged in industry, commerce and services, an unusually high proportion in Bengal. The Hooghly jute mills could draw on the poorer weavers, on men and women from neighbouring Bankura and even from Chota Nagpur and Cuttack.[6] Thus, the Rishra Mill was soon followed by India Jute Mill, Hastings Jute Mills and Presidency Jute Mill.

The first successful jute mill was established in 1859 in Baranagar, a hub of manufacturing and engineering industry.[7] The other early centre of the industry was Howrah. Its wagon was hitched to Calcutta's star. It prospered as new docks were opened at the port. The Howrah town had a flourishing trade in country and imported cloth. The first flour mills were established there in 1855. Jute mills followed and by the 1870s there were five mills in the vicinity of the railway station.[8]

In the 1880s, when new mills were mushrooming, the Jubilee Bridge

---

[1] *Imperial Gazetteer*, Calcutta, IX, Oxford, 1908.
[2] *Annual Report on the Administration of the Bengal Presidency*, 1879–80.
[3] D. R. Wallace, *The Romance of Jute*, 2nd edn., London, 1928, p. 8.
[4] *Imperial Gazetteer*, Bengal, VII, pp. 266–9.
[5] Hameeda Hossain, *The Company Weavers of Bengal: The East India Company and the Organization of Textile Production in Bengal, 1750–1813*, New Delhi, 1988.
[6] *Imperial Gazetteer*, Hooghly and Howrah, XIII, pp. 165–6, 208.
[7] J. C. Marshman, 'Notes on the Right Bank of Hooghly', *Calcutta Review*, 5, 1845.
[8] S. R. Deshpande, *Report on an Enquiry into the Family Budget of Industrial Workers in Howrah and Bally*, Delhi, 1946.

over the River Hooghly was opened. Entrepreneurs were attracted to the relatively rural and undeveloped east bank. Kankinara, Alliance and Anglo-India mills were erected around Naihati and Titagarh; and Standard, Kinnison and Kharda mills were established near Kharda Railway Junction. Mill owners chose isolated sites in order to draw on the labour of the surrounding agricultural population and built near railway junctions hoping to attract migrants as they got off.

Until the 1870s, Bengal mills appeared to have had no great difficulty in obtaining labour. There were workers from surrounding villages, from Calcutta and from neighbouring districts of Bengal. From the late 1880s it began to seem as though the halcyon days of labour abundance were over. The increased competition for workers among mills, especially the loss of skilled workers like weavers to rival mills, troubled managers. They now began to complain of serious labour shortages. '[T]he scarcity has been felt for some time past, and which is now so acute that, speaking generally, most of the Mills in the Association could find employment for at least 10 per cent more work-people than they at present have.'[9] Against these complaints about labour shortage must be weighed the evidence of stagnant wage rates.[10] The apparent paradox might be explained by short-term local bottlenecks in the supply of labour in a period of rapid expansion, which occurred in Titagarh and Shyamnagar.[11] It may also be the case that the volume of complaints by employers reflected their anxieties about securing not simply sufficient labour but more crucially, an adequate supply of disciplined and skilful workers.

Even towards the close of the nineteenth century, Bengal had a seasonal and localised labour market. Throughout the eighteenth and nineteenth centuries, East India Company servants and other employers grumbled about the scarcity and the high price of labour in Jessore, Faridpur, Hooghly, Howrah and 24 Parganas.[12] Calcutta appeared to be suffering chronic labour shortage from the eighteenth century onwards. As the demand for artisans, labourers, porters and domestic servants increased in the city, wages were pushed up by shortage of food. The East India Company commissioned contractors of various

[9] H. M. Haywood, Acting Assistant Secretary, IJMA, *IJMAR*, August 1899.
[10] Ranajit Dasgupta, 'Material Conditions and Behavioural Aspects of Calcutta Working Class 1875–1899', *Occasional Paper No. 22*, Centre for Studies in Social Sciences, Calcutta, 1979, pp. 40–1.
[11] DUL, TDP, Directors' Minute Book, Shyamnagar Jute Factory, 17 December 1899.
[12] F. H. Buchanan, *A Geographical, Statistical and Historical Description of the District or Zilla of Dinajpur in the Province or Soubah of Bengal*, Calcutta, 1833; Henry Mead, 'Work and Wages', *Calcutta Review*, 37, 73, 1861, pp. 149–59; WBSA, General Miscellaneous, August 1868.

kinds – *sardars*, *buxies* and *daffadars*. It pressed the Zamindars in the 24
Parganas to mobilise labour. Both incentives and intimidation failed.
Moreover, the East India Company's rhetoric of a 'free labour market',
its dependence on agricultural prosperity for a high tax yield and for the
supply of many of its chief export items made it impractical to plunder
the immediate environs of Calcutta for cheap labour.[13]

There were, however, short-distance and temporary streams of migration even in the early eighteenth century. By the close of the century, the
districts were able to draw on the ruined weavers and a few destitutes. In
times of famines and shortages, as in 1769–70 and 1788, there was
more concerted movement towards the city.[14] In the harvesting season,
workers came from Midnapore, Orissa and Chhotanagpur. Calcutta
attracted artisans and poor peasants from neighbouring 24 Parganas,
Nuddea, Hooghly, Burdwan and Midnapore. By the end on the nineteenth century, such migration had increased considerably and the last
four districts accounted for about half the immigrants in Calcutta.[15] Yet,
when more concentrated inputs of labour were required, as in road and
canal construction, workers had to be imported from outside Bengal.[16]
Presumably the costs of importing labour were offset by much lower
wages.

Most temporary migrants were men. Of women migrants, it was
mostly widows and deserted wives of low castes like *Haris* and *Muchis*
who came alone to Calcutta.[17] In fact, the scope for women's employment was limited. They were employed as domestic servants and in food
processing, and they played ancillary roles in some artisan occupations
like textiles and pottery. They also participated in retailing, as carriers in
the building trade and in some menial services. There were lodging-
house keepers, washerwomen, barbers, sweepers, midwives and large
numbers of women were reported as prostitutes. By the late nineteenth
century, some of even these occupations in which women predominated
were declining.[18]

[13] P. J. Marshall, 'The Company and the Coolies: Labour in Early Calcutta', in Pradip
Sinha (ed.), *The Urban Experience: Calcutta, Essays in Honour of Professor Nitish R. Ray*,
Calcutta, 1987.
[14] *Report of the Commissioners appointed under the Chairmanship of George Campbell, to
enquire into the famine in Bengal and Orissa in 1866*, I.
[15] W. W. Hunter, *A Statistical Account of Bengal*, I, London, 1876.
[16] Dhangars were brought from Chhotanagpur 'at enormous expense' for the Rajpur
Jheel. Lord Dufferin, Report Submitted to the Viceroy, P. Nolan, *Report on the
Condition of the Lower Classes of Population in Bengal*, Calcutta, 1888 (henceforth
Dufferin Report).
[17] Usha Chakrabarty, *Condition of Bengali Women around the Second Half of the Nineteenth
Century*, Calcutta, 1963.
[18] *Report of the Census of the Towns and Suburbs of Calcutta*, H. Beverley, Calcutta, 1881,
pp. 44–50. Other than 19 per cent in 'stated occupations', women were recorded

On the whole, the labouring poor were chary of higher wages in Calcutta. They preferred wages in combination of cash and kind. In 24 Parganas, Howrah and Hooghly, jute cultivation and trading increased rapidly.[19] There were winter crops, turmeric, sugarcane, chillies and tobacco.[20] Anyone with some access to land could grow vegetables (especially potatoes) for the urban market.[21] These offered the poor a variety of employment. By contrast, the city held little attraction. Women, especially, suffered from the crowded living conditions in the city. The loss of communal facilities like segregated and secluded ghats for bathing and the relative dearth of 'subsistence' activities like the gathering of fuel and food may have made Calcutta both uneconomic and unpleasant.

It is then not surprising that mills experienced periodic shortages of labour when they depended on local sources. Their problems were solved by long-distance migrants. From the mid-eighteenth century, Bengal had begun to draw non-Bengali labour from Orissa and Bihar.[22] The so-called 'hill coolies' – adivasis from the Chhotanagpur hill areas – were on the move from the beginning of the nineteenth century and could easily be induced to migrate to Calcutta. By 1868, workers began to come from further afield.[23] By the end of the nineteenth century the trickle became a torrent. Men from Bihar, eastern United Province, Orissa and northern Andhra Pradesh changed the contours of Calcutta's labour market.[24]

Calcutta and the surrounding mill towns lay in the way of three major routes of inter-provincial migration. First, there was the well-documented annual seasonal exodus of agricultural labour from Bihar, especially Muzaffarpur, Saran, Gaya, Patna, and Bhagalpur, and some west Bengal districts, especially Midnapore, Bankura and Birbhum, to east Bengal at the time of harvesting. Workers left home at the beginning of the winter for temporary employment in the harvest fields, roadworks, railways or other casual employment and returned in summer.[25]

under the category 'indefinite and non-productive'. Of the women in 'stated occupations', 45 per cent were in 'domestic service', about a quarter were in 'hard manual labour' and about another quarter were in petty trades and retailing.

[19] Hem Chunder Kerr, *Report on the Cultivation of and Trade in Jute in Bengal: The Bengal Jute Commission, 1873*, Calcutta, 1877.

[20] Dufferin Report, 1888.   [21] *Report on the Internal Trade of Bengal*, 1876–88.

[22] Marshall, 'The Company and the Coolies', p. 24.

[23] 'Labour Difficulty in Bengal', *Calcutta Review*, 47, 1868.

[24] Between 1881 and 1891 the proportion of migrants increased by 11.8 per cent; in the decade of the 1890s this increase was by 40.7 per cent. Between 1901 and 1911, the share of migrants rose by another 32.6 per cent. The increase was even more evident in jute mill towns where, by 1930, migrants outnumbered the local population in the ratio 2:1. *Report of the Census of the Towns and Suburbs of Calcutta*, 1881, II; *Census of India*, 1891, III; *Census of India*, 1901, VI, 1; *Census of India*, 1911, V, 1.

[25] See chapter 2 below.

Second, there were 'indentured' labourers for the British and foreign colonies. Agents and contractors recruited workers from United Provinces, Bihar and Central Provinces. Recruits were taken to the depot in Calcutta and shipped to various colonies like Fiji, Mauritius, Natal, Trinidad and Surinam. Third, there was both organised and unorganised recruitment for the tea gardens of North Bengal, Assam and the Surmah Valley. Workers were brought to Naihati or Calcutta, sent by steamer to Goalundo and despatched to the various gardens. A series of laws from 1859 enabled planters to recruit labour on coercive contracts.[26] The system was controlled by the Calcutta-based British Managing Agencies who also managed the jute mills. Their various interests were brought together in the Bengal Chamber of Commerce.

The jute industry, by virtue of its location, could draw on all these streams of migration.[27] Calcutta and Naihati were two major centres through which migrants passed and these urban centres offered them a variety of alternative employment. Naihati, an important railway junction in the east–west traffic, also lay at the heart of the greatest concentration of jute mills – the Jagaddal–Naihati–Bhatpara belt. Calcutta and Naihati had the two most important labour depots from which workers were despatched to (Assam and overseas) plantations. From 1904, Naihati took over from other smaller depots like Bhatpara, Ranchi, Palamau, Madhupur and Purulia, as the only halting place for labour recruited from Orissa, Madras Presidency, Central Provinces and Midnapore.[28]

Inter-provincial seasonal migration was well entrenched long before jute mill migration started. The districts supplying the largest numbers of such seasonal migrants were also over-represented among mill labour – Saran heading the list. The classic pattern of industrial migration – male and circular – corresponded more closely to the seasonal migration of agricultural labour than the relatively long-term or settled family migration offered by plantations. Wages in plantations were lower than in the jute industry.[29] Distance and ease of communication too must have contributed to the migrant's decision to opt for 'free' migration to

---

[26] Even after the Workmen's Breach of Contract Act was actually abolished in 1926, the gardens continued to intimidate labourers with the threat of penalties for 'desertion' or 'absconding'. R. K. Das, *Plantation Labour in the Indian Tea Industry*, Bombay, 1954.

[27] Bagchi has called jute mill migration a 'by-product' of plantation recruitment. A. K. Bagchi, *Private Investment in India 1900–1939*, Cambridge, 1972, pp. 133–5. Chakravarty points out that the influx into jute mills started when colonial emigration was falling off. Lalita Chakravarty, 'Emergence of an Industrial Labour Force in a Dual Economy – British India, 1880–1920', *Indian Economic and Social History Review*, 15, 3, 1978.

[28] WBSA, General Emigration, April 1904, B6–9.

[29] Wage-differentials are difficult to establish. But it appears that jute workers were better paid than, at least, the plantation labour. Bagchi, *Private Investment in India*, p. 123.

Calcutta rather than the greater security of 'contract' migration. In the aftermath of the famine of 1874, when the government sought to encourage emigration to the tea districts, many from the worst affected areas came instead to Calcutta.[30]

It is likely that rural migrants knew something about the areas to which they were migrating. Intending migrants would use the advances made by sardars, recruiters and agents to pay debts or to tide over a bad patch. They would take a free ride to Calcutta and then complain to the Protector that they were 'unwilling' to proceed or had been coerced.[31] Sometimes even sardars refused to honour the 'contract'. Local recruiting agents complained that sardars refused to return to the gardens after the expiry of their licence and would not give an account of the advances paid to them. An unwilling migrant had to be returned to his place of registration at the expense of the agents. In 1916 the Chairman of the Assam Labour Board complained,

[A]dvances and payments [are] made to prospective emigrants for the purpose of paying off debts or for the support of members of families left in the recruiting districts or on other grounds ... Cases in which emigrants, who have received such payments and who have subsequently, when en route to Assam, declared themselves unwilling to proceed have lately arisen, and in some instances the same emigrants have repeated these tactics on more occasion than one.[32]

To prevent destitution, the government had ruled that in all cases, the agents would be responsible for 'repatriation' of prospective emigrants to the place of their origin, that is to say, to the place where they were recruited and registered. Agents responded by delaying registration after recruitment. They registered workers in Calcutta in order to avoid the costs of repatriation. Many 'intending' or 'returned' migrants were thus stranded – a floating labour pool around the Calcutta and Naihati depots. There were many like Sikdar Pod and his wife, Khiro. They were promised employment in Calcutta and taken to a depot. They escaped but could not return home. There were two men from Arrah and Fyzabad who escaped before they reached the depot, but found it impossible to make their own way home.[33] There were men like

---

[30] WBSA, General Emigration, July 1904, A6–15. In a case instituted against four garden *sardars* accused of kidnapping six women and two men, all the testimonies indicated that the men and women had been decoyed to the gardens with promises of employment in Calcutta.

[31] The 'Protector' was appointed by the Government to 'protect' prospective emigrants and also to oversee recruitment and migration for the plantations. WBSA, General Emigration, June 1911, B7–24.

[32] Lt. Colonel W. M. Kennedy, *Report on the Working of the Assam Labour Board for the Year Ending 30 June 1916.*

[33] Kennedy, *Report on the Working of the Assam Labour Board.* Also see WBSA, General Emigration, December, 1911, B4–9.

Bindeshwari Prasad, who managed to escape from the Calcutta depot and wandered destitute looking for work in the city.[34] These and the few 'paupers' returned from the plantations in the overseas colonies joined the urban labour market.

By the end of the nineteenth century, adult men poured into Calcutta, the largest commercial centre in the region, to swell the crowds at the jute mill gates. So far as labour supply was concerned, the mill owners' locational calculations finally paid off, and paid off handsomely.

Shift to migrant labour – implications for women workers

Since it was long-distance migrants who met the jute mills' staple labour requirements, the fact that they primarily comprised men had a significant impact on employment patterns in the mills. First, women already working in the mills were disadvantaged by the influx of migrant men. Second, a few women did migrate. But they did so in conditions which confirmed their marginalisation.

It has been mentioned that when the industry depended on 'local' labour, they drew on poor peasants, artisans and destitutes. Women, more often, belonged to the last category. Widows and deserted wives were forced to work for hire when they were deprived of familial resources. The pattern of women's participation in visible economic activity was not regionally uniform. In the areas where the jute industry was concentrated – Calcutta, 24 Parganas, Hooghly and Howrah – women's workforce participation rates were the lowest.[35] The relative prosperity of the region which allowed local men to opt out of mill employment also allowed them to retain cultural sanctions against women's induction into jute mills. Thus it would be only single women – deserted wives and widows – who would seek employment in the mills.

Although it is difficult to arrive at a precise estimate of the proportion of women among jute workers in the nineteenth century, it appears to have been highest at the turn of the century. In the 1890s there were about 17–20 per cent women in the total workforce.[36] In these years, a 'good proportion' of the women came from within a radius of two or three miles away from the mills.[37] But in addition to local women, there were migrants from Midnapore, Birbhum and Bankura. Some of them

[34] *Dasi*, 1, 1, 1891; 2, 2, 1894.   [35] See chapter 2 below.
[36] The figures are difficult to ascertain. My own are taken primarily from IJMA reports and the Census. Also see Arjan de Haan, *Unsettled Settlers: Migrant Workers and Industrial Capitalism in Calcutta*, Rotterdam, 1994, p. 201.
[37] B. Foley, *Report on Labour in Bengal*, Calcutta, 1906, para. 29.

came to Calcutta and the mill towns, though a large proportion also went to the plantations and collieries. Many families left Midnapore to settle in the Sunderbans, '[o]thers came as millhands and coolies in the metropolitan districts'.[38] Before 1890, many women working in jute mills were from these three districts.[39] Quite consistently and even in the 1920s, among the various streams of migration to Calcutta and suburbs, the proportion of women was highest in the migration from Midnapore (at 56.8 per cent), followed by Hooghly (at 49.7 per cent).[40]

In the 1890s, women comprised 29 per cent among the workers of Shyamnagar Jute Mill. Of these, 9.3 per cent were 'locals', i.e., they came from within a five-mile radius of the mill, and 10.4 per cent migrated from further afield in Bengal. By the beginning of the twentieth century, the proportion of Bengali women in the total labour force was considerably reduced. In 1905, when women constituted 22 per cent of the total workforce in the jute industry, only a very insignificant proportion was 'local'. The Preparing Department alone employed more women than men – about 80 per cent in Victoria, Shyamnagar and Titagarh.[41]

As in the case of the men, the growing flow of migrants tended to diminish the share of locals among women in the workforce. But in the case of women the decrease was sharper. Men from Bihar and UP tended to displace Bengali women who worked in departments designated 'unskilled'. Bengali men, to some extent, retained their hold over the more 'skilled' jobs. Indeed, after 1900, Bengali men were over-represented among the 'skilled' category, though they formed only one-fifth of the total labour force. In 1921, 39 per cent of 'skilled' workers came from districts where the mills were located, while only 20 per cent came from UP. Equally, Bengali men seemed to have been better represented in the 'skilled' category (31 per cent) than in the 'unskilled' (17 per cent).[42] The 'skilled' workers earning higher wages were able to support their families in the jute mill area or in districts which permitted weekend commuting. Women from these families rarely worked in mills. As a result, the number of Bengali women in the workforce decreased

[38] Emigration from Midnapore amounted to nearly 4.8 per cent of the population, some of which went to Assam in the tea gardens and some to Mayurbhanj coal mines. L. S. S. O'Malley, *Bengal District Gazetteers* (henceforth *BDG*), Midnapore, Calcutta, 1911, pp. 32–8; Birbhum, 1910, pp. 30–6; Bankura, 1908, pp. 44–6.
[39] WBSA, Home Judicial, February 1896, A423–440. Also see *Indian Factory Commission* (henceforth *IFC*), Calcutta, 1891, pp. 77–87.
[40] *Report of the Royal Commission on Labour in India* (henceforth *RCLI*), V, 1, pp. 4–8.
[41] *Labour Enquiry Commission*, Calcutta, 1896 (henceforth *LEC*), Appendix O.
[42] It appears that 'skilled' referred to any job involving work with machinery. *Census of India*, 1921, V, 2.

rapidly. By 1923–4, the few Bengali women found in the industry were either widows or single women.[43]

From the beginning of the twentieth century, Bengali men tended to concentrate in mills south of Calcutta such as Budge-Budge and Fort Gloster, where the number of women employed had always been low.[44] Even in the 1930s, a mill like Budge-Budge continued to employ workers who drifted in from the surrounding districts rather than those who came from Bihar and U.P.[45]

It is not clear how managers viewed the declining presence of women in their mills. They expressed widely divergent opinions regarding the viability of employing women. Some mills seemed to have considered women troublesome. The IJMA repeatedly threatened to dispense with them altogether if the government imposed restrictive legislation on their hours of work and rest. Their stance in these debates suggested that they had no particular interest in employing women.[46] Though these avowals cannot be accepted at face value, the first Factories Act (1881) did come precisely when the industry was expanding rapidly and hiring more workers. The IJMA's failure to prevent legislation alerted them to the dangers of regulation of female labour on the British pattern and employers began to discourage the extensive employment of women.

While the formal position of the industry was unfavourable to employing women, individual employers or their managers continued to have contrary preferences. Some managers periodically expressed a preference for employing women. In 1875, the Gourepur Mill manager told the inspector, 'A few young girls among them [boys] [were] brought in to counteract the threat of strikes among the boys.'[47] Later in 1921, one manager averred that he liked a few women around to 'keep the men content', or to have girls around, though they were less efficient than boys, because they were more tractable than the boys who were prone to strikes.[48]

In either case – preference or aversion – managers accepted that the option was between *a few women* or no women at all. They did not contemplate a predominantly female workforce. Indeed, they would not

---

[43] Dagmar Engels, *Beyond Purdah? Women in Bengal, 1890–1939*, Delhi, 1996, pp. 212–13.
[44] *Annual Report on the Workings of the Factories Act in Bengal* (henceforth *FA*), 1911.
[45] *RCLI*, V, 1, R. N. Gilchrist, Memorandum of the Government of Bengal.
[46] WBSA, Judicial, November 1892, No. 95; *IJMAR*, 1887, 1899, 1907.
[47] WBSA, General Miscellaneous, September 1875, A 6–27.
[48] Curjel Report, Appendix B, Manager, Lawrence Jute Mill, Sl. No. 8. Das also reported similar views of managers. R. K. Das, 'Women Labour in India', *International Labour Review*, October–November, 1931, p. 397.

have found it easy to exercise such an option. To begin with, only a limited section of the local women had taken to jute mill employment. By the end of the nineteenth century, in any case, local labour was increasingly marginalised by the migrant workers. And the migrant workers were usually men. There was little family migration to the cities and only very few women migrated on their own. Mostly, men came alone or with a brother, a son or a cousin. Wives and daughters remained in the village. As a result, very little of this migration was permanent. Permanent migration was usually undertaken in family groups and included women. For officials, the number of women present in migrant groups constituted an index of the permanency of migration.[49] Some of the movement to the tea plantations of Assam, to the coal mines of Bengal, or to the settlements of the Sunderbans, represented family migration.

But this kind of permanent migration was rarely directed towards the city except in times of extreme distress and scarcity. A settled population of labouring poor from which large numbers of women could periodically be drawn into the labour force eluded Calcutta. The railways made temporary and circular migration easier. Workers could not only go to the city, but they could also return to the village more frequently. The need for permanent migration, and therefore migration in family units, was thus reduced. Men came without their wives and children from surrounding and more far-flung villages. They came to earn wages in Calcutta to supplement their agricultural earnings, but still retained the freedom to move between the city and the countryside.

In 1921, the Census Officer, Thompson, commented, 'a few workmen have children with them who were born since they immigrated but practically none have settled down to maturity to swell the numbers of the native born. They are no more than their temporary habitants.'[50] Calcutta had always had fewer women, but by the 1920s, Calcutta and the surrounding mill towns became an overwhelmingly male world. In the female population older women and children were preponderant.[51] In the adult population, there were eight men to three women in Calcutta and eleven men to four women in mill towns.[52]

Certainly, women from Bihar and UP often migrated without their families. Individual female migration over short distances often outstripped male migration, especially in rural–rural migration. Women also contributed large numbers to casual and inter-district migration,

[49] *BDG*, Midnapore, Calcutta, 1911, p. 33.   [50] *Census of India*, 1921, V, 1, p. 116.
[51] *Report on the Municipal Administration of Calcutta*, 1920–1, I, p. 67 and table 9.
[52] *Census of India*, 1901, VI, 1, paras 71 and 109. In Titagarh and Bhatpara women were about 25 per cent of the population. *Census of India*, 1921, V, 2.

and only some of this could be attributed to marriage.[53] Temporary and seasonal migration for agricultural labour, for instance, accounted for large numbers of immigrants in Saran. In 1921, of the 44,736 total immigrants, 20,000 casual immigrants came from contiguous UP districts – 'and the majority of these are women'.[54]

Such migration was usually casual or seasonal. Women from labouring families travelled alone or in groups during peak agricultural seasons to undertake transplanting or weeding work, or peasant women may have travelled to their natal villages to participate in harvesting as part of their household's survival strategy. These seasonal women migrants neither revoked nor even challenged familial control over their labour. Rather, a pattern of periodic migration became integral to the deployment of women's labour by the family. The dominant values of seclusion and segregation did not preclude labouring women's participation in field and other visible work, even when it involved travelling long distances.

Women's individual migration to the cities was usually of a very different character. Many women who came to the city were single: widows, deserted or deserting wives who came alone, or 'with men who were not their husbands'.[55] Some women were those cast off by their families for a variety of reasons. Widowed or barren women, those suspected of infidelity, wives whose husbands had married again, found it increasingly difficult to survive in the village without familial support. Their earlier independent occupations – spinning, husking and food processing – were being gradually eroded. Their access to resources was increasingly dependent on their relational and behavioural role fulfilment within the family. The city offered them anonymity and wages. But married women or widows who left their villages alone or with their lovers, often abrogated all possibilities of returning to their village. For such women permanent migration to the city could have been either a preferred choice, or the last desperate alternative.

The most common incidence of such deprivation seems to have been through widowhood, as is evident from statements collected by the various labour commissions. Except one, all the women interviewed by the Indian Factory Commission of 1891 were widows who held that all their colleagues were widows too and that widowhood alone drove

[53] A. Menefee Singh, 'Rural-to-Urban Migration of Women in India: Patterns and Implications', in J. T. Fawcett et al. (eds.), *Women in the Cities of Asia*, Essex, 1984.
[54] A. P. Middleton, *Bihar & Orissa District Gazetteer* (henceforth *BODG*), Saran, Patna, 1930, p. 32.
[55] See chapter 5 below.

Bengali women into mill work.[56] Many widows, who were denied their customary right of maintenance by both their natal and conjugal families, came to the city in search of jobs.[57] Narsama Kurmi came to work in the jute mill because 'after the death of her husband the witness found that she could not earn a living in her native place, and her brothers were not willing to receive her back into the family on account of the extra work it would give them to keep her'. She had no children and so she came to Calcutta alone and secured work in the Howrah Jute Mill. Young Bochu Nilkanto came to Serampore with his mother when his father died. Noor Muhammad's mother 'compelled him to join the mill' when his father died. Mangari came to Titagarh with her husband who 'died of cholera' and she was compelled to join the preparing department of the mill. Her 'widowed mother' worked in the same department. Mangari's sister was 'a barren lady' and she too worked in the mill.[58]

Many women came to the city to escape social and familial harassment. Sometimes women escaped persecution by their husbands or in-laws. Or a domestic quarrel might trigger off flight. Such women had little access to resources outside the family and migration might have seemed a viable option providing some economic independence. Often they left with men who held out prospects of high wages and good working conditions. Some of these women took up jute mill work. Some migrants sought refuge in the impersonality of urban life after violating kin or caste rules in the village.[59] Sociologists in the 1920s and 1930s cited such cases, often to demonstrate the social anarchy they associated with the mills' neighbourhoods.[60]

A young caste Hindu woman, wife of a railway officer, ran away with Biswanath Singh, a weaving *sardar*, and came to Naihati. The *sardar* got her a job in the Finishing Department.[61] Women who wished to marry outside caste or community often had little option but to migrate. For instance, Maharajia, a married Hindu girl, left her husband to marry a Muslim. Her second husband's family rejected her; she and her husband were forced to seek employment in Calcutta.[62] The extent of

---

[56] *Report of the Indian Factory Commission*, Calcutta, 1891 (henceforth *IFC*), pp. 88–9.
[57] See chapter 2 below.   [58] *RCLI*, XI, pp. 335–65.
[59] Curjel Report, Appendix B, Mr Niyogi, Organising Secretary, Servants of India Society.
[60] G. M. Broughton, *Labour in Indian Industries*, London, 1924, p. 15; S. G. Panandikar, *Industrial Labour in India*, Bombay, 1933, p. 219.
[61] Interview, Dr Kamala Basu, Naihati, 28 October 1989.
[62] WBSA, Finance Emigration, February 1913. A little support for this kind of statement can be had from newspaper reporting of petty criminal cases. In the seven months between June and December 1929, the *Amrita Bazar Patrika* reported eight cases of 'abduction' and 'enticement' from villages to jute towns, while the *Ananda Bazar*

such 'individual' women's migration cannot be ascertained but it is beyond doubt that women were less mobile in long-distance village-to-city migration. Jute mill managers would have to intervene actively in this pattern of migration if they wished to employ more women. They already had male labour at their gates; and the costs of organising women's recruitment seemed steep by comparison.

The Managing Agents had a ringside view of organised recruitment: Assam and overseas colonial planters financed migration on a large scale. Both these groups of employers operated from a situation of acute labour shortage. Assam planters, faced with remote, uninhabited and inaccessible gardens, needed to 'settle' labour. The abolition of slavery had prompted colonial planters into alternative modes of recruitment. Both these employers particularly needed women (or 'families'). Assam planters wanted a self-reproducing workforce. The colonial planters were concerned about a possible 'social anarchy' from the skewed gender-ratio among their Indian labour. They did not wait for the free operation of the labour market to bring forth women. They deployed their own coercive apparatus with the collusion of the colonial state. They kidnapped, 'enticed' and recruited. In the process they ran the gauntlet of patriarchal opposition.[63]

Women's migration outside the family context was characterised as deviant. Such migration, voluntary or involuntary, threatened familial control over women's labour and sexuality. These dominant patriarchal values, the norms of seclusion and gender segregation, were undergoing changes in the nineteenth century, eroded in some aspects and reinforced in others. But these changes did not by any means contribute towards 'freeing' women from family control or towards their large-scale employment in the modern capitalist sectors. Of course, there was a massive demand for labour – in the urban labour market of Calcutta, in Bengal's three industries, tea, coal and jute, and in the overseas plantations. But specific demand for women's labour was neither so large nor so compelling. The industrial sector in India, even in the 1930s, was indeed quite small as consequently was its demand for labour.[64]

Patrika reported fifteen in the same period. The *Amrita Bazar Patrika* again reported nine similar cases of 'abduction' and 'enticement' in 1935, eleven in 1937 and sixteen in 1939.

[63] Samita Sen, 'Unsettling the Household: Act VI (of 1901) and the Regulation of Women Migrants in Colonial Bengal', in Shahid Amin and Marcel van der Linden (eds.), 'Peripheral Labour? Studies in the History of Partial Proletarianization', *International Review of Social History Supplement 4*, 41, 1996, pp. 135–56.

[64] In absolute terms, India's industries were doing well – at a steady 4–6 per cent annual growth rate. But in 1900–1, the secondary sector accounted for just 11.7 per cent of the national income and 10 per cent of the labour force. The jute industry contributed about 0.4 per cent to the national income. K. Mukherji, 'A Note on the Long Term

In the matter of women's migration, the colonial state was caught between the interests of British capital and the displeasure of indigenous elites, missionaries and some of their own district officials. The state's reliance upon the collaboration of various, shifting sections of the local elites gave force to opposition against 'greater freedom' and migration for women. Moreover, the state's revenue policies were premised on small peasant agriculture which in turn increasingly depended on the intensification of 'family' labour. From the middle of the nineteenth century, the Government of India introduced a series of legal and administrative measures to entrench familial control over women's labour. The widening of women's migration options could threaten these equations.[65] In the late nineteenth century the debate about the rights and wrongs of women's recruitment reached a peak. When the Assam Labour and Emigration Act (Act VI) of 1901 was finally passed, it included several clauses dealing specifically with women's recruitment. Together these clauses denied women the right to take migration decisions. The Act accepted that husbands and children were to be 'protected'; and women who wished to escape them had to be prevented or punished. Its provisions were invoked by fathers and husbands to stop women leaving 'home', either alone or with lovers. Doubtless, the Act did very little to stop the 'enticements' and kidnappings which it avowed to address. Most district officials were indifferent to, if not actively in sympathy with, recruiting agencies, many of which were owned and run by Europeans. But ineffective as it was, the Act made women's recruitment more difficult and expensive.[66]

Managing agents were not only fully alive to the trials of women's recruitment. They were chary of any 'active recruitment' that involved investing in workers' migration for jute mill labour. Some of them undertook 'active recruitment' for tea plantations – they constantly complained of labour shortage, generated stacks of paper, devised networks of agencies and regulations and resorted regularly to fraud and kidnapping to meet their targets. For the jute industry, they did relatively little. The Labour Enquiry Commission of Bengal, 1896, confined itself to only a perfunctory mention of the jute industry in an appendix because the IJMA displayed no interest. The IJMA, in fact, declared that they needed no 'system of recruitment'. The jute mills did not require recruiting agents or contract migration. They were not

Growth of National Income in India 1900–01 to 1952–53' in V. K. R. V. Rao et al., *Papers on National Income and Allied Topics*, Bombay, 1962; O. Goswami, *Industry, Trade and Peasant Society: The Jute Economy of Eastern India, 1900–1946*, Delhi, 1991, p. 11.
[65] WBSA, Judicial Police, August 1873, A95–98.
[66] Sen, 'Unsettling the Household'.

willing to finance recruitment. The labourers 'came and went as they pleased'. This proved sufficient for the industry's needs.[67]

The mills eschewed even *sardari* recruitment. Between 1870 and 1905, when the industry was continually and dramatically expanding, *sardars* were probably used. But this never developed into an organised system of recruitment and its significance declined over time. *Sardari* recruitment was never the single method of recruitment, nor a very important source of labour for mills. By the beginning of the twentieth century the mills were refusing to pay railway fares for intending migrants. One weaver told Foley, 'If the mills sent *sardars* for men and paid them their railway fares, they would obtain men. If he himself was sent ... for 50 men and paid their railway fares, he could obtain 50 men.'[68] Foley suggested that there was a certain amount of *sardari* recruitment, but by 1905 this had already become negligible. Though official and management statements often refer to the *sardar* and his role in recruitment, by the time of the Royal Commission very few workers were brought to the city by a *sardar*.[69]

It would appear that the manner in which migrants found their way into the city and into jobs in the unorganised sector was not very different from the way they entered mill work. Large numbers of migrants from Bihar and Orissa sought temporary or permanent employment in mills, warehouses, tank-digging, brick-making and in a vast range of casual and manual work like *palki*-bearing, *punkha*-pulling and as *coolies*.[70] Jute mill labour was in no way set apart from the urban poor engaged in a variety of casual and unskilled employment. Rickshaw pullers and carters, for instance, were often attracted through agents like *chaudhuris* and *sardars*, old and trusted employees from UP and Bihar, who usually recruited from their own areas. But entry into these occupations was not restricted to those who came in through intermediaries.[71] Jute mill workers too were a part of this vast urban labour market encompassing Calcutta, Howrah and Naihati.[72]

---

[67] W. Parson, Secretary, Bengal Chamber of Commerce, WBSA, General Department, Emigration Branch, August 1905, A26–39.

[68] Foley Report, Appendix I.

[69] Only four out of twenty witnesses were recruited by *sardars*. Many more found employment through kin and village network. *RCLI*, V, 2, pp. 76–80; XI, pp. 355–65.

[70] *Report on the Administration of the Bengal*, 1878–79, p. 124.

[71] Labour Investigation Committee, Ahmed Mukhtar, *Report on Rickshaw Pullers*, Delhi, 1946.

[72] Bala Missir operated a carters' network. WBSA, Home Political Confidential (henceforth HPC) 199 (1–5) of 1925. In 1923, Jagdeo Bania secured employment with 'the notorious cart chowdhury Bala Missir'. WBSA, HPCO, 908 of 1930. Also see M. K. A. Siddiqui, 'Caste among the Muslims of Calcutta', in S. Sinha (ed.), *Cultural Profile of Calcutta*, The Indian Anthropological Society, Calcutta, 1972, p. 42.

'Active recrutiment' of workers involving payment of advances, commissions and the costs of transportation was viable for the plantations because these were covered by contracts. Briefly, in the 1890s, the IJMA sought ways and means of tying down labour. Managers complained that workers brought to the city at their expense to work in their mills disappeared altogether or were found working in neighbouring mills or in other employment. They contemplated criminal prosecution to deter 'deserters'. Bengal Chamber of Commerce and IJMA tried to persuade the Government of Bengal to extend to them the facilities of the Workmen's Breach of Contract Act, enacted in 1859 specifically for the benefit of tea plantations. The mills in Howrah were already under the operation of the Act, but the Government of Bengal felt that the Act would be 'unsuitable for the Calcutta side of the river'. Another existing instrument was Section 492 of the Indian Penal Code which bound a worker brought at the expense of the employer 'by lawful contract in writing' for a period of at least three years. To invoke this law against deserting workmen, mills would have to enter into individual written contracts once at the place of origin and have these affirmed at the mill gates. The Government's response to IJMA's overtures was unenthusiastic. Mills crowded together in a small area and competing incessantly for skilled labour would be unable to enforce these laws.[73]

The Government of Bengal was equally lukewarm about IJMA's proposal that local officials should actively encourage migration to jute mills. Given the competing demands for labour by agents for overseas emigration, tea planters and local landed interests, the Government was unwilling to play an obviously partisan role. Instead, they recommended the employment of recruiters.[74] But therein lay the hub of the matter. Recruitment through agents or *sardars* involved payment of travel expenses and a commission which could only be recovered from the worker over a period of time. Mill owners were not particularly keen on incurring these costs. The mills' labour shortage was not acute enough, they were not willing to commit themselves to continued employment of individual workers, and their ability to prevent desertion seemed uncertain.

Jute mill owners preferred their casual and informal recruitment. While this involved temporary labour shortages and a high turnover of labour, it also left them free to hire and fire at will. In any case, the remoteness of plantations not only made some women's presence desir-

[73] Haywood, *IJMAR*, 1899; Secretaries of Dunbar Mills, 24 Parganas, *Miscellaneous Annual Report of the Presidency Division, 1902–3*, WBSA, General Miscellaneous, November 1903, A 19–22.
[74] *IJMAR*, 1899 and 1907.

able; it permitted a degree of control over the women thus expensively recruited which jute mills were not in a position to ensure. Thus the jute industry rejected a system of modified indenture which would entail any responsibility on the part of the employer, or state recruitment which would bind them to employ workers, women or men, sent down by Government.[75] Mill managers also realised that while any form of indentured employment or *sardari* recruitment would protect their investment in individual workers, their investment would bind them to their workmen as surely as the written contract would bind the worker. A manifest preference for women workers through organised recruitment was thus inimical to the industry's interests. Although there were very few women in the industry, the mills had found a ready labour force. To ensure a similar supply of women workers, they would have to attempt specific and direct recruitment of women, invest in agents and pay rail fares, run the gauntlet of patriarchal legal restraints and win the co-operation of local officialdom. Women may have been cheaper on the shopfloor, but it cost too much to get them there. Without incurring any of these costs, the mill owners had got the labour supply they wanted in the male migrants.

The jute mills' labour strategy

It has been argued that local labour failed to meet the industry's expanding demand in the 1880s. It was the accelerated scale of migration from Bihar and UP that really provided for the mills. But the complaints about labour shortage persisted up to 1905, well after migrants had glutted the labour market. Thus some interesting questions about the mills' labour strategies arise. The mills' owners required not just 'sufficient' labour; they needed a flexible labour supply allowing for fluctuations in production. Labour surplus, placing them in an unassailable bargaining advantage, was crucial to their operational strategy.

In the 1870s, Calcutta mills had cut into Dundee's markets and made unprecedented profits. This had prompted a sudden rush of investment. In 1884, when overproduction threatened to take the bottom out of the export market, the mills combined to form the Indian Jute Manufacturers' Association.[76] The main purpose of the Association was voluntary restriction of production in order to maintain price levels. In 1886, they agreed to reduce the running time of the mills. This was called the

[75] W. Parson, Secretary, Bengal Chamber of Commerce, WBSA, General Emigration, August 1905, A26–39.
[76] The name was changed to Indian Jute Mills Association in 1902.

Short Time Working Agreement, a device to be tried, tested and strained in the years to come. But the IJMA was not able to unite the industry's interests and wield monopolistic power. Researchers have recently pointed out that the Association was, in fact, riven by internal rivalries. The IJMA found the first agreement difficult to reach and even more difficult to maintain and enforce.[77] Towards the close of the decade several new mills were floated at the cost of the full working capacity of existing mills. The IJMA was powerless to prevent the erection of new mills, even by its own members.[78] The Hastings mills, having secured 'the bulk of the woolpack orders' and working longer with electric light, thumbed their noses at the IJMA. Some mills retaliated by under-selling – a 'breach of the spirit and aim of the association', which the IJMA found 'impossible' to stop.[79] Thus, even when the jute industry served a buoyant market, intra-industry competition proved too strong for effective producers' combination.

The IJMA was also unable to eliminate 'time-cribbing'.[80] This referred to the practice of running mills longer than permitted by the agreement. Thus mills usually employed more labour than their official production figures warranted. Mr Nicoll of the IJMA, for instance, admitted that 'shortage' often referred to their inability to procure the 10 or 15 per cent additional labour that mills preferred to carry.[81] Ostensibly, this was an insurance against absenteeism and the dilatory habits of Indian workmen.

No legislation can alter the nature and ingrained habit of Indian workers. They have been in the habit of leaving their work at odd and uncertain periods ... [f]or taking food, smoking, drinking water and necessary purposes ... [E]fforts have been made but with only limited success, to stop, or at any rate curtail these practices ... [T]he Indian mill hand takes frequent unauthorised holidays.[82]

Accordingly, the mills averred that they carried almost '100 per cent more hands' than a similar mill would in Dundee.[83]

Mills certainly required their 'superfluous' workers for clandestine production during short-term working. Since most mills worked more hours and more looms whenever possible, a certain amount of 'floating' labour was essential for their operational flexibility. The 1880s and 1890s, although by and large profitable for the industry, were also

[77] DUL, TDP, Shyamnagar Jute Mill papers, July 1885 to May 1886; Directors' Minute Book, Titagarh Jute Factory, 24 June 1885.
[78] Ibid., October 1888.
[79] DUL, TDP, Directors' Minute Book, Shyamnagar Jute Factory, 14 May 1890.
[80] DUL, TDP, Shyamnagar Jute Mill papers, July 1885 to May 1886.
[81] IJMAR, 1899.   [82] IJMAR, 1907.
[83] WBSA, General Miscellaneous, August 1893, A1–36.

marked by remarkable fluctuations in the jute goods market. A series of short-term working agreements contributed to these uncertainties. In these circumstances most mills preferred casual employment from a surplus labour pool, allowing them to recruit or retrench according to need.

The jute industry largely produced secondary goods for a volatile international market. At the beginning of the twentieth century, it exported nearly 85 per cent of its total manufacture.[84] Until the First World War the expanding trade in wool, wheat and cotton proved profitable. In the war years, there were unprecedented profits in supplying sandbags. However, as Omkar Goswami has shown, by 1913 the US market alone consumed about 40 per cent of Calcutta's jute products.[85] The industry became heavily dependent on the vagaries of one national market. Their output flexibility depended on two elements of their variable cost: raw material and labour.

The price of raw jute was relatively unpredictable. Jute growers, operating on small margins, sold immediately after the fibre was separated. But post-harvest prices were subject to massive fluctuations. The mills tried to depress prices by manipulating the gradations of raw jute, but this had only a limited effect.[86]

Until the First World War, the mills were run almost entirely by European managing agencies. However, a very small proportion of the capital came from outside India. Most of the joint stock companies were floated in the Calcutta stock exchange. The managing agents controlled these companies, not by virtue of majority holding, but by ensuring that no one else acquired a large holding and by acquiring proxy votes from small shareholders. They took a commission on the gross turnover as well as their share of the dividend income. They were thus committed to a high level of output even if stocks mounted.[87] They were also committed to high dividend payments – to ensure an initial oversubscription of shares, of course, but also to attract capital. In the early years, when machinery and skilled personnel had to be imported at enormous cost, capital was not easily forthcoming. Very soon jute shares began to be snapped up in the Calcutta stock exchange because of the industry's reputation for high dividends.

In their attempt to balance high levels of output with high dividend payments, the mills were caught in a dilemma. In the short term, overproduction and a slump in international prices left them with few

---

[84] *IJMAR*, 1907.   [85] Goswami, *Industry, Trade and Peasant Society*.   [86] Ibid.
[87] Parimal Ghosh, 'Colonial State and Colonial Working Conditions: Aspects of the Experience of Bengal Jute Mill Hands, 1881–1930', *Economic and Political Weekly* (henceforth *EPW*), 30 July 1994.

alternatives. They were unable to influence prices. They attempted to combine in order to contain domestic competition and restrict output. However, their initial difficulties of combination grew increasingly insoluble. Five mills, called the 'outside' mills, who did not join the Association, battened on the Association's policy of voluntary cut-backs to earn large profits. In 1912 the Association almost split over short working.[88] Though the outbreak of the war in 1914 shelved these questions, the evident profitability of the industry attracted indigenous investment. Indian competition grew after the First World War. In 1911 there was only one Indian on the Board of Directors of one mill but by the 1930s the growing Indian component offered IJMA formidable competition.[89]

Even if not fully effective in themselves, the short-time working agreements made control of labour in general, and control of labour supply in particular, vital for the industry. To individual mills it seemed as though labour was the one significant factor of production they could control.[90] Workers' wages accounted for about 50 per cent of the total conversion costs in an average jute mill.[91] In 1897, the Shyamnagar mills desisted from installing electricity because of 'the great increase involved in wages'.[92] Since wages were such an important component of the cost of production, the managing agencies responded to short-term crises by reducing the level of employment and attempting a more intensive use of labour. In effect, restriction of production by shorter hours of work, or by sealing off a portion of the looms, cut into labour time and either increased the workload on individual workers or decreased wages by shortening the hours of work.

Between 1889 and 1900 labour mobility was the major source of friction among the 'Association' mills.[93] Also, their moves to cut wages and increase workloads often became the immediate cause of labour discontent. The 1890s were especially troublesome. About ten new mills were set up between 1896 and 1900. Many mill towns were

[88] *Sixth Half-Yearly Report of the Indian Jute Mills Association*, 31 December 1887; Wallace, *The Romance of Jute*.
[89] B. R. Tomlinson, 'Colonial Firms and the Decline of Colonialism in Eastern India, 1914–47', *Modern Asian Studies*, 15, 1981, pp. 455–86.
[90] For Bombay cotton textile industry, see R. S. Chandavarkar, *The Origins of Industrial Capitalism in India: Business Strategies and the Working Classes of Bombay, 1900–1940*, Cambridge, 1994. The difference between the two cases is that while Indian mill owners in Bombay failed to win from the government protection against textile lobbies of Britain and often also against labour troubles, the jute industry was much more successful in persuading the Government of Bengal to co-operate. See chapter 3 below.
[91] D. H. Buchanan, *The Development of Capitalist Enterprise in India*, New York, 1934, p. 250.
[92] DUL, TDP, Directors' Minute Book, Shyamnagar Jute Factory, 29 September 1897.
[93] DUL, TDP, Shyamnagar Jute Factory, 1900.

dogged by epidemics. In 1897–8, the weaving and spinning departments, where workers were not as easy to substitute, were the worst
affected by 'sickness'.[94] Meanwhile, in 1895–6 a series of labour strikes
and riots took place. Some of these were directed against the management, the municipal authorities and the police. There were occasional
disputes among workers, especially between Hindus and Muslims. The
mills became concerned about security and the need to forge a more
coercive apparatus in alliance with local government and the police to
ensure greater control over workers. Their financial contribution helped
the police to improve both direct and indirect vigilance over workmen's
activities.[95] Increasingly, the control of labour emerged as the key
element in their business strategy.

By the 1880s managers were vexed over control and discipline. The
local labour market, largely casual, comprised villagers who sought to
supplement agricultural earnings by working for wages. Managers
grumbled that these workers stayed away at harvest time or for rituals
like weddings and local festivals like the *rathyatra* and the many *pujas*. If
they were not let off, they took casual leave. Spinning 'boys' would go
on strike over 'trivial' issues like a small increase in wages or as an
excuse to take a day off work. The men who came from areas within
weekend commuting distance returned home frequently.[96]

Such absenteeism has sometimes been interpreted by historians as an
agricultural population's inability to adjust to the rhythm of industrial
work.[97] The levels of such truancy in the mills, and indeed the actual
disjuncture between agricultural and factory work, have perhaps been
exaggerated. The invocation of rural life as a colourful and harmonious
mosaic of work and leisure owes more to an urban nostalgia than to the
hard realities of agricultural work. It was as difficult for the poor peasant
to interrupt a day's harvest as for the artisan or the poor labourer to take
the odd day off during peak seasons. Besides, not all jute mill workers
had been agriculturalists. They came from a tremendously heterogeneous range of occupations. In Hooghly and parts of 24 Parganas a
variety of small-scale paper, oil, rice and other mills were already
familiar. From accounts of early mills, it appears more as though
workers were able to assimilate factory work within their established
pattern of life. Occasional stoppages for festivities were facilitated by
fluctuations in employment. At the same time, workers needed their

[94] DUL, TDP, Directors' Minute Book, Shyamnagar Jute Factory, 1889–90; Titagarh
Jute Factory, 1889–1900.
[95] WBSA, Judicial Police, June 1896, A8–9.
[96] WBSA, General Miscellaneous, September 1875, A6–27.
[97] Dasgupta, 'Material Conditions'.

wages and would not easily risk their jobs by excessive truancy. Managers were bound to exaggerate the levels of absenteeism, since mill owners justified low wages on gounds of low productivity and inefficiency. But the actual number of holidays depended on their bargaining success. It is quite clear, for instance, that in the early 1890s, when the mills were competing for labour, workers stepped up their holiday demands. When in Baranagore Jute Mill, in 1894, workers fought for a holiday on Bakr-Id, the manager found them 'more exacting' than previously. In 1893, the mill had not closed for either Id or Muharram. Mr Orr, Manager, Gourepore Jute Mill, stated that in 1896 for the first time workers demanded holidays on Id, Muharram and Rath Jatra. In many of the mills holidays had been routinely declared for Hindu festivals. As the Muslims grew in number, they began to claim their own holidays.[98]

The mill owners felt that men from Bihar and eastern UP were 'more satisfactory and regular'.[99] The owners were not engaged in a relentless quest for any ideal standards of labour efficiency. Managers were concerned with the supply and recruitment of labour and with the maintenance of discipline and attendance in the face of wage cuts, increasing hours and higher workloads. The established mills were concerned with preserving their workforce, especially older and skilled workmen like weavers and spinners. The newer mills attempted to 'lure away' the skilled workers of older mills. While managers were happy to employ workers on a relatively casual basis, the simultaneous loss of many workers destabilised production and caused disciplinary problems. In 1890, Titagarh faced some of these problems:

In some weeks the whole of the weavers have been changed and daily a considerable number of looms have been standing on account of no hands being available to work them ... [T]he average of the hands is far below par, many of the looms being worked by untrained coolies, who are only taking off a very poor production and thus greatly interfering with the results.[100]

Managers sought to constrain workers by keeping one week's wages in hand. Workers resisted. When weavers wanted to leave Kankinara Mill for higher wages at Shyamnagar, they attempted to collect their arrears from the manager. The police had to be called in to contain the ensuing riots.[101] But such measures were not always successful. Often workers

---

[98] WBSA, Judicial Police, June 1896, A8–9. The managers of Kankinara, Kamarhatty and Fort Gloster mills complained that workers were demanding many more holidays than previously.

[99] S. H. Fremantle, *Report on the Supply of Labour in the United Provinces and Bengal*, Calcutta, 1906.

[100] DUL, TDP, Directors' Minute Book, Titagarh Jute Factory, 1889–90.

[101] *FA* 1895.

abandoned their week's wages to move to a mill which paid more even if it meant longer hours of work. The introduction of electric lighting in some mills troubled Gourepur, Union and Kharda mills who 'feared that their labour would go to mills which worked with electric light'. In the end, they joined a short-term working agreement 'to get their labour in hand and not [for] the curtailment of production'.[102]

A series of violent strikes in 1895–6 further convinced managers that they needed stronger mechanisms of control over their expanding work-force. Many of them ascribed the disturbances to the 'cheapness of rice' that year and the activities of 'outside agitators' who were able to approach and influence Bengali workers. Some managers averred that 'old hands . . . [were] teaching the younger ones their rights or supposed rights'.[103] The manager of the Victoria Mill believed that Bengali workers were 'disaffected' because 'they are too well off' and that the fall in rice prices made them more independent.[104] The IJMA agreed that a fall in food prices induced local workers 'to take more holidays' and these in turn led to confrontations, often violent, with the managers. Attempts on the part of managers to enforce punctuality and punish latecomers led to a strike in Serampore. Another strike in Howrah was precipitated when an attempt was made to increase the length of the working day. The police had to feel their way because 'influential persons in Calcutta' were thought to have backed these strikes.[105] Compared to such volatile Bengali workers, 'the up-country men work steadily and they go home with their earnings once a year and in due course come back again'.[106]

But the managers' preference for 'up-country' men was not actualised without opposition.[107] The migrant 'surplus' drove wages down. It is highly unlikely that in an overstocked labour market, where the urban poor were competing for the relatively lucrative jute mill jobs, existing workers would accept lower wages and a longer working day without demur. Some workers, who walked a few miles from neighbouring villages to the mills, gave up their jobs in despair when their mills used electric light to extend the working day to fifteen hours.[108] Others clung to their jobs and tried to resist the induction of migrant workers and the

[102] WBSA, Judicial Police, January 1896 A5–7. Also see *IJMAR*, entry for 20 January 1899.
[103] WBSA, Judicial Police, June 1896, A8–9, Gourepur Jute Mills.
[104] Ibid., Victoria Jute Mill.
[105] *The Administration of Bengal under Sir Andrew Fraser*, 1903–8, pp. 26–7.
[106] WBSA, Judicial Police, June 1896, A8–9, Victoria Jute Mill.
[107] Ranajit Dasgupta, 'Factory Labour in Eastern India – Sources of Supply, 1885–1946', *Indian Economic and Social History Review*, 8, 3, 1976. For a 'cultural' argument, see de Haan, *Unsettled Settlers*.
[108] *IJMAR*, 1895.

wage depression. The Howrah Mills had used their proximity to the railway terminus to employ 'up-country' migrants. By 1893 these workers outnumbered the local men. In October, the police were summoned to quell a 'disturbance between old hands and new workers'.[109] In Kankinara, in April 1895, when the induction of new workers enabled the manager to cut wages by 4 annas, older spinners violently resisted.[110] But the 'old hands' were fighting a rearguard battle. The flood of migrants had so glutted the Calcutta labour market that their bargaining position was irredeemably weakened. By the 1890s nearly half the jute mill workers in Bengal were 'up-countrymen'.[111]

If the jute mill managers had thought that isolation from the local population of Bengal and the commitment to send their savings regularly to their native village would make the workers from Bihar and UP unresisting, they found by the late 1890s that their confidence had been misplaced. The 'up-country' workers quickly acquired a reputation for pugnacity and the Muslims a special notoriety as 'turbulent' and violent.[112] Local Bengali *bhadralok*, police, government officials and mill managers concurred on the threatening potential of these masses of alien men with their different languages and distinctive lifestyles. They were associated with overcrowded *bastis*, dirt, promiscuity and crime: results of the breakdown of the caste system, sexual mores and the moral order. In 1897, *Samay* wrote:

Just at present very large numbers of up-country Hindus and Muslims can be seen in Howrah, who are very stout and strong in physique . . . In the majority of theft cases . . . these upcountrymen are sent up as criminals . . . [They are] addicted to ganja and bear a turbulent character. The religious difference between up-country Hindus and Muslims is not very great and they will live in the same room.[113]

Earlier, in 1895, workers of several industrial establishments in Titagarh, about 35,000 people, had taken possession of a mill. The managers and the local government lost their nerve and decided to create more municipalities, to strengthen the police presence and to increase magisterial powers because these 'workpeople . . . are not as amenable to discipline as natives of Bengal'.[114] In the disturbed year of 1897 the 'possibility of a riotous spirit' was sometimes associated

---

[109] WBSA, Judicial Police, June 1896, A8–9, Howrah Mills. Wages were reduced in 1893, when Bengalis had already become a minority in this mill.
[110] *FA*, 1895.   [111] WBSA, Judicial Police, June 1896, A8–9.
[112] Parimal Ghosh, 'Emergence of an Industrial Labour Force in Bengal: A Study of the Conflicts of the Jute Mill Hands with the State 1880–1930', Ph.D Thesis, Jadavpur University, 1984.
[113] Report of Native Newspapers, *Samay*, 3 September 1897.
[114] WBSA, Judicial Police, January 1896, A5–7.

particularly with the 'masses of ignorant up-country mill hands'. The Tollah riots helped to focus such fears especially on Muslims. The Managing Agents for the Alliance Mill wrote to the IJMA, 'an urgent representation should be made … on the question of the present disturbed state of the Mohammedan labouring community'.[115]

Thus, the local Bengali workers and the up-country workers, especially the Muslims, were successively styled as volatile and turbulent. In other words, when the mills sought to manipulate labour by cutting wages and increasing workloads, the steadily expanding workforce began to combine in resistance along various axes – language, region and religion. The manoeuvres of the mill owners gave more potency to these identities and deepened differences among the workers. In many cases strikes began in an attempt to induce managers to grant holidays on religious festivals, increase wages, shorten working hours or dismiss corrupt and brutal supervisors. The managers faced with demonstrations opened fire at crowds of thousands of workers, and called upon the police who dispersed the 'mob' with guns or lathis and arrested workers indiscriminately.[116] These police interventions intensified strikes which often extended to the streets of mill towns. The grievances of Muslim workers increased when their collective religious festivities were dismissed as 'innovations' in areas where they were minorities. Their attempts to carry out cow sacrifices against local Hindu opposition and police prohibition precipitated several confrontations among Hindu and Muslim workers and the police.[117] Besides, the Muslim *Julahas* had begun to predominate in the weaving departments and to establish some degree of control over their jobs. Some managers, whose challenge to their monopolistic claims over weaving jobs failed, felt threatened.[118]

Some managers observed shrewdly that the troubles of the 1890s were being exacerbated by the competition for labour among mills. They predicted a complete capitulation of workers once the extensions of old mills and erections of new mills had been completed and the market settled down.[119] They got it nearly right. A major influx of migrants after the famine of 1896–7 did once again 'overstock' the labour pool. In 1905, there were only occasional seasonal shortages.[120]

[115] IOL, Judicial Police, 92, 7 July 1897.   [116] Ibid.
[117] The Rishra Cow Killing Case, WBSA, Judicial Police, August 1896, A1–13. For a debate on the 'communal' character of these riots see Dipesh Chakrabarty, *Rethinking Working Class History, Bengal 1890–1940*, Princeton, 1989; Parimal Ghosh, 'Communalism and Colonial Labour: Experience of Calcutta Jute Mill Workers, 1880–1930', *EPW*, 28 July 1990.
[118] WBSA, Judicial Police, June 1896, A8–9, Champdany Jute Mill. The Bombay cotton textile mill owners' attempts to attack the position of weavers has been explored in Chandavarkar, *Origins of Industrial Capitalism*.
[119] WBSA, Judicial Police, June 1896, A8–9   [120] Foley Report.

By 1914, labour scarcity was a distant memory.[121] Moreover, the flood of migrant labour and the Short Time Working Agreement had facilitated the depression of wages. While the manager of the Titagarh Jute Factory was being troubled by new and untrained workers, the directors were cheerfully contemplating a saving of Rs 1000 in the weekly wage bill.[122]

The jute mills did not conform to the conventions of large-scale industry in attempting a steady level of production with a stable workforce. Facing an uncertain world market, producing cheap and unstandardised secondary goods, unable to smooth the fluctuating prices of their raw material, the mill owners chose the policy of tailoring production to the vagaries of demand. Attempts at artificial restriction of production through a cartel failed as often as they succeeded. Their survival strategy became crucially predicated on a malleable labour market. In the male migrants from Bihar and the UP they got the labour supply they wanted: a supply large enough to enable them to manipulate labour, enforce wage reductions, intensify workloads, retrench and rehire at will.

It was because the effects of this large-scale migration were so favourable to the mills, that the IJMA explored ways of facilitating and expediting further migration. But they no more than toyed with the notion. The flow of migration was firmly established, they realised, without let or hindrance.

The 'working-class family' – reproduction of labour

The incessant flow of male migration more than adequately renewed the workforce. The jute industry did not require women to ensure a stable labour force that was locally self-reproducing. Moreover, the costs of reproduction of the labour force were in part provided by the continuing 'rural link' of the migrant workforce: the men earned a wage in the city while women and children remained in the village to procure subsistence through a range of waged work, gathering and foraging.

This migration – single, male and temporary – suited mill owners. The 'unsettled settlers', as de Haan has called them, were torn from their communities to live and work for a period of years in a hostile environment. The mill owners believed that they would be eager to save as much they could as quickly as possible and would, therefore, be susceptible to intensive working. They also believed that migrants

---

[121] *RCLI*, V, 2, pp. 161–2.
[122] DUL, TDP, Directors' Minute Book, Shyamnagar Jute Factory, 21 October 1885 and Titagarh Jute Factory, 1885–1890.

moving between the city and the countryside would provide the kind of flexible labour they needed; workers used to the seasonal rhythm of agricultural work would easily accept retrenchment when mills were forced into cutting labour supply and would return in equal or larger numbers when the mills wanted to rehire.

The reproductive role of the 'rural connection' came to the forefront in the 1920s and 1930s when the Government (prompted by the International Labour Organisation) and trade unions pressed for welfare measures like maternity benefit, sickness insurance or unemployment benefit. Their attempts were countered on the grounds that workers went home to their remote villages when they were pregnant, sick or unemployed. Mill managers conjured visions of the beauracratic nightmare involved in administering welfare schemes for, they claimed, an incessantly nomadic workforce.[123] Towards the 1940s, when they began to lose the argument, casual employment helped them to ensure that few workers fulfilled the minimum required period of service to be eligible for benefits.[124]

Managers found a relatively casual employment of workers more useful. If the mills had been required to invest in training workers, they might have pursued more assiduously the possibility of 'settling' down some categories of labour. But there is no evidence that this was the case. Even weavers acquired their skill at their own cost and time, by unpaid and informal apprenticeships.[125] Typically, the average length of service in individual mills was very short. In 1930, in eleven mills, an average of 62.2 per cent of workers had less than five years' service in a mill.[126] Angus Mill had a 12 per cent turnover per month in 1932, and this was a low figure compared to other mills.[127] There is very little evidence to show whether such turnover differed between various categories of workers. Nor is there any statistical evidence available to estimate labour turnover for the whole industry. The evidence for Bombay suggests that high labour turnover in individual mills may not have precluded relatively long-term 'commitment' to an industry, the workers being mobile between mills within the industry.[128] Doubtless, managers 'produced' high turnover figures to 'prove' that workers were unsettled and manipulated records to deny workers 'continuity of service' which would entitle them to the rudimentary social security benefits introduced in the 1930s. The oral evidence given by workers to

[123] *IJMAR*, 1925 and 1935.   [124] See chapter 5 below.
[125] Chakrabarty, *Rethinking Working Class History*, pp. 90–2.
[126] WBSA, Comm. Comm., April 1930, A19–20.
[127] G. T. Garratt, 'The Indian Industrial Worker', *The Economic Journal*, 42, 167, 1932, p. 399.
[128] Chandavarkar, *The Origins of Industrial Capitalism*.

the Royal Commission, however, suggests that workers in fact frequently left one mill for another.[129]

The managers' need for at the least a group of casualised workers was reflected in the *badli* system. The system seems to have run thus: a large number of men and women would present themselves at the mill gates at the beginning of each shift to a supervisor, a clerk or a *sardar*. The day's vacancies would be filled from these women and men. Their employment was for the day and their wages were estimated by shifts. It was possible for workers to work months and years together on this basis. There was no guarantee of employment from day to day, except the goodwill of the supervisor or the clerk concerned. Such goodwill could of course be obtained at a price. Supervisors, clerks and *sardars* ran a profitable trade in allotting daily assignments. It is thus that the *sardars* emerged as important players in the control of the labour market, not as recruitment agents. On the one hand, they had to ensure the availability of sufficient workers from day to day, on the other, they carried the powers and obligations of distributing patronage among the workers. In the 1930s, when this delicate balancing act could not be sustained anymore a Labour Bureau and a quasi-formal system of *badli* registers were introduced in an attempt to establish some degree of direct control over daily hiring.[130] Although many sources allude to this as a widely practised system, it is impossible to estimate the proportionate share of *badli* workers, since they were not registered in factory records. But this system enabled the mills to create a sufficiently large pool of labour, with the necessary skills, to keep wages depressed, and yet not to suffer the costs of carrying extra labour.

While the fluctuations of production and the consequent uncertainty of employment forced mill workers to retain their base in the village – as an insurance against unemployment, as a place to go to when they were ill or pregnant or more usually when they retired – the presence of this rural link also in turn contributed to the instability of the labour market. In order to maintain their rural base, a homestead and perhaps some land, some members of the family, usually the wives and children, remained in the village. So the village remained the home, with functional and emotional associations, to which the migrant workers returned every year for periods of one to three months.[131] The system of informal and personalised recruitment in the mills also meant that

[129] *RCLI*, V, 2, pp. 76–80; XI, pp. 335–65.
[130] DUL, TDP, Victoria Jute Mills, Manager's Report to the Directors, 1939 (henceforth, MRD).
[131] De Haan, *Unsettled Settlers*. He has argued that the instability of the labour market and the personalised recruitment were as much, if not more, the chosen alternative of the migrant workers as dictated by mills' policies.

access to jobs could very often depend on relationships carried over from the village to the city. Chandavarkar has argued, in the case of Bombay, that this could include a range of services besides employment; access to credit and housing could also depend on a range of caste, religious and village associations.[132] A *deshvali bhai* ensconced in the mill neighbourhood was an invaluable asset to the fresh migrant.

In many ways, then, migrants with a 'rural connection' in contributing to the casual nature of the urban labour market were useful for the industry, useful enough to offset the disadvantages of high labour turnover and more useful than a 'settled' population of labouring families. The earnings of wives and children in the villages enabled the male workers to 'come and go as they please' but the inadequacy of the rural earnings ensured that male workers actually came and went more according to the mills' requirements.

The mills passed on the entire cost of migration to the workers as well as the costs of the maintenance and reproduction to the rural household. The jute mill workers' wages were insufficient for the maintenance of a family in the expensive cities and towns; they were insufficient even for the survival of the man in the city and his household in the village. As a result, the men in the city were caught in a vicious cycle of indebtedness. An enquiry in 1930 revealed that, 'most of the families are in a chronic state of indebtedness and the apparent savings of 8 per cent are spent on the payment of debts and interests, except a few families, who really do make a saving'.[133] Though a certain part of the debt was incurred in the village, a large part, perhaps the major part, was incurred in the mill area itself. Apparently, Rs 45 of the total debt of Rs 60 incurred by Hindus from UP, and Rs 75 out of a total debt of Rs 94 incurred by the *madrasis*, were actually incurred in the mill area itself.[134] Annual interest rates ranging from 72–150 per cent were paid by 75–90 per cent of the workers. The average debt per head among 30,000 workers was calculated to be Rs 189. The margin of savings was, of course, too low for them ever to be able to repay their debts, though interest was cut off at source.[135] The practice of moneylenders queuing up before the mills on pay day has been mentioned frequently. Migrating to the city and securing a jute mill job was at times a means of augmenting access to credit. Credit obtained in the city could go towards the maintenance of the rural base – cash to pay taxes, to buy seeds or service the debts

[132] Chandavarkar, *The Origins of Industrial Capitalism*.
[133] A. C. Roychoudhury, *Report on an Enquiry into the Standard of Living of Jute Workers in Bengal*, 1930, para. 28.
[134] Roychoudhury, *Report on an Enquiry into the Standard of Living of Jute Workers*, para. 57.
[135] *RCLI*, V, 1, pp. 48–9.

accrued in the village.[136] Remittances from the city to the village certainly played an important role in the rural economy, though figures are difficult to obtain and untangle.[137]

The women and children worked for wages and at 'subsistence' occupations in the village. Thus the 'working-class family' made ends meet. Ranajit Dasgupta has argued that they existed at a 'sub-subsistence' level, the rural household invisibly subsidising the industry through the intensified work of women and children.[138] Unfortunately, wages and cost of living indices are an uncertain guide to a statistical evaluation of this thesis. The notion of 'subsistence' is, of course, highly relative and nailing it to precise figures an exercise fraught with difficulties. It has been argued that the lack of housing and the mills' policy of paying individual subsistence wages rather than a 'family wage' discouraged family migration.[139] There appears no obvious reason why the mills would pay 'family wages' – they were not concerned with family migration, they were not even willing to bear any part of the costs of efficient reproduction of the labour force, in terms of quantity, health or skills.

So far as the working poor were concerned, men, women and children had always laboured to enable the household's survival. In the case of the Bengal jute workers' household, the men worked in the city and the women and children in the rural economy. The higher cost of living in a city which offered women fewer opportunities for work within the social and cultural parameters of conventional gender differentiation must have influenced their migration decisions. Women coming to the city were usually concentrated in the lower-paid end of the wage market, and were deprived of the collecting and gathering activities that were so crucial to rural survival patterns.

In order to maintain the flexibility of the workforce, the mills im-

[136] Chandavarkar, *The Origins of Industrial Capitalism*.
[137] Gail Omvedt, 'Migration in Colonial India: The Articulation of Feudalism and Colonialism by the Colonial State', *Journal of Peasant Studies*, 7, 2, January 1980, pp. 195–6.
[138] Ranajit Dasgupta, 'Migrant Workers, Rural Connexions and Capitalism: The Calcutta Jute Industrial Labour, 1890s to 1940s', Indian Institute of Management (Calcutta) Working Paper Series, April 1987, Mimeograph.
[139] Arjan de Haan's data points in a completely different direction. He argues that debt was not related to poverty and that most mill workers could save about half their earnings. De Haan, *Unsettled Settlers*. I have argued in my Ph.D thesis that lower-paid workers could not afford to maintain their families in the city and therefore it was much more economical to leave women and children in the village. Samita Sen, 'Women Workers in the Bengal Jute Industry, 1890–1940: Migration, Motherhood and Militancy', Ph.D Thesis, Cambridge University, 1992, pp. 33–7. For a more detailed discussion of the relative notion of 'subsistence' and 'family wage' see Chandavarkar, *The Origins of Industrial Capitalism*, pp. 307–26.

printed on the labour market an unstable and casual character, aided by an informal and personalised system of recruitment. The nature of migration – male and circular – reinforced these tendencies. But the mill owners' expectations that temporary migrants would be necessarily more amenable to their manipulative strategies were badly misplaced. The informal system of recruitment brought into full play social identities based on gender, caste, religion, language and region. The way these relationships mediated access to jobs, credit and housing hardened identities and deepened differences within the workers. While these differences served at times to divide the workforce along various axes, they also allowed solidarities to be forged from these relationships.

Although casual and flexible labour was important to the industry, female labour, which has in various historical conjunctures proved the most amenable to fluctuating employment, was not required or desired by the jute mills. This was partly because the abiding 'rural' link of male migrants gave them some of the desired flexibility, but also because men came alone to the cities in large numbers to supplement their household income. The recruitment of women involved long-term investments in individual workers and costs which jute mills did not have to incur in the case of male labour, because they did not have to recruit men actively. There was an additional advantage in employing men. Women tended to respond more to the needs of the household economy than to the ebb and flow of the labour market. Married women often entered the labour market when a downswing in the economy had reduced male earnings and withdrew when things improved. This helped in keeping women's wages depressed, but it also involved an uncertainty of supply.

So far as the migrant workers were concerned, one or more male members of their family might spend the greater part of their lives in the mill towns, while the other members of the family lived and worked in their villages in various parts of Bengal, Bihar, Orissa or UP. Despite the long distances involved, it is necessary to overcome the habit of treating the city and the village, industry and agriculture as such distinctly separate entities that an investigation of the former can be undertaken without any reference to the latter. For the workers who often lived in two households, in the city and in the village, strategies of survival encompassed both these spheres. And it is in the context of the migrants' household strategy that the immobility of women in rural–urban migration must be understood.

2 'Will the land not be tilled?': women's work in the rural economy

In the nineteenth and early twentieth centuries, industrial and plantation employers found women expensive and difficult to recruit because of the family's prior claims on women's labour. It appears that pre-colonial rulers used the ideologies of family and caste to manufacture consent for a highly coercive labour arrangement. The colonial state drew on this available system of labour.[1] The family in particular continued to serve as the vehicle for the quotidian application of labour. Within the household, division of labour was according to gender and age; control was maintained through familial roles. The family remained crucial in the regular organisation of work and operated within other local caste and community affiliations when labour was required in greater quantities. Thus kin ties were the most important means of recruiting labour. Even the very large-scale and long-distance migrations overseas tended to operate on grounds of kin, caste and local networks.[2]

The colonial state reinforced gender controls within the family to facilitate small peasant agriculture which depended on unremunerated family labour. In fact, capitalist development itself 'rested heavily on the forcing up of labour intensity within family units actually tilling the land'.[3] Consequently, the division of labour in the household economy sharpened – men concentrated control of capital and capital-intensive labour in their own hands, relegating women to labour-intensive tasks with low status and poor reward. From the 1860s, two significant processes transformed the functioning of the rural household: the increase in the unpaid component of women's and children's labour and the decline in its paid component.[4]

---

[1] Ranajit Guha, 'Dominance Without Hegemony and its Historiography', *Subaltern Studies VI*, Delhi, 1989.

[2] Michael R. Anderson, 'Work Construed: Ideological Origins of Labour Law in British India to 1918', in Peter Robb (ed.), *Dalit Movements and the Meaning of Labour in India*, Delhi, 1993, pp. 87–120.

[3] Sugata Bose, *Peasant Labour and Colonial Capital. Rural Bengal since 1770*, New Cambridge History of India, III-2, Cambridge, 1993, pp. 66–111.

[4] Discussed more fully in Samita Sen, 'Unsettling the Household: Act VI (of 1901) and

As agrarian surplus dwindled, small and marginal peasant families began to depend more heavily on household tasks geared to subsistence and social production. Women usually undertook these tasks – not just wives and mothers but older female siblings and widows who were associated with familial roles and rewarded with a disproportionately low share of the family resources. Women were losing their mainstay in the rural economy as first spinning and then grain husking were taken over by mills. They were propelled into increasingly intensified activity in household and subsistence tasks which underpinned all other forms of production and independently accounted for a large proportion of productive activity but were socially invisible. The household tasks women undertook were not recognised as productive activity unless they entered the exchange network.

Women became hostages to a sharpening differentiation within agrarian society even as their work became increasingly invisible. In particular, as the returns from labour and crafts declined, poorer peasants and labourers were compelled into increasingly wider and more intensive deployment of women's and children's labour to procure subsistence. Thus, women's household tasks, though socially invisible, acquired critical importance.

Simultaneously, as labour cheapened, the holders of land and capital were able to replace family labour with hired labour. Men from across various segments of rural and urban society withdrew women relatives from visible productive activities to signify their higher status. These social groups initiated new adaptations of notions of domesticity, seclusion and segregation to a remarkable variety and combination of practices and activities. They also gave the ideology of seclusion and segregation a new valence and invested considerable social capital to keep women's work invisible. They also sought to reproduce their class status through women's 'unproductive' domestic work.

Urban migration enhanced both these tendencies. As rural households released the surplus adult men for the urban labour market, the difference between men's and women's contribution to the household increased. Men now earned regular wages and the cash crucial for rent and debt-servicing, while women merely took on greater responsibility for the continuance of the family economic activity and continued to maintain the rural end of the household out of their varied but intermittent foraging and gathering activities.

Thus, on many counts, many more women worked much harder at a

the Regulation of Women Migrants in Colonial Bengal', forthcoming in *International Review of Social History* (special edition on Labour outside Europe and America).

wider range of occupations, but on the whole they received poorer material rewards and less recognition of their productive contribution.

An ideology of domesticity in nineteenth-century Bengal

In the nineteenth century, the Bengali elite was engaged in elaborating an ideology of domesticity. They located a newly constituted notion of 'tradition' in an increasingly sharply defined domestic sphere, providing the bedrock for the emergent 'nationalist' discourse. The 'domestic' turned on the figure of the woman. It was she who created and protected the sanctuary of the home where the colonised elite sought refuge from negotiations and collaborations with alien rulers.[5]

Women, as denizens of the 'domestic', were in the eye of reformist storms. There was a long and bitterly fought debate on the proper content of women's education.[6] Some felt that formal education was inappropriate – colonial education, with its westernising influence, would corrupt the 'pure tradition' of 'true womanhood' and hinder women's fulfilment of their primary roles as wives and as mothers. Not everyone agreed, however, that midwifery, childrearing, hygiene and health, home medicine, adjuncts relevant to training 'good' housewives and mothers, should supplant geography and grammar taught in schools. There was, nevertheless, a general consensus of opinion that one, if not the primary, justification of women's education was in the social ills inflicted by an ignorant housewife and mother. Reformers advocated 'educating' women in housewifery and motherhood. A vast didactic literature proliferated in the domestic manuals and women's journals prescribing and circumscribing the women's domain. The *sugrihini* and *sumata* were presented as the ideal.

The construction of a domestic space within which women were to remain as custodians of the spiritual autonomy of the subject race has been interpreted exclusively in relation to a hegemonic project of elite

[5] Samita Sen, 'Motherhood and Mothercraft: Gender and Nationalism in Bengal', *Gender and History*, 5, 2, 1993. Also see Ratnabali Chatterjee, 'The Queens' Daughters: Prostitutes as an Outcast Group in Colonial India', Report, Chr. Michelsen Institute, 1992. For a discussion on 'domesticity', see Tanika Sarkar, 'Hindu Conjugality and Nationalism in late Nineteenth Century Bengal', in Jasodhara Bagchi (ed.), *Indian Women: Myth and Reality*, Calcutta, 1995.

[6] The positions often differed according to the desired mixture of 'traditional' and 'modern' elements appropriate to the social role ascribed to women. Sri Bangesh Chandra Maitra, MA, *Stri Swadhinatar Hujug*, Grihastha Mangal, 10, *Magh* 1929, p. 302. *Adarsha Ramani, Bamabodhini Patrika*, 10, *Magh* 1913, p. 300. Also see Himani Banerjee, 'Fashioning a Self: Educational Proposals for and by Women in Popular Magazines in Colonial Bengal, *EPW*, October 1991, pp. WS51–62.

'nationalism'.[7] What has been ignored is the crucial issue of women's work which lay at the heart of this particular definition of domesticity. The valorisation of the domestic woman involved a confirmation of women's exclusive responsibility for domestic work – both for immediate consumption and for material and social reproduction – and simultaneously the divesting of all such work from their earlier productive associations.

Middle-class colonial intellectual men were locked in a contradiction – they had to defend 'tradition' against the intrusion of the colonial state but they also had to redefine that tradition to meet new compulsions of professional and service employment. It is often forgotten that, in the nineteenth century, a large proportion of the urban middle classes in Bengal were, in fact, migrants and they were quite often, as were the mill workers, 'single male' migrants. They too had 'rural' links. When the 'family' of the *bhadralok* did indeed accompany the men to the city, either their common economic interest in land or their nostalgic associations tied them to the *bhita*, the ancestral plot. The city provided the *basha*, where men alone or in many cases men with wives and children lived and worked, truncated from the putative 'joint' family.[8]

In the urban context, women undertook new forms of domestic work. In areas in which the housewife came under criticism – employment of servants, domestic hygiene, cooking, household medicine, and management of finance – extremely complex changes were taking place.[9] The middle-class women were devoted to tasks which upheld the professional and service elite's status aspirations: interior decoration, embroidery and macquillage. They thus elaborated the 'leisured lady' of Victorian imagination. Many housewifely activities became the stuff of a new domestic 'science' which sought to define the ideal homemaker and lay down prescriptive norms. The dispensers of advice were mostly men, with professionals like doctors lending their weight to such 'scientific' lore.

[7] Partha Chatterjee, 'The Nationalist Resolution of the Women's Question', and Lata Mani, 'Contentious Traditions: The Debate on Sati in Colonial India', both in K. Sangari and S. Vaid (eds.), *Recasting Women: Essays in Colonial History*, Delhi, 1989. The assumption of hegemony has been challenged by Tanika Sarkar, 'A Book of Her Own, A Life of Her Own: Autobiography of a Nineteenth Century Woman', *History Workshop Journal*, Autumn 1993, pp. 35–65.

[8] Joya Chatterji, *Bengal Divided. Hindu Communalism and Partition, 1932–1947*, Cambridge, 1995.

[9] The domestic manuals addressed the young and educated bride, not the mistress of a joint family. They sought to teach what the old housewife never had to do. Finance management particularly acquired a new relevance where the small margin between income and consumption required careful husbanding and rationalisation for long-term gain. Women's ability to keep accounts was considered a significant advantage of female education. Chatterji, *Bengal Divided*, pp. 186–7, 204–5.

Domesticity was simultaneously nature, art and science. The contradictions that flowed from such a construction fuelled fears of imminent moral degeneracy. The employment of servants was held up as a corruption peculiar to educated women. They were seen to have withdrawn their labour and rejected the manual part of housework. The substitution by servants depersonalised domestic service and added to household expenditure. Such denunciations ignored the fact that elite households had always hired servants. Even in the changed social milieu, the employment of servants was a crucial mark of family status.[10] And this was implicit in the domestic manuals which always devoted lengthy sections on the proper management of servants.[11]

The home as a site of reproduction of labour and as a moral entity was underlined by collapsing the ideal homemaker, the *lakshmi*, with the norm of chastity as embodied in the *sati*. A sharper enunciation of gender division of labour accompanied a renewed emphasis on gendered spaces. Thus there was greater resistance to women's acquisition of skills that would enable them to earn a living. From a violation of the 'natural' roles of men and women to a complete moral degeneracy and a collapse of the social order was but a short step.

This furore over women's awakening on the basis of individual liberty – God knows what may be the consequences. Marriages based on sexual desires . . . divorce . . . the demand that women have the power to earn, that women be given enough value . . . all these are imported rebellion against men . . . The old sages have said that independence does not suit women . . . this is not only true for Hindus but it is entirely and unmistakeably true for the welfare of the entire human race . . . anything else will bring chaos and destruction.[12]

Assertions of tradition in the idealisation of womanhood reflected a desired rather than a real continuity. Many *bhadramahila*, in the nineteenth and twentieth centuries, experienced a greater degree of seclusion. Control over women's behaviour was an additional means of determining social status in the fluid and uncertain social atmosphere of the city. Women's behaviour was brought under closer scrutiny.[13]

Simultaneously, in the closing decades of the nineteenth century, the *bhadramahila* also began to take the first tentative steps towards new professional and service employment. The trend heightened after the First World War with increasing educated unemployment and rising costs of living. The kinds of work women could undertake were limited

---

[10] Chatterji, *Bengal Divided*, pp. 198–9.
[11] Sarat Chandra Das, *Satidharma*, Calcutta, 1911; Dinesh Chandra Sen, *Grihasri*, Calcutta, 1915; Nandalal Mukhopadhyay, *Swami-stri*, Calcutta, 1933.
[12] Hemantakumari Debi, *Striswadhinata*, Grihastha Mangal, 12, Chaitra, 1929, p. 365.
[13] Meredith Borthwick, *The Changing Role of Women in Bengal, 1894–1905*, Princeton, 1984, pp. 5–7.

to those considered respectable. There was, moreover, an attempt to co-opt such work within the discourse of 'domesticity' on the ground that paid work was undertaken for familial survival.

But if the earning husband falls ill, will women stay crying by their bedside? That day, if necessary, the woman will leave her home to earn money, will stand in the workplace with hundreds and thousands of other men and women. If the husband is weak and the son dead, will the land not be tilled? Will she stand by the door starving with tears in her eyes? ... Today we need such women who combine womanliness and *shakti*.[14]

Segregation itself was an argument for women's engagement in services and professions. The needs of women students and women patients justified some women's employment in teaching, doctoring, nursing and midwifery. Women could extend their nurturing and servicing roles into these 'public' activities for economic gain more legitimately when they were deprived of male earnings or familial resources.

[If] our bhadramahila will not become nurses, at least they can care to collect the homeless orphan young girls and train them for it. This would be easy and would allow these poor girls to find a way of earning their living ... Widows and spinsters can take charge of it and women doctors could teach them ... It is women's responsibility to undertake this venture.[15]

Some middle-class reformers argued that widows, orphaned girls and deserted wives had to acquire a means of earning a respectable livelihood because their only other alternative was prostitution. They thus set up 'homes' for deserted women, unsupported widows and other destitute women. The Saroj Nalini Dutt Association, for example, provided a range of vocational training.[16] In the process, they reinforced the association of paid work with women deprived of family resources. They defined women's work as an extension of 'domestic' needs which delayed a more general entry of middle-class women into paid employment.

At the same time, the 'housewife' in the city was disengaged from a range of activities integrally associated with domesticity in the village – food processing, market gardening, livestock tending and spinning. Instead, she became responsible for the performance or supervision of tasks geared to immediate consumption. Rather than also 'producing'

---

[14] *Adarsha Ramani, Bamabodhini Patrika*, 10, *Magh* 1913, p. 301.
[15] *Antahpur*, III, 8, *Bhadra* 1898, pp. 151–3.
[16] A list of such women's associations and their activities was published in *Bangalakshmi*, 1932, pp. 511–14. The purpose, among others, was to assist 'helpless widows' and the spread of 'cottage industry'. The *Netrokona Narimangal Samiti* had five looms to produce towels and wicks, a society in Jessore had one Industrial Home, *Kalyanisangha* in Chakradharpur had similar training programmes for cottage industries and 'household arts', and a branch of Saroj Nalini Dutt Association in Bagura had training programmes and a loom for towels and carpets.

some of the food the household consumed, she was now restricted to cooking or even supervising the cooking of raw food procured in exchange for cash. These tasks, increasingly elaborated and divested of 'economic' value, became the essential 'domestic' repertoire of middle-class urban 'new women'. The urban household depended on a daily disbursement of cash, and even middle-ranking rural households were becoming increasingly integrated into the cash economy. The cash which supported these households came from the men – as income from land or as fees and salaries. The ideology of domesticity was predicated on a particular understanding of this gradual differentiation in the roles of men and women, a dissociation of production and consumption, the economy and the family. The ideological valorisation of the 'domestic' was not merely a matter of marking out an autonomous domain where the 'nation' was to be located. It was also part of a larger social movement whereby the confirmation and maintenance of elite status became increasingly dependent on a sharply enunciated separation between domesticity and productivity, locating women in the first and men in the latter. As a result, women's activities had to be divested of any association with productive work.

Purdah – **work and status**

The *bhadralok* ideology of domesticity drew both from Victorian and brahmanic social values. The 'westernised' Brahmos emphasised women's social presence and basic education. But the *sati-lakshmi* owed not a little to the brahmanic ideal of chaste and self-immolating womanhood. Rosalind O'Hanlon has argued that the nineteenth century saw a gradual diffusion of brahmanic religious values and texts throughout Hindu society.[17] Much of the overt expressions of this Hinduisation involved a reinscription of gender relations. Many dominant upper and middle peasants, and the intermediate artisanal and trading castes who had previously not practised strict *purdah*, dowry, child marriage or enforced widowhood began to adopt these customs. Alongside, in the process of Hinduisation, the new elites secluded their women and pursued the domestication of women's work by increasingly excluding women from production-related activities. Thus, they participated in a new construction of 'Hindu' identity which seemed to turn on the seclusion of women and the occlusion of their work. Many middle-ranking groups adopted brahmanical customs whose practice became prime signifiers of status and symbols of upward social mobi-

---

[17] Rosalind O'Hanlon, Introduction to *For the Honour of My Sister Countrywomen: Tarabai Shinde and the Critique of Gender Relations in Colonial India*, Oxford, 1994.

lity.[18] It was, in fact, a highly selective and exclusionist interpretation of the brahmanic norms of chastity and elite practices of seclusion that acquired this generalised value. Even low-caste peasant and artisan women were drawn into its ambit through an appeal to a shared past which, ostensibly, had been disrupted in the Muslim interregnum. These middle peasants, traders and artisans, however, could only adopt the practices and values of seclusion and domesticity by redeploying their household labour. They could, moreover, effectively undertake such reorganisation because women's work was being increasingly cheapened and devalued.

The significance of this social phenomenon in nineteenth-century Bengal has been, by and large, ignored. But it is of great importance. And it must be understood in the context of the wide-ranging changes in the political economy which have preoccupied so many historians. First, in the eighteenth century, land and not labour was the scarce commodity. By the turn of the century, labour was being released from the declining artisanal industries, the army and the courts to flood agriculture.[19] Second, the economic imperatives of colonialism were sharpening social differentiation within rural Bengal. The spread of cash crops and services benefited some agrarian groups directly. The cultivators' desperate need for cash to meet rent and revenue demands increased the returns of usurious capital. Those who possessed some capital gained from the increasing competition for land. Thus, landholders and moneylenders were acquiring dominance over cultivators and labourers. The imperative was now to cheapen rather than to immobilise labour.

The eighteenth-century social strategies were thus turned on their head. Social exclusionism was becoming more apparent. Access to political power became dependent on clearly demarcated caste identities and 'caste privileges' involved prior claims to economic resources. For increasingly rigid and caste-bounded communities, the adoption of

[18] Attempts at caste mobility among the Kurmis involved restructuring gender relations within a community. Gyan Pandey, 'Peasant Revolt and Indian Nationalism: The Peasant Movement in Awadh, 1919–1922', in Ranajit Guha (ed.), *Subaltern Studies I*, Oxford, 1982. In Oudh, in the 1920s and 1930s, notions of a 'pious and austere' woman underwrote a realignment of caste hierarchy. Kapil Kumar, 'Rural Women in Oudh, 1917–1947: Baba Ramchandra and the Women's Question', in K. Sangari and S. Vaid (eds.), *Recasting Women: Essays in Colonial History*, New Delhi, 1989, pp. 344–65.

[19] The period from 1850 to 1880 marked for Bengal a change from a labour-scarce to a labour-surplus situation. Partha Chatterjee, 'Agrarian Structure in Pre-Partition Bengal', in Asok Sen et al., *Perspectives in Social Sciences 2: Three Studies on the Agrarian Structure in Bengal*, Calcutta, 1982. Also see O. Goswami, *Industry, Trade and Peasant Society: The Jute Economy of Eastern India, 1900–1947*, Delhi, 1991.

brahmanic values and high-caste practices – *purdah*, child marriage, the payment of dowry and the progressive restriction on widow remarriage – became the most effective means of upward social mobility.[20] Their wider diffusion was aided by the colonial state's juridical sanction to selective elite practices in marriage and succession.[21] Customary rights of lower-caste women were often eroded through such reinforcement of brahminical ideology.

The high-caste practices of seclusion and segregation, which were increasingly being defined as the 'Hindu tradition', were symbolised by the *purdah* system. The construction of the home as an affective space, *griha*, drew on the older tradition of the *andar*. Typically, in rural Bengal in the late nineteenth and early twentieth centuries, men and women were allocated separate living spaces. Houses were built around court-yards – women would occupy the 'inner' (*andar*) rooms, inaccessible to men outside the immediate kin group. Men inhabited the 'outer' (*bairer*) rooms coming into the inner rooms only to sleep. But such a division of living space was only a culturally specific articulation of *purdah*. The definition of *purdah* cannot be restricted to the more obvious aspects of elite practice – the strict physical incarceration of Hindu women or the wearing of *burqua* by Muslim women. There was no one *purdah* system 'traditional' to Bengal. It included a wide range of cultural practices: from modest veiling, the down-cast eye to separate meals for men and women.[22]

In the delta areas of eastern Bengal, settlements were often small and dispersed with the basic unit being the *bari* or home, a unit of four to ten houses where members of a single kinship unit lived in several households. Muslim village women, especially, were supposed to remain within the *bari*.[23] In nineteenth-century Bengal and Bihar, seclusion of

---

[20] Rosalind O'Hanlon, *Caste, Conflict and Ideology: Mahatma Jotirao Phule and Low Caste Protest in Nineteenth Century Western India*, Cambridge, 1985, pp. 15–49; David A. Washbrook, 'Progress and Problems: South Asian Economic and Social History c. 1720–1860', *Modern Asian Studies*, 22, 1, 1988; C. A. Bayly, *Rulers, Townsmen and Bazaars: North Indian Society in the Age of British Expansion, 1770–1870*, Cambridge, 1983, pp. 31–2, 208–9, 407–8.

[21] P. Chowdhry, *The Veiled Women. Shifting Gender Equations in Rural Haryana 1880–1990*, Delhi, 1994.

[22] A basic difference between Hindu and Muslim *purdah* is said to be that while the latter was a symbolic shelter of closely related kin against the outer world, the Hindu *purdah* was aimed more at regulating sexual behaviour within the joint family. Hanna Papanek, 'Purdah: Separate Worlds and Symbolic Shelter', in H. Papanek, and G. Minault (eds.), *Separate Worlds: Studies of Purdah in South Asia*, Delhi, 1982.

[23] Papanek, 'Purdah', p. 13. The author quotes Florence McCarthy, 'Bengali Village Women: Mediators between Tradition and Development', MA Thesis, Michigan State University.

women appeared to be common in affluent peasant families.[24] The poorer cultivators and lower artisanal castes did not impose strict seclusion but women's appearances in public were regulated by a variety of codes. According to R. C. Dutt, the wife of the Tanti, Kumor or Chhutor 'will stand aside when a stranger is passing by the same road'.[25] The most stringent *purdah* was observed by young brides of high castes. While older women and daughters of the house were free to go outside to work, attend religious functions and social events, the young brides stayed in the house. Young wives in lower-ranking families, though they also veiled themselves, observed stringent seclusion for a shorter period of time.

Even as generalised values of *purdah* were being increasingly disseminated, its specific expressions varied according to caste, class and region. In Bengal, a gradual Hinduisation of *purdah* entailed a reconstitution of gender division of labour which, in turn, was facilitated by a sharpening differentiation in rural society. Increasing gains of capital were accompanied by declining wages, employment opportunities and land availability.[26] The middle peasant and trader found it easier to adopt seclusion by forgoing unpaid women's labour in the family farm or in retailing. They withdrew women from visible activities because it implied the ability to hire others. In many districts of Bihar, the more affluent cultivating and artisan families employed the *panibharin* women to eliminate any possibility of the public appearance of their women.[27] As dissociation from manual labour defined the *bhadralok* from the *chhotolok*, the withdrawal of women from 'visible' work marked out the social elite. Those who could free women from outside labour signalled their ability to dispense with women's contribution to household income. Only those men who were certain of the adequacy of their own earnings and resources could insist that women keep to their homes. Most secluded women prided themselves on their strict observance of *purdah*. When high-status women made an appearance in the field or on

---

[24] F. H. Buchanan, *An Account of the District of Bhagalpur in 1810–11*, Patna, 1939, p. 172; and W. W. Hunter, *A Statistical Account of Bengal, 24 Parganas*, I, London, 1876, p. 108.

[25] R. C. Dutt, 'The Aboriginal Element in the Population of Bengal', *Calcutta Review*, 1882, quoted in *BDG*, Bankura, Calcutta, 1908, p. 69.

[26] Real wages are, of course, notoriously difficult to calculate. For some estimates of declining wages compare F. H. Buchanan, *An Account of the Districts of Bihar and Patna 1811–12*, Patna, 1928, p. 556; Dufferin Report, Main Report, p. 11 and L. P. Shirres, *Memorandum on the Material Condition of the People of Bengal in the years 1892–93 to 1901–02*, pp. 13–14. Also see Anand Yang, *The Limited Raj: Agrarian Relations in Colonial India, Saran District, 1793–1920*, Delhi, 1989, p. 51.

[27] F. H. Buchanan, *An Account of the District of Shahabad in 1812–13*, Patna, 1934, p. 165.

the threshing floor, they did so only to bring food to men supervising labour.

For secluded women, ideally, the allocation of work followed the logic of the allocation of living space. Women would work inside the house and the courtyard at tasks which included food preparation, cleaning and maintenance of house and possessions, childcare and handicrafts such as spinning, weaving or embroidery. They also played important roles in agriculture and artisan manufacture, but were usually assigned tasks which did not conflict with their household duties. The processing and preparation of food for consumption, for instance, remained exclusively their responsibility. Thus their primary association with child-rearing and housekeeping was reinforced. They undertook a variety of agricultural and manufacturing tasks which were, moreover, subsumed within the daily routine of domesticity. By the very association with domesticity, women's activities in household production became designated as non-economic. Instead, their work was naturalised within normative definitions of femininity, acquiring, as they did, emotive and aesthetic value: a fulfilment of womanhood, not an integral part of the household's productive activity.

As a mark of social status, the value of seclusion lay in the contrast it offered between the rich who could afford to hire labour and the poor who were forced to use family labour. The elite woman's leisure contrasted sharply with the poor woman's toil. It was only the needy who were forced to deploy, visibly, women's labour for household survival. Neither *purdah* nor any ideology of domesticity ever kept poor women away from manual and visible work. The decline in the price of labour that allowed the relatively affluent to dispense with women's labour outside the home obviously had a different implication for those who were dependent on wages for survival.

In such households – the marginal peasant, the agricultural labourer or the individual small artisan – reduced earnings increased dependence on women's and children's contribution. As the individual worker's earnings declined, all members of the family were required to work more. In these circumstances, observance of complete seclusion was impossible. Within a few months after the consummation ceremony (*garbhadan* or *gauna*), brides would begin to fetch water and work in the fields. In fact, more women were being forced to undertake wage labour (in agriculture and earthwork) and sell products previously retained for household consumption (fuel and processed grain). In larger numbers and in more diverse ways, they were impelled to participate in visible economic activity. Yet, increasingly, such work was being excluded from the normative ideal of legitimate feminine activities. The diffusion of a more rigidly defined ideal of gender division of labour thus reinforced the social marginality of poor women.

Women's work and migration

In Bihar and UP, many women stayed behind while the men in their households went to the city to work for wages. These men often preferred jute mill jobs not only because of the better wages, but because wages were 'regular' and were paid in cash.[28] By contrast, the woman in the village had to eke out a livelihood on low and intermittent returns. As a result, women bore the main brunt of poverty. With loss of land, the material basis for a great deal of women's tasks was lost – market gardening, cattle-rearing, rice husking and food preparation. In addition, other non-agricultural occupations for women were declining. The establishment of cotton and rice mills drastically reduced women's earnings from husking and spinning.

The narrowing opportunities for women's employment did not, however, force them into towns and cities. While men in most cases migrated as a strategy of familial survival, women usually left when there was no hope of subsistence at home.[29] As mentioned earlier, single women often migrated when deprived of familial resources. Whole families migrated in periods of exceptional distress, as in the famine of 1918.

The majority of jute workers were men who came to the city alone or with other male kin. It is difficult to say, from the fragmentary evidence available, whether these men came from the category of marginal peasants who had very little land or tenancy rights over small plots. The numbers of relief workers during the famines declined in June. This coincided with the time when the jute workers usually came to the village for their annual visit. Were the mill workers from the same kind of agrarian group who sought relief in times of famine? In Saran, Chamars, Noonias, Jolahs, Dusadhs, Binds and Ahars filled relief registers. In Patna, 75 per cent of relief workers were landless, and in Bhagalpur, too, landless labourers predominated. Except in the case of

[28] There is some evidence that wages were higher in Bengal proper than in Bihar or Orissa, and eastern districts of Bengal had even higher rates than the Bengal average. Dufferin Report, Main Report, pp. 7–9. Also see *Final Report of the Survey and Settlement Operations in the Muzaffarpur District, 1892–1899*, C. J. Stevenson-Moore, Calcutta, 1901 (henceforth Stevenson-Moore Report) pp. 23–4; *Final Report on the Survey and Settlement Operations in Saran District, 1893–1901*, J. H. Kerr, Calcutta, 1903 (henceforth Kerr Report), p. 36. Average wages were higher in Dacca and 24 Parganas than in Saran in 1911. Yang, *The Limited Raj*, pp. 196–7.
[29] Chandavarkar has set out this argument for migration to the Bombay cotton textile industry. R. S. Chandavarkar, *The Origins of Industrial Capitalism in India: Business Strategies and the Working Classes in Bombay, 1900–1940*, Cambridge, 1994.

about 10 per cent of the workers, most were accustomed to earthwork.[30] At the beginning of the twentieth century, Foley had noted that most jute mill workers did not have access to land. 'In Shahabad I was informed that the Musalman Jolahs and Dhunias, who went to the jute mills, did not possess land.'[31]

Set against this is Foley's own evidence that a substantial number of workers had, if not ownership rights, at least tenancy rights over land.[32] In twenty-two villages surveyed in Muzaffarpur, most long-distance migrants had some earnings from cultivation.[33] Grierson's evidence also supports this hypothesis. He had considerably discomfited the Government of Bengal by depicting a steady impoverishment of Gaya peasants. In his estimate, a family of six did not have 'sufficient clothing or two meals a day' from anything less than 20 *bighas* of land.[34] Only 10 per cent of the population of Gaya district, which sent nearly one-third of its total emigrants to Calcutta, had that much land.[35] Almost half of the cultivators held less than 5 *bighas*, which made them crucially dependent on supplemental income from various sources.[36] But the totally landless with absolutely no income from land was a small proportion of the population.[37] The agricultural labourer, in almost all accounts of the nineteenth century, was one who depended primarily but not only on wages. And given that this was a labour-surplus district, migration was an obvious strategy of supplementing household income. Remittances

[30] Report on the Famine in Bengal, 1896–97, WBSA, Judl. Police [Revenue, Agricultural (Famine)], July 1898, B101–102 (henceforth Famine in Bengal).

[31] Foley Report. According to Census estimates, 30 per cent of workers came from low-caste and artisan occupations. Another 30 per cent were Muslims, a large number of whom (Jolahs, for example) also belonged to artisan castes. *Census of India*, 1911, V, 2, Appendix to Table XVI.

[32] Foley Report. Dasgupta calculated that about one-third of the workers had some amount of land. Ranajit Dasgupta, 'Migrant Workers, Rural Connexions and Capitalism: The Calcutta Jute Industrial Labour, 1890s to 1940s', Indian Institute of Management (Calcutta) Working Paper Series, April 1987, 1987.

[33] Stevenson-Moore Report, p. 362.

[34] G. A. Grierson, *Notes on the District of Gaya*, Calcutta, 1893, p. 90. According to Yang, in Saran, at the turn of the twentieth century, 20 per cent of the peasantry had below-subsistence holdings, and 10 per cent were in the landless category. Yang, *The Limited Raj*, p. 48.

[35] *Final Report on the Survey and Settlement Operations in the District of Gaya, 1911–1918*, E. L. Tanner, Patna, 1919.

[36] This evidence is corroborated for Saran, Muzaffarpur and Darbhanga in the Dufferin Report.

[37] Grierson, *Notes on the District of Gaya*, pp. 87–9. Stevenson-Moore talks of three categories: the 'pure' cultivators (60 per cent of the population) were 'those principally dependent on cultivation'; the 'cultivating labourer' (19 per cent) typically derived only one-third of his income from his own fields; and the 'pure' labourers (9 per cent) were those whose 'principal income derived from labour in others' fields'. Stevenson-Moore Report, p. 26. Also see Kerr Report, para. 36.

from single migrants increased the staying power of the rural household in areas where the margin between subsistence and starvation was perilously small.

Later, however, in 1930, when the Royal Commission collected twenty life histories of jute workers, there were thirteen workers who had almost no income from land. The Labour Investigation Committee of 1944 also noted that there were some workers who had small plots and others who had just tenancy rights.[38] The Jagaddal survey found that 41.3 per cent of the workers owned some land but almost 60 per cent had very little or no land.[39]

A definitive conclusion is far from easy. It would seem that the size of landholding or lack of any would not explain migration. Other factors supervened to form the decision to migrate. It can, however, be argued that in labour-surplus districts, households released surplus adult male labour for the urban market. But, for one thing, that would beg the question of the size of households in rural areas. For another, it would lead to an investigation of the totality of household resources *qua* household liabilities.

If the evidence on landholding is contradictory, the evidence on household sizes is very thin on the ground. Theoretically, the average extended family consisted of three or four generations of the male line – father, mother, unmarried daughters and sons, married sons and their wives and children. Widows often returned to their parental homes, so the widowed sisters or daughters often joined the household. Actually, poorer households rarely approximated this norm. High mortality, epidemics and famines regularly split up families. For the poorer peasants, small households appeared to have been more common (see Table 2.1).

A rough estimate of the average household sizes among those holding 4 to 7 *bighas* of land would thus appear to be about 5–6 persons. Elsewhere in the Dufferin Report we have similar evidence. Another village in Midnapore shows average family sizes ranging from 5.6 of the better-off cultivator to 5.8 of other cultivators. In Burdwan the cultivator had an average family of 8, and the agricultural labourer of 5.[40] In the evidence from Gaya, average family sizes ranges from 7 for the pure

---

[38] *RCLI*, V, 2, pp. 76–80. Labour Investigation Committee (henceforth LIC), *Report on an Enquiry into Conditions of Labour in the Jute Mill Industry in India*, Government of India, Calcutta, 1946.

[39] K. P. Chattopadhyay, *A Socio-Economic Survey of Jute Labour*, Calcutta, 1952, p. 30. In a later study 40 per cent workers were found to have no land at all. N. Bhattacharya and A. K. Chatterjee, *A Sample Survey of Jute Workers in Greater Calcutta* (mimeo), Calcutta, 1973.

[40] N. S. Alexander, Burdwan Division, pp. 9–14, Dufferin Report. There is no explanation of the categories or how the data was collected.

68   Women and labour in late colonial India

Table 2.1. *Size of households in three mouzas of Midnapore in 1888*

	Mouza A		Mouza B		Mouza C		Total	
	Culti-vator	Labo-urer	Culti-vator	Labo-urer	Culti-vator	Labo-urer	Culti-vator	Labo-urer
Family size	3.80	4.03	7.70	6.40	4.20	6.19	5.20	5.54
Number of children	0.29	1.30	2.18	1.80	1.60	1.86	1.60	1.60
Family landholding (in *bighas*)	6.45	4.50	4.70	2.60	5.60	3.50	5.58	3.50

Source: Dufferin Report, 1888. From N. S. Alexander, Commissioner of the Burdwan Division to the Secretary to the Government of Bengal, 16 April 1888, Tables A-E pp. 22–32. The mouzas are in Ghatal sub-division - Banpore, Aguria and Naihati.

cultivators to 3.9 for the landless labourers.[41] A survey of twenty-two villages in Muzzaffarpur found the average family size of the cultivating labourer to be 5.06, and that of the pure labourer 3.94. The former had an average of 1.81 children, while the latter had 1.29 children in each family.[42] At a later date, a survey of village Malheri in Hardoi district showed an average of 7 persons per family.[43] Given the very high mortality, and the especially high infant mortality rates, an average household of 6–8 can be presumed to be fairly large and including more than 2 adults (see Table 2.2).[44]

A variety of economic interests bound the extended family. The common ownership of immovable property may have kept upper and middle peasant families together, especially in cases where partition would result in less than economic holdings. For those at the bottom of rural society, the almost landless low castes, larger families may some-times have allowed more efficient distribution of resources, or reflected the difficulties of mobility in a labour-surplus economy.[45]

Households that needed to supplement their landed income would

[41] *Report on the Material Condition of Small Agriculturists and Labourers in Gaya*, C. J. Stevenson-Moore, Calcutta, 1898, p. 16.
[42] Stevenson-Moore Report, p. 364.
[43] Krishna Sahai Asthana, 'A Social and Economic Survey of Village Malehra, District Hardoi', in R. Mukherjee (ed.), *Fields and Farmers in Oudh*, Calcutta, 1929, pp. 4–9.
[44] In a study of household sizes in China in the 1930s, the use of computer simulation has shown that an average mean household size of seven can indicate as high as 40 per cent of the population living in extended families. Zhangwei Zhao, 'Demographic Influences and Household Formation in Chinese History – A Simulation Study', paper presented to the 6th International Conference of the Association for History and Computing, Denmark, 28–30 August 1991 (unpublished).
[45] In the Presidency division of Bengal, the 'lower classes' appeared to live together in a joint family. Dufferin Report, p. 17. In Malhera, the average family size in general was about seven but among some low castes, like the Lohar, Dhanuk, Chamar and Arakha,

Table 2.2. *Size of households in Mouza Banpore, District Midnapore, in 1888*

In averages	Low caste – Dule	Intermediate castes
Family size	5.05	3.62
No. of children	0.88	2.15
Land held per family		
(in *bighas*)	1.89	6.12
Per capita land (in *bighas*)	0.39	1.77

Source: Dufferin Report, 1888. From N. S. Alexander, Commissioner of the Burdwan Division to the Secretary to the Government of Bengal, 16 April, 1888, Table B, pp. 23–4.

then send one or more adult males to neighbouring districts, or even further afield. Iswar Chandra Boistab had 15 *bighas* of land. But he worked in a jute mill because his three brothers looked after the land.[46] For such single migrants mobility was a means of augmenting household income. The rest of the family would stay behind in the village to continue to work on the land and crafts while these men would send home what little they could save. The Royal Commission's interviews indicate that many men migrated thus, as a strategy of familial survival. Noor Muhammad who came from Arrah, said, 'We do small weaving work at home, but that is not enough to support the whole family ... I send money home to my wife.' Kalil's wife, brothers and parents remained in the country. He said, 'I send them a monthly remittance ... The reason why I came to work in the jute mills is that I was hard up in my country, could not get food, and was becoming indebted.' This spells out one major reason why migration was important for small and marginal peasants. Remittance from the city was their only source of cash essential for debt-servicing.[47]

Though crucially dependent on the supplemental income from the city, these male migrants did not contemplate permanent migration since land, though inadequate, was an insurance against starvation. The landless labourers were after all the first to go hungry in times of scarcity. If, however, a male migrant wished to retain his interest in the land and the homestead, he had to keep some part of the family – usually the wife and children – in the village.[48]

the average family size was 11.7. Asthana, 'A Social and Economic Survey of Village Malehra', p. 6.

[46] A. Smith, Presidency Division, p. 21, Dufferin Report.

[47] Others like Abdul Hakim, Sheikh Babu Jan, Gobardan and lastly, Behari Rai, a rare Brahmin from 'up-country', stressed the importance of their remmittance to the rural household. *RCLI*, V, 2, pp. 76–80 and XI, pp. 355–65.

[48] Sen argues that single and temporary migration was the best way for the migrant to

It has already been mentioned that unlike in the case of single male migrants, 'family' migration was motivated by the exhaustion of rural resources. Women's mobility was accelerated by acute shortage. The famine in 1891, for instance, prompted greater family migration.[49] In 1905 and again in 1911, as the Central Provinces rapidly recovered from famines, emigration from almost all districts declined. Significantly, the proportion of women emigrants fell more sharply. In 1910, in Chhatisgarh, the principal recruiting ground of the province, several years of good harvests had made recruitment of women extremely difficult. Moreover, the local building projects like the railways in Nimar and the road and irrigation works in the Nagpur Division offered women an alternative to migration.[50] Women preferred waged employment in the vicinity of their village to long-distance migration.

It follows that whole families of workers came to the mill towns when other alternatives were exhausted. The 1891 Commission interviewed six women, of whom only one said they 'have house and fields at home'; all the others had no land. Two men came to Baranagar with their families because they had no land in Hooghly.[51] The Royal Commission recorded similar cases in the 1920s. Tulsi and Tilasari, who migrated with their children from Gorakhpur, had no land at all. Habib, a woman worker in Anglo-India Jute Mill said, 'I was poor, all my folk came here and I also came.'[52]

For the overwhelming majority of male jute mill workers, the wages in the city were only a part of a survival strategy that embraced the urban and the rural economies, their own labour in the mills and their wives' and children's labour in the village. It was when the rural resources were completely exhausted that men took their wives and children to the city. Even then, ritual and economic links with the village were usually maintained over generations. In some cases, marriage ties provided the crucial connection; in some rare cases city wages allowed families to acquire land in the village; and in any case kin ties were not totally severed. Such strategies were, however, predicated on male control over household migration decisions. In labour-surplus areas there was a high premium on labour mobility. Male control over migration decisions and

retain his rights in the family land and property however low its productivity. A. K. Sen, *Employment Technology and Development*, Delhi, 1975.
[49] *Report on the Famine in Bengal, 1896–97*, Calcutta, 1903.
[50] *Report on the Working of the Inland Emigration Act in the Central Provinces for the Year Ending 30 June 1905*, Calcutta, 1905. *Report on the Emigration from the Port of Calcutta to British and Foreign Colonies for the Years 1910 and 1911.*
[51] *IFC*, pp. 86–8.
[52] Karu, Babuniyah (from Arrah), Gauri (from Ganjam) and Mongal (from Bilaspur) who worked in the mills with their families said that they had no source of subsistence in the village. *RCLI*, V, 2, pp. 76–80.

the near exclusion of women from urban occupations enhanced the already existing difference in wage-earning potential between men and women. Remittances, however inadequate, reinforced the importance of male earnings as the primary mainstay of the family. In Gaya, remittances came primarily from men in service as *durwans*, peons and weavers in the jute mills of Calcutta, Hooghly and 24 Parganas. Except cattle-rearing, which was mainly women's and children's work, this was the single most important source of supplementary earning in the villages. Remittances were also the chief source of cash and migration to the city allowed access to new sources of credit. As Grierson pointed out, 'Besides all the rest is received in kind ... this alone, apart from cultivation, brings hard cash. So it enables him [the cultivator] to pay rent and and to pay the money lender ... and enables the money lender to lend to him.'[53] Thus, migrant men earned cash wages; women's occupations (cattle-rearing, husking and transplanting) were paid in kind. It was the men's remittances that paid the rent or serviced debts.

The premium placed on male earnings obscured the intensification of women's work in rural Bihar. The inability to hire labour meant that 'family has to take much more active part in cultivation'.[54] Skrine noted in North Bihar that 'except in the case of superior castes, every member of the cultivator's family labours in the fields'.[55] In the Patna district 'the women gathered crops and cleared the fields of weeds'.[56] Grierson noted, 'the women of a labourer's family work at the seasons of transplanting and reaping. They also work at tapping *toddy*-heads and collecting the opium.'[57] Women also hired out their labour. In Gaya, the agricultural labourer's wife was expected to work for wages, husk, grind or collect fuel to make ends meet.[58] In Halia, where agricultural labour was poorly paid, women and children 'eke out the family income' by small earnings from occasional employment.[59]

Male migration intensified women's direct involvement in and responsibilities for agricultural operations in Bihar and UP. The *Jaunpur District Gazetteer* noted, 'All the eastern districts [of UP] now exhibit preponderance of females ... probably emigration [of males] is the principal factor ... [women] remaining at home to till the fields'.[60]

[53] Grierson, *Notes on the District of Gaya*, p. 107.
[54] *Census of India*, 1911, VI, 1, p. 548.
[55] F. H. B. Skrine, *Memorandum on the Material Condition of the Lower Orders in Bengal during the Ten Years from 1881–82 to 1891–92*, Calcutta, 1892, p. 52.
[56] Ibid.   [57] Grierson, *Notes on the District of Gaya*, p. 111.   [58] Ibid.
[59] *Bihar and Orissa District Gazetteer* (henceforth *BODG*) Puri District, 1929, p. 196.
[60] H. R. Neville, *District Gazetteer of the United Provinces* (henceforth *DGUP*), Jaunpur, 1908, p. 75. Also see *DGUP*, Ghazipur, 1909, p. 80. In late 1920s, '[e]xcept in the case ... of the higher castes women play a very important role ... by working both on their

By the beginning of the twentieth century, women in Bihar began to predominate in several occupations.[61] They took part in most of the field operations other than ploughing, i.e., sowing, weeding, reaping, threshing, winnowing and removal of dry grass. Women's participation in both agriculture and non-agrarian occupations was the highest in Saran, the district supplying the largest number of migrants to Calcutta.[62] The *Gazetteer* remarked, 'female labour is employed more extensively than in any other province'.[63]

These observations are strengthened by an enquiry into crop patterns in Bihar and UP. It is widely held that the major purpose behind the periodic visits of the workers to their village home was to look after their land and cultivation. The *Report of the Indian Factory Labour Commission of 1908* was widely quoted to 'prove' the semi-rural character of mill workers on the basis that mill workers returned to the village to harvest their crops.[64] But the relation between harvesting operations and the annual exodus of workers from the mills seems tenuous.

The Foley Report had found that the main season when migrant workers returned home was in May and June, when there was little by way of cultivation in Bihar and eastern UP. In most UP districts, for instance, May and June were the two months in the year unoccupied by field work. 'I enquired in Bihar what sort of cultivation there was to attract him, and the reply was that it was the toddy season and that there might be a little sugarcane work to do seemed hardly adequate . . .'.[65]

It is evident from Table 2.3 below that in the high-migration Bihar districts the most important crop was the *aghani*. This winter crop was reaped in November, December and early January. The next in importance was the *rabi*, which was harvested in March, April and May. The *bhadoi*, which was not very important in Bihar but quite extensive in western districts of Bengal, was sown in these months.[66]

Seasonal migration of agricultural labour, as indeed the annual return of mill labour to their villages, did not coincide with the harvesting of the major crop. Thousands of migrant workers visited their homes in May and June, after the *rabi* was off the ground, and left before the *aghani* sowing. It was precisely at the time of harvesting this *aghani* crop – at the beginning of winter – that the seasonal eastward migration of

own and others' farms as hired labourers'. Asthana, 'A Social and Economic Survey of Village Malehra', p. 119.

[61] *Census of India*, 1911, V, 1, para. 1101.

[62] Ranajit Dasgupta, 'Factory Labour in Eastern India – Sources of Supply, 1885–1946', *Indian Economic and Social History Review*, 8, 3, 1976, pp. 277–329, Table 4.

[63] *BODG*, Patna, 1930, p. 86.

[64] *Indian Industrial Commission*, 1908, VI, pp. 115–16.   [65] Foley Report, para. 83.

[66] *Famine in Bengal*, pp. 11–16.

Table 2.3. *Percentage of net cropped area under each crop in some Bihar districts, 1905–12*

	Percentage of net cropped to total area	Bhadoi	Aghani	Rabi	Others
S. Monghyr	53	19	54	50	1
N. Monghyr	69	43	29	66	
Saran	79	41	34	62	
Champaran	70	46	38	55	
Muzaffarpur	80	38	48	60	
Darbhanga	80	28	63	47	
Purnea	61	34	56	39	
Bhagalpur	70	27	64	41	2
N. Bhagalpur	77	34	60	36	3
S. Bhagalpur	56	18	69	48	1

Source: Final Report on the Survey and Settlement Operations (under Chapter I of the Bengal Tenancy Act) in the District of Monghyr (south), 1905–1912, P. W. Murphy, Settlement Officer, South Bihar, Ranchi, 1914, p. 74.

agricultural labourers, from districts of Bihar and UP to Bengal districts, also took place. These agricultural labourers returned to their villages only at the end of the summer and in time for the sowing of the *aghani* in their own district. Tilling the land, reaping the crop and other major agricultural operations were usually done by the family members in-cluding women and children who stayed in the village. The annual exodus of jute mill labour back to the village during the summer dovetailed into this pattern.

Thus, the worker did not visit the village in order to participate in field work. On the whole May was a lean month – the *rabi* harvests almost completed and the *aghani* sowing awaiting the monsoon. At the end of the month, there was some employment in weeding paddy and in indigo fields. The other lean month was October – when the profits from reaping the *bhadoi* was the only supply of grains available.[67] This evidence is further strengthened by the figures from the famine relief operations of 1896–7. In both the 1896–7 and the earlier 1873–4 famines, the numbers in relief works were at their highest in May. In March cutting the *rabi* provided some employment, but there was a steady increase in numbers requiring relief throughout April and May. The turning point came in June, and the main break came in July when, with the coming of the rains, opportunities of field employment increased.[68]

It is especially notable that men found it more lucrative to go to

[67] John Beames, A schedule from Purnea, Dufferin Report.
[68] *Famine in Bengal*, p. 40.

Bengal for field or earthwork rather than to stay at home to reap the most important crop of the region. This relatively less rewarding task devolved on women, enhancing the wage difference between men and women. The gender ratio in famine relief works is also indicative of this wage differential.

[S]ome inconvenience was felt ... for the excess of women and children over males ... [in] Shahabad and Saran ... [A] considerable temporary emigration of the male members of families goes on for the crop-cutting in Eastern Bengal and elsewhere and it was their womenfolk and children who were left behind who crowded upon the works ... showing a natural tendency to rise as distress deepened, and latterly when at the breaking of the rains, the men went off to field-work ... piece-work had a tendency to increase the proportion of men.[69]

Thus, only the more remunerative piece-work attracted male labour to relief works. Otherwise, it was more rewarding to trek to eastern Bengal than to work for government relief projects. Even in times of scarcity, poorly rewarded relief work was availed more by women and children.

Women's wages seem to have been generally lower than men's. Buchanan reported an average daily agricultural wage of 7 *pies* for men and 4 *pies* for women. Among artisans, women earned 6 *pies* a day and men 10 *pies* a day.[70] But this was not uniform. Elsewhere, 'the women as day labourers make almost as much as the men, as they are employed to beat and transplant rice receiving the same allowance as men'.[71] In 1880s, the Dufferin Report indicated that wage differences between men and women were sharper in Bihar than in Bengal.[72] By the twentieth century women were mostly paid lower wages for agricultural labour. 'Women who are extensively employed in the lighter forms of field work ... customarily obtain two-thirds of man's wage.'[73] Ploughing and sowing (exclusively undertaken by men) were often paid at double the rate for weeding and watering (undertaken mostly by women).[74]

Women's work and the household economy

A rare attempt at quantifying women's contribution to the household budget was made by Grierson. According to his estimates, artisans in Gaya derived 44 per cent of their earnings from 'supplementary' activities, of which women contributed at least 30 per cent. Women worked on the family farm, for hire in transplanting seasons and reared

---

[69] Ibid.   [70] Buchanan, *An Account of the District of Bihar and Patna*, pp. 565, 616.
[71] Buchanan, *An Account of the District of Bihar and Patna*, p. 558.
[72] Dufferin Report, Main Report, pp. 3–14.   [73] *DGUP*, Ballia, 1907, pp. 48–9.
[74] *DGUP*, Ghazipur, 1909, p. 79. Also see J. H. Kelman, *Labour in India*, London, 1923, p. 39.

cattle.[75] In the household of the agricultural labourer, men, women and children worked for wages. But the 'supplemental' income, amounting to 40 per cent of total earnings, derived primarily from women's miscellaneous activities. In cultivating families, who had about 5 *bighas* of land, women not only worked in the family farm but provided about 20 per cent of the supplementary income by cattle-rearing, and grain processing.[76] We do not know how Grierson collected his data. So one may not take his quantitative assessment as absolutely precise. But it does give an idea of how important women's labour was for the maintenance of the household in Bihar at the close of the nineteenth century.

Earlier, Buchanan had found that though women were paid very poorly for grain processing, their principal sustained work throughout the year, they made up for it by weeding. Among agricultural labourers, women's total earnings exceeded those of the men. In Purnea, 'the low allowance given to women for beating rice cuts off the great part of that grand support which the poor in Dinagpur and Ronggopur enjoy and which almost always ensures their subsistence'.[77] By the early twentieth century, in Muzaffarpur, more than half the 'supplementary' income of the agricultural labourer, crucial in the lean periods of March and October, was provided by women.[78] In Saran, for instance, women predominated in many occupations.[79] Even in Bengal, women were associated with a wide range of non-agrarian activities.[80] In most western districts of Bengal like Midnapur, Birbhum or Bankura, and in some Bihar districts, like Gaya, Saran and Muzaffarpur, an accelerated agrarian crisis after the First World War increased the small and marginal cultivator's dependence on 'supplementary' income.[81] Women's work became more critical for the household.

Women thus contributed almost, or even more than, half the household income. Why was this contribution less valued? One clue was

[75] Grierson, *Notes on the District of Gaya*, p. 121.
[76] Ibid., p. 112.
[77] F. H. Buchanan, *An Account of the District of Purneah in 1809–10*, Patna, 1928, p. 444.
[78] Stevenson-Moore Report, p. 364.   [79] *BODG*, Saran, 1930, p. 85–6.
[80] In Bengal, as against 1.2 million engaged in agriculture, there were some 500,000 in grain processing, 200,000 in making and selling of agricultural produce and 340,000 in caste-specific occupations. In 1901, there were 1.4 million women in agriculture, 462,000 in grain processing and 200,000 in making and selling of forest products. *Census of India*, 1901, VI, 1, p. 197.
[81] General agrarian conditions appear to have been worse in western and central Bengal and Bihar. In the eastern and northern districts of Bengal the agrarian crisis was delayed by a few decades due to the lucrative jute crop. Dufferin Report, Main Report, pp. 7–9; Stevenson-Moore Report, pp. 23–4. See also Chatterjee, 'Agrarian Structure in Pre-Partition Bengal'; Sugata Bose, *Agrarian Bengal: Economy, Social Structure, and Politics, 1919–1947*, Cambridge, 1986, pp. 18–30.

provided by Grierson himself. He accepted the income from male
resource (land, craft or labour) as the 'main' earnings. The rest,
including women's varied activities, was labelled supplementary. Consequently, women's work were perceived as marginal. The range and value
of their work were disguised. The extent to which they contributed to
household survival could remain unacknowledged.

Women's work was perhaps labelled as marginal and supplementary
because such work was associated with poor returns, was casual and
intermittent. In Bengal and Bihar a very large number of women traded
in fuel.[82] Women collected cow dung and litter and made cow dung
cakes with them and carried them to the market to sell.[83] It was a
labour-intensive and poorly rewarded occupation: 'they sell the cakes of
cowdung fuel in the hot weather, a basketful every two or three days,
for Gorakhpuri *pies* (a third of an *anna*)'.[84] Thus women collected and
sold firewood, grass and fodder, made baskets, ginned cotton, cleaned
and sold farm or cottage products. Grierson remarked that women
usually made up the household's deficits 'by odds and ends, supplemental sources of income, such as cutting of fuel in the *jangal* and the
like'.[85] In Halia, where agricultural labour was very low paid, women
and children 'eke out the family income' from jungle roots, fruits and
fuel.[86] Towards the end of nineteenth century many of these 'subsistence' activities along with some of women's staple occupations were
actually declining.

Some skills were widely disseminated and often handed down to
generations of women. Spinning, for example, was compatible with
domesticity and seclusion, undertaken at home and in intervals from
housework. Thus spinning employed the largest number of women in
Bengal. At the beginning of the nineteenth century Buchanan presumed
that in Bihar all adult women spun.[87] According to him, 'all castes are
permitted to spin ... [A] large proportion of women spin cotton ... and
this is an employment suited well to the jealousy of the men. [sic]'[88] He
added:

[b]y far, the greater part of these spin only a few hours in the afternoon ... But
there are many women who spin assiduously and who have no interruption of

---

[82] *Census of India*, 1911, V, 1, para. 1101 and VI, 1, p. 549.
[83] Also in the Central Provinces where 411 men and 6,428 women were returned under
this head in 1881. *Census of the Central Provinces*, 1881, II, p. 117. 'Poorer women
gather the cow dung from the roads, mix it with water, and make into rough round
cakes, which they spread out to dry on the ground ... When baked, these cakes are
taken to the market to sell for fuel.' Kelman, *Labour in India*, p. 38.
[84] Grierson, *Notes on the District of Gaya*, p. 111.
[85] Grierson, *Notes on the District of Gaya*, p. 112.   [86] *BODG*, Puri, 1929, p. 196.
[87] Buchanan, *An Account of the District of Bihar and Patna*, p. 647.
[88] Buchanan, *An Account of the District of Bhagalpur*, pp. 607–11.

children and family, where the thread is fine ... As the demand ... for fine goods has for some years been constantly diminishing, the women had suffered very much.[89]

Hand-spinning had been hard hit by competition from cotton mills and women were only able to earn one *anna* a day. Yet, A. C. Chatterjee pointed out, hand-spinning would continue so long as 'it provided a small income for purdah women and widows who were not prepared to leave their village to enter factories'.[90] A 22-year-old widow from Santipur, who maintained her parents-in-law and three daughters by her earnings from spinning, wrote with pride that 'others in the field were no match for her in quality spinning'. As her income declined, she pondered over the depths of poverty to which Englishmen had been reduced to have to undersell even her cheap yarn.[91] Despite its declining fortune, cotton spinning and weaving remained in popular memory as a most suitable occupation for women. In 1931, 'hand spinning and weaving were still carried on in the household with the help of women'.[92] A woman writing in a popular journal argued:

Dependent women are not always welcome. Economic pressures on the family are increasing ... cannot women earn something instead of being totally dependent? ... earlier they would weave or spin ... if they were not poor their earnings would form their *streedhan* ... 'Charka is my husband and son, *charka* is my grandson, it is due to *charka* that there is an elephant tied to my door' ... whether, as in the old saying, one could actually have an elephant tied to one's door, I do not know. But it certainly provided a means of earning money within seclusion.[93]

Spinning, however, as in some other superior crafts for extended markets where women worked in the household unit as helpers, did not always give direct access to markets. Many women spun thread for the male members of the family to weave.[94]

There were some tasks which women generally performed for their

---

[89] Buchanan, *An Account of the District of Bihar and Patna*, p. 647. Also see *An Account of the District of Purnea*, p. 536.

[90] A. C. Chatterjee, 'Notes on the Industries of the United Provinces', 1907, quoted in G. M. Broughton, *Labour in Indian Industries*, London, 1924, p. 59.

[91] In a letter dated 5 January 1828 to *Tatwabodhini Patrika* quoted in Brajendranath Bandopadhyay (ed.), *Sambadpatre Sekaler Katha*, Calcutta, 1977, 1384 BS, pp. 156–7.

[92] R. K. Das, 'Women Labour in India', *International Labour Review*, October–November 1931, p. 383.

[93] Manorama Ghose, *Banganarir Kaaj* (Bengali women's work), *Mashik Basumati*, *Baishakh*, 1329 BS, p. 33.

[94] Traditionally, women did the spinning and men the weaving. *Report of the Census of the Town and Suburbs of Calcutta*, 1881, H. Beverley, p. 144. For every 1,000 men, there were 19,737 women spinners but only 207 female cotton weavers, 442 cotton cleaners, pressers, and ginners, 498 yarn and thread sellers, and 624 dyers. *Census of India*, 1901, VI, 1, p. 497. Also see *Census of the Central Provinces*, 1881, II, p. 109 and *Census of India*, 1921, XVI, 2, p. 385.

own families but occasionally extended for sale in the market. These included animal husbandry, making and selling of milk products, preparing vegetable oil and producing and selling forest products. Much the largest employment in this category was in grain and food processing. In textile industries men were still three times as numerous as women but in food processing women, chiefly employed as rice pounders, huskers and flour grinders, were six times as many as men. The processing of grain was usually a part of most women's domestic routine, often undertaken also for sale. Thus, 'husking and boiling rice ... is done entirely by women'.[95] The twenty most common preparations of rice – *mooree*, *cheerah*, *khoyee*, *moorkee*, etc. – were all undertaken by women.[96] In Calcutta, too, the industry of 'rice-pounders and huskers' employed chiefly women.[97] Flour was usually ground at home by women. In Patna, however, it was 'ground in hand-mills at which both men and women are employed. The labour is very hard so that the people seldom work more than 3 hours in the cool of the morning, and two women at the same length do not in a morning grind more than 20 *seers* of wheat.'[98] In the early nineteenth century this provided earnings in cash or kind for many women. Buchanan noted in Patna that:

They are all women, many of them, however young, generally sit in streets with a little fire place parching for all the people in the neighbourhood and receiving a little of the grain from each ... A few are able to purchase grain, parch it in their house, and retail it in their shop.[99]

In Shahabad, he noted that:

Scarcely any of the women who parch grains have shops. All are of the Kandu tribe and are called Bharbhunas ... Two women usually sit in the same shop or house ... Each woman makes 4–5 seers a day. They collect whatever fuel they require.[100]

Smyth also mentioned the physical strain of husking rice. The *dhenki*

[95] Major Ralph Smyth, *Statistical and Geographical Report of the 24 Pergunnahs District*, Calcutta, 1857, p. 27. It was usual for children to assist at the looms which only the man operated and for the wife to spin. Such a unit made a profit of Rs. 4 per month. Buchanan, *An Account of the District of Purnea*, pp. 539–42.

[96] Smyth, *Report of the 24 Pergunnahs District*, p. 27. The 'domestic work' of rice pounding and husking employed 30,000 persons 'which was carried on almost exclusively by women'. *BDG*, 24 Parganas, 1914, p. 145. Also see *BDG*, Hooghly, 1909, p. 176. The 'domestic' industries of rice-pounding and husking and the parching of grain 'naturally fall to the women's lot': to every man, in Bengal there were twenty-seven women and in Bihar and Orissa there were sixteen. *Census of India*, 1911, VI, 1, pp. 548–9.

[97] In the city proper there were 122 men to 640 women, while in the suburbs, there were 3 men to 165 women. *Census of India*, 1901, VII, p. 86.

[98] Buchanan, *An Account of the Districts of Bihar and Patna*, p. 636.   [99] Ibid.

[100] Buchanan, *An Account of the Districts of Bihar and Patna*, p. 402.

was used for cleaning and husking rice which was part of the daily routine of housework though sometimes women would sell cleaned rice.

The cleaning or husking [of rice] is effected by means of an instrument called a dhenki ... Two women work this machine, one alternately presses down the end of the lever with her foot to raise the pestle and then by removing her foot allows the pestle to fall. The other removes the beaten grain and puts fresh into the mortar.[101]

Quite frequently, women assisted the men in the household by selling the products of the business. Among the Agraharis in Bihar, 'the women are not secluded as among the Agrawalas, but take part in business of their husbands by selling rice, flour'.[102] Among the Mallahs, the fishermen and boatmen caste, 'their women work in the village and sell fish'.[103] In Hooghly, half the fish-sellers were women.[104] Among the Gauras of Cuttack, the women sold milk and milk products but they eschewed field labour of all kinds.[105] In Saran, '[Ahir] women, who are very hardworking, add to the family earnings by making and selling cowdung cakes, milk, ghi, and curd'.[106] In fact, 'it is regarded as a woman's job to dispose of the articles that her husband makes, grows, or catches, such as pots and household utensils, milk, ghee and fish.'[107]

Women also participated in some caste-specific artisan (handloom and pottery) and service (laundry and sweeping) occupations. In these, women usually had no independent role but had to work as part of the household team.

There were a few independent professions followed by women without reference to their male relatives.[108] But such activities were strictly limited and the largest such occupation for women – midwifery – was devalued by ritual pollution. Only low-caste women could practise as midwives. In most districts of Bihar, midwives were chamar women. In Bengal proper, women from Hari, Muchi, Dom and other castes could practise midwifery.[109]

Among the low castes, men and women often worked together as in basket weaving, tea gardens, coal mines, field labour and *jhum* cultivation.[110] While women did not usually work on the cotton loom, they wove jute, which was much heavier work. In Bengal, apart from prostitution and midwifery, women were registered as actually out-

---

[101] Smyth, *Report of the 24 Pergunnahs District*, p. 27.
[102] *BDG*, Monghyr, 1909, p. 134.   [103] Ibid.
[104] *BDG*, Hooghly, 1912, p. 176.   [105] *BODG*, Cuttack, 1933.
[106] *BODG*, Saran, 1930, p. 45.   [107] *Census of India*, 1911, V, 1, p. 549.
[108] The 1901 Census returned some male midwives who were either dependants or, as in Decca, assistants who cut the cord but took no part in the delivery. *Census of India*, 1901, V, 1, p. 478.
[109] *Census of India*, 1901, V, 1, p. 479.   [110] *Census of India*, VI, 1, p. 482.

numbering men in three occupations. 'Two of these are domestic industries to which women are well-suited' – silkworm-rearing and the making of twine or string.[111]

Many of these customary occupations declined in the twentieth century. The characteristic features which had made them more accessible to women also made them vulnerable to 'modernisation'.[112] Many of women's crafts were basically for daily use and, therefore, had potentially large markets. Competition had already substantially eroded the textile handloom industry and some other artisan industries. Women, limited by time, skill and capital, used easily available raw materials and locally made crude implements. Consequently their productivity was low. With development of transport these commodities became items in a large network of trade involving capital, information and mobility. Their production was easily and profitably mechanised. Women could not compete with the new machines because of their initial low productivity. Factory-produced goods, such as utensils and clothing, gradually replaced women's handmade products. In addition, commercialisation and the pressure on land curtailed access to forests and commons – to food and fuel. In 1881 women were engaged in a third of the agrarian occupations and in two-fifths of 'making and selling' occupations. By 1921–31 women were reduced to a little over a quarter of the latter. The biggest losses were in food processing, forest products and caste-specific occupations.[113]

Apart from the secular decline in women's non-agrarian occupations their association with domestic work led to a systematic undercounting of women's work.[114] Only visible work by women in fields or markets was taken into account. Many European government officials made a curious and arguable connection between impoverishment and women's visible work. Some of them used the invisibility of women as an index of the prosperity of a region.[115] To give only two examples:

---

[111] *Census of India*, 1911, VI, pp. 548–9.
[112] Nirmala Banerjee, 'Working Women in Colonial Bengal: Modernization and Marginalization', in K. Sangari and S. Vaid, (eds.), *Recasting Women: Essays in Colonial History*, New Delhi, 1989, pp. 283–8.
[113] Banerjee, 'Working Women', pp. 286–7.
[114] One problem is the unreliability of the statistical data. The definition of women's work changed in each of the first three decennial census. The census of 1881 registered women in the husband's occupation. In 1901 and 1911 'great stress was laid ... [that] women and children who work at any occupation, of whatever kind, not being merely an amusement or of a *purely domestic character* ... must be entered' (emphasis added). *Census of India*, 1901, VI, 1, p. 486. In addition, respondents often did not register women's employment. The figures provided by the successive census should be taken as rough guides.
[115] Such a connection could reflect a remembered rather than an actual prosperity and the rules of sexual division of labour pertaining to a community applied to all its

Women are very rarely seen either at work or at the market and on the whole the people are, as compared with the ryots of the same class in the north, very comfortably off.[116]

And:

The people are well off. The absence of women from markets and the fields, showing that they are not required to work except for domestic purposes, is tolerable evidence of the fact that their husbands are able to earn enough for the support of their family. In most other districts the females of the lower classes work in the fields, weeding and transplanting crops: they form the majority at the markets and hats, but in this district few seem to stir abroad beyond the precincts of their own village.[117]

The low workforce participation rates of women in eastern and northern Bengal relative to western and central Bengal and Bihar, may reflect only the proportion of women who worked outside the home. In 1911, in Bengal proper, the ratio of workers to dependants was 36:64, while in Bihar and Orissa it was 48:52. This ratio was more marked in the case of agriculture: in Bengal, 1:2 and in Bihar and Orissa, 4.7:5.3.[118] Women's participation in agricultural work would thus seem to be the lowest in eastern Bengal. Yet, in Rajshahi, where 'women do not work for wages', they helped in cultivation, in weeding crops, husking rice, and weaving gunny bags.[119] In contrast, in Bihar districts, or among the poor of western Bengal, like in Bankura and Birbhum, women were seen to be far more active in agricultural operations and in subsistence activities like fuel gathering or in petty trading.

Lower wages and the perception that their earnings were secondary meant that women often entered the labour market when they had exhausted other alternatives.[120] Sometimes they were pushed into the labour market by the inadequacy or deprivation of male earnings. Non-economic reasons like widowhood, desertion or barrenness might force women 'to go out to work'. It appears that in the early part of nineteenth century in parts of Bihar it was difficult to get female domestic servants except widows and old women 'who have lost all

---

members – individual misfortunes were not justifiable exceptions. Banerjee, 'Working Women', p. 289.

[116] *General Administration Report*, Chittagong Division, 1880–1, p. 10.

[117] The Magistrate of Tipperah, *General Administration Report for the year 1884*, para. 21.

[118] In total, women's workforce participation rate in Bengal was about two women to every seven men, as compared with Bihar and Orissa which had one woman to every two men workers. In Bengal only 2 million women against 6.5 million in Bihar and Orissa were deemed employed. *Census of India*, 1911, V, pp. 548–9. For district-wise breakdowns see Banerjee, 'Working Women', Table 6, p. 289.

[119] E. E. Lewis, Rajshahye Division, pp. 3–4. In Chittagong, a labourer could maintain his family on his wages, but his wife would husk grain and his children would tend cattle. D. R. Lyall, Chittagong Division, p. 4, Dufferin Report.

[120] Chandavarkar, *The Origins of Industrial Capitalism in India*.

their kindred'.[121] In a much later period, at the close of the century, district officials reported from various districts of Bengal, Bihar and Orissa that widows and old women without children formed the largest proportion of destitutes in the village. The Collector of Burdwan wrote, 'the only individuals among them who have no margin, or but the slenderest margin ... are old widows'.[122] The Commissioner of the Presidency division reiterated that those destitute or living on charity were 'chiefly destitute females or old or childless persons'.[123] Such women might either migrate or hire out their labour. Married women, especially those with children to support, were often forced to work outside the home by the fluctuations of male wages and employment.

Women did not work at similar occupations all the year round.[124] They provided labour on family lands during the busy season when wages were higher and the demand for labour was greater. In the lean season, when men could not find work, women would undertake either subsistence activities with low returns or hire out their labour at exceptionally low wages. In twenty-two villages of Muzaffarpur, the supply of labour exceeded its demand by 68 per cent and 'only one-third of the female labouring population found work after the male population was satisfied'.[125] Women might often enter the labour market when the demand for labour was at its lowest and withdraw when the situation was improving. This not only kept women's bargaining strength in the labour market very low but it also helped maintain women as a flexible supply of labour.

The gender division of labour in agriculture is illuminating. Ploughing and sowing were mainly done by men, while transplantation and weeding were the duties of women. They 'are said to be more proficient in this light but tiresome work than men, and some women are so proficient, that they will not work for others at daily rates of wages, but will earn much more by taking contracts for definite areas ... sometimes women are seen to be reaping though it's tougher and usually men do it'.[126] In most cases such divisions of labour appeared in the form of long-established custom. In Bengal, for instance, women were not seen to do any ploughing. This could be due to the symbolic and ritual

[121] Buchanan, *An Account of the District of Bhagalpur.*
[122] Dufferin Report, Main Report (Burdwan Division), 1888, p. 5.
[123] A. Smith, Presidency Division, p. 7. A Bauri widow of about 20 years was 'an instance of absolute pauperism, just short of mendicancy'. N. S. Alexander, Burdwan Division, p. 3, Dufferin Report.
[124] Or they might not even work for wages all the year round. From A. K. Roy, Joint Settlement Officer, p. 6, Dufferin Report.
[125] Stevenson-Moore Report, p. 364.   [126] *BDG*, Bankura, 1908, p. 104.

importance of the plough in Bengali culture.[127] The same was true of sowing: it was 'unusual to see women sowing. This may be because of the ceremonial significance of the act'.[128] Yet, in certain districts of the Central Provinces wheat sowing was normally done by women.[129] The widely held custom of women participating in transplanting can, however, also be attributed to the increase in demand for labour in that season, since transplanting was a relatively labour-intensive job. This was also the season when prices of grain rose.[130] For families without stores of grain it might become more imperative for a larger number of women to work for hire. Depending on the supply of labour, however, women were paid either equal or less wages than men. Where there was a higher incidence of landlessness, the rise in prices of grains[131] would probably force a larger number of labourers into field work, and this might, despite the higher demand for labour, depress wages. Nor were rules for such division of labour universal. In some areas, like in eastern Bengal, women were not seen taking part in field work even in busy seasons. However, in other parts they were extensively employed.

Work, *purdah* and dowry

The social and economic devaluation of women's work must be seen within the configuration of social and cultural perceptions of gender and the close correlation between work, status and *purdah*. The uneven demand for women's labour among different social groups in different areas led to protean practices of segregation and domesticity. A particular social group's ability to manipulate customary rules of *purdah*, however, influenced in turn the extent to which they were able to deploy women's labour. Both economic and status considerations were inevitably involved. Poor women usually constituted a mobile labour force to be deployed where the demand was greatest. Either natal or conjugal

[127] The sharing of bodily substance is an important basis of kin relations, symbolised and daily reconstituted by shared *anna* (usually rice or other grains cultivated by the use of the plough). Ronald B. Inden and Ralph W. Nicholas, *Kinship in Bengali Culture*, Chicago, 1977, p. 52.
[128] *BDG*, Bankura, 1908, p. 103.
[129] *Census of the Central Provinces*, 1881, II, p. 102.
[130] 'The price of paddy rises as usual during the transplanting season, and falls as soon as the aus paddy is in the market'. Anundoram Borooah, Noakhally, p. 3, Dufferin Report.
[131] In Gaya, women were employed in planting out the seedlings, the men as *kabariyas* (uprooters of seedlings), *dhowas* (carriers of seedling from seed-bed to field) and *chhitas* (distributors). Men were paid four seers of grain and women three seers. Grierson, *Notes on the District of Gaya*, p. 111.

kin, if not both, would insist that a woman visit them at particularly busy times.

The withdrawal of elite women from visible or manual work and the simultaneous compulsions on the poorer women to participate in such activities impelled socially aspirant families to devise different forms of *purdah*, like the Maratha variant of working in the field and veiling at home.[132] When a woman worked in the family farm, she veiled her face to avoid appropriate affines. Hard-working young women would work long hours in the sun harvesting wheat with their faces veiled from elder male affines working nearby. As more women participated in general and field labour, some adaptations of *purdah* were devised to ensure security from sexual harassment. This might have prompted the common practice of women working together separately from men in most agricultural operations. In other non-agricultural labour too, women were seen to band together when working alongside men.

The need for security may have been greater for wives who remained in the village when men migrated, either to the city or for seasonal agricultural labour. Even in the home, the need for security and protection from sexual advances of male affines might have prompted more women to adopt forms of *purdah*. Many folksongs of the period refer to unwelcome advances:

Thou thief, my husband's younger brother thou have plundered my youth . . .
Had my husband been at home, I would have had you maimed and got you
    hanged.[133]

. . . While sweeping the yard, the skirt of my cloth flew away, O Rama!
And my wicked brother-in-law began to gaze on my breast, O Hari!
I would get such a brother-in-law killed, O Rama!
If my 'knife-thrusting' (husband) were at home, O Hari![134]

In eastern Bengal, even the small peasants had the natural possibility of two rice crops in the year and they could draw cash advances in the lean season against the jute crop. They could afford to hire labour from outside in the busiest season. Hence, the stricter seclusion was practised in East Bengal. But these *purdah* practices were elastic too, often modified to accommodate the demand for women's labour. In Dinajpur, among *khodkasht* ryots, 'females do not work for their livelihood, but for their own household and cultivation work'. Among agricultural labourers, women would work, but, 'the females of these people are not

---

132 O' Hanlon, *For the Honour of my Sister Countrywomen*.
133 Translation in original. G. A. Grierson, *Seven Grammars of the Dialects and Sub-dialects of the Bihari Language*, Calcutta, 1883, p. 129.
134 Translation in original. W. Irvine, 'Baiswari Folk-songs collected by J. N. Rae', *Journal of the Royal Asiatic Society*, 53, 2, 1, 1884, pp. 236–7.

allowed to work for hire'.[135] In Chittagong, 'The women hold a good position and are not allowed to do any field work beyond the light task of gathering the *rabi* crops, nor are they permitted to work on the road or in any other public place or even go to the market.'[136] Such adaptations of *purdah* were relatively cost-free because they did not involve loss of women's labour when and where it was most required. At the same time they allowed poorer families to aspire to higher status associated with seclusion of women. In a period of enhanced competition for dwindling agrarian resources such marks of status acquired greater importance.

It follows that manual and visible work was associated chiefly with poor, low-status and low-caste women. In western districts of Bengal, participation of women in agriculture was noticed most among the low caste or the landless labour. In Birbhum, field labourers, 'being mostly low caste men, were assisted by their women and children'.[137] Even so, in most agricultural work women and men had strictly separate roles and it was more common for women to work together separately from men. Among the Bauris, who were mainly landless labourers, nomadic cultivators (sharecroppers) or under-ryots, women undertook even general labour. Dutt noted the range of work such 'semi-aboriginal' women performed. 'Household work', he admitted, 'is the lot of Hindu women', but among the low castes 'men and women work together' in the field, at digging and carrying. '[W]ives often carry things for sale to the village market while husbands work in fields ... the Bauri women of Bankura are the best *coolies* for carrying luggage or portmanteaus, often 20 to 30 miles a day.'[138]

In the long term, the devaluation of women's productivity is best reflected in the movement in the twentieth century towards a general practice of dowry. More and more castes were abandoning the payment of brideprices in favour of paying dowries. In the late nineteenth century, payment of brideprice was still common among several agricultural castes.[139] Curiously, the twentieth-century conventional wisdom

---

[135] C. R. Marindin, Dinagepore, Dufferin Report.

[136] *General Administration Report for the year 1879–80*, Chittagong, para. 13.

[137] *BDG*, Birbhum, 1910, p. 67.

[138] Dutt, 'The Aboriginal Element in the Population of Bengal', p. 69. Also see *BDG*, Bankura, 1908, pp. 59–60. 25 per cent of the general labour employed in Hooghly were women. *BDG*, Hooghly, 1912, p. 176. In Saran, Dusadh and Nunia women 'work as hard as men'. *BODG*, Saran, 1930, p. 45.

[139] In 1901, most Aguri, Tili, Sadgop, Chashi Kaibarta still paid brideprice. But some of them, like the Chashi Kaibarta of Howrah and Nadia, and better-off Aguri, Tili and Sadgop were switching from brideprice, because 'they know that this is looked down upon by high castes'. As a result, the dowry rates were increasing rapidly. *Census of India*, 1901, VI, 1, p. 251.

of the financially crippled father of daughters has an ancestry in nine-teenth-century official descriptions of families ruined by demands of brideprice. An officer wrote from Khulna:

The excessive expenses incurred by the marriage of a male member of a family involves the family in debt for years, and unless this expense is to some extent met by the 'pan' received for females when given in marriage, it becomes a serious drain on the family resources. In fact, but for this, the majority of the poorer classes would be much better off and able to live without feeling the pressure of poverty as long as crops and prices remained normal.[140]

From the Burdwan Division, the Commissioner wrote:

I found on enquiry that the debts were very often incurred not to procure food for the debtors, but to enable them to marry, as among the lower classes of the people, the intending bridegroom has to pay a pretty considerable sum to the father of the bride.[141]

By 1930, when the Government of Bengal was investigating popular reaction to the Sarda (Child Marriage Restraint) Act of 1930, the picture had changed radically. There were reports from various parts of Bengal that families were finding it difficult to find grooms because deteriorating economic conditions made it difficult for them to pay the requisite dowry.[142] By 1931, there were forty-two out of fifty-one Census-registered castes paying dowries, which according to the Census was a change in the last forty to sixty years.[143]

This development coincided with an increasing acceptance of the brahmanical custom of hypergamy among lower castes like the Sadgops, Pods, Chasa and Dhobas, who had previously had to buy their brides. Unlike the high-caste urban elite, these castes previously had some incidence of adult marriages. In the nineteenth century they tended to shift more towards child marriage and the practice continued among them even after the *bhadralok* had abandoned it. It was not merely a concern to preserve young daughters' chastity and the desire to improve ritual status that lay behind this. The devaluation of women's work meant that parents were less willing to undertake the maintenance of daughters for longer periods. L. G. Durno, the Magistrate of Faridpur, having canvassed Hindu and Muslim opinion, reported that raising the age of marriage 'will place on the father expenditure which the bride-groom's people bore; the girl's whose marriage is postponed must be kept at home and is one more mouth to feed.'[144] The District Officer of Chittagong read the opposition against the Sarda Bill in similar terms:

[140] Dufferin Report, Main Report (from Khulna), p. 18.
[141] N. S. Alexander, Burdwan Division, p. 17, Dufferin Report.
[142] WBSA, HPC 73(1–8) of 1930.   [143] *Census of India*, 1931, I, p. 399.
[144] WBSA, HPC 73 (1–8) of 1930.

'The longer the parents have to maintain their daughters unmarried, the greater the drain on their income ... economically, therefore, the act will be felt especially by the poorer amongst the community.'[145] Besides, the costs of marriage, in an inflationary period, were best undertaken early to obviate the devaluation of more long-term savings. There were a few who greeted the Sarda Act with relief – families in Burdwan, Faridpur and Chittagong were finding it difficult to meet dowry demands for even young girls.[146]

In the Bengal context, dowry can be related more to the relative devaluation of women's productive capacity than to the daughter's pre-mortem share in the parental property. The dowry was paid not to her but to the husband's family. More interestingly, dowry was spreading to poorer classes who had little property to leave.[147] By the same token, dowry cannot be regarded as a contribution to the girl's maintenance since it was paid increasingly for women who made an active contribution to the income of the conjugal household.

Buying a bride did not, of course, involve any benefit to the women who were bought since the price was paid to the father and was more in the nature of a compensation for the loss of her labour. Hence, a 'female child does not earn anything, but she brings at her marriage about Rs. 100–200 to the father, and is useful to the mother as she learns to work'.[148] The system of brideprice recognised, if not respected, women's productive contribution to the conjugal family. By that token, brideprice could also be paid for widows. It appears that usually older women fetched a lower price. But experience counted: 'amongst a few functional castes, a widow of mature age, who is an expert in the work by which the people of the caste ordinarily live, commands a higher price than one who is younger and more attractive but less useful from a professional point of view'![149] In some agrarian communities of Bihar,

[145] Ibid. Among the Gauras, a trading and pastoral caste, child marriage was 'more stringent' and if an unmarried girl reached puberty, either she would be given in a mock marriage to a bow and arrow or she would be taken to the forest and they would 'tie her to a tree' for the 'wild beast or the first comer'. It was apparently usual to arrange for someone to come and carry her off. K. G. Gupta, *Census of India*, 1901, VI, 1, p. 249.
[146] WBSA, HPC 73 (1–8) of 1930.
[147] Anthropological convention has tended to concentrate on the relation of dowry and property. In many cases it is regarded as the daughter's pre-mortem share in the parental or ancestral property. H. L. Moore, *Feminism and Anthropology*, Blackwell, 1988 (reprint, 1991), pp. 65–72. But women often had limited access and rights to such property. Ursula Sharma, *Women, Work and Property in North-Western India*, London, 1980.
[148] A. Smith, Presidency Division, p. 13, Dufferin Report.
[149] *Census of India*, 1901, VI, 1, p. 251. For a fuller discussion of widow remarriage, see chapter 5 below.

the widow of one brother was married to another. Thus, the conjugal family retained her labour, and avoided another brideprice for the second brother.

The perception, however, of a widening gap between men's and women's earning capacities and their material contribution to the conjugal household that led to spread of dowry, also explains the increasing restrictions on widow remarriage and the move towards child marriage. Among some castes who continued to pay brideprices (Sadgops of Bankura), dowry was paid for grooms with jobs in the organised sector, salaried jobs or university degrees which carried expectations of better employment and higher income.[150] In a situation where a woman's status was embedded in her conjugal family the competition for employment was reflected in the competition for grooms and, as in the case of hypergamy, dowry was the price paid for the desired marriage. Where sons were sent to work in the modern sector to supplement landed income, the relative exchange-value of women's contribution to the family income declined. Even those women who worked outside the home worked mostly in occupations with smaller returns, while men who went to work in the modern sector – in mills, mines and plantations – received higher wages.

[150] Dagmar A. E. Engels, *Beyond Purdah? Women in Bengal, 1890–1939*, Delhi, 1996, pp. 41–56.

3   'Away from homes': women's work in the mills

In recent years scholars have feverishly debated the rival merits of class and community in understanding the social and political action of industrial workers in Bengal. In elaborating and pursuing these alternatives, they have focused on a false problem. It has been assumed either that the experience of factory work does (or even should) in the long run subsume social identities based on religion, region and language or that, partly as a result of economic backwardness such 'pre-capitalist' identities remain well-entrenched, dividing workers and weakening their resistance to capital. The first scenario is supposed to obtain in advanced capitalist societies, especially in Britain, where class cohesion is deemed to have followed the industrial revolution. In fact, of course, it is now recognised that a narrow focus on 'class' issues has obscured the politics of race, region, language and gender on which the profits of mobile European capital thrived in the nineteenth and twentieth centuries. There never was, anywhere, a unitary 'class'. Historians, however, have been preoccupied with explaining the reasons and conditions of its absence in Bengal. Workers' experience of factory work, particularly in the jute industry, is supposed to have been structured by economic backwardness and the enduring strength of 'pre-capitalist' cultural norms. As a result, it is argued that, though industrial employers reduced, or even eliminated, skill differentials, thereby creating the conditions for solidarity in the workplace, these processes did not significantly impinge on their pre-existing differences which survived and resisted homogenising pressures of capitalist policies.[1] Such explanations obscure the process of industrial labour-force formation. Many pre-existing 'differences' were, indeed, reinforced but they also acquired new functions, meanings and significations in the context of colonial industrialisation since capitalism worked through and amplified such differences. That is to say that the social relationships of inequality which segmented and structured the labour force and the

[1] Dipesh Chakrabarty, *Rethinking Working Class History, Bengal 1890–1940*, Princeton, 1989.

labour process were also in turn reinforced by the latter. No existing social relationship was simply and mechanically translated into the shopfloor, the trade unions and the urban neighbourhoods. Social networks of caste, kin and community influenced access to credit, employment and housing; they contributed to particular structuring of occupations. In the case of the Bombay cotton textile industry, industrialisation played an active role in perpetuating, deepening and modifying existing social differences. In some cases capitalist strategies even created new hierarchies within the working classes.[2] The relationships and identities defined by gender, caste and religion remained but were also profoundly transformed by the experience of urban employment.

This chapter isolates gender in reading the history of this transformation. It examines the role of gender division of labour in the formation of the labour force and in the labour process itself. It argues that gender was an important axis along which the industrial working class developed, and highlights questions of why, how and with what results the jute industry increasingly became a male preserve. The employers created hierarchical skill differentiations which separated jobs into men's work and women's work within the mills. In order to do so, they drew on existing perceptions of gender, but the ways in which they differentiated between men and women workers often heightened their differences and exacerbated the divergence of their interests.

A circular logic underpinned the association of women with lower skills in wider public discourses current in the late nineteenth and early twentieth centuries. Employers and workers – men and women – sometimes shared these perceptions of gender. Employers paid women less than men because women performed tasks designated as 'unskilled'. Conversely, employers deemed certain tasks unskilled and fixed lower wages for them if these tasks were habitually undertaken by women. Men workers associated low wages, low skill and lower status with women's tasks. These tasks, designated as 'women's' work, very rarely bore any special relationship to the needs of biological reproduction, though employers and male workers often advanced specious arguments about their suitability in relation to childbearing and lactation. The ideological constructions of skill and suitability became clearer as male workers began to lay exclusive claim on the better-paid jute mill jobs, leaving women access to only a very few low paid 'suitable' jobs. The proportion of women in the mills decreased rapidly and to the extent

---

[2] R. S. Chandavarkar, *The Origins of Industrial Capitalism in India: Business Strategies and the Working Classes in Bombay, 1900–1940*, Cambridge, 1994. Some of his basic arguments about the nature of colonial industrialisation, capitalist policy and labour politics can be applied to the Bengal jute industry.

industry continued to employ women, they were progressively concentrated in two or three tasks.

In the case of the jute industry, most women of what may be called the 'working-class family' remained in the village to undertake agriculture or otherwise procure the means of subsistence. The few women who came to the cities concentrated in unskilled and manual work, petty services and retail trades where rewards were poor and the conditions of work unregulated. In these urban occupations, as in the rural workforce, gender division of labour was pervasive. In the silk industries women mainly spun and turned reels. In indigo factories, they carried the fresh plants to the vats, removed the refuse, and carried the cakes to the godowns.[3] In 'modern' industries, large numbers of women in rice mills were 'drying, spreading, and turning rice, moving it from the hullers and winnowing bran in rice mills'; in the shellac industry they were 'stripping, grinding and sieving'; in earthwork and the building trade they were mainly 'carriers'.[4]

Among the 'organised' sector, which had begun to be brought under the purview of legislation from the late nineteenth century, tea planters were the most assiduous employers of women.[5] Planters in remote and sparsely populated tea gardens actively sought a self-reproducing 'settled' labour force and they needed women. In addition, women and children undertook for low wages the labour-intensive task of leaf-plucking. Over time, the 'nimble' fingers required for the task became constituted as a specific 'feminine' skill. Not only was women's labour valued in garden work, but also it was considered the most 'suitable' employment for women.[6] Government officials, middle-class British and Indian reformers considered conditions of work in mines and mills, in contrast, to be highly unsuitable for women. In coal mines, women worked underground and carried heavy loads which were supposed to injure their health.[7] Jute mill work too was 'unsuitable' for women – mill owners and even male workers agreed. These attitudes enabled mill owners to nail women's wages at the lower rates that female labour commanded across the urban economy and to depress the wages of men who worked at jobs commonly associated with female labour.

[3] WBSA, General Miscellaneous, September 1895, A27.
[4] R. K. Das, 'Women Labour in India', *International Labour Review*, Oct.–Nov. 1931, p. 397.
[5] N. Banerjee, 'Working Women in Colonial Bengal: Modernization and Marginalization', in K. Sangari and S. Vaid (eds.), *Recasting Women: Essays in Colonial History*, New Delhi, 1989.
[6] Curjel Report, pp. 3–5.
[7] *Annual Report of the Chief Inspector of Mines in India*, Calcutta, 1905, p. 2. Women also carried loads in iron and salt mines.

In the early years of the industry, in the nineteenth century, women were scattered across various processes of the mill. From about the 1890s, when the industry was expanding rapidly, migrant men replaced women in most departments. Women were retained in a few 'unskilled' and low-paid jobs. This trend, clearly discernible in the 1920s, may have been in part the employers' response to 'protective' legislation: the Factories Acts of 1881 and 1891 placed restrictions on hours of work, rest intervals, and night work for women and children but not for men. Employers did not immediately retrench women but they further pushed them into the unmechanised jobs.

It has been argued earlier that jute entrepreneurs relied on flexibility of production and labour supply. Mill owners manipulated labour through casual hiring and variable hours or speed of work. In periods of crisis women proved particularly useful. The widely current ideologies of gender defined women primarily as housewives and mothers and their income as 'supplementary'. Women, thus, even more than men, could be used as a floating labour reserve, hired when necessary but easily dispensed with in a slump.

In the 1930s the jute industry faced a major crisis. With their backs to the wall, the IJMA became vulnerable to the government's attempt to standardise wages and employment conditions. 'Rationalisation' became the new watchword. Yet, despite a great deal of talk, the attempts at labour efficiency remained ad hoc and piecemeal. While a few Managing Agents undertook renovation, introduced new machinery and some technological upgrading, the mill owners' common and sustained strategy was to reduce labour costs through wage cuts, increased workloads and even outright retrenchment.

Obviously, 'rationalisation' did not affect the workforce uniformly. The changing market conditions and employers' policies affected different sections of the workforce in different degrees and in diverse ways, exposing and even exacerbating their internal differences. Mechanisation, for instance, affected women more adversely. The practice of employing women primarily in the less mechanised sections of the mill had become well entrenched by the 1920s. The introduction of machinery in these jobs often entailed retrenchment of women and the recruitment of a few men in their places. By long habit, the assumption that women were unable to handle sophisticated machinery had been naturalised. Besides, with prospects of unemployment looming large, male workers and trade unions were more than happy to encourage this myth. In the Bombay textile industry, the crisis and the subsequent 'rationalisation' helped women workers to define their specific common interests. The effects of such consolidation became evident in the women's strikes of 1928. Women in the Calcutta jute industry did not experience rationalisation in the same way.

In the jute industry, despite the increasing gender segregation of jobs, women were not exclusively departmentalised as they were in reeling and winding in cotton textile mills. The hierarchies of perceived gender-specific skills did not result in gender segregation by departments and the creation of predominantly female enclaves. There was no task in the jute industry, unlike in tea plantations, that was considered 'women's' or specifically related to perceived 'feminine' skills. Women were neither encouraged to settle, as in plantations, nor did they work in male–female units, as in coal mines. It follows that in the jute industry there was no strict division of labour between men and women in the production process. But by the 1920s and 1930s, though there was no exclusively women's work, some work was designated as men's work, or rather, as work that women could not do. Women were distributed across a few of the lower-paid jobs in the mills. So even when increasingly fewer women were being employed, they worked along with men distributed throughout the mills. It was thus less likely that their position would be specifically and systematically attacked. However, since some of the labour-intensive tasks like feeding, receiving and hand-sewing in which women predominated became susceptible to mechanisation, their jobs were more threatened than those of men in the 1930s. Employers used the trade unions and the male workers' fears of unemployment to undermine women's hold over their jobs. The women workers, whose interests were not obviously cohesive in the workplace, found it difficult to combine against employers.

Era of protection – 1881–1919

The jute mill owners' success in marginalising women in the 1930s owed not a little to their ability to draw on stereotypes of women workers that had been in wide circulation ever since women's induction into jute mills in the nineteenth century. Even then, government officers and reformers – British and Indian – had expressed doubts about women's ability to endure the physical strain of factory work. Employers stressed women's need to work and the importance of their earnings in ensuring family survival, but reformers were uncertain about the comparative value of women's wage contribution to the family. The reformers emphasised the ill-effects of women's employment on do-mestic life and the immorality of unrelated men and women working together.

These arguments became interwoven with questions of skill and wages and began directly to impinge on the employment of women in the wake of the Factories Act of 1881. Until 1911, factory legislation did not intervene into conditions of adult male employment but regulated the hours of work and rest for women and children, fixed the minimum age at which children could be employed, determined the extent to which women should use moving machinery and prohibited night work for these categories of workers.

It is commonly believed that these legal provisions reduced women's employment in the organised sector, that the 'protective' legislation in effect became 'restrictive' legislation – and without due and proper wage compensation. Thus, women and children earned less because they were forced to work fewer hours, and not to work at all in night shifts and with moving machinery. It does not appear, however, that these laws led employers to directly reduce the number of women employed. Neither the restrictions on women's and children's hours of work and rest (Act of 1881 and its Amendment in 1891) nor the prohibition on women's night work (1920s) led to any immediate retrenchment of women.

In the jute mills, in fact, the effects of many of these laws were cushioned. First, the IJMA successfully lobbied the Government of Bengal for formal exemptions from many laws. Second, the government and the inspectorate tended to overlook what they regarded as minor infringements. In any case, the inspector's office was ill-equipped to deal with the rapidly proliferating factories. Overworked inspectors could not or would not untangle the confusion created by personalised recruitment, casual employment, multiple shifts and the enormous parallel system of relieving workers who never appeared on registers. Factory laws were thus in general evaded, and more particularly so in the case of women and children.

Nevertheless, the mill owners, through the Bengal Chamber of Commerce and the IJMA, put up fierce resistance against 'protective' legislation. It has been shown earlier that some managers used women, who were paid less, to counter male aggression and solidarity. Managers were loath to give up these advantages, especially at a time when the industry was expanding at a stupendous rate. They therefore dwelt on the 'light and easy' nature of the work given to women and children, their own liberality in allowing women to 'come and go as they pleased' and the importance of women's and children's wages to the household's survival. Besides, the mill owners quite correctly believed that once the principles of labour legislation had been conceded, these would eventually be extended to adult male labour.

Not much is known about the hours worked by women and children before 1881. They probably worked the same hours as men – from dawn to dusk. The amendment in 1891 to the Factories Act of 1881 fixed women's hours of work at eleven per day. However, by 1896 most mills adopted electric light. This resulted in the lengthening of an average working day from about twelve hours to about fifteen or sixteen hours.[8] In the jute industry shift work made it possible to retain women without contravening the letter of the law. Mill owners insisted that because of the practice of working shifts no women worked longer than ten hours.[9] Nevertheless, they argued long and hard to prevent a legal maximum of eleven hours being imposed. Perhaps they were unwilling to have the existing situation formalised because it jeopardised future flexibility. It is more likely that women did in actual fact work longer than the ten hours which they admitted.[10]

In most cases the 'protective' laws, especially those regarding women and children, were subject to wholesale evasion. A. G. Clow, examining the efficacy of factory legislation, found, 'no provisions were so consistently evaded as those designed for the protection of women'.[11] By 1896, the working shift in jute mills became a cause for concern. A special Commission initiated by the Dundee lobby found that in some mills, particularly in the Hastings Jute Mill, women and children (under 14 years) were employed for twenty-two and fifteen hours respectively. Messrs Birkmyre Bros. even provided a 'sleeping room' for infants.

It is easy to be misled by the long and laboured controversies over the exact age which separated 'children' and 'young persons' for the purpose of the Factories Acts. The precise age of prospective young workers was impossible to determine and certificates falsifying the workers' ages could be readily obtained. In the early years, the carefully drafted rules and regulations had no visible effect on recruitment practices of the Bengal mills. It was very common to find children of 5 or 6 years at work. Reform and protection came very slowly. Fifty years after the first 'protective' law, 30–40 per cent of children in jute mills were under the legal minimum age of 9 years and 25 per cent of the young full-timers were under 14 years. A list of prosecutions of mill

---

[8] *Bengal Administration Report for 1896–97*, 2, pp. 134–48. By 1908, 'cribbing time' (working illegally from 4.30 a.m. to 8.30 p.m.) became common. *Report of the Indian Factory Labour Commission* (henceforth *IFLC*), 1908, para. 11.
[9] WBSA, Home Judicial, February 1896, A467.
[10] A census taken in 1928 found that 61 per cent of the men and 56 per cent of the women worked more than fifty-four hours per week. C. M. Matheson, *Indian Industries – Yesterday, Today and Tomorrow*, Oxford, 1930, pp. 20–8.
[11] A. G. Clow, 'Indian Factory Law Administration', *Bulletin of Indian Industries and Labour*, 8, February 1921, p. 28; *IFLC*, p. 45.

owners from August 1925 to April 1927 revealed at least 123 cases involving illegal employment of women and children.[12]

The system of shifts in multiple shift mills offer every opportunity for employment beyond the legal limits and in some mills children are actually working as many as 11–12 hours per day. In single shift mills, two or more mills are adjoining, children have the opportunity to work the morning shift in one mill and the afternoon shift in another ... approximately 25 per cent of the children employed in jute mills work longer hours than the law permits ... Detection ... is exceedingly difficult ... false name and particulars (are provided) ... it is common practice for parents to disown their children and children their parents if they have the slightest suspicion that trouble may arise from the admission.[13]

The widespread practice of double employment was corroborated by the IJMA.[14] The *sardars* and clerks extracted bribes from the workers to conceal ages and identities and therefore had an interest in the continuance of the system. The parents needed extra money and were eager to bypass the law. It was finally by an amendment to the Factories Act in 1926 that parents were made liable for children working double shifts. Even so, in the 1930s, children were covered with an upended basket when the inspector was around.[15] The factory inspector found, not surprisingly, that 'instructions have been attended to and ... may now be said to be properly kept ... the provisions of the law regarding hours of working ... and number of holidays have been observed'.[16]

As in the case of children, so in the employment of women, the multiple shift concealed infractions of the law. It allowed time-clerks and *sardars* to keep workers longer hours than officially admitted. They took a cut out of the extra wages workers thus earned. Managers did little to enforce regulations and even less to restrain the clerk and the *sardar* (see Table 3.1).[17]

The laws prohibiting women's and children's employment before 5.30 a.m. and after 7 p.m. were repeatedly challenged by the IJMA. Since the introduction of electric lighting in 1896, some mills worked all day and through the night. Soon after, a commission was sent from Dundee to inspect labour conditions in the Bengal jute mills. This commission suggested that women employed in night shifts worked elsewhere during the day and therefore argued that night work by women should be

[12] WBSA, Comm. Comm., January 1929, B261–8. Miss Sorabji, a member of the Royal Commission, quoted forty-two cases of infractions regarding women and children. *RCLI*, V, 1, p. 239.
[13] Certifying Surgeon, *RCLI*, V, 2, p. 334.   [14] *RCLI*, V, 1, p. 298.
[15] Bejoy Hazra, Interview, Radhanagar Colony, Bauria, 4 November 1989 and Mathur Naskar, Interview, Santoshpur, Bauria, 2 December 1989.
[16] *FA*, 1935.   [17] WBSA, Comm. Comm., January 1929, B261–8.

Table 3.1. *Timetable of a multiple shift system*

Time-workers
A Shift – 5.30 to 8.30 a.m.; 9.30 a.m. to 3.30 p.m.
B Shift – 5.30 to 9.30 a.m.; 2.00 p.m. to 7.00 p.m.
C Shift – 5.30 to 2.00 p.m.; 3.30 p.m. to 7.00 p.m.
Piece-workers
A Shift- 5.30 to 7.00 a.m.; 8.00 a.m. to 12 noon; 1.30 p.m. to 7.00 p.m.
B Shift – 5.30 to 8.00 a.m.; 9.00 a.m. to 1.30 p.m.; 3.00 p.m. to 7.00 p.m.
C Shift – 5.30 to 9.00 a.m.; 10.30 a.m. to 3.00 p.m.; 4.00 p.m. to 7.00 p.m.
D Shift – 5.30 to 10.30 a.m.; 12.00 noon to 4.00 p.m.; 5.00 p.m. to 7.00 p.m.
Half-timers
A Shift – 5.30 a.m. to 10.00 a.m.
B Shift – 10.00 a.m. to 2.30 p.m.
C Shift – 2.30 p.m. to 7.00 p.m.

Source: WBSA, Comm. Comm., January 1929, B 264.

prohibited.[18] The Government of Bengal took the view that women should work the same hours as the men who had to accompany them to and from work.[19] They were willing to permit jute mills to employ women because, they argued, the tropical climate made night work physically less taxing and therefore the women themselves preferred to work at night. They believed that the shift system would ensure that the working day would be limited to eleven hours.[20] Dissenting voices were also heard within official circles. Dr Murray, the Civil Surgeon, insisted that under no circumstances should night work be allowed for women. While agreeing that a woman 'in this country ... was accustomed to night work', the Chief Inspector of Factories, Walsh, pointed out that shifts allowed serious infringements of the law. Even on night shifts, women worked more than eleven hours. He was in favour of further restrictions. Walsh's opinion, based on informal discussions with mill managers was none the less in total contradiction to the position of the IJMA as well as the Government of Bengal.[21]

The issue of night work and its prohibition was centred on women. It resurfaced in the 1920s. The International Labour Convention, 1919 (later ratified by Government of India) fixed a minimum of eleven hours night's rest for working women. Yet, in 1926, investigations by the ILO revealed that only 13,000 out of 53,000 female jute workers in Bengal enjoyed the full eleven hours of rest at night. The ILO wrote to the

---

[18] IOL, Home Judicial, February 1896, A405–68.
[19] Secretary, IJMA, *IJMAR*, 1895.
[20] IOL, L/J&P/3/404–7, Indian Factories (Amendment) Act, 1891.
[21] WBSA, General Department, November 1895, A5–17.

Government of India to enquire whether the climate in Bengal or the special circumstances of shift work justified such exemptions.[22]

In the nineteenth century, the Government of India, prompted by British and Indian labour reformers, argued that some labour legislation was necessary to protect women and children who were 'weak, helpless creatures'.[23] They argued that factory work threatened the health and well-being of women and children and this was usually offered as a clinching argument in favour of curtailing their hours of work. The Bengal Chamber of Commerce and the IJMA sought to circumvent this argument by pleading special climatic conditions. '[T]he health and welfare of the workers are ... the deciding factor in this matter .... Thus [we] urge no other consideration ... (and) claim exemption from Articles 2 and 3 of the Washington Convention on grounds of climate.'[24] The Chief Inspector of Factories rejected this argument because, 'shortening the period of night rest for working women can not be anything but detrimental to their health'.[25]

Jute mill owners thus adopted various strategies – disputations, evasions and the multiple shift system – to neutralise 'protective' laws. Where these failed, factory managers were certainly not willing to reduce factory time to accommodate women and children. So long as adult male labour remained outside the pale of the Factories Acts, jute mills were able to carry on, dispensing with the few women who might throw their schedule out of gear. Also, the laws introduced limits. Inspections, however cursory, and interference were all resented by managers. Legislation thus handicapped the 'protected' categories in the labour market. The chances of their employment in registered factories were reduced. Read pointed out:

If women are not allowed to work the same number of hours as men, the possibility is that they will not be employed in many departments where men generally work. The hours of work and intervals of rest should be the same for both men and women.[26]

In the 1920s, when Read put forward this argument, the thrust of 'protective' laws had changed. Men were not forbidden night shifts but their hours of work had been curtailed as well.[27] Some of the issues

---

[22] Article 7 of the convention made a special exemption for climatic factors but not for shift work. WBSA, Comm. Comm., May 1929, B196–9.

[23] The Deputy Commissioner of Nagpur wrote, 'they [men] are quite capable of taking care of themselves, while women and children are helpless'. IOL, L/E/9/290–5.

[24] WBSA, Comm. Comm., May 1929, B196–9.   [25] Ibid.

[26] She was the woman member of the Royal Commission of Labour. Margaret Read, *From Field to Factory*, London, 1927, pp. 203–4.

[27] The Indian Textiles Factories Act of 1911 introduced restriction on the hours of work of adult male labour. This became applicable to the jute mills by the 1922 amendment.

raised in this era of 'protective' legislation thus became redundant. But
not entirely. First, some of the 'protective' laws – as in the case of night
work – were revived in the 1920s. The earlier strategies of evasions and
avoidance adopted by jute mill owners had begun to run aground.
Adoption of single-shift working in the 1930s made the maintenance of
workers' registers relatively straightforward. The provincial government
found it increasingly difficult to protect jute mill owners in the face of
the combined pressures from the ILO, the Government of India and the
trade unions. The inspectorate could not continue to ignore obvious
violations of factory laws by the mills. Second, after the First World
War, women's factory work became increasingly enmeshed in conflicting
discourses. On the one hand, there was a move towards equalising the
conditions of men's and women's work – they were given the same hours
of work and rest. On the other hand, a new strand of reformists actively
appealed to familial ideology: if a woman was to take up paid employment at all, it must certainly fit into her prior domestic commitments.

These two trends converged in the 1930s. The emphasis on domesticity and motherhood devalued women's role as earners. The existing
attitudes towards women as unskilled, low-paid and marginal workers
became more deeply entrenched. Mill owners were able to draw on
these discourses when 'protective' laws became too irksome. Faced with
the depression and the need to reduce labour costs, jute mill owners
seized the new opportunities for mechanisation and were able to
dispense with the majority of their child workers and a substantial
proportion of the women.

Fewer jobs for women: gender, skill and wages – 1920–29

The jute mill owners were able to dispense with women workers by
mechanising their tasks because women were already concentrated in
the kinds of tasks that were susceptible to mechanisation. This gendering of work in the jute mills followed the seemingly universal pattern
of allotting the most manual and repetitive tasks to women. Thus, they
could be paid less and conferred unskilled status. At various stages mill
managers explained why women were not employed in handling machinery or in jobs requiring skill or training. Women married young;
they usually came to mill work too late to go through the apprenticeship
required to train for a skilled job. The demands of housework and
childcare limited their commitment to work. Moreover, women would
have to be apprenticed to male workers – an arrangement not acceptable
to either. Thus, women's work became characterised as 'unskilled'. It is
necessary, however, to interrogate the category 'skill'. In jute mills, for

instance, the classification of tasks as 'unskilled' often bore very little relation to the actual amount of training or ability required for them. Skill definitions were saturated with gender and age perceptions. The work of women and children, usually lumped together, was deemed inferior precisely because it was done by women and children, rather than because of any intrinsic quality in the work itself. These women and children carried into the workplace their socially subordinate status which served to define the value of their work. Far from being an objective economic fact, calculable from investment or productivity, skill became an ideological category imposed on certain kinds of work by virtue of the social subordination of the workers who undertook them. In turn, the encapsulation of gender and power in the way the notion of 'skill' was applied, confirmed, perpetuated and even intensified the marginalisation of women's and children's work.

In the late nineteenth century and even in the early twentieth, women and children worked in practically all the departments of a jute mill.[28] Most commonly they worked at sack-sewing, winding, assorting jute, filling cans, drawing and ranging frames.[29] Although many fewer women than men were employed in the mills, or perhaps because of it, managers did not adhere rigidly to these occupational divisions. It was towards the close of the nineteenth century that certain tasks began to be officially designated as 'suitable' for women and others as 'suitable' for men. The work designated as suitable for women tended to be poorly paid.

By the 1920s gender-ghettos had become clearly discernible. Janet Kelman, a researcher, suggested that though in a few mills women worked only in sack-sewing and finishing, 'their occupation in different departments right through the mills is much more general'.[30] Almost simultaneously, Dagmar Curjel, officially appointed to survey Bengal industries, found that, 'On the whole, women are mostly employed on less skilled work, in the lesser paid parts of the mill, the preparation and hand-sewing departments.'[31] Women were being increasingly concentrated in the unmechanised departments with low-paid work. By the 1930s, some jobs like weaving, spinning and beaming were dominated by men while women tended to cluster at the beginning and the end of the process – in the preparing and finishing departments.[32] Children generally changed bobbins in the spinning department. Even in pre-

[28] *IFC; LEC*, Appendix O.
[29] WBSA, General Miscellaneous, September 1895, A27.
[30] Janet Harvey Kelman, *Labour in India*, London, 1923, p. 80.
[31] Curjel Report, Appendix B.
[32] A survey undertaken in 1931–32 concluded that more than half the women employed in jute mills were in preparing. The rest were distributed mainly between batching and

Table 3.2. *Wages for selected occupations in a jute mill in 1896*

Occupation	Wages (in Rs. as. p)	Suitable for
Wage work – 50 hours per week		
Jute carrying	3–6–0	men
Batching	1–8–0	women
Jute cutting	2–2–0 to 2–6–0	men
Preparing	1–4–0 to 1–9–0	women
Preparing	1–12–0 to 2–4–0	men
Spinning	1– 8–0 to 2–10–0	men
Spinning	1–2–0 to 1–4–0	children
Piece-work		
Winding	1–4–0 to 1–12–0	women
Winding	1–8–0 to 2–4–0	men
Beaming	3–0–0 to 4–0–0	men
Weaving	4–0–0 to 6–0–0	men
Finishers	1–8–0 to 2–0–0	men
Sack-sewing	1–8–0 to 2–4–0	men, women and children
General coolies	1–10–0 to 2–4–0	men
Native foremen	7–0–0 to 12–0–0	men

Source: Labour Enquiry Commission, 1896.

paring and finishing, women were associated mainly with two jobs – breaker-carding[33] and hand-sewing.[34]

Inside a jute mill

In the 1920s, scholars, reformers and government officers were concerned about the conditions in which women worked in the mills. They wrote detailed accounts of the gender-wise distribution of workers in different stages of jute hessian and sacking production.[35] Many of these authors shared the employers' and managers' perceptions about allotment of tasks according to women's abilities and domestic responsibil-

sewing. WBSA, Comm. Comm., January 1932, A2–6, M. I. Balfour, 'Report of a Survey of Women Workers in Jute Mills, 1931–2', 1932 (henceforth Balfour Report).

[33] *Ghari-kal* (*ghari* meaning clock and *kal* meaning machine) because there was a timer to control the rhythm of the operation.

[34] *Maagi-kal* (*maag* colloquially meaning woman) because many women worked there.

[35] This description has been based mainly on G. M. Broughton, *Labour in Indian Industries*, London, 1924; Kelman, *Labour in India*; Curjel Report; CSAS, BP, Box No. XVII, 'Indian Jute Industry'. Though mills are now more mechanised, the basic process remains very similar as noted in Titagarh No. 2, Fort Gloster (North), Howrah Jute Mill and Bally Jute Mill. I am very grateful to the factory managers, particularly Mr S. Dhara, Personnel Manager, Fort Gloster Mill, for explaining the 'production flow-chart'.

ities. These perceptions, of course, served to justify differentiation of men's and women's tasks and also the contention that skill hierarchies were technologically determined. An examination of the production process is, therefore, necessary to fully appreciate how the gender division of labour came to be constructed and how the gender-wise distribution of workers in mill occupations was established.

As soon as the jute came into the mill, it had to be sorted. Managers, assisted by *sardars*, selected the better-quality jute for hessian. The women, working under the *sardars*, opened up the bales to separate the jute meant for hessian and lay aside the others for coarser sacking. Then the jute was passed through a softening machine consisting of fluted rollers under heavy pressure with an emulsion of oil and water. The 'batching oil' often caused women a skin disease called jute dermatitis.[36] By the 1920s, it was usual for men feeders to place the jute in the softening machine and the women to act as receivers.

Next, the jute was cut, usually by men. In the Preparing Department, however, women worked in carding to break down the long stalks or strips of fibre into a continuous broad ribbon of fine fibres and to lay the fibres parallel to one another. It was monotonous and labour-intensive work at which women were thought to be better. Breaker cards broke and hackled the stalks of the fibre to make a broad ribbon termed a sliver. Here women would both feed and receive, usually working together in groups of three. Two women fed and one managed the cans at the delivery end. This was heavy work requiring constant attention since a scantily fed machine wasted engine-power. The finisher card needed twelve slivers fed manually (mostly by women) and the carding continued on a finer scale.

The next process of drawing was also done by three women. One arranged the slivers side by side at the feed end, another took delivery and the third carried the finished product to the next machine. Then slivers were doubled in a frame. Drawing thinned out the sliver, doubling counteracted it by combining two or more such drawn-out slivers.

Slivers thus prepared went to the Roving Department where women fed the machine and men did the actual roving. Here slivers were strengthened with a partial twist called a 'rove'. The rove was then taken for spinning. Here very few women worked full-time but a few girls might have been employed as half-timers.[37] The spinning frames drew

---

[36] Hindus were said to be more badly affected because they used *saji mati*, a kind of soft clay, instead of soap. Dagmar Curjel and H. W. Acton, 'Jute Dermatitis', *Indian Journal of Medical Research*, 12, 2, 1924–5.

[37] Kelman, *Labour in India*, p. 82. Women and girls were 'extraordinarily deft at this operation', Broughton, *Labour in Indian Industries*, p. 133.

out the rove further and spun the yarn. Warp yarns were twisted harder than weft yarns.

'Winding' followed next and the warp yarn was wound round large bobbins for a greater continuity in length. The weft yarn was wound into 'cops' to fit the weaving shuttles. Equal numbers of men and women were employed in the warp spool winding but only men in the weft cop winding. The warp yarn, saturated with starch to prevent breakage, was drawn onto larger beams (beaming) and placed at the back of the loom for weaving. This work was considered heavy and undertaken exclusively by men.

Next came weaving. While most observers in the the 1920s and 1930s agreed that women did no weaving at all, Kelman noted, 'in several mills two or three women, brought in by their husbands, who are in the same shop, weave sacking'.[38]

The final stage in the manufacture constituted the finishing process whereby the woven cloth was passed through the heavy rollers of a calendering machine for ironing and eventually cut and sewn into bags. The bags were made into bundles of twenty-five or thirty and packed in a hydraulic press. Usually, men worked at the machines for sewing sacks, at the calender machines and also packed the bales in the Finishing Department. Some sacks were machine-sewn on the sides and needed only to be hemmed at the mouth. Others were totally hand-sewn. In the Hand-sewing Department whole families worked together – men, women and children.

Only 'light and easy' work for women

Even though jute production involved no specific feminine skill, it did involve specific masculine skills which women, of course, could not offer. The tasks of weaving and spinning, for instance, became exclusive male enclaves. Employers used arguments about women's lack of skill to exclude them from these higher-paid 'skilled' tasks. In 1900, the IJMA reported that whereas it took a week to train a *coolie*, or even 'women', it could take up to a year or more to train weavers and spinners.[39] Nevertheless, it is frequently supposed that 'skill' was not particularly important for jute mill work and that this imparted a certain homogeneity to jute labour.[40] But such a view would not account for the relationship affirmed between 'skill', or the lack of it, and gendering of labour. If 'skill' was indeed so irrelevant as to create a homogeneous workforce where individual workers were replaceable, then gender differentiations

[38] Kelman, *Labour in India*, p. 82.   [39] Foley Report, Appendix.
[40] Chakrabarty, *Rethinking Working Class History*, pp. 90–2.

would not have existed and would, in any case, be unnecessary and expensive.

In 1937, the IJMA declared that 'up to spinning ... most of the work is mechanical or routine and can be easily learnt, and labour for these departments is plentiful; winding, weaving and (machine) sewing required skilled labour'.[41] This prompted managers to make 'every effort ... to encourage likely workers to train as spinners', when spinners were short.[42] Obviously, managers gave some importance to the 'training' required for spinning. In contrast, it was maintained that 'a few weeks at any of the machines was enough to make a worker proficient in preparing'.[43] This difference in perceived skill requirement was reflected in the wage differential between 'skilled' and 'unskilled' workers which was about 66 per cent in 1896 (Table 3.2). Jute mill owners constituted weavers and spinners as a group of 'skilled' and, therefore, better-paid workers. This allowed them to pay wages at lower rates to the large mass of 'unskilled' workers. In 1921, over 55 per cent of the jute labour force, numbering 280,854 persons in all, were 'unskilled *coolies*' who were not required to handle any machinery.[44]

Undoubtedly, the higher rate of wages in weaving was partially maintained by the attempts of the *Julaha* Muslims to pursue something like a 'closed shop'.[45] In the 1920s, and even after, theirs were the highest-paid jobs in the mills.[46] Fearing that the high wage rates commanded by them would be whittled down, the male weavers resisted the entry of women into their trade. Their attempt at a 'closed shop' was, of course, never fully successful because men from other castes and regions did gain entry into weaving in many mills. But the sanctions against women proved effective. Associations with 'skill', physical strength and long hours of work gradually defined weaving as a purely masculine occupation. Although weavers in Dundee Jute Mills were mostly women, managers and weavers in Calcutta held fast to the belief that women could not weave.[47] Ironically, 'female operatives' were recruited from Dundee to work the first weaving looms in the Howrah Jute Mill. Similarly, in 1818, some Lancashire girls were brought out to Bengal to introduce factory methods of work at the old cotton mill at

[41] CSAS, BP, BOX XII, J. R. Walker, 'Jute Strike Situation', 1927.
[42] DUL, TDP, Victoria Jute Mill, MRD, 1939.   [43] *RCLI*, V, 1, pp. 280 and 298.
[44] *Census of India*, 1921, V, 2, Table 22.
[45] *IJMAR*, 1886–7, 1891 and 1894. P. S. Gupta, 'Notes on the Origin and Structuring of the Industrial Labour Force in India, 1890 to 1920', in R. K. Sharma (ed.), *Indian Society – Historical Probings in Memory of D. D. Kosambi*, Delhi, 1974. For the Bombay case see Morris D. Morris, *The Emergence of the Industrial Labour Force in India: A Study of the Bombay Cotton Mills, 1854–1957*, Los Angeles and Berkeley, 1965, p. 79 and Chandavarkar, *Origins of Industrial Capitalism*, pp. 230–1, 320.
[46] *Census of India*, 1921, V, 1, p. 406.   [47] *IFC*, p. 65.

Bowreah.[48] In the early years of the industry, there were probably some women weavers. The jute factory at Serajgunj employed women in 'preparing, weaving, spinning, and sewing bags'.[49] By the 1920s, however, most observers categorically stated that 'Indian women' did not weave. In the 1930s, the Royal Commission noted that there were no women weavers at all.[50] Thus weaving and spinning were constituted as the only two 'skilled' jobs and women excluded from these for that reason. Even in other jobs presumed to be 'unskilled', women were relegated to the least-paying tasks. Women's tasks became in some way more 'unskilled' – because they were allowed to take time off or because they were thought less committed to their work. To sustain their incoherent claims, managers used varying definitions of 'skill'.

The intention here is not to imply that weaving and spinning did not actually require any skill, or that skill requirements were uniformly low or homogeneous in any degree; rather, to suggest that managerial pronouncements about 'skill' should not be taken at face value. In factories and mills, there were always numerous and minute gradations of skill, status and wages which rarely followed technologically deter-mined modes and needs of production.[51] Such hierarchies of skill and income more often reflected social perceptions shared by employers and workers. Often, too, wage differentials even between skills were more a function of the disparate strengths in the collective bargaining process. Thus, women and young men were more easily bunched together as 'unskilled' and paid less. The workforce preferred to retain existing wage differentials among themselves most often as betokening a measure of self-esteem. Mill owners played on existing hierarchies of age, gender, caste and community, deepening and perpetuating differ-ences and disunities among workers. Since some workers and trade unions also had an interest in upholding these perceptions regarding gender, age and wage hierarchy, they failed to grapple with the em-ployers' divisive policies. In fact, such disunities gained prominence as trade unions became more closely allied with political parties whose electoral strategies often emphasised community-based gender ideolo-gies.

[48] *Handbook and Directory of the Jute Industry*, IJMA, 1967. Also see Kelman, *Labour in India*, p. 82.
[49] WBSA, General Miscellaneous, September 1895, A27.
[50] Even now most managers and workers agree that women cannot operate looms. In one exceptional case a Bengali woman was employed as weaver in the Howrah Jute Mill.
[51] Samita Sen, 'Class or Gender? Women and the Bengal Jute Industry', in Arjan de Haan and Samita Sen (eds.), *A Case for Labour History. The Jute Industry in Eastern India*, Calcutta, forthcoming. For a detailed discussion of this point in the context of the Bombay textile industry, see Chandavarkar, *Origins of Industrial Capitalism*.

Mill owners were quite willing to abandon these stereotypes in times of labour scarcities. In 1922, women worked consecutive shifts in two mills.[52] Women were even employed in customarily 'male' occupations. In jute mills, said R. K. Das, women usually did the drawing, roving, moving receivers and hand-sewing. 'Only in those districts where there is scarcity of labour are women found in other departments of a jute mill.'[53] However, stereotypes once instituted could also defeat managers. Male workers would not undertake 'women's' jobs easily and strongly resisted employment of women in male departments. In 1942, after the bombing of Calcutta, male workers fled to their villages.[54] The Clive Jute Mill, for instance, was short of selectors and the manager hired women for the job. The men objected, but capitulated in the face of the management's insistence.[55] Elsewhere, women were employed as weavers and spinners. Although some mill managers were of the opinion that there was no difference in efficiency between men and women, and others that women were in fact more efficient, the system was discontinued soon after because 'they [women] were unsuitable'. In fact, the managers could not continue to employ women in these jobs once male labour became available.[56] In the *roja* month, Muslim women found the legal ban on night work particularly onerous. Managers, when they were unable to persuade the government to relax the rules, were often forced to run the mill without the Muslim women.[57] New problems cropped up when some of the feeding and sewing operations were mechanised. Feeding and sewing, hitherto 'women's tasks', when reconstituted by the introduction of machinery became acceptable to, even desired by, men. Gradually men took over many such tasks. By the 1950s, women were to be found only in the Breaker feeder and the Hand-sewing Departments.[58]

Factory inspectors and reformers insisted that women working with moving machinery were more at risk, prone to accidents and that it was more 'dangerous'. So women were excluded from machines like the openers in cotton mills. The jute mills' counterpart was the softener feeder section (known as *haathi kal* or the elephant machine because of its size). A large number of women were employed at the *haathi kal*; many died because the work was 'decidedly arduous, and bangles on

[52] Curjel Report, Main Report, p. 12.   [53] Das, 'Women Labour', p. 397.
[54] CSAS, BP, Box XVI, George B. Morton to Edward Benthall, 6 January 1942. Oriyas particularly seemed to have left the mill towns en masse.
[55] Ibid. Also see *Social and Economic Status of Women Workers in India*, Labour Bureau, 1953, pp. 16–17.
[56] *Social and Economic Status of Women Workers in India*, p. 17.
[57] DUL, TDP, Shyamnagar, Victoria and Angus, MRD, 1938–40.
[58] *Social and Economic Status of Women Workers in India*.

their arms and wrists, and anklets on the feet, have, on several occasions, been the direct cause of fatal accidents'.[59] In the 1890s, there was a systematic effort to remove women from this task. By 1900, only five mills employed women for feeding softeners. One manager said, 'owing to a recent accident, he has taken the opportunity of clearing all women from these machines'.[60]

Accidents on the softener machine were, however, not confined to women. The moving tables were the same length as in Dundee but 'owing to the looser clothing of workers in India' many men too were drawn in and killed.[61] After women were replaced by men as feeders, however, accidents involving women continued to occur. Managers blamed the women workers for these accidents arguing that the women rubbed the running rollers with tow to save oil to take home.[62] In the 1920s, Mr Williamson, Manager of Serampore Jute Mill, introduced the automatic stop thus improving safety standards. Yet women were not re-employed as feeders.[63] Feeding was no longer the simple manual task it had been earlier; by association with complex machinery it had acquired the status of 'skilled' work.[64]

Women did meet with accidents on other machines as well: clothing and jewellery got caught in them. In 1898 one woman died in the Clive Mill when jute became entangled with her bangles and drew her arm into the rollers of the softener. Another women was killed in Sibpur when the jute fibres around her foot pulled her into the machinery. Yet only a small proportion of the accidents reported had women victims. In 1909, out of a total of forty-four accidents reported, six involved boys and only one involved a woman who was killed in the Ganges Rope Works when her hands were entangled in the flyers of a spinning machine. In 1910, seventy-seven accidents were reported. Of these, five involved children and two women; one was hit by a trolley working between the Finishing Department and the export jetty and the other when her hands jammed between the rollers of a breaker card. In 1911, of forty accidents reported, there were two accidents to children and only one to a woman. At the Kankinara B Mill, a woman was scalped when her hair caught in the revolving vertical shaft as she stooped to get

[59] FA, 1898.
[60] Chief Inspector of Factories quoting Manager of Delta Jute Mill, WBSA, General Miscellaneous, June 1900, A1–8. Central Jute Mill employed four women at the feed end; Ganges Jute Mill employed women at both ends; Sibpur had women especially at the feed end; Delta felt unable to turn out the woman who had been working there 'for many years' but would not reappoint women; in Baranagore there were several women and the manager was asked by the inspector to discontinue the practice.
[61] Ibid.   [62] Curjel Report, Appendix B, Sl No. 2.   [63] Ibid.
[64] Dagmar Engels, Beyond Purdah? Women in Bengal, 1890–1939, Delhi, 1996, p. 222.

something from inside the roving machine.[65] The reported accidents to women all seem to have been fatal. Perhaps, like other factory laws relating to women and children, the Workmen's Compensation Act was usually ignored and only very serious accidents reported.

As their assumed lack of physical strength defined the jobs women could not do, so the jobs that women did undertake were considered suited to their special requirements. Both the proponents and detractors of 'protective' legislation took it for granted that certain kinds of work were more suited to women. Jute mill managers bent backwards to demonstrate that women's work was 'light' and 'easy', that they allowed women to sit most of the day and to leave periodically to attend to their housework and childcare. In 1879, D. Cochrane of the India Jute Company said that the women's work was of a 'very light nature'. H. H. Risley concurred.[66] In the early 1920s, Curjel felt that 'the work done by women in a jute mill cannot be said to be heavy ... in the hand-sewing department ... women sit at their work'.[67] Kelman gave contradictory statements about the strain involved in women's work. She found in sewing 'all depends on rapidity' and sewers 'work at it in a way that seems altogether too strenuous for the hot Indian climate'.[68] Curjel too described the heavy work in preparing, drawing and roving which involved moving 'fairly heavy receivers filled with jute', 'many hours of continuous standing' and maintaining 'a certain speed of work'.[69]

In fact, the mills were noisy and jute was a heavy material. Feeding breaker cards meant lifting loads and constant attention. At the finishing card three women worked to match machine speed – one arranged the sliver side by side at the feed end, one took delivery at the other, and one carried. In the Spinning Department, the shifting of bobbins 'must be done quickly for with a bulky material such as jute, the bobbins fill fast' and have to be changed frequently.[70]

The Hand-sewing Department was usually the worst maintained. The low status of women's work and the poor condition of the departments where they worked went hand in hand. Hand-sewing was piece-

[65] *FA*, 1898, 1909–11.
[66] Quoted in Ranajit Dasgupta, 'Material Conditions and Behavioural Aspects of Calcutta Working Class 1875–1899', *Occasional Paper No. 22*, Centre for Studies in Social Sciences, Calcutta, 1979, p. 8.
[67] Curjel Report, Main Report, pp. 3–4.   [68] Kelman, *Labour in India*, p. 82.
[69] Curjel Report, Appendix A, p. vii. She also wrote, 'women workers were crowded together ... where through ventilation was inadequate, and the air contained much dust and fluff ... [P]ractically there was no free circulation of air ... [F]loors ... were often uneven and in a bad state of repair ... [T]he glare was often considerable.' Curjel and Acton, 'Jute Dermatitis'.
[70] D. H. Buchanan, *The Development of Capitalist Enterprise in India*, New York, 1934, p. 247.

rated. Managers were thus exempted from close supervision. Women were, apparently, allowed to come and go as they pleased to feed their babies, to attend household duties, or for rest. The managers' 'liberal-minded' license was, of course, circumscribed by very low piece-rates.[71] The pace and volume of work were critical to women.

Nevertheless, women may have preferred the relative flexibility of the Sewing Department,[72] which was maintained by treating it as 'outside' the factory. In the Union (North) Mill

The Department where the Hand-sewers sit has a partition separating it from the part of the Factory where the Machinery is placed. This separate section is dark and badly ventilated. By means of this separate partition, women can work for 12 hours daily, and young children with them. According to the Chief Inspector of Factories, Bengal, this separate partition should not effect the minimum age limit being enforced, but the Manager evidently consider it does.[73]

Very often children helped their mothers in sewing, which was an easy way to get around the law and earn money necessary to feed the family.[74] After 1912, legal restrictions had rendered children unecono-mic in any work other than shifting and doffing. But under the conditions in the Hand-sewing Department it was easy to ignore the law. Women worked long hours because they needed the money but they did not have to work continuous or regular shifts. Others could take their places.

Wages – for men, women and the family

Employers justified and rationalised the lower wages they paid women by adverse job ranking. Though almost all accounts from the 1920s and 1930s agreed that there was no discrimination in rates of wages in the jute industry between the men and women, they also, in every case, quoted lower rates of wages for women. Foley reported lower rates for unskilled female labour than male. An 'ordinary man', presumably male workers, on average earned Rs. 2.25, while an 'ordinary woman', again presumably female workers, on average earned Rs. 1.25. A 'trained' man earned Rs. 2.75; a 'trained' woman about Rs. 2.06. Only in sewing were the rates the same for men and women.[75] Managers explained that

[71] Secretary, IJMA, *IJMAR*, 1908.   [72] See chapter 4 below.
[73] Curjel Report, Appendix B, Sl, No. 8. Also Fort Gloster Mill, Sl, No. 14.
[74] Ibid., Sl, Nos. 7, 9 and 14.
[75] Foley Report, p. 9. Others quote lower rates for women. See Broughton, *Labour in Indian Industries*, pp. 135–6; Das, 'Women Labour'; and R. B. Gupta, *Labour and Housing in India*, Calcutta, 1930, p. 82.

in each specific job, wage rates were the same for men and women, but women worked at less skilled tasks and, therefore, earned less.

Managers routinely justified the low wages across the industry by invoking the 'inefficiency' of Indian workmen.[76] Government officers tended to confirm these stereotypes. One official remarked, 'Both men and women stop work and go out for drinking, eating, and other purposes at unauthorised hours, spending thus about one-fourth of their regular time on an average.'[77] But women, especially, were charged with tardiness. A manager complained that 25 per cent of the women workers were at least an hour late. The women were mainly pieceworkers; by coming late, without taking the half-hour midday interval and going home as soon as possible, they might have been better able to balance factory and housework. This, however, lowered their wages. Women were paid about Rs. 1 per month less on the ground that they were allowed to 'come and go as they please'.[78]

Even as 'skill' did not follow technologically justifiable categories, the relationship between skill and wages was equally arbitrary. There was no straightforward criterion to differentiate wages among occupations. Though, on the mill managers' own admissions, women's and children's tasks were arduous and required considerable dexterity and speed, their wages could be and usually were fixed at the lower rates they earned in unskilled work in the city. Wages were determined by a complex mix of custom, competition and struggle.

As it is, only very scanty and unreliable statistics for wages and cost of living indices are available. The index of real wages declined from 62.3 in 1900 to 52.5 in 1929 and rose to 87.5 by 1939.[79] These figures, based on one single jute mill, are clearly untenable since the most remarkable feature of the industry was the inchoate wage rates prevailing throughout this period.[80] Wages were complicated by cryptic job descriptions, by time and piece-rates.[81] Each mill attempted to negotiate the lowest possible rates and graded their jobs differently. As a result,

---

[76] Dasgupta, 'Material Conditions and Behavioural Aspects', p. 13.

[77] Quoted by Das, 'Women Labour', p. 537. 'The Indian worker is as a rule exceedingly difficult to drive. He is not likely to be a good subject for efficiency engineers.' R. N. Gilchrist, *Labour and Land*, Calcutta, 1932.

[78] Kelman, *Labour in India*, pp. 199–220.

[79] K. Mukherjee, 'Trend in Real Wages in the Jute Textile Industry from 1900 to 1951', *Artha Vijnana*, 2, 1, March 1960.

[80] *RCLI*, V, 2, pp. 124–63. For a fuller discussion and comparison between different industries of India, see A. K. Bagchi, *Private Investment in India, 1900–1939*, Cambridge, 1972, pp. 121–31.

[81] Chandavarkar has argued that the differences between piece- and time-rates have been exaggerated. Piece-rates could not be arrived at without a time component calculation, while time-rates had to bear some relation to productivity. Chandavarkar, *Origins of Industrial Capitalism*, p. 86.

Table 3.3. *Rates of wages in the Spinning Department of the Union (North) Mill in 1935*

Job description	No.	wages per week (Rs. as. p.)
Spinner (sacking weft)	25	3–8–0
(Sacking warp & hessian warp and weft)	68	3–3–0
Line *sardar* (sacking & hessian – warp & weft)	4	6–8–0
Rove bobbin *coolie sardar*	1	3–8–0
Coolies carrying full rove bobbin	14	2–8–0
Rollerman	1	4–4–0
Listman	1	3–4–0
Sweepers	2	2–0–0
Spinning bobbin *coolie sardar*	2	3–8–0
Spinning *coolie* for full & empty bobbins	24	2–8–0

Source: CSAS, Benthall Papers, Box X, John Williams to Bird and Co., Enclosure 6, 12 August 1935.

simple comparisons are misleading. The averages gloss over minute and varied gradations of wages that the mills typically followed. An example of the complex graded wage system is the Spinning Department of Union (North) Mill (see Table 3.3).

It is in this context that the differences between men's and women's wages must be understood. The mill owners stressed the 'light and easy' nature of women's work. The manager of Anglo-India Jute Mill said, 'they [women] were not paid at a lower rate than men for the work they did because they were women but ... the parts of a mill where women are usually employed required less skilled work and, therefore, the rates were lower'.[82] In fact, women were paid less because they were women, that is to say, they had to accept lower wages because they could not in any case have commanded more in any other occupation in the city. Some of the jobs at which men and women worked together were the lowest paid in the mills. Yet, even in departments where 'women worked alongside of men', like preparing, winding and sewing, women earned less (see Table 3.4).[83]

In the Preparation Department which employed large numbers of women, women did only a few particular jobs as shown below – breaker-feeding, and carrying between breaker and finishing cards and between first and second drawings. The highest-paid woman was paid less than the lowest-paid man and the highest-paid men earned double what the

[82] Curjel Report, Appendix B, Sl, No. 19.
[83] In winding women were paid Rs. 1–4 to Rs. 1–2 while men were paid Rs. 1–8 to Rs. 2–4. *LEC*, Appendix O.

Table 3.4. *Rates of wages in the Preparing Department of Union (North) Mill in 1935*

No. employed	Job description	Sex	Wages per week (Rs. as. p)
10	Dollop weighers	male	2–8
30	Braker feeders	female	2–4
10	Between breaker cards and finishing cards	female	2–2
8	Between finishing cards and first drawings	male	3–0
15	Between first drawing and second drawing	female	2–2
14	Roving feeders and delivery from second drawing	male	3–0
10	Rovers	male	3–0
32	Rove shifters	male	3–0
4	Rove shifter *sardars*	male	2–9
3	Line *sardars* – breaker feeder	male	3–4
3	Line *sardars* – between breaker and finishing	male	4–0
3	Line *sardars* – between Finisher and first drawing	male	4–0
3	Line *sardar* – between second drawing and roving	male	4–0
10	Pickers from breaker and cards	n.a.	2–8
1	Beltman	male	4–8
2	Sweepers	female	2–0

Note: The figures for roving have been calculated from the Naihati Standard Mill Rate for male productive operatives on ten head roving. Group Mill Standard Rates have been assumed in case of all other operatives.
Source: BP Box X, John Williamson to Bird & Co., Enclosure 6, 12 August 1935.

highest-paid women earned. There is no record of demands for an equal wage. Possibly, it did suit women to come and go as they pleased. In the case of piece-rated workers, however, this meant lower earnings. Overall, such arguments justified women's lower wages.

In the debates over protective legislation, the opponents of legislation had emphasised the working-class women's need to work. Employers, especially, stressed that these women *had* to work. In a period when domesticity defined elite women, working-class women could be seen as units of labour, capable of working long hours. Until almost the end of the First World War, the poor women's role as workers was not subordinated to their maternal and reproductive roles.[84] Mill owners argued that they paid higher wages. The industry provided women 'an easy earning of their living'. Factory work was 'more remunerative than domestic service ... they eat well ... build houses ... even buy orna-

[84] Mr Wells, Magistrate, 24 Parganas, WBSA, General Miscellaneous, September, 1875, A6–27. A doctor remarked, 'The women working in the factories (are) ... a particularly healthy lot and quite capable of working the same hours (as men)'. *IFLC*, p. 28.

ments'. If the government insisted on legislation, employers threatened to dispense with female labour, causing 'immense injury by throwing them out of work',[85] 'especially when male workmen and half-time children are always available ... poorest class of women [will be] driven to starvation for want of employment'.[86] They turned maternal and housewifery arguments on their head:

by common consent and standing custom of the country, girls are married far below that (14 years) age. Nor does it unoften occur that females in this country become mothers of children even at an age below 14. To shut them out then from whole-time labour until the boys and girls reach the age of 14 would be a hardship to them.[87]

Much later V. D. Thackersay said much the same thing in the Legislative Assembly debates over the Act of 1922.[88] It would be 'a fatal error to restrict in any way the wage-earning capacity of a family' was the argument against prohibiting night work for women.[89] In fact, the Factories Acts did not take into account the danger of abruptly reducing the earnings of women and children, beacuse it was assumed that their maintenance would be subsidised by adult male earnings.

In the 1920s and 1930s mill owners succumbed to the Government's reasoning. They too dwelt increasingly on the 'supplementary' nature of women's earnings. It has been pointed out earlier that the jute mill owners were not interested in women for their material or social reproductive roles; on the same count, their concern over the 'working-class family' was at best tepid. However, they seized on the post-war interest in 'family' ideology as a convenient means of marginalising women in the workforce. In the 1930s, this helped them undertake massive retrenchments. Throughout the 1920s, the mills quite success-fully used two contradictory arguments. They fought off the welfare reforms on the grounds that the jute mill workers were migratory, mobile and of a 'non-family' character: wives and children did not live in the city; and workers returned to their villages in case of unemploy-ment and illnesses. They also argued that the women who did work in the mills were not married to the men with whom they lived and were, therefore, not entitled to be treated as 'family'. Simultaneously, they latched on to the argument that given the primary earning role of the men in the 'family', women did not need to earn as much as men. In any

---

[85] Sitanath Roy, Hony Secretary, Bengal National Chamber of Commerce, WBSA, Judicial Department, November 1892, A95.
[86] *Report of the Annual General Meeting of the IJMA*, 1895.
[87] Sitanath Roy, WBSA, Judicial Department, November 1892, A95.
[88] IOL, L/E/3/213. Legislative Assembly, 10 January, 1922.
[89] Secretary, Calcutta Trades Association, WBSA, Judicial Department, November 1892, A95.

case, of course, the 'need' of workers – men, women or the working-class family – was not, as it never is, of any importance in the determination of wage levels.

The government officials, middle-class philanthropists and trade unions, in their zeal to protect the 'family' and ensure 'family wages', continually emphasised the 'supplementary' nature of women's earnings.[90] These convictions were reinforced by Curjel's finding that the major proportion of women workers in jute mills handed over their earnings to their 'protectors'. One manager remarked that there was no point in increasing women's wages or paying maternity benefit in cash because the money was bound to be handed over to the 'protector'.[91] The desirability of a male breadwinner was the basis of 'family wage' arguments. *Amrita Bazar Patrika* wrote, 'millions of bread-winners, men, and women and children are sweated and fleeced off their pitiful wages which are reduced almost to a vanishing point ... How can a man burdened with a family maintain himself on Rs. 10 or 12 a month?'[92] Gilchrist suggested to the IJMA, 'The incentives to women's work should also be lessened, for the women would be well occupied in the home and in the plot.' This was offered as one means of reducing the unemployment problem and avoiding payment of unemployment insurance.[93] It was in this context that Gilchrist said:

In respect of both income and expenditure it is the family and not the individual that is important in relation to the standard of living ... It is impossible under the present standards of earnings for the men to be considered the 'rice-winner' of the family. The women must go out to work also ... From all parts of India evidence is forthcoming that it was necessity which drove women to work in the mills and mines ... The most serious indictment of the recent industrial situation is the extent to which families depend on the children's earnings to meet the necessary expenditure.[94]

The prohibition of women from underground work in coal mines became controversial because men and women worked in units and women miners received their pay as part of their men's wages. There were, however, 20 per cent women who were the sole breadwinners of the family. Also, 80 per cent of the women had to supplement their income by working in the fields in the sowing and harvesting seasons.[95]

---

[90] '[T]he reason advanced in support of [lower wages for women] has been that while owing to the universality of marriage and the joint family system men have to support a large number of dependants, women workers ... have not to support even themselves fully.' S. G. Panandikar, *Industrial Labour in India*, Bombay, 1933, p. 187.

[91] Curjel Report, Appendix B, Sl, Nos. 7 and 15.

[92] 'Politics and Labour', *Amrita Bazar Patrika*, 4 April 1928.

[93] Gilchrist, *Labour and Land*.   [94] Ibid.

[95] *RCLI*, V, 2, pp. 108, 119–20; Curjel Report, Appendix E; K. Roy, 'Women Labour in Mines', *Modern Review*, April 1923, pp. 511–13.

The All India Women's Conference sought a solution in 'the fixing of adequate minimum wages for men mine workers'.[96] The view that the loss of women's earnings would merely 'have the practical effect that women and children would become dependent on men' ignored the needs of single women.[97]

The payment of a 'family wage' to the man did not help female-headed households. Curjel had found that women jute workers' earnings were appropriated by male 'protectors'. But, Matheson's Sholapur Enquiry showed that the average woman worker supported several dependants.[98] So did many women jute workers. In mill towns unemployment and mobility destabilised the household. Divorce and desertion were common. Children almost invariably remained with the mother. Among the women interviewed by Curjel, at least one woman in every mill was the sole supporter of her children.[99] There was also a high proportion of widows. A large number of women workers were, in fact, the sole or the principal source of family subsistence. The policy of treating women's earnings as 'supplementary' and paying them lower wages on that basis, was, in practice, misconceived.

A widening gender divide: the depression and rationalisation – 1930–39

Mill owners' arguments about the supplementary nature of women workers' earnings did not imply any aversion to employment of women. Mill owners and managers defended their employment of women and argued against 'protective' legislation even in the 1880s. From the beginning of the twentieth century, as the jute industry expanded, they devised ways and means of evading the law and the inspectorate. After the First World War, employers selectively appropriated arguments about the maternal and housewifely responsibilities of women which were being touted in the international arena under the auspices of the ILO. They used such arguments to keep women's wages down and to increasingly concentrate them in the lower end of mill jobs. But they continued to employ women. While the proportion of women in the jute workforce declined at the turn of the century, thereafter it remained steady right up to the mid-1930s. In the 1920s, some mills toyed with maternity benefit, crêches and clinics, but on the whole managers resisted rather than upheld suggestions about dispensing with female

[96] *Modern Review*, June 1929, p. 717.
[97] IOL L/J & P/ 3/ 404–407. Bengal Chamber of Commerce, February 1890.
[98] Matheson, *Indian Industries*, Appendix II.
[99] Curjel Report, Appendix F, Sl, No. 131.

labour. Their attitude to women workers changed significantly in the early 1930s and soon after the proportion of women in the workforce steadily, though very gradually, declined.

Up to 1930, the jute mills had done well. Despite the increase in the number of mills and the spectacular expansion in loomage between 1900 and 1914 – in only fourteen years the capacity set up over forty years was doubled – jute goods manufacture and export were still enormously profitable. While business remained good, the IJMA had by and large ignored the 'investment restriction' clause. Market fluctuations prompted occasional short-term working agreements. But these proved increasingly difficult to negotiate, maintain and enforce.[100] On the balance, however, the IJMA did not entirely fail as a cartel in this period.[101]

The outbreak of the First World War created an unprecedented demand for sandbags. The IJMA abandoned all restrictions. The Factories Acts were suspended. The disruption of exports slashed raw jute prices and the difficulties of machinery import discouraged new mills. The existing mills made enormous profits. Dividends went up to as much as 330 per cent.[102] At the end of the war, a drop in demand and steep inflation created some problems. The industry, as usual, tried to put the squeeze on labour. In 1920–21, they faced widespread labour discontent. By 1923, the export market had looked up again. Profits were comfortable if not as spectacular as in the war years.

Meanwhile, war profits had attracted another rush of investment. In the 1920s, twenty more mills were set up increasing the loomage by 31 per cent. The industry reached a state of chronic excess capacity. In the pre-war years extra loomage were reserves to be mobilised for a demand hike. By 1929, the industry had 30 per cent capacity permanently in reserve. The Government calculated that if the mills worked day and night they would produce '400 per cent in excess of the present demand and about 300 per cent in excess of the highest demand ever known'. Even working fifty-four hours in the week, the industry's capacity exceeded by 25 per cent the highest known demand.[103]

The internal dissensions within the IJMA were exacerbated. New entrants could no longer be wooed into voluntary production restrictions. The new mills had been expensive to set up: capital was dearer,

[100] *IJMAR*, 1911, 14, 19.
[101] Goswami, *Industry, Trade and Peasant Society: The Jute Economy of Eastern India, 1900–1947*, Delhi 1991, pp. 54–63.
[102] Goswami, *Industry, Trade and Peasant Society*, pp. 95–7.
[103] Memorandum from the Additional Secretary to the Government of Bengal, Finance, Commerce and Marine Departments, 1935 (henceforth Goevernment Memorandum). CSAS, BP, Box X.

machinery and building costs higher.[104] These mills had to work long hours to fully utilise their capacity and to recover their initial investments. They argued that they had neither the war reserves to tide them over nor the advantage of having recovered their investments many times over like the pre-war mills.[105] Thus even when a short-term working agreement was hammered out, some of the new mills stayed out of the Association. According to an independent census, almost 10 per cent of even the Association's capacity came from 'clandestine' looms.[106] While the market remained buoyant, these problems were manageable, but even as the IJMA was persuaded to relax working hours from fifty-four to sixty in the week, the depression took the bottom out of the world market.[107] Until the outbreak of the Second World War in 1939, the industry faced the truly formidable task of riding a long recession with a huge over-capacity.

The IJMA could have declared an all-out price war. Some of the newer and smaller mills may have gone under. The older mills would have had to pare profits to the bone but their reserves would have carried them through. But such a scenario might have been disastrous for the Managing Agents who retained their control by a delicate mechanism of ensuring proxy votes. They did not have the majority holdings which would have ensured their control over the mills. So instead of attempting to undercut the market, the IJMA petitioned the Government to impose on recalcitrant 'outside' mills the limitations that they failed to achieve by agreement: a maximum working week of fifty-four hours and entry restrictions. In reply, the Government recommended rationalisation, 'better organisation', a shutting down of 're-dundant units'; the industry must be 'prepared to rationalise itself by concentrating production in a limited number of mills securing adequate use of their machinery and [be] content with reasonable profits on that amount of capital which is necessary to meet demand'. The Government held that the solution to overproduction and unreasonable competition was 'increased efficiency and technical progress'.[108] Dr Barker's report on the technological obsolescence of the mills confirmed these views.[109] The mill owners' failures to pursue technological sophistica-

---

[104] Ibid. Memorandum from B. N. Birla to E. C. Benthall, 14 March 1934.
[105] Government Memorandum.
[106] IJMA, Memorandum to Outside Mills, 22 August 1935. CSAS, BP, Box X.
[107] E. C. Benthall, Diaries, entry for 20 June 1930. CSAS, BP, Box VII. He noted that the 'piecegoods market is utterly dead'.
[108] Government Memorandum.
[109] S. G. Barker, *Report on the Scientific and Technical Development of the Jute Manufacturing Industry in Bengal with an Addenda on Jute, its Scientific Nature and Information Relevant Thereto*, Calcutta, 1935.

tion has been considered an additional proof of their 'mercantile' character.[110] However, these were tricky options for the old mills whose main advantage lay in the fact that their machinery was amortised many times over. Undertaking large capital costs, installing new machinery and streamlining production at a time when the market showed no signs of recovery seemed very risky.

Indeed, rationalisation and mechanisation would have required enormous outlay. Jute manufacture was a linear process, and piecemeal mechanisation would lead to production bottlenecks. The entire reconstruction of a mill, as undertaken by Bird and Co. in Union North, was not possible to replicate across the industry.[111] B. D. Bhatter and L. Nemenyi have been called 'ideologues' of the jute industry.[112] Perhaps for that very reason they came close to the heart of the problem: 'if new manufacturing methods and processes are now developed suddenly, the outcome would be nothing short of the necessity of replacing practically all the existing machinery by new ones'.[113] Besides, it was felt that serious rationalisation would have to be undertaken right across the industry. Benthall, in the light of the Dundee experience, cautioned against too quick a commitment to technological sophistication. '[I]t must not be forgotten that once a modern mill goes up on the Hooghly, all the other mills become out of date, including new mills. That is the experience of Dundee and although Calcutta conditions are somewhat different, the principle will, I think, apply there also in due course.'[114]

In 1930, mills like Victoria had assiduously avoided any additional costs except 'ordinary routine maintenance'. 'This year has been one of retrenchment and economy', wrote the manager, 'consequently no new work of any magnitude has been initiated ... [I]mprovements ... have been small and inexpensive.'[115] In fact, even the 'reconstruction' of the Union North mill did not inspire a zealous adoption of every new technology. The plan had been prompted by high maintenance costs. The machinery dated 'back to 1874 – a good long life!' no doubt, but in the 1930s the 'machines are done ... there is hardly one sound machine in the place', they were 'only fit for scrap' and bills for 'renewals and

[110] Chakrabarty, *Rethinking Working Class History*, pp. 40–5.
[111] There is a series of correspondence dealing with the reconstruction of the Union North Mill in CSAS, BP, Box X. The costs were estimated at Rs. 6,000 per loom. Letter from E. C. Benthall to G. B. Morton, 24 June 1935. The mill 'gained 35 years life at the cost of Rs. 23 lakhs'. This was 'high' but cheaper than a new mill. Letter from G. B. Morton to H. P. Bennett, 12 August 1935.
[112] Chakrabarty, *Rethinking Working Class History*, p. 45.
[113] B. D. Bhatter and L. Nemenyi, *The Jute Crisis*, Calcutta and London, 1936, p. 68.
[114] Letter from E. C. Benthall to G. B. Morton, 20 September 1935, CSAS, BP, Box X.
[115] DUL, TDP, Victoria Jute Mill, MRD, 1930.

repairs' mounted.[116] It was, however, the carding machines and the looms that were in particularly bad shape; the other old machinery that could be used was still used. In fact, the Managing Agents refused to put in new winding machinery because 'there was no loss of efficiency' in the old, but more importantly, 'labour is paid on piecework'. The burden of efficiency in this case could thus be shifted to the winders; so far as the mill managers were concerned, 'the cost remain the same'.[117]

While most mills remained unwilling to undertake large-scale reconstruction, they gradually acquired some new machinery, especially labour-saving devices. But the mills carefully calculated whether the savings in wages would offset the initial costs. In Shyamnagar, Teasers were rejected because the installation and maintenance costs were too high. The 'high speed' system being introduced from 1930 caused many problems. The Calcutta mills worked on fifteen systems which were gradually being reduced to twelve, but Frasers' scheme of high-speed working required only eight systems and a series of Roll Formers. To save a weekly wage bill of Rs. 158, the mill would have to invest £6,772. It is not surprising that the manager found that the scheme 'cannot be at present considered'. The high-speed self-doffing spinning frames in the North Mill proved recalcitrant when they were not 'worked in conjunction with either the Roll Formers or the Can Trumping systems'. If the rove continued to be prepared in the usual way, high-speed spinning proved unsteady and produced yarn of poor quality. These problems could only have been avoided by new machinery in the Preparing section.[118]

The mills, determined on stable dividend payments even at the cost of raiding their reserves, did not wish to tread the uncertain and expensive path of technological efficiency.[119] The mechanisation they undertook was ad hoc and piecemeal and directed more towards labour saving. To this end, while the IJMA was still able to function as a group, the mills reverted overnight in February 1930 to a single shift-method of working, rendering one-fifth of their labour force redundant. Their carefully calculated strategy paid off: 60,000 workers 'melted like snow in summer'. Despite the government's deepest forebodings, the industry had crossed the first hurdle without any labour resistance whatsoever.[120] Thereafter, the mills concentrated on eliminating surplus labour. In the

---

[116] Letter from G. B. Morton to H. P. Bennett, 12 August 1935, CSAS, BP, Box X.
[117] Ibid.
[118] DUL, TDP, Shyamnagar Jute Factory (North and South), MRD, 1932.
[119] 'I certainly see every argument for not increasing our financial commitments.' Letter from E. C. Benthall to P. Hoerder, 18 July 1935. CSAS, BP, Box X.
[120] Gilchrist, Labour and Land.

Titagarh Jute Factory in 1932, the manager reported, 'with a view to bringing down working costs ... departments have been carefully scrutinised and any surplus hands paid off'.[121] In Shyamnagar in 1932, rates of pay were reduced and further wage cuts contemplated.[122] In 1933, 'reductions in labour and wages were carried out ... to economise ... and ... hands were paid off whenever it was found possible to do so'.[123] The short-term working agreement finally reached in 1932 helped to lighten labour costs. The sealing of 15 per cent looms 'greatly' reduced the labour complement in Titagarh.[124]

The reduction of labour inevitably increased the load on existing workers and an elaborate system of inspection was initiated to ensure more direct control over quality and speed on the shopfloor. Shyam-nagar, Victoria, Titagarh, Empire and Presidency Mills developed a three-tier inspection system – the mill clerks followed by salesmen undertook daily inspections while the management carried out occasional checks.[125]

The main concern of the industry remained the control and reduction of labour costs. They paid lip-service to the Government's pursuit of 'better organisation'. By dint of talking loudly and often about 'rationalisation' and 'efficiency' they sought to win legislative support. In essence their policy was geared to retrenchment, wage cuts, larger workloads and increasing direct control over labour. Even their limited mechanisation aimed towards these ends. T. G. Morrow, appointed to look into the possibilities of mechanisation, got the hang of the industry's needs more clearly than Barker. His report was headed, 'Labour Saving Devices for Jute Mill Machinery'.[126] He stated:

Mechanical Can Trumpeters and Sliver Roll Formers are mainly labour saving devices, and if, incidentally, they help to make a better yarn (as they certainly do) this is not their chief recommendation ... Mills fitted out with one or other of the above devices, are working with one quarter to one third of the labour previously employed.[127]

The Mechanical Can Trumpeters and Roll Formers in the Preparing Department became essential in conjunction with high-speed spinning. Mackie and Boyd frames both carried larger numbers of higher speed spindles and, though these employed fewer spinners, they required each

[121] DUL, TDP, Titagarh Jute Factory (Mill No. 1), MRD, 1932.
[122] DUL, TDP, Shyamnagar Jute Factory (South), MRD, 1932.
[123] DUL, TDP, Shyamnagar Jute Factory (South), MRD, 1933.
[124] DUL, TDP, Titagarh Jute Factory (Mill No. 2), MRD, 1932.
[125] DUL, TDP, Shyamnagar, Victoria and Titagarh, MRD, 1933.
[126] T. G. Morrow, 'Labour Saving Devices for Jute Mill Machinery', 1932, DUL, TDP, Shyamnagar Jute Factory (North), MRD, 1932, pp. 15–27.
[127] Ibid.

spinner to tend many more spindles than earlier. As a result, most mills were able to 'pay off a considerable number of hands resulting in a saving of wages'. The Titagarh Mills retrenched about 175 workrs to save about Rs. 296 on weekly wages.[128]

It was the introduction of self-doffing frames and not protective legislation or the zeal of the factory inspectorate that eased out children from the mills. The children were primarily engaged as doffers and shifters in the spinning department; both these jobs were practically eliminated.[129] Though the proportion of children began to gradually decline from 1922, much the sharpest fall came in 1930–36, when the new spinning frames were gradually being introduced. In fact, in 1930, the total reduction of male labour was about 15 per cent, of female labour about 19 per cent, while children were reduced by about 70 per cent. (See Table 1.)

In the preparing department men replaced women. The jobs most stringently reduced in this limited mechanisation of the 1930s were batching, spinning, breaker, carding and preparing. The batchers suffered heavy retrenchments. Spinners were either retrenched or required to put in much more intensive effort: they not only had to 'look after a greater number of spindles than is customary', but the higher speeds entailed more sustained effort, greater alertness and quickness of movement.[130] The spinners' resentment was expressed in the many strikes of the period. Having always been, along with weavers, at the forefront of labour agitations, the spinners became the mainstay of unions in the 1937 general strike, while weavers remained more quiescent over this period. It is hardly surprising that the Angus Jute Mill found, in 1939, that the chief 'troublemakers' came from the batching, preparing, spinning and winding departments.[131]

The Breaker and Carding Departments were reorganised to employ fewer women. The rhythm of feeding was speeded up resulting in fewer women having to do much more intensive work. But the women in the Preparing Department suffered the heaviest retrenchment.[132] Preparing needed reorganisation because there were only two ways of high-speed spinning: one was to select better quality jute or 'higher batch', an option that Dundee adopted; the other was to streamline the preparing machinery. The Calcutta industry had been increasingly lowering the

[128] DUL, TDP, Titagarh (Mill No. 1), Shyamnagar (North and South), MRD, 1932.
[129] Especially after the introduction of the Angus All-Geared Spinning Frames in 1932.
[130] DUL, TDP, Shyamnagar and Titagarh, MRD, 1937.
[131] DUL, TDP, Angus Jute Works, MRD, 1939.
[132] Workers were reduced by eighteen batchers, twenty-three spinners and twenty-five from the Preparing section. DUL, TDP, Titagarh Jute Factory (Mill No. 2), MRD, 1933.

standard of raw jute to cut costs and were unwilling to tamper with 'normal Indian batch conditions'. The only solution was 'modern preparing machinery' which involved reducing workers, especially women workers in these jobs.[133] The number of workers reduced in this department in the 1930s does not indicate the scale at which women were paid off, since in many cases women were replaced with a few men. Morrow had already argued, 'The Can Trumpeting arrangement would also require change from female to male labour as the weight of the can averages 50 lbs.'[134] No such obvious reasons were cited for eliminating women from Roll Formers, though perhaps the managers anticipated less trouble from women, and unions were more willing to go along with retrenchment if some men were employed in place of the women.[135]

These changes in the Preparing Department were accompanied with far greater attention to the work of the women who remained in some of the feeding sections. Women were thought to be especially dilatory and under-utilised. In Titagarh, 'strict attention is given to the weighing of dollops, feeding of jute at breakers, and splicing of ends at cards and drawings ... [W]omen are instructed to pick out any roots when the sliver is attended.'[136] At the breakers, diagonal feeding was adopted to ensure a more level yarn by preventing the root ends entering the feeder at the same time. This made the women's jobs more onerous: they had to gauge the different distances at which to throw the jute on the feed table. This operation was also simultaneously quickened by speeding up the clocks attached to the feeders or by dividing the dollops.[137] Angus introduced 'several youths into the preparing departments to work in place of women'. A few of them were asked to take over the heavier cans. The others were trained in breaker and second drawing – no reason was offered for preferring 'youths' to women. Indeed, women continued to dominate the breakers across the industry. The Angus manager's determination to progressively 'introduce several more men' in these jobs increased after women in the Preparing Department walked off in a body during a strike.[138] Earlier in the year, Shyamnagar and Victoria Mills had also suffered protracted strikes begun by women in preparing. Thus, the managers who had believed that the women workers' indifference to unions meant greater complaisance were proved mistaken. Women put up stiff resistance when their jobs were attacked,

---

[133] 'Note', 31 July 1935. CSAS, BP, Box X.
[134] Morrow, 'Labour Saving Devices for Jute Mill Machinery'.
[135] See chapter 6 below.
[136] DUL, TDP, Titagarh Jute Factory (Mill No. 2), MRD, 1930.
[137] A diagonal feeding was increasingly adopted by most mills. DUL, TDP, Titagarh (Mill No. 2), Shyamnagar (North and South), MRD, 1933.
[138] DUL, TDP, Angus Jute Works, MRD, 1939.

though the unions' disinclination to take up their issues often meant that their struggles were short-lived and generally unsuccessful.

Later in 1941, Anglo-India (Middle) Jute Mill, Jagaddal, retrenched 118 women from the preparing department or 'gradually rendered [them] unemployed over the past four months' because of 'introduction of modern machinery in the Preparing Department following a policy of mechanisation'. Ninety-three roll formers and feeder-banks had been introduced between the breaker and finisher cards and first drawings. Since feeding was done mainly by women, 118 women were paid off and dismissal of another seven was contemplated. These jobs were now associated with complex machinery and higher productivity; they were now regarded as more skilled and were to be better paid. Eighteen men were employed instead of the women. The 'services of men are required' because, apparently, heavier loads needed to be carried. The net result of this reorganisation, succinctly expressed by the IJMA, was the retrenchment of 125 women and the employment of twenty-two men. The unions did not take up the matter.[139]

One other women's job was seriously reduced in this period. Gunny bags, earlier sewn by hand by women, began to be sewn by the Herakles sewing machine which only men operated. The Hand-sewing Department which had employed large numbers of women now merely counted, bunched and sewed together bundles of bags.[140] This further reduced the overall proportion of women employed in mills. Wages for sewing were initially low, and conditions for work had often been worse than elsewhere. Neither in wages nor in the changes in working conditions did this job keep pace with other departments.[141]

The rather unsatisfactory agreement IJMA achieved in 1932 wore thinner after 1935. The 'outside' mills worked long hours and were weathering the recession better than IJMA mills. The new mills within IJMA were worst hit. Benthall called for a price war: 'I am anxious to see a period of smaller margins in order that some of our friends may have a lesson that it is not so easy to make profits in jute after all'.[142] A gradual unsealing of looms began in 1934. By 1937 all restrictions were aban-

---

[139] WBSA, Comm. Comm., March 1941, B181–4.
[140] CSAS, BP, Box X, Kinnison Jute Mill to Bird and Co. Head Office, August, 1935.
[141] *In the Matter of Industrial Disputes in the Jute Textile Industry in West Bengal between the Employers of 9 specified Jute Mills and their Workmen: An Award*, Government of West Bengal, Calcutta, 31 August 1948.
[142] Letter from E. C. Benthall to A. Wilson, 18 July 1935, CSAS, BP, Box X. There was a 'panic in the market' and a rush to sell jute shares. Mills covered by the agreement, Birla and Hukumchand, were threatening to resign. The IJMA was still trying to convince the 'outside' mill to reach an agreement on an 'equal footing'. But by September, it looked as though there was a 'virtual break up of the present agreement'. The IJMA tried to patch things up and it took them almost a year and a half to

doned.[143] Many mills began night shifts. Since women were prohibited night shifts, these mills dismissed women across the board.[144] But IJMA did not sustain the price war for long. The 'outside' mills were quickly shaken and the Krishak Praja Party-Muslim League coalition ministry came forward with the Bengal Jute Ordinance of 1938 restricting working time to forty-five hours in the week, a considerably better deal than the fifty-four hour demand in 1930. By 1939, IJMA had most of the industry under its fold. The reduction in working hours led once again to a round of dismissals. Predictably, more women than men were retrenched.[145]

Some perceptions of gender – recruitment, housing and *purdah*

Jute mill owners were able to dismiss women in large numbers in the 1930s without much opposition except, of course, in some cases, from the women themselves. The existing negative perceptions about women's participation in factory work drew the male workers and trade unions into collaboration with mill management when it came to replacing women workers with men. Clearly, the mill managers, men workers and the trade union leaders shared some perceptions about the gendering of work within the factory. These perceptions contributed to gender segregation of jobs on the shopfloor which in turn had important implications for the gender division of labour outside the mill gates. That is to say, the low status of women's 'unskilled' and low-paid work inside the mill adversely affected their role and position in the household and the neighbourhoods. To begin with, many women seem to have had little direct control over their own earnings. In the 1920s, Curjel noted that migrant workers often 'appropriated' one wife's mill wages to live in the city and saved from their own earnings to remit to the other wife in the village household.[146] In such households, women's higher wages would have, no doubt, augmented the common kitty, but male control

officially abandon the already dead agreement. Letters from G. B. Morton to H. P. Bennett, 2 and 6 September 1935. CSAS. BP. Box X.

[143] Letter from E. C. Benthall to J. A. McKerrow, 31 August 1937, CSAS, BP, Box XII.

[144] Letter from Paul Benthall to E. C. Benthall, 11 October 1937, CSAS, BP, Box XIV.

[145] E. C. Benthall's note, 4 May 1937. CSAS, BP, Box XII. DUL, TDP, Angus Jute Works, MRD, 1939.

[146] Curjel Report. Also see Diptesh Bhattacharya, 'Growth of Class Consciousness among Jute Workers in early 20th century in Bengal', Ph.D Thesis, Australian National Universsity (n.d.), quoted in Vina Mazumdar and Kumud Sharma, 'Sexual Division of Labor and the Subordination of Women: A Reappraisal from India', in Irene Tinker (ed.), *Persistent Inequalities. Women and World Development*, Oxford, 1990.

was better assured if women earned less than men. Mill owners faced little challenge in their efforts to characterise women's wages as 'supplementary'; trade unions, ironically, took the argument a step forward by periodically demanding 'family wage' for the men. Indeed, in the 1920s, industrial employers, government officers and inspectors, reformers, labour philanthropists and trade unionists rediscovered the virtues of the male 'rice-winner' system. There did not seem to exist great possibilities of autonomy for women through their access to wages outside the context of the family, if they handed over their earnings to men. Moreover, their very access to jobs and earnings was mediated by a group of men within the workforce who were able to exercise considerable control and authority over women. This privileged group of men consolidated their position though mill owners' policies which inscribed male control into the system of recruitment and supervision. Thus, both mill owners and male workers upheld the ideology of women's inferiority. In the long run, the spread of such practices as dowry were facilitated.

Recruitment

The mills' personalised system of recruitment enhanced women's dependence on men for access to jobs, as well as to credit and housing. It has already been argued that the *sardar* rarely acted as a direct recruiting agent. It was a role rendered superfluous by migration from Bihar and UP at the turn of the century. The migrants arriving in Calcutta or the suburban mill towns found their way into the mills through caste, kin, community or village contacts. The mills eschewed any formal system of recruitment, depending on these personalised channels. Thus in effect the clerks and *sardars* emerged as key intermediaries responsible for ensuring a full complement of labour.

The *sardar* was typically a labour supervisor – and there were three or more *sardars* in every department of a mill. The line *sardars*, supervising a small group of workers were under a head *sardar*.[147] The *sardars* were always men. The jute mills, in not pursuing a strict horizontal segregation of genders on the shopfloor, rigidified the vertical segregation of women into the lower echelons of jute mill work. Since men could and often did work in the departments where women also worked, and since male workers would not be amenable to supervision by women, there were no women *sardars* in jute mills. In contrast, in the cotton mills where women had their own departments, they were headed by women supervisors.

---

[147] *LEC*, Appendix O.

The *sardars* as labour supervisors were a bridge between the management and the workers – their value to the management lay in their ability
to control labour and regulate its supply to mills, while their control and
authority over labour in the workplace depended to some extent on
networks of power outside the mills. In the absence of formal recruitment channels, the informal networks of caste, village and kin became
crucial for access to jobs as well as providing a safety-net in an uncertain
urban environment where migrants had very few sources of sustenance.[148] The system of *badli* or temporary workers, who were employed on a 'daily' basis or in the very short term, typified the informal
system of recruitment. To the management, this was an easy means of
ensuring a flexible labour supply – to be deployed when necessary,
either as blacklegs or for expansion of production. For workers, it meant
chronic insecurity of employment and a higher premium on permanent
jobs. A group of workers were constantly dependent on patronage.[149]

It has been shown earlier that the low level of wages entailed chronic
indebtedness. The worker was embedded in a complex network regulating his access to employment, credit and housing. *Sardars*, clerks,
darwans and *jamadars* within the mill, and traders, shop-keepers, the
local toughs (*goondas*) outside the mill, were involved in servicing the
workers. The scope of a few clerks in the Bally Jute Mill has been
described thus:

> the case of the workers is that they had to pay the various clerks of the Jute
> Department for securing employment. Homage in cash was also exacted from
> time to time as security for tenure of jobs, while religious festivals became
> occasions for special peace offerings. It is alleged that registers were so
> manipulated that the men received more wages than were due to them, the
> arrangement being that they would refund the excess amounts to the Babus ...
> There was the further allegation that Tripura Babu forced many of the men to
> buy their provisions from his brother's shop at Uttarpara on pain of dismissal ...
> Mr Kitching wondered why the men should, all of a sudden, have experienced
> righteous indignation at the clerk's dishonesty ... There is little doubt that the
> wages of these bogus tickets had to be drawn through the workers, who must
> have exacted a price for their connivance, so that when there was a hitch among
> the partners the truth leaked out.[150]

[148] A. K. Bagchi, 'The Ambiguity of Progress: Indian Society in Transition', *Social
Scientist*, 13, 3, March 1985. Of the ten workers interviewed by the Royal Commission, two had been recruited by a *sardar*. The others had come through 'relatives' and
'friends'. In case of Abdul Halim, the *sardar* was the friend who provided cash in times
of need and ensured the security of his job. *RCLI*, V, 2, pp. 76–80.

[149] *Sardars* had to pay a deposit to the mill clerk which they subsequently extorted from
the workers. Ritlall Sardar was charged Rs. 100, Piro Shaftier Rs. 75 and Chhattu Rs.
50. Pearilall, line *sardar* was charged Rs. 40 for a transfer. DIG CID IB, 168 of 1922.

[150] *Report of the Court of Enquiry appointed under Section 3 of the Trade Disputes Act, 1929
(Act VII of 1929), to investigate the Trade Dispute between Messrs. George Henderson &*

The power of *sardars* and clerks on the shopfloor and in the working-class neighbourhoods had two significant implications for women workers. First, male supervisors' notions of what kind of work was appropriate for women influenced the pattern of their employment. Male values of segregation and male workers' interest in retaining control and use of women's sexuality and labour were written into the hiring practices of the mills. Moreover, the *sardars* and clerks could extract sexual favours from women in return for access to jobs, which increased the opprobrium of jute mill jobs for women and ensured their withdrawal from such jobs when higher male earnings allowed them to do so. Second, women had no scope for upward moblity in jute mills: neither could they expect promotion within their own jobs nor could they shift to other more lucrative jobs in the mills.

The better paid male workers used the informal recruitment system effectively to exclude women from jobs like weaving and spinning. Possibly they feared that induction of women would threaten their ability to maintain the high wage levels. But why did weavers and spinners not use their 'personal' channels to recruit their own mothers, wives, daughters or sisters to high-paying jobs thereby augmenting their household resources? Their 'nepotism' was extended to brothers, sons, nephews or fellow villagers rather than to female kin. Obviously, since most men left their female relatives in the village, the few who might have desired better incomes for their women relatives were unable to contravene established gender segregation in the mills. So, weaving jobs had to go to male protégés while wives and daughters were given jobs in preparing or finishing. In part, this reflected the preference for male rather than female earners in the family. The better paid workers were better able to maintain non-earning adult female relatives, and often did so. To have wives living in various modified forms of *purdah* in the city signalled higher social status, and this may have prompted some weavers and *sardars* to bring their wives to the mill areas. In turn such practices contributed to the clustering of women at the lower rungs of the job ladder. Since their 'own women' did not work, *sardars*, weavers and spinners had no obvious interest in promoting women for better jobs.

The relationship between *sardars* and workers was shot with many contradictions. The *sardar*'s unique position derived from the tightrope he walked between the employers and the workers – at moments of crisis he could be caught in the crossfire. The personalised recruitment

Co. Ltd., of 101/1, Clive Street, Calcutta, Managing Agents, Bally Jute Mill, Bally, district Howrah, and the Workmen of the Weaving and Jute Departments of the said Mill, Government of Bengal, Calcutta, 1941.

through *sardars* created vertical loyalties within the workplace – loyalties which in turn reinforced the social identities of caste, community, language or region through which recruitments operated in the first place. These could be used as instruments of control by the management; equally they could become a significant cohesive force. *Sardars*, in a sense, epitomised this duality. *Sardars* could become women's allies in their attempts to protest against sexual harassment by European assistants, managers, *jamadars*, *durwans* or men of other communities. Equally, women could tap managers' or male workers' support against sexual exploitation by *sardars*.[151]

The ambiguity of the *sardar*'s role extended further. They provided leadership to workers and thus became the first target for dismissal. Workers often struck for the reinstatement of *sardars*. In July 1920, in Bally Jute Mill, three *sardars* went out with 100 men of the Spinning Department when a brother of one of them was dismissed. In the protracted negotiations, the reappointment of the brother and the three *sardars* became the main sticking point. In 1921, the Hastings workers went on strike against the dismissal of a *sardar*. In Caledonian Mill in 1921 'The workers left at the instigation of the sardar and next day wanted to return but the manager refused ... [he] dismissed some 200 sardars believed to be ringleaders of this trouble.'[152]

But the *sardars*' role in strikes was always ambiguous. They often successfully initiated strikes, but their influence over workers was limited. They failed at times to effect terms of settlements. In May 1928, this was proved in two major strikes in Wellington and Hastings Jute Mills.[153] The general strike of 1937 demonstrated to mill managers the futility of depending on the *sardars* and clerks to maintain control over workers. In April 1937 'a compromise was reached between the representatives of the management of Budge-Budge, Caledonian, Cheviot, Lothian, and Oriental Jute Mills and some sardars ... The mills were opened on the appointed date but ... only a small minority of the workers had returned to work.'[154]

By the late 1930s, workers were trying to cut *sardars* down to size. In Angus Sectional Working Committees (not unlike Benthall's 'workers' panchayats') were formed comprising four workers from each 'section' to bypass the *sardars* and to 'assert authority'.[155] But managers could not entrust such committees – whose aim was to represent grievances –

---

[151] Samita Sen, 'Honour and Resistance: Gender, Community and Class in Bengal, 1920–40', in Sekhar Bandopadhyay et al. (eds.), *Bengal: Communities, Development and States*, New Delhi, 1984. See also chapter 6 below.
[152] DIG CID IB, Secret Reports, 1921.   [153] Ibid.
[154] WBSA, HPC 484 of 37.   [155] DUL TDP Angus Jute Works, MRD, 1937.

with the task of disciplining workers. At the same time, it was quite clear that the heyday of the *sardar* was over. The manager of the Shyamnagar Mill acknowledged, 'the *Burrababoos* [head clerks] and Sirdars have very little influence over the labour nowadays; in fact, the trend of events at present is to have them ousted, the workers maintaining they are offenders in cases of bribery '.[156]

The mills were willing to assist in the 'ousting' of *sardars* from certain functions.[157] The mills' labour needs were contracting. The managers' expectations changed. The emphasis was on productivity despite the poorer quality jute used. They required more intensive effort from skilled workers and swift adaptation to new machinery. As a result, managers needed more direct control over labour than *sardars* offered. Under pressure from Managing Agents, managers were quick to deny their dependence on *sardars* and clerks. The IJMA took it upon itself to assert that 'Jute mill managers and Assistants are in close touch with labour' and they gave considerable importance to the 'personal touch' in containing or redressing workers' grievances, a manifest failure in the protracted general strike of 1937.[158] Benthall rejected the suggestion that extensive 'welfare work' helped avoid strikes in Clive Mill. Rather, he believed that the manager, Wallace, had won the 'quiet' backing of the Muslim leaders. He suggested that Bird and Co. should 'encourage all the men to establish closer contact' both with the workers and the municipality.[159]

To attack the *sardars'* positions effectively, managers had to undercut their powers of patronage, especially their ability to provide employment. In 1939, 'to have a supply of relieving workers ... it was decided to register all relieving workers'.[160] Many jute mills inaugurated Labour Bureaux to formalise *badli* hiring. Thus the role of the *sardar* at the mill gates reduced. A centralised system of casual employment also cut into the powers of the departmental overseers. Managers (through registers if not through identity cards) could now keep track of workers and weed out 'troublemakers'. Workers, particularly women, put up stiff resistance to these innovations.

As the *sardar*'s role as a patron declined, so did his role in supervising and disciplining begin to be challenged. *Sardars* became a target of the

---

[156] DUL TDP Shyamnagar (North) Jute Factory, MRD, 1937.
[157] Arjan de Haan, 'Towards a Single Male Earner: The Decline of Child and Female Employment in an Indian Industry', *Economic and Social History in the Netherlands*, 6, 1994.
[158] Walker, 'Jute Strike Situation', 1937.
[159] CSAS, BP, Box XII. Paul Benthall to E. C. Benthall, 5 July 1937.
[160] DUL TDP Victoria Jute Mill, MRD, 1939. Also see reports for Angus, Shyamnagar (North and South) and Titagarh (Nos. 1 and 2) for the same year.

workers' anger. Complaints against 'bribery' and 'corruption' were not new. In February 1921, in Wellington Jute Mill, the 'real cause behind the trouble between the Assistant Manager and the workers was the demand of the workers that Bhaglu Sardar be dismissed'. The charges against Bhaglu included extortion, bribery and sexual harassment. Later on 7 March, the spinners of Northbrook Jute Mill demanded the dismissal of Ismail Sardar. In November in the same year, weavers of Shyamnagar Mill demanded the dismissal of two *sardars* who extorted money to appoint weavers.[161]

The *durwans* and *jamadars* were seen as more direct agents of the management, and were primary targets of violence when industrial relations were tense. Sexual harassment of women workers by *durwans* was a recurring theme of protest. Gourepur Jute Mill had gone on strike on 9 September 1923 over an alleged insult offered to a woman worker by a mill *durwan*. In 1928, Meghna closed because some *durwans* had used improper language to the woman workers on the occasion of the *Holi* festival.[162] In the 1930s, strikes demanding dismissals of *sardars*, *jamadars* and *durwans* proliferated and acquired a new intensity.[163]

Housing

The attack on the *sardar* in the workplace was often extended to the mill neighbourhoods because of the control they exercised over one key resource of urban survival – housing. Of course, he was by no means the only player in the game. Mill clerks, local shopkeepers, moneylenders and neighbourhood toughs shared the spoils from 'slum' territory. Many of these 'big men' of the mill towns controlled the *bazar* areas where migrants congregated. They put up shacks and makeshift cottages to meet the enormously enhanced demand for accommodation and could command high rents.

The harsh condition of life in these 'slums', it has been argued, discouraged women's migration.[164] In the writings of contemporary officials and sociologists, the lack of 'privacy' features as the crucial deterrent to 'family life' in the poorer quarters of the city. Their arguments often reveal their middle-class assumptions about what constituted 'family life', but they were also emphatic in pointing out that

[161] DIG CID IB, Secret Reports, 1921. In the strike wave of 1920–21, there were two strikes by spinners over this issue. J. H. Kerr, *Report of the Committee on Industrial Unrest in Bengal*, Calcutta, 1921, Appendix.
[162] DIG CID IB, Weekly Report, Secret, 1928.
[163] In 1937, the Ganges and Wellington strikes were over extortion. WBSA, HPC 484/37.
[164] Banerjee, 'Working Women in Colonial Bengal'.

rural women, however poor, were used to gender-segregated spaces, in private and in public.

Until the 1890s, Bengali labourers were housed in huts in nearby villages which was a cheap option that also allowed for 'privacy' and 'family life'. The problems arose with the growing flood of immigrant labour. The mill areas showed some of the heaviest concentrations of population. There were two main options available to the worker – the mill *lines* and the privately owned *bastis*. The *lines* were built by jute mill owners specifically to attract migrant labour. Some of the mills situated outside Calcutta had to provide housing for about 50 per cent of their employees.[165] Most official sources emphasise the advantages of the *lines* and their superior quality of sanitary and living arrangements.[166] In the better *lines* the space between the houses was paved with brick and there were *pucca* drains with arrangements for flushing. Fear of epidemics and their effect on labour supply prompted rudimentary public health measures.[167] The *lines* were generally rows of one-roomed back-to-back tenements, each with a *verandah*, two to four feet wide, for cooking and washing. The mills usually placed restrictions on the number of people living in a room, but such rules only existed on paper.[168] The total available space provided per worker was 64 to 120 square feet, and the *verandah* provided an additional 30 to 60 square feet. Each of these rooms was meant to be occupied by three to four workers, providing about 25 square feet per worker.[169] 'In spite of the abundance of land in jute towns, single-room houses, meant for four adults, are sometimes occupied by eleven or sixteen adults,' said Curjel.[170] Rents were lower than market prices and varied from 8 annas to Re 1 per month per room.[171] However, the accommodation in the *lines* was limited and they housed only a part of the workforce of the mills.[172]

The majority of the workers were housed in the *bastis* in rooms rented from the *sardars* or the shopkeepers.[173] Mill managers sometimes complained that workers preferred the private *basti* of the *sardar*.[174]

---

[165] Bagchi, *Private Investment*, pp. 127–30.   [166] *BDG*, 24 Parganas, 1914, p. 68.
[167] Chakrabarty, *Rethinking Working Class History*, Chapter 1. Public money was used for the housing of workers through the 'Mill Municipalities' – municipalities controlled by jute mill managers. IJMAR, 1904.
[168] Gupta, *Labour and Housing*, p. 184.   [169] *RCLI*, V, 1, p. 31.
[170] Curjel Report, Main Report, pp. 5–6.
[171] Dr Batra, Director of Public Health, *RCLI*, V, 1, p. 31.
[172] In the early years, only 13.8 per cent of workers were housed in *lines*. This increased to about 39 per cent by 1937. *LIC*, p. 29.
[173] *RCLI*, V, 1, p. 282.
[174] The reason was thought to be lower rent and intimidation by the *sardar*. IJMA, *RCLI*, V, 1, p. 282. Private housing rent in Calcutta was very high, despite the Calcutta Rent

Some workers did not like to live in accommodation provided by the employer because it implied inspections, a loss of liberty and vulnerability to managerial vengeance.

Living arrangements in the *lines* were not considered suitable for women.[175] The *lines* were 'highly in demand' because of 'healthy surroundings' but 'married upcountry Muhammedans and Hindus preferred private rooms outside because there was no privacy in the lines, particularly for the womenfolk'.[176] The oft-mentioned practice of closing all windows and apertures with bits of rags or sacking in already ill-ventilated rooms was explained by the need to secure some 'privacy' in back-to-back tenements. But it is difficult to envisage how *basti* conditions could have offered more 'privacy'. Indeed, we do not know much about the use of space in poorer neighbourhoods. Usually, huts were built very close together. The lower paid workers could only afford dormitories – four to eight strangers living in one small room. In fact neither the *lines* nor the *basti* could have provided 'privacy', if that is indeed what was desired, for women. The immigrant labourers 'accordingly, do not bring their families with them'.[177] For many long-distance migrants the choice was seen as one between 'family life' in degrading conditions or separation from their families.

This need for 'privacy' was usually related to the *purdah* system and the custom of seclusion. Women who lived in some variations of the *purdah*, were almost always trapped within ill-ventilated houses. In mill *lines* and *bastis*, they lived in very small rooms which were 'screened off with sacking and were much lacking in light and ventilation'.[178] Window spaces were closed up. Roof ventilation existed in some houses, but back-to-back houses did not permit through ventilation. Most women cooked in the same room and there was no escape for the smoke.[179] Women would spend hours in unventilated quarters squatting on the mud floor cooking over an open coal fire. The effect of such

Act of 1920. An average family spent about 5 per cent of its income on rent if they were living in *lines* and 10 per cent if they were living in a *basti*. Gupta, *Labour and Housing*, p. 81.

[175] Curjel Report, Main Report, pp. 5–6; *RCLI*, V, 1, pp. 150, 282 and 2, pp. 27, 208–9.
[176] Nalinakshya Sanyal, Jute Mill Operatives at Sibpur, *Welfare*, I, January–December 1923.
[177] Gupta, *Labour and Housing*, p. 18.
[178] Curjel Report, Appendix B, Sl, no. 9. 'The better-off Mahomedans (sirdars, weavers etc.) may bring their wives for periods to live with them ... The mill quarters as they stand, allow of very little privacy. These women are accustomed to either complete seclusion or to considerable privacy. Therefore, the quarters in mill lines are shut off by means of sacking hung all round. I went into such houses, they were very dark and stuffy', Curjel Report, Appendix B, Sl, No. 3.
[179] *RCLI*, V, 2, p. 208.

living conditions was reflected in the higher death rate among women from tuberculosis.[180] Besides, seclusion became difficult when water had to be collected from and utensils and clothes washed at communal taps and hydrants, often a considerable distance from the home.

Mill owners made no provision for single women to live alone. The IJMA claimed that, 'Indeed, in many cases, a certain amount of accommodation is provided free, chiefly to Madrasis and Bilaspuris, and also to poor Hindusthani women living alone.'[181] But when Miss Powers brought up the question of separate 'single' *lines* under special protection of the management for single women, there was no response from either the Government or the employers.[182] The price for physical protection often had to be paid in sexual currency. Sometimes single women clustered together for protection and the houses where such single women lived were often known as the 'prostitute lines'.[183]

Seclusion, work and status

The issue of 'privacy' in mill housing tied in with the larger question of a perceived conflict between domesticity and work. Women's employment in factories had sharpened these oppositions. There was a tendency to idealise the 'household' nature of women's work in the rural economy. In contrast, factory work was felt to violate the physical and symbolic separation between the home and the public world of men.[184] The

---

[180] 'To secure privacy in a congested city, light and air have to be shut out and the women consequently live in the darkest and worst ventilated rooms .... The high death rate amongst females from ... tuberculosis and other respiratory diseases ... is further proof of the evil effects on health of the purdah system.' *Report on the Municipal Administration of Calcutta*, 1920–21. Also see Gupta, *Labour and Housing*, p. 122.
[181] *RCLI*, V, 1, p. 282.   [182] *RCLI*, V, 2, p. 237.
[183] Curjel Report, Appendix B, Sl, No. 1.
[184] The following passage illustrates a typical urban middle-class nostalgia for the idyllic village. In constructing village life as the unchanging essence of Indianness, the nationalists contributed not a little to these stereotypes. 'In the villages and the countryside the woman is a helpmate to the peasant farmer and the field labourer. Cooking food and doing all her work of the household is not her only occupation. She renders invaluable service during the sowing season and again at the harvest time, and not infrequently takes the grain to the market for sale and makes the necessary purchases. She feeds the cow and the buffalo, milks them and prepares *mattha* and *ghee* the former for home consumption and the latter for sale. Besides she spins yarn and adds to the family income in other ways during leisure hours. Thus she helps her husband in his daily toil, gets him healthy and delicious food, and proves in every way a useful and valuable member of the family. She keeps a healthy constitution, because she works mostly in the open air, and gives birth to strong children, who grow healthful and happy because they get plenty of space and open air to play about. *All this is, however, reversed in the city, where social conditions forbid much outdoor life to the females*. The dearth of space and the consequent high rents compel the labourers and other poor folk to live in ill-ventilated and insanitary single-room tenements, which

'private' and 'public' binary was implicitly overlain with the rural and urban divide. The village was the proper milieu for women – there their work and the home were harmoniously integrated. The urban slum and factory work were necessities with which men had to contend. Read expressed the problem directly in terms of a perceived separation of home and work: 'Modern industrialism has taken a good deal of work away from homes to factories and women have naturally followed it . . . The nature and condition of work [in factories] have subjected them to moral and physical deterioration.'[185] The conditions of factory work, the long hours, night shift, the conditions of life in the city tenements or the mill *lines* were all seen to contribute to the deterioration of working-class family life.[186]

The system of shifts and the long hours of work meant – for men and women – that their lives were organised around the workday. The effect of multiple shifts on women and their domestic work provided the Chief Inspector of Factories with an argument for a changeover to the single-shift system.[187] The question of night-shift work by women became important, as pointed out earlier, in the context of the introduction of electric lighting. It was felt that children would either be taken by the mothers into the mill or left uncared for at home, and both were undesirable alternatives.[188] The question of a day's rest in the week was also prompted by such concerns. The weekly rest was 'not only a physical but also a psychological necessity . . . for women who had to do a great deal of household work on the weekly holiday'.[189]

Arguments against women's work in the factory or in favour of its restriction or regulation were often touched with a piquant moral flavour. In his masterly Minute of Dissent to the Factory Commission of 1908, Dr T. M. Nair insisted, 'The large majority of Indian women will never work alongside of men in the spinning room or the weaving shed.'[190] M. Muhammmad Habibullah was more direct: 'the Bill does

afford neither sufficient light and fresh air nor adequate accommodation to the inmates. Of privacy there is little or none. Add to all this, the woman seldom finds adequate and suitable work for herself in the city. Long hours in the factory or the workshop in unnatural surroundings are *peculiarly harmful to her constitution*. The result is that she feels exhausted and tired after coming from the works. She can neither enliven the spirits of her husband after the day's labour, nor prepare good food for him, nor take due care of the children. *No wonder, therefore, she has no preference for her home in the city bustee, nor is her husband anxious to keep her there*' (emphasis added). Gupta, *Labour and Housing*, pp. 46–7.

[185] Read, *From Field to Factory*, pp. 203–4
[186] Broughton, *Labour in Indian Industries*, p. 103.
[187] WBSA, Comm. Comm., January, 1929, A261–8; May 1929, B196–9.
[188] *Report of the Textile Factories Labour Committee*, 1907, p. 11.
[189] Das, 'Women Labour', p. 539.
[190] T. M. Nair, Minute of Dissent, *IFLC*.

not provide that males and females should not work together. I trust that the rules framed under the law will make sufficient provision for their segregation.'[191] To the threat that women workers might be replaced by men if not allowed the same hours of work, Dr Nair retorted, 'In India, men and women do not compete for the same work.'[192] The Government agreed that 'it is probably not desirable that women should compete with men'.[193] Such objections to women's work in factories derived obviously from a culture of segregation.

But how did women negotiate their economic compulsions? In jute mills there was no occupational mobility between men and women and between women and women. There was thus absolutely no opportunity for promotion for women. Over time, while some jobs designated as 'women's work' were divested of recognised skill, others associated with skill and strength increasingly excluded women. According to Kelman, in the 1920s, 'weft-winding . . . [i]s better paid, and men may be more willing to do it, or it may need more skill and therefore be avoided by the women'.[194] The gendering of 'skill' and wages became more evident after the 1930s. The 1953 enquiry reported that, 'due to employment of women in certain occupations for a long time . . . a sort of convention has developed whereby these occupations have come to be known as *magh* jobs . . . Men do not like to take up such jobs.'[195]

A great deal was said about how factory work cut into domestic time but the incessant drudgery of domestic labour was rarely recognised. In a survey of women workers in the jute industry 50 per cent (132 women) reported that they felt more fatigued after housework than after factory work. Fifty-seven women complained of fatigue all the time.[196]

There can be little doubt that *basti* conditions made housework particularly difficult and women who also worked in the factories had a very heavy schedule.[197] A most conservative estimate of the time a working woman spent on housework would be three to four hours daily (and this would be in addition to an eight to ten hour working day). The working day would usually begin at 6 a.m. The woman would be up at 4 a.m. or 5 a.m. to make food for the family and rush to work. She would,

---

[191] IOL, L/E/3/213, Officiating Collector of Shahabad, 10 September 1909.
[192] T. M. Nair, Minute of Dissent, *IFLC*.
[193] IOL, l/E/3/213, Government of India, 1 April 1909.
[194] Kelman, *Labour in India*, p. 82.   [195] *Social and Economic Status*, p. 17.
[196] M. N. Rao and H. C. Ganguly, 'Women Labour in Jute Industry of Bengal – A Medico-Social Study', *Indian Journal of Social Work*, 2, 1950–1951, pp. 185–6.
[197] The household schedule has been reconstructed from several sources. Broughton, *Labour in Indian Industries*, pp. 131–2; Matheson, *Indian Industries*, pp. 186, 215–24; Margaret Read, *Indian Peasant Uprooted*, London, 1931, p. 168.

if she lived near the mill, return at half-time to cook lunch, feed the children, have her own meal – all in the one and a half hours that were given to her by the 1922 Act as the minimum period of rest to enable her 'to attend to her domestic duties' – and rush back to the mill. In most mills there were no arrangements for meals. The one and a half hour interval was felt to be sufficient for women working in split shifts to go home, eat and come back. The woman on a continuous shift would have to eat before coming to work. A woman might have to cook her meal in the morning and take it to the mill. She would eat in the open or at her machine since the mills had no provision for shelter or eating. The children on most shifts got home for meals, but intervals for different shifts were at such different hours of the day that, in the great majority of cases, family members on different shifts would have to eat at different times and this made domestic tasks more burdensome. The woman returned from work in the evening via the *bazar* to cook again for dinner, wash utensils, and very often wash clothes. And her work was never over before 10 p.m. or 11 p.m. In addition, water had to be fetched daily from a distance and took time to collect, for every woman had to wait her turn in a queue. Sometimes, even utensils had to be taken to a street hydrant to wash. Given these constraints, it is not surprising that wherever possible women tended to depend on 'cheap bazar stuff to eat in place of cooked meals' or even semi-parched grains. *Chapatis* were replaced by ready-made bread, with adverse nutritional consequences.

Women were inducted into household responsibility at a young age. To begin with they married very young, usually between 6 and 10 years of age. Though it is unlikely that girls so young became responsible for the entire housework immediately after marriage, there are some indications that fairly young girls were co-opted into housework. Given a working mother's constraints, it was quite usual for a young daughter or daughter-in-law to help out extensively with the housework. In fact, the lack of amenities and facilities meant that women had to depend to a great extent on the female support network of relatives, neighbours and daughters. Sobartan, who was the only earning member in a family of seven and supplemented her earnings from the jute mill by making paper toys in the evening, depended entirely on her mother and her daughter to do the housework.[198] In a survey in 1950–51, 81 per cent of the women interviewed said that they had to cope with the burden of housework alone. Almost every woman who got help, got it from a daughter.[199] A few also got help from other female relatives, like a sister-

[198] *Social and Economic Status*, Sobertan, p. 78.
[199] Rao and Ganguly, 'Women Labour in Jute Industry of Bengal', p. 183.

in-law or mother.[200] Fuel collection was often the responsibility of young girls[201] as were fetching water from the nearest street outlet or even a distant tank,[202] going to the market, or to the 'corner shop' for provisions, washing utensils and, if necessary, washing them at the street hydrant, as in the case of 10-year-old Dilia.[203] Such duties were definitely the lot of young daughters, who had very short childhoods. It was often the task of an older brother or sister to mind young infants and babies at home, to carry them to the mother or cook and carry lunch to the mill. While the mother considered it her primary duty to 'feed' her children it was often the duty of the children, especially daughters, however young, to help with housework.

The economic compulsions behind factory work and the requirements of family survival allowed an expansion of the concept of the *samsar* (typically, household). So long as a woman justified her waged employment in terms of 'need of the family' her commitment remained basically directed towards the home and family.[204] In this sense, the concept of *samsar* could be expanded beyond the home.[205] This flexibility strengthened the ideology of domesticity – it became more ubiquitous and almost inescapable. An exceptional economic need, especially that of the family, became the only acceptable justification for women's work across classes and communities. It then became easier to co-opt and appropriate women's waged work within the familial context. As a result, women's ability to wrest any degree of autonomy on the basis of their cash earnings was severely circumscribed. The potential conflict between domesticity and factory work was somewhat resolved and the familial control of men over women retained.

Given the conditions in which women had to bear the double burden of domestic and mill work, some women, not surprisingly, preferred to shed a part of their workload.[206] Since domestic work was unavoidable, they often chose not to work in mills.[207] For the middle-class observer, Indian and British, this was an affirmation of the ideology of domesticity. In a sense they were correct. Middle-class women could engage in 'respectable' work, which, even if paid, did not seriously compromise the status of the family. In contrast, working-class women were engaged

---

[200] Ten-year-old Amala collected cowdung, *Ananda Bazar Patrika*, 4 May 1935. Eleven-year-old Tasi collected firewood, *Amrita Bazar Patrika*, 3 April 1940.
[201] Ibid.   [202] *Amrita Bazar Patrika*, 3 May 1939.
[203] *Amrita Bazar Patrika*, 21 September 1939.
[204] Mary Higdon Beech, 'The Domestic Realm in the Lives of Hindu Women in Calcutta', in H. Papanek and G. Minault (eds.), *Separate Worlds: States of Purdah in South Asia*, Delhi, 1982, p. 131.
[205] This was true of the political participation of women too. See chapter 6 below.
[206] Matheson, *Indian Industries*, Appendix II.
[207] Read, *Indian Peasant Uprooted*, pp. 178–9.

in ill-paid jobs in poor conditions, most of which were considered demeaning. Since poor women could not aspire to the 'respectable' professions, their aspirations concentrated on domesticity which alone could confer a degree of status to working-class families. Besides, most women enjoyed little control over their earnings – their wages were swallowed up in the family budget.[208] Their one form of saving was buying jewellery.[209] Thus, they may have preferred to remain confined to the household when male earnings made this possible. The men in the family were equally eager, when earnings permitted, to withdraw women from factory work.

The nature of the work available to a poor women – its monotony and its physical demands exacerbated by sexual harassment – tended to push her further into the family; a trend reinforced by the difference in the earning potential between husband and wife, as in the case of factory workers.[210] Possibly the wife did not actually believe her 'place' was in the home. But a minimal advancement in the household living standard often prompted her preference to be a housewife.

The systematic replacement of female labour by adult male workers from the 1930s thus produced surprisingly little protest. Women themselves put up stiff resistance against direct retrenchment, increasing workloads and stringent inspections, but in most cases they found no support from the male-dominated trade unions. Besides, straightforward retrenchment was carried out only in fits and starts. More sustained strategies were forced early retirement and 'natural wastage'. In either case, the women who retired were replaced with men workers. Trade unions, dogged by spiralling male unemployment, mostly approved these measures. Even women may have been more happy to relinquish their jobs to a son or a son-in-law than to another unrelated woman. For most women, aspirations for a daughter or a daughter-in-law rarely included jute mill employment. Rather, marriage to a man who could afford to keep them out of the mills was more desirable. These attitudes were not universal, but women who preferred to continue to work rather than hand over their jobs to sons on whose wages they thereafter became dependent, often found it impossible to withstand the combined onslaught of the management, the unions and the family. It is, then, not particularly surprising that researchers in the

---

[208] *Social and Economic Status*, p. 17.   [209] Matheson, *Indian Industries*, p. 215.
[210] Though the wife consistently earned less than her husband, she contributed typically one-third of family income and her job was steadier. But usually skilled workers earned more by overtime and part-time work than women working full-time. Beech, 'The Domestic Realm in the Lives of Hindu Women'.

field find 'the decline of female labour was not seen as something entirely negative'.[211]

Only workers who earned a 'family wage' could afford to withdraw women from factory work. Thus the association of status with women's seclusion and domesticity was confirmed and emphasised. Poor women, if not visibly restricted by *purdah*, suffered a loss of status when economic deprivation forced them to take up wage labour outside the home. Curjel noticed how non-working women emphasised their superior status. In the *basti* outside Howrah Jute Mill, 'A number of Mahomedans, upcountry workers, of the better paid class lived here with their wives ... These women did not work outside. They were not strictly purdah, but told me they stayed mostly in their homes.'[212] Inside the mills, she met some Bengali women. The old *Doctor babu* of the mill, working there for forty years, told her, 'Bengali women do not work in mills as long as their husbands are alive, or they are living with their husbands. He pointed out that the women, who on my questioning said, "husband dead" did not mean that they lived alone ... but they are ashamed to own this to us.'[213]

Some wives of better paid workmen appear to have maintained *purdah*. This seems to have been especially true of *sardars* and Muslim weavers. These women were 'accustomed to either complete seclusion or to considerable privacy ... the women told me that they rarely (if ever) went about the lines'.[214] As in the case of the *bhadramahila*, the unfamiliarity of the city might have increased restrictions on some women.

For working-class women in the *bastis* of Calcutta and other jute towns, maintaining *purdah* often meant incarceration in tiny airless cubicles. In overcrowded *bastis* where water taps were shared, complete seclusion required hiring domestice services. Only wives of a few better paid workers could afford to maintain *purdah* in these conditions. In the odd case, men would would take over some domestic responsibilities – marketing, fetching water and fuel – to enable young wives to maintain rules of seclusion.[215] Thus, *purdah* in the slums, as elsewhere, signalled family status, since it implied the ability to dispense with women's

---

[211] De Haan, 'Towards a Single Male Earner', p. 160. For a more detailed discussion see Samita Sen, 'Gendered Exclusion: Domesticity and Dependence in Bengal', in A. Janssens (ed.), 'The Rise and Decline of the Male Breadwinner Family?', *International Review of Social History Supplement 5*, 41, 1997, pp. 65–86.
[212] Curjel Report, Appendix B, Sl, No. 12.   [213] Ibid., Sl, No. 11.
[214] Ibid., Sl, No. 3.
[215] Basmati Debi, Titagarh, 14 April 1991, Interview in collaboration with Arjan de Haan. Her neighbour said, 'We are Muhammedans, my mother did not work .... She would go out to fetch water and things. Otherwise she stayed at home. Earlier she did not go out even for that. Father did all that.'

contribution to family income and hire domestic service. Curjel made this connection:

I went in the lines to some of the houses of better paid workers – the weavers. They had their womenfolk, and their rooms were screened off with sacking. I talked to these women and it seemed doubtful if they were really these men's upcountry wives. They said they wore purdah, but, I found, did not mind showing themselves before the Mill Manager. Their behaviour was quite different from that of the purdah women seen at the Kharda Jute Mills. It is noteworthy that here as elsewhere the weavers were the autocrats of the mill, and their womenfolk did not usually work. The rooms screened off with sacking were much lacking in light and ventilation – (? was the 'Pseudo-purdah' rather a sign of social superiority).[216]

The rules of *purdah* may have been modified as in other communities.[217] Women workers probably did not reject its underlying value system. Even when separate living quarters were impossible, separate meals remained a visible practice of the ideal of gender segregation. Some rules, like the showing of respect to elders, the avoidance of male affines and obedience to the mother-in-law, showed remarkable resilience.

The general movement in Bengal from brideprice to dowry affected women workers in the jute industry too. Chattopadhyay noted an increasing trend towards dowry in the 1940s, along with a decrease in instances of widow remarriage. He also noted a correlation between payment of dowry and improving economic circumstances of the groom's family.[218] It is possible that, as elsewhere, the difference in the earning potential of men and women in the mills sharpened the move towards dowry payment. Nabin and Gopal Ghose bought land from mill wages and moved up in caste from Ujania to Bhatak. Their descendant Akrur Ghose commented, 'and now that the girls do not work, it has become very difficult to get them married. Earlier, if there were two daughters, selling them would fetch four cows. Now, if there are two daughters, one has to sell one's *bhita* [homestead] for their marriage.'[219] Women interviewed have seen, in their lifetime, the change from 'no payment' or brideprice marriages to dowry marriages. These women, who worked in the mill after their marriage, were given a few utensils and a few sarees at their marriages, but they pay cash, jewellery

[216] The comment in brackets has been quoted verbatim. Curjel Report, Appendix B, Sl, No. 9.
[217] Basmati Debi said that some women observed *purdah* for a few years after marriage and would be free to work in the factory if necessary after the birth of the first child. She, however, never maintained *purdah*. Interview, Titagarh, 14 April 1991.
[218] Chattopadhyay, *A Socio-Economic Survey of Jute Labour*.
[219] Bhupati Ranjan Das, 'Paribaric Kahinite Chatkaler Itihas' (The History of the Jute Industry in Family Stories), *Baromash, Saradiya*, 1988, p. 81.

and other consumer items, like bicycles and watches, to marry their daughters and granddaughters in the hope that they, at least, will not have the misfortune of having to work in the mills. Basmatia, who bitterly watched her retirement benefit go up in the smoke of the sacramental fire at her granddaughter's marriage, remarked, 'Now you have to give so many things – money, furniture ... Earlier this was not there. At my daughter's wedding I gave five utensils and the money she got as presents from family, nothing else ... At my wedding there was nothing.'[220]

[220] She worked in the Titagarh No. 2 Mill since she was ten years old (in the 1930s). Her retirement was spent for the granddaughter's marriage. So she worked in *bhaga* (job-sharing) at the Kinnison Mill for a few years. An old woman, she said, 'Will I get money if I sit idle?' She wanted to continue working but could not get a job. There was a bitter frustration against her complete dependence on her son. Other women also commented on the change to dowry. Lachhmania Debi, who worked for twenty-six years in Nuddea Jute Mill, had no dowry paid at her marriage, but comments on the spiralling dowry demand in her community. Interview, Gourepur, February 1989. Munia Debi was born in 1934 and worked in a mill after marriage. There was no 'tilak' paid at her marriage, but she paid cash for her daughter's marriage. Nuddea Mill, Gourepur, February 1989.

4 Motherhood, mothercraft and the Maternity Benefit Act

It has been suggested earlier that the 1920s witnessed a shift in the nature of state regulation of factory labour. Before the war, the Factories Acts had targeted the 'weaker' sections of the workforce, accepting on the whole the principle that adult male labour was able to deal with the 'market' without external interference. After the war, faith in the paramountcy of free trade over the labour market was losing ground and the newly instituted International Labour Organisation made a spirited attempt to monitor working conditions across the globe.[1] Workers were now seen as an identifiable social group with a claim on the state's protection. The growing 'public' commitment towards workers' wellbeing was no longer limited to 'weaker' sections of labour, that is women and children, but embraced the working people as a whole. Apart from a few variations in permitted hours of work and special restrictions on night work, increasingly women and men workers were being treated at par while children faced progressively more stringent restrictions. Welfare measures like accident compensation, trade union rights, sickness and unemployment insurance were at least ostensibly gender-neutral.

Women workers' lives, however, began to come under scrutiny in other more diverse ways. In the pre-war debates about the 'protective' legislation, while women's domestic and mothering roles were often brought into play both by proponents and opponents, the laws were directed towards the woman in the workplace and they sought to regulate, primarily, her conditions of work. In the early years of industrialisation, access to cheap labour was seen as India's chief advantage over Dundee and Lancashire. Industrialists, and to some extent state officials, had defended women's employment in factories on the grounds that, even if 'supplementary', their earnings were essential for their own and for their households' survival. Thus, women figured in

---

[1] This was not, of course, the first. The International Labour Conference in Berlin, 1890, had attempted similar measures.

142

the state, capitalist and reformist discourses in their capacity as workers, albeit as workers less able to uphold their specific interests.

In the post-war era a major change took place. Factory women were regarded less as workers with particular problems calling for separate remedies than as special kinds of mothers and wives – ones who also worked. Alongside debates about whether they should in fact work and what adverse effects such work had on their housewifery and motherhood, there were attempts to isolate and remedy the specific disabilities of working wives and mothers.

The burgeoning discourse about a state committed to the well-being of its large working population also found strong resonances in growing concern about the 'family'. To aid the family in repopulating war-ravaged nations, in bringing up the next generation of citizens and reproducing labour was one important function of the welfare state. The social reconstitution of the family drew on assumptions about its fundamental 'natural' functions. In so doing, it gave rise to a range of conflictual characterisations of the working-class family and women's role within it. The older arguments about full and unqualified parental rights over children were on the one hand being systematically discredited; on the other, simultaneously, there was an increasing emphasis on the duties and responsibilities of mothers in ensuring that families played their socially desirable role. Thus it was the 'working-class woman', by virtue of marriage or motherhood, who now qualified for attention rather than the 'woman worker', in her capacity as a factory worker, who had earlier attracted legislation. State and capitalist welfare now, at least putatively, embraced wives, mothers and daughters of 'workers' even if they did not themselves work in the factory. Much of the ILO's concern for women was focused on maternity and motherhood and this provided a context for the redefinition of women's role in the working-class family.

How far these international trends influenced government policy and managerial attitudes in India is, of course, open to question. It is, however, undeniable that the ILO's interventions stirred up prolix controversies. These brought to the fore the disagreements among the Government of India, the provincial governments, British expatriate and Indian business interests as well as the conflicts within the trade union movement. The result was a rich archive on working-class 'welfare' which continued to proliferate despite the absence of material and ideological conditions for concrete welfare policies.

The Government of India could not, after all, entirely avoid the issues pressed by the ILO. For a while it effectively pleaded India's less-developed status to opt out of many welfare commitments. But in 1922

India replaced Switzerland as the eighth most industrialised country in the governing body of the organisation. The obligation to ratify and enforce ILO conventions increased.[2]

Other concerns meshed with international pressure for reform. The First World War had directed the government's attention to the industrialisation of India.[3] The growing trade union movement raised the uncomfortable spectre of communism. Government feared social and political dislocation among the city's poor. The footloose migrants who had, in the late nineteenth and early twentieth centuries, seemed to promise compliance and regularity began to present the Bengal jute mill owners with determined and even violent resistance. They posed, increasingly, a threat to 'law and order' and caused grave anxieties to the managers, the police, the local and provincial governments. A large concentration of adult male workers, unhampered by immediate responsibilities for the security and maintenance of women and children, no longer appeared quite so appealing. But the British solution – the rationalisation of the working-class family through the extension of public welfare – was hardly an attractive prospect for the colonial state. They wrote uneasily about the 'family wage', conducted 'family budget' surveys and sought to square these concerns through the argument that Indian industrial labour was in fact of a 'non-family' variety. This latter term, used frequently by contemporary sociologists, was intended to describe the predominance of workmen who left their wives and children in the village. The 'working-class family' in the Indian urban context began to seem to be a social category of doubtful value to makers of policy.

Industrialists also seized on the 'non-family' argument in the immediate post-war years to resist the welfare measures being mooted. The jute industry were able to maintain high profits in the post-war decade, but internal competition pushed them towards increasing reliance on low labour costs. They put up fierce resistance against the Government's attempts, at the instance of the ILO, to institute accident compensation, sickness, unemployment, retirement and maternity benefits. In the first case they could not prevent the legislation, but were able by and large to circumvent its worst consequences by evading the rules. The others, tentatively put forward by the Government in the 1920s and 1930s, were staved off on the grounds that the workers usually returned to their villages when they were old, sick, unemployed

[2] IOL, Industries & Overseas Department, 2408 of 1922.
[3] C. Dewey, 'The Government of India's "New Industrial Policy", 1900–1925; Formation and Failure', in C. Dewey and K. N. Choudhuri (eds.), *Economy and Society*, Delhi, 1979. The theme is explored further in chapter 5 below.

or pregnant. So, argued mill owners, the proposed welfare measures were unnecessary. But they were also impossible to implement without a bureaucratic network which only the Government had at its diposal. The colonial state, equally chary of avoidable financial burdens, countered with the argument that these measures would increase the efficiency and productivity of labour and were, therefore, in all fairness, the employers' responsibility. Besides, the industrial workforce constituted too minor a proportion of the population to claim so heavy a share of the state's resources. The employers and the state were each trying to foist on the other the responsibility for financing labour welfare.

An idealised standard of labour efficiency was gaining popular currency in Western Europe and the USA: a reasonably healthy, energetic and contented workforce was more productive, and therefore of more value to employers. The Government tried to convince mill owners and managers that 'rationalisation' in the workplace would be more effective if accompanied by welfare schemes in the neighbourhood – leisure clubs, cinema screenings, health exhibitions and baby shows should be instituted to wean workers away from liquor shops, gambling dens, indigenous doctors and midwives. In the 1920s, when the jute industry was doing well, production was expanding and profits were steady, some mills had adopted a variety of these schemes ad hoc and piecemeal. The health exhibitions and the baby shows were particularly popular. Jute mill mangers were at that stage still keen to retain cheap female and child workers in some of the more labour-intensive processes. The welfare schemes with their emphasis on supervision, reporting and home visiting also provided a means of extending their direct control over the labour force. In tea plantations, where female labour was more numerous and regarded as more vital, these schemes were adopted with even greater alacrity.

Quite obviously, jute mill owners' notions of labour management were far removed from ideal standards of effciency. In the 1930s when profits were down, when the IJMA was facing recalcitrant 'outside' mills, labour welfare was the least of their anxieties. They sought to reduce labour costs while the Government advocated 'rationalisation' and 'welfare'. They retained the 'voluntary' schemes of maternity and child welfare because these were no longer a mere sop to public conscience or an argument against legislation overriding the mill owners' spontaneous munificence. More importantly, mills were undertaking heavy retrenchment, especially of women. Mill owners found an emphasis on family and mothering roles helped to delegitimise women's factory employment. Besides, the threatened women were taking recourse to collective resistance, from within or outside the unions. The welfare schemes offered an ideological and practical means of controlling their activities.

The issue of maternity benefit for working-class women was first raised in earnest in the wake of the Washington Convention of the International Labour Organisation (1919). This provoked various debates over working-class practices regarding childbirth, childcare, infant and maternal mortality through which emerged a new definition of motherhood applied unsystematically to poor urban women. Public debates over issues of childbirth and maternity were of course not new in India. The colonial state had already committed itself to providing some rudimentary medical facilities to Indian women, particularly to elite women. A number of *zenana* hospitals were founded, meant explicitly for women in 'true *purdah*', upper-class women, who were thought unable to approach male doctors. The establishment of the Dufferin Fund in 1885 was the first organised attempt to provide such medical care for Indian women and there had been spasmodic missionary efforts even earlier. Some of these endeavours were supported by Indian men who either believed in the beneficial effects of Western medicine or saw in financial donations to the Government's projects a means of acquiring greater honour and power. The missionaries and medical women from England were enthusiastic about this benevolent face of the civilising mission especially since for many of them India proffered a route to professional advancement. Yet, since these efforts had been provoked by the concern for high infant and maternal mortality rates, they were consciously limited not only to 'true *purdah*' women, but also to specific gynaecological and obstetric facilities. The medical personnel fixed on the Indian woman 'between the breasts and the knees'.[4]

The concern over high infant and maternal mortality rates also entered the nationalist discourse from the end of the nineteenth century. Various shades of Indian opinion sought to highlight the critical importance of infant life – quantitative and qualitative – as a forerunner of a healthy and numerous population, a national resource. Early efforts in this direction, as in the case of the *zenana* hospitals, were restricted primarily to elite women. The rhetoric began to broaden and include poor women in the 1920s and 1930s.

The numerous champions of the mother's right to medical and other facilities – missionaries, medical professionals, the colonial state and

[4] Geraldine Forbes, 'Medical Careers and Health Care for Indian Women: Patterns of Control', *Women's History Review*, 3, 4, 1994; 'Managing Midwifery in India', in D. Engels and S. Marks (eds.), *Contesting Colonial Hegemony: State and Society in Africa and India*, London, 1994.

Indian nationalists – drew out really alarming statistics of infant and maternal mortality. The Censuses of 1872 and 1881 gave strength to the debate. The stagnant, and even negative, growth rate of the population drew public attention.[5] These concerns continued in a small way in the early years of the twentieth century,[6] but took on a greater momentum in the 1920s.

The first independent study on the subject was undertaken by Curjel in 1920 who reported a 49 per cent survival rate of infants in Bengal while stillbirths, miscarriages and abortions alone accounted for 34 per cent of pregnancies.[7] In Calcutta, female mortality rates were found to be higher than male mortality rates and the excessive female mortality was characterised by an even higher rate of maternal mortality. In 1920–21, female mortality was over 5 per cent whereas the rate of male mortality was 3.3 per cent. The difference was sharper between women of childbearing age – 15 and 40 years – and men of the same age.[8] As for infant mortality, Calcutta was second only to Bombay. In 1920 the infant mortality rate in Calcutta was 386 per thousand births. In 1920, in Ward XXIV of Calcutta, a slum area, the infant mortality was higher than the Calcutta average at 582 deaths per thousand births.[9] These statistics were only the tip of the iceberg given the inefficiency of the registration system. Nor did things change much in the next two decades. In 1944 Dr Jean Orkney calculated that the death toll in India from childbirth was higher than plague, smallpox or even cholera. And these figures left out those with permanent injury to health from post-natal complications.[10]

Motherhood and mothercraft

In Bengal, in the closing years of the nineteenth century, motherhood had emerged as the central and defining element in the dominant discourses of gender. It had played a key role in the social reform debates. The elite men in favour of widow remarriage had persuasively argued against the injustice of denying child widows the ultimate fulfil-

---

[5] *Report of the Census of the Town and Suburbs of Calcutta*, H. Beverley, 1881, II; *Bamabodhini Patrika*, 3, III, 258, 1886; *Education Gazette*, 6 December 1889.

[6] A lady sanitary inspector was appointed in 1908. *Amrita Bazar Patrika*, 13 November 1908. Raja Mahendra Raychaudhuri proposed a committee of enquiry in the Bengal Legislative Assembly. WBSA, General Sanitation, March 1914, B91–2.

[7] Dagmar Curjel, *Improvement of the Conditions of Childbirth in India*, Calcutta, 1918.

[8] *Report of the Municipal Administration of Calcutta*, 1920–21, pp. 67–8.

[9] *Annual Report on the Public Health Commissioner with the Government of India*, 1920–25.

[10] J. M. Orkney, 'The Health of Indian Women and Children', *Journal of the Association of Medical Women in India* (henceforth *JAMWI*), 32, 1944, p. 5.

ment of a woman – motherhood.[11] Stagnation of population, high infant and mortality rates had also drawn out social reformers on the subject of childbirth and childrearing. They concentrated on social 'evils' like child marriage, the absence of widow remarriage,[12] and the superstitions and rituals surrounding childbirth.[13] In the late nineteenth century, as the reformists lost ground to the preservers of 'tradition', the problems of infant and maternal mortality were appropriated within the 'nationalist' discourse in different ways.

The idealisation of womanhood as the repository of tradition and the construction of the domestic sphere as the proper and rightful domain of women, involved a general valorisation of motherhood. The ideal woman was not only the creator and protector of the sanctuary of the home, but the good and chaste mother who, empowered by spiritual strength, was the iconic representation of the nation. This idealisation found support in the notion that children were crucial for nation-building and for 'the maintenance of the race'. The responsibility for bearing and rearing children lay with women. But it was too vital to be left to women unaided. If the ignorant and careless housewife was a threat to the social order, the neglectful and indifferent mother spelt national disaster. Women had to be taught to be good mothers. As domestic manuals sought to train a new kind of housewife, so the new mother had to be inculcated with a self-conscious responsibility for the nation's future. Along with the *sugrihini*, the *sumata* faced a barrage of advice and prescriptive norms on childrearing.[14]

The Washington Convention encouraged the extension of these discourses on motherhood to working-class women. It gave a new focus to anxieties regarding the physical deterioration of the working population of the country. Debating a shorter working day for factory women, A. C. Chatterjee, Secretary to the Government of India, Department of Industries (later delegate to the ILO) declared, 'as a patriotic Indian, I think it is our duty to see that girls grow up sufficiently strong in order to become healthy and capable mothers'. Jamnadas Dwarkadas argued, 'we are stunting the growth of the future labourers of the country'.[15]

Work outside the home, specifically factory work, was regarded as impairing women's childbearing capacity. This stressed the 'natural' or the biological and physiological aspects of motherhood. Increasingly,

[11] Uma Chakravarti, 'Social Pariahs and Domestic Drudges: Widowhood among Nineteenth Century Poona Brahmins', *Social Scientist*, 21, 9–11, 1993, pp. 130–58.
[12] *Education Gazette*, 6 December 1889.
[13] Hemantakumari Choudhury, *Sutikagriha, Antahpur*, V, 9, 1902, p. 133.
[14] These arguments have been elaborated in an earlier article. Samita Sen, 'Motherhood and Mothercraft: Gender and Nationalism in Bengal', *Gender and History*, 5, 2, 1993.
[15] Legislative Assembly Debates, 10 January 1922.

also, explanations for maternal and infant mortality were sought not in poverty, environment or lack of medical services but in the working mother's neglect, carelessness and ignorance. The solution was sought not in crêches, maternity benefit or health facilities but in teaching mothers how to take care of their children.

The 'enlightened motherhood' advocated for the *bhadramahila* required comprehensive education – hygiene and health, childcare and housework, and geography and literature jostled each other. It was quite clear from the beginning that the 'education' of working-class mothers did not imply formal education. Rather, it involved the kind of education becoming popular in Britain as 'mothercraft'.[16] The term itself was borrowed by concerned Indians. The arguments promoting formal education for middle-class women and mothercraft for poor women were, however, based on similar assumptions. It was agreed that uneducated women endangered the physical development of children and ignorant women perpetuated harmful 'traditional' and 'superstitious' practices.

This social construction of motherhood, grounded in the biological fact of women's childbearing and lactation capacities, sought, on the one hand, to transcend class differences. On the other hand, its configuration in discourses about the poor and its application through myriad social and welfare policies highlighted class differences. It explicitly gave middle-class women – medical professionals and voluntary social workers – the authority to condemn and thereafter concretely intervene into the lives of poor women. The new mothercraft was being defined by the medical profession – doctors, nurses, trained midwives and trained health visitors. The standards of hygiene, nutrition and childcare they set were derived from the middle-class context. Middle-class convention took it for granted that the proper context of childhood was the family and the person most responsible for childrearing was the mother. In working-class families, mothers considered it their primary duty to earn to 'feed' their children and children reciprocated by helping with housework or earning towards household expenses. The mothercraft formulae did not take into account the possibility that their application to the working classes would be fraught with difficulties and frustrations. The more unsuccessful they were, the greater was the urge to look for reasons for failures in custom, tradition or the lack of co-operation of the poor. Mothercraft thus became an important terrain of contest – working-class women subverted the dominant notions of motherhood

[16] Anna Davin, 'Imperialism and Motherhood', *History Workshop Journal*, 5, Spring 1978. The term was indigenised as *Matritva Vidyar Siksha*, Pushpa Basu, Special Supplement on Child Welfare, *Ananda Bazar Patrika*, 20 March 1941.

through which middle-class professionals sought to control and characterise them.

Mothercraft had various facets. There was, first, a growing concern that factory work or any other strenuous work of that nature impaired women's actual physical and biological capacity for childbearing. Researchers and reformers sought to establish, statistically, that women who worked in factories suffered greater post-natal complications to the detriment of their own and their children's health, even life. There was, as a result, a call from some quarters to ensure, by legislation, women's withdrawal from factories and mines. But the problems were not entirely biological. There was a serious physical and health risk to children left unattended by working mothers. Poor working mothers often devised alternative childcare methods but these were unacceptable to professional welfarists who emphasised the mother's personal supervision of the child's well-being. In the case of poor mothers, they argued, rudimentary 'education' was necessary to ensure efficient and effective care of children. They thus advocated the establishment of voluntary welfare centres to 'instruct' mothers in the scientific wisdom of motherhood. These 'centres' bolstered a conviction that instruction would prove more valuable than maternity allowances in cash for working mothers. Moreover, the new social construction of motherhood was attended by a gradual evolution of standards of nutrition, the importance of breastfeeding, other elevated standards of childcare and a simultaneous denigration of the traditional methods of childbirth symbolised by the 'indigenous *dai*' whose ignorance constituted a danger for mothers and children.

Factory work and childbearing

Academic research attempted to give a 'scientific' basis to the belief that factory work was detrimental to women's childbearing capacity. Experiments were undertaken in Italy, France, Germany and England: 'it is now a well-established fact that infant mortality is shockingly high among the babies of women who work in factories and mills ... infant mortality increases progressively according to the increase in the proportion of women obliged to work outside their homes'.[17] Similar research was undertaken in Indian industrial areas to demonstrate the universality of this dictum. Curjel's shocking statistics[18] were confirmed by Dr Margaret Balfour of the Women's Medical Service of India. Her

---

[17] C. W. Saleeby, *The Eugenic Prospect*, London, 1921, p. 916. Also see A. B. and M. E. Olsen, *Health For the Millions*, London, 1908, p. 176.

[18] About 41 per cent of children were born while the mother was working in the factory.

Table 4.1. *Maternal mortality rates per hundred births among jute mill workers, 1929–31*

Year	Benefits	Maternal deaths	Deaths per 100 births
1929	816	18	2. 2
1930	1857	21	1. 1
1931	1882	15	0. 8

Source: M. I. Balfour, 'Report of a Survey of Women Workers in Jute Mills, 1931–2', 1932, p. 10, WBSA, Comm. Comm., January 1932, A2–6.

Bombay and Calcutta studies revealed that the rate of stillbirths and miscarriages doubled when women worked in mills (see Table 4.1). Her conclusion, widely quoted in official and sociological treatises, was that 'factory work' was 'injurious to the mother and the unborn child' and 'adverse to childbearing itself'.[19]

These figures compared favourably with the official statistic for Calcutta given as 2 per cent.[20] But records of mills' health personnel showed much higher rates.[21] Such evidence strengthened the feeling that factory work was inimical to women's health and, specifically, to childbearing. Research on the negative effects of factory work on mortality and fertility continued in the 1950s.[22]

If the physical strain of factory work was the main cause of the higher mortality, one possible solution was the removal of women from industrial work. A body of philanthropic opinion did in fact advocate such a course.[23] They sought to clinch the debate on women's underground work in coal mines by advancing arguments about its adverse consequences on the reproduction of the race: 'no attempt is being made to

She calculated a 12 per cent rate of miscarriage and 5 per cent rate of stillbirth. Curjel Report, Appendices B and F.

[19] Dr M. Balfour, 'The Maternity Conditions of Women Mill Workers', Bombay, July 1929, quoted in M. Read, *Indian Peasant Uprooted*, London, 1931, p. 174. Balfour Report, pp. 10–13. A later survey revealed that 50 per cent of women reported more fatigue after housework than from factory work. Others complained of fatigue all the time. M. N. Rao and H. C. Ganguly, 'Women Labour in Jute Industry of Bengal – A Medico–Social Study', *Indian Journal of Social Work*, 1, 1950–51, pp. 185–6. The issue of housework has been discussed in chapter 3 above.

[20] *Health Officers Report*, Calcutta, 1929.

[21] For maternal mortality rates, Reliance report was 9.6 per cent, Union South was 8.9 and Shyamnagar North was 4. Similarly, the official benefit figure for infant death rate was 7.2 per cent in 1929, 5.3 in 1930 and 5.2 in 1931. According to health visitors the rate was 19.3 per cent in Budge-Budge, 19.6 in Kankinara and 13.3 in Union South. Balfour Report.

[22] Rao and Ganguly, 'Women Labour in Jute Industry of Bengal', p. 190.

[23] '[T]he women of India must be kept away from the mills and their family life preserved'. C. M. Matheson, *Indian Industries – Yesterday, Today and Tomorrow*, Oxford, 1930, p. 101.

face the effects of work in the mines on women and children and through them on the race'.[24] In fact, they fully realised that women could not be prevented from employment in factories, plantations and mines. The solution was a compromise – to teach them mothercraft to lessen as far as possible the harmful effects of ignorance and neglect. Instead of pursuing the institution of maternity leave, compensatory pay, and health services, they helped the state and employers to bring under their scrutiny individual childbearing and rearing practices of poor mothers.

Strategies of childcare - opium vs. crêches

Going out to work long hours in the factory posed, in the case of women with young children, an intractable problem. The evils attached to an unattended child became, for sociologists and social workers, the strongest argument against women's particpation in factory industry. Contemporary scholars who investigated working-class conditions elaborated these concerns.[25] According to R. K. Das, who investigated the condition of women workers in India for the ILO, 'The employment of women in factories (and) ... their continued absence from home has affected the home life and especially the welfare of children'.[26]

These were questions inextricably related to the mills' use of female and child labour. Up to the 1920s, IJMA resisted legislation. In some important respects, crucially in the working hours of women and children, they failed. However, jute mills were able, with the factory inspectorate's connivance and the complicated multiple shift system, to nullify existing regulation. From the mid-1920s when single-shift work began to come into vogue, their interest in child labour began to decline; from the crisis of the early 1930s, they attempted more systematically to eliminate both child and female labour from the mills. Thus their attitudes changed – to the presence of children in the mills, to children's work, to the unattended child at home and to the provision of crêches and schools.

In 1921, Dr F. Barnes's discovery that 90 per cent of children in

[24] IOL, Industries and Overseas Department, File 2536, 1921. Newspaper cutting, unnamed and undated. The Indian Mining Federation retaliated against exclusion of 'women from underground work in mines on the ground that women have worked in Indian mines without impairing in the least their capacity to bear healthy children'. *Daily News*, 25 August 1928.

[25] 'In all factory towns, very high infantile mortality is seen, due largely to the employment of mothers in the factories and hence neglect of babies who require constant care from the mother'. *Modern Review*, January–June, 1931, p. 187.

[26] R. K. Das, *Factory Labour in India*, Berlin, 1923, pp. 203–4.

Bombay *chawls* were fed opium by their mothers provoked great public outrage.[27] At that stage, jute mill managers were still defending the practice of children below the legal age of employment accompanying mothers to the factories. The possible alternatives and their desirability became closely intertwined with managers' interest in employing child labour. Mill managers argued that in the absence of supervision at home, children were better off working in the factory. The other alternatives – creches for young children and schools for the older ones – required considerable financial commitments. The state provided no schooling, and the employers categorically refused any responsibility. Calcutta's jute mill managers were dismissive also of the value of creches. They argued that women neither liked nor used creches provided by employers. They even argued that attempts to change the 'custom' of women bringing their young children into the factory would evoke strong resistance. Thus, unlike the Bombay mills, Calcutta jute mills had no creches. Even social workers were convinced that the Hand-sewing Departments were not unsuited to young children. This section of the mill was usually separated from the rest and contained no 'dangerous' machinery.[28] Reliance Mill ruled that children would not be allowed anywhere in the mill except the Sewing Department.[29] But many mill managers argued further that the sewing section of the mill was actually the more desirable environment for young children. They rejected the demand for four weeks' leave after childbirth on the grounds that a new-born child was better off in the factory: '[it is] generally to the child's advantage as it lies in some quiet corner of a well-ventilated work-shed instead of living in a dark, dirty, insanitary home'.[30]

There was, of course, another point of view. Even some managers pointed out that young children were being exposed to the fluff, dust, heat and noise for very long hours.[31] The dangers of respiratory diseases and jute dermatitis were compounded for children 'who toddle about and live in that dust-laden atmosphere during the working hours of the mills'.[32] When jute mills employed women on night shifts, Walsh, the Chief Inspector, was worried about children who slept night after night

[27] Dr F. Barnes, 'Final Report of the Lady Doctor, Maternity Benefits to the Industrial Workers', *Labour Gazette*, September 1922.
[28] A. G. Clow, 'Indian Factory Law Administration', *Bulletin of Indian Industries and Labour*, 8, 1921, p. 28.
[29] Mrs Cottle and Miss Headwards, *RCLI*, V, 2.
[30] Bengal Chamber of Commerce, WBSA, Comm. Comm., December 1924, A40–54. Also see evidences, *RCLI*, V, 1: Manager, Birla Jute Manufacturing Company, p. 429 and IJMA, p. 298.
[31] Mrs Cottle and Miss Headwards, *RCLI*, V, 2.
[32] O'Connor, Senior Certifying Surgeon, *RCLI*, V, 1, p. 331.

in the unhealthy and noisy atmosphere of the mill.[33] The issue gained more urgency because of the increasing numbers of accidents involving children left lying around unattended in the mills.[34]

Yet there seemed to be no alternative, especially for nursing mothers. The mills made no provision, women either took their children with them to the mill to feed them at intervals or they left their work to go and nurse them at home. The employers insisted that women were allowed to come and go as they pleased and the Act of 1922 allowed them a one and a half hour break.[35] In the Fort Gloster Mill special gate-passes were issued to nursing mother.[36] To allow for these contingencies, successive commissions refused to recommend the exclusion of children from mills. Even in the 1920s, 'it was not an uncommon sight to see a woman at work with her infant at her breast'.[37] H. H. Brailsford described how he found some women in jute mills holding a baby in one hand and operating the machinery with the other hand.[38]

Not all women took their children to the factory. Some may indeed have used opium, whether or not children were left at home unattended. Barnes's figures may have been exaggerated, but the practice was in vogue.[39] In villages children were often fed opium to keep them quiet allowing women to carry out their domestic chores.[40] There are other stray references to its use in Calcutta, not specifically in the context of the poor.[41] But the doped and completely unattended child was possibly not a frequent occurrence. Working women relied on a relative, a neighbour or an elder child to attend young children. Very often older women in the household, who could no longer work in the factory, would take over housework and childminding. In some cases there were neighbourhood networks – many women workers would leave their

[33] Clow, 'Indian Factory Law Administration', pp. 28–9.
[34] In 1929, for instance, the Chief Inspector of Factories reported twenty-three cases of accidents involving children under 12 years (the legal age for employment). One 4-year-old suffocated under a pile of jute. *FA*, 1929. Next year in 1930 there were twenty-one accidents to young children of which four were fatal. *FA*, 1930.
[35] D. B. Meek, WBSA, Comm. Comm., December 1924, A40–54.
[36] Interview, Mathur Naskar, Bauria, 2 December 1989.
[37] A. Marr, Secretary to the Government of Bengal, 2 October 1920, IOL L/E/3/222.
[38] H. H. Brailsford, *Amrita Bazar Patrika*, 11 August 1928.
[39] For Kanpur see B. Shiva Rao, *The Industrial Worker in India*, London, 1939, p. 142. For coal mine workers see Matheson, *Indian Industries*, p. 155. For Calcutta mills see M. Read, *From Field to Factory*, London, 1927, p. 175. Also see *Social and Economic Status of Women Workers in India*, pp. 56–8. In Calcutta, a baby died of an overdose. The mother, Mehrunnisa, fed her two-month child opium because it had a cold and cried. *Ananda Bazar Patrika*, 23 August 1923.
[40] Curjel, *Improvement of the Conditions of Childbirth*.
[41] *A Text Book of Sanitary Science for the use of Senior Students in English and Anglo-Vernacular Schools in India*, Simla Government, 1890.

babies with an older woman and pay her a small weekly sum.[42] Migrant women often lacked the usual support from a larger kin group, properly defined. They evolved networks of female support based on caste, community or sheer neighbourhood proximity.[43] However, such strategies of childminding were frequently condemned. The mother was the only person really responsible for childrearing and any other alternative was automatically less desirable or, even, dirty, incompetent and irresponsible. As a result reports of accidents involving infants when under the care of an elder sibling were used as an argument against leaving children 'unattended' (by the mother) at home whereas the really large numbers of accidents to children within the factory were given less importance, especially where they might argue the need for crêches.

Employers clung to the notion that working-class mothers were not willing to use crêches. The conviction of the employers rubbed off. The absence of crêches in Calcutta and the failure of some attempts at crêches in Bombay were explained away by the 'prejudice against crêches on the part of the worker'.[44] Even welfare workers like Mrs Cottle and Dr (Miss) Headwards of the Bengal Presidency Council of Women who actually ran welfare centres in mill areas were convinced by this comforting traditionalism. The women's recalcitrance was attributed to caste prejudices and superstition. In fact, their suspicions were not unfounded – crêches were often ill-kept and in unsavoury conditions. An enclosure in the department of a jute mill found only twelve takers. Not surprisingly, since there seems to have been no one in charge.[45] In another case, a room was reserved in the coolie *lines*. Mothers were asked to leave their children there and come at intervals to nurse them. The scheme failed because this crêche, if it can be called that, 'was not under supervision'.[46] Margaret Read argued, 'The success of infant welfare clinics at Titagarh and Kankinara show that trained women in charge can overcome prejudice and caste scruples among women workers. It is a matter of patient education.'[47] It is doubtful whether even 'patient education' was required. Many women used the well-run crêches at Kankinara, Howrah and Nuddea.[48]

[42] Dr Pownes, Titagarh Mill. WBSA, Comm. Comm., May 1939, A7–22.
[43] In Titagarh, a number of neighbouring women paid an older woman to mind their children during working hours. The arrangement was restricted to *Madrassi* women.
[44] P. S. Lokanathan, *Industrial Welfare in India*, Madras, 1929, pp. 137–8.
[45] *RCLI*, V, 1, p. 45.
[46] Dr Pownes, Certifying Surgeon, Calcutta and Barrackpore, to Government of Bengal, WBSA Comm. Comm., May 1939, A7–22.
[47] Read, *Indian Peasant Uprooted*, p. 45.
[48] Interview, Parmesri, Nuddea Jute Mill, January 1989; interview, Durgi Rajvar, Fort Gloster (North Mill), 2 December 1989; interview, Dr Kamala Basu (formally of Nuddea Mill), Naihati, 28 October 1989.

Many attempts at providing crêches failed because the rule of excluding children from factories was not enforced. Even the IJMA in their evidence to the Royal Commission admitted that crêches 'will be utilised to the extent infants are prohibited to enter mills'.[49] Act II of 1922 empowered the Factories Inspector to prohibit admission of young children, but in Bengal it was not until May 1932 that the first systematic effort was made to exclude from mills children under 12 years of age. IJMA held that the rule would create difficulties for individual mills.[50] But as more mills adopted high-speed spinning, their requirement for child labour reduced. Many managers, already committed to a gradual phasing out of child labour from spinning, began to crack down on worksharing in the sewing shed. The tacit understanding between workers and managers which had made the 'presence of children' in the factories a means of evading legal restrictions on children's work began to break down. The fear of a minimum wage legislation in the offing pushed managers to pare down informal workers. It was no longer viable to put to work children who merely accompanied their mothers. Finally, thus, the factories inspectorate was able, in a remarkably short time, to report a surprisingly easy and 'ready compliance' with the exclusion rule. For the first time, the managers played an active role in ensuring this compliance.[51]

Breastfeeding

The debates about children's presence in the mills focused on alternative modes of supervision, schooling and work. The terms in which the questions were cast were drawn from current understanding of the socially desirable role of children and how best to achieve these: whether poor children should be allowed to work as a means of 'on the job training' or whether the value of a general school education cut across classes. But the various strands of opinion agreed that the problem was most intractable in relation to children too young to be set to work in the mills, especially nursing children. The importance of breastfeeding was being gradually defined by the medical profession and was becoming a part of the idea of good motherhood in this period. An Expert

[49] *RCLI*, V, 1, p. 283.   [50] *IJMAR*, 1932.
[51] A manager pushed a heavy bale of jute from the top of a pile and narrowly missed killing a child. He forbade the women to bring in their children. Three-hundred agreed; thirteen left their jobs. The Chief Inspector concluded that the ban could be easily enforced. *FA*, 1931. Even now, children play about in the Hand-sewing Department. The managers say exactly what they must have said fifty years ago – that the women insist and they are powerless to stop it. Interviews, Fort Gloster North Mill, November–December 1989.

Committee of the League of Nations set the standards: 'Breast-feeding which is superior to artificial feeding should be continued up to the age of 6 months.' The bottle was condemned and 'medical persons are in favour of breast-milk ... [it] contains proteins and fats easily digestible by children and anti-bodies to fight with foreign elements in the body'.[52] The problem of inadequate feeding of children was invariably related to poverty and ignorance.

In our country due to ignorance and carelessness of ordinary people, a large number of children die when young. To eradicate this evil, wet-nursing and child-rearing has to be well explained to our mothers ... lack of healthy food and absence of hygiene are the two major causes of infant mortality ... if these two areas are looked after, many hundreds of babies will be saved from death.[53]

The other problem was, of course, that the standards set could not be met by poor and working women. As pointed out earlier, women workers were provided very little facility for nursing. They would take the babies with them and feed them when they got an opportunity. This was completely against the new principles of disciplined and routine feeding patterns prescribed by welfare centres and health visitors. A doctor, Amritalal Basu, writing a series of articles on 'Breast-milk and Baby's Food' insisted that, 'breast feeding must be regular and disciplined, otherwise it will cause much harm'.[54] Even presuming that such prescriptions made sense to busy mothers, the women working in jute mills could not follow the rigid routine of feeding patterns when they worked in shifts which changed from week to week. Often, working mothers had to evolve their own alternatives. These 'failures' reinforced ideas of the careless, negligent and ignorant working-class mother. For instance, most women continued breastfeeding long after the prescribed six months. Some even continued to breastfeed after the next conception which warred against popular belief. Breastfeeding was popularly believed to be a method of contraception, and lactation was often continued only to reduce the chance of conception. In Bengal, however, women (especially of the upper classes) 'generally believe that the practice of suckling her child when she is pregnant is not desirable as the milk becomes unsuitable'.[55] But, for working-class mothers this may have been the cheapest and most convenient practicality.

Often too women would wean their children very early to accommo-

---

[52] W. R. Aykroyd, 'The Nutritive Value of Indian Foods and the Planning of Satisfactory Diets', *Health Bulletin No. 23*, 1935–38, pp. 23–5; *Welfare*, August 1924, pp. 482–9 and February 1926, p. 614.

[53] *Bamabodhini Patrika*, V, 9, 1910.   [54] *Bharat Mahila, Baishakh*, 1913, p. 14.

[55] N. Sengupta and K. Bagchi, 'Dietary Habits of Bengali Pregnant and Lactating Women of Low Socio-Economic Groups in Calcutta', *Alumni Association Bulletin, All India Institute of Hygiene and Public Health* (henceforth *AIIH*), 10, 19, 1961.

date their routine. For instance, in the 1960s, Sethna noticed the practice of giving children barley water or *misri* (sugar water) or cow's milk diluted with water even if there was sufficient breast milk. These 'supplements were started either by seeing a neighbour give them or as is more often the case, to quieten the child during the busy working period of the mother' and this also meant that others like an older sibling could feed the child if the mother was too busy. The vicious circle of poverty and high morbidity and mortality often forced poor mothers to postpone weaning and continue breastfeeding despite inconveniences. Sometimes women continued with breastfeeding for fear of diarrhoea.[56] These strategies, dictated by practical convenience, were judged against the standards set by welfare centres and provided the basis for a comprehensive denunciation of childrearing practices of the poor.

The indigenous *dai*

A concerted attack on the role of the indigenous *dai* in traditional childbirth practices began from the late nineteenth century and gathered momentum in the 1920s and 1930s. This has sometimes been seen as a poignant example of the conflict between 'rival systems of ideas and authority', the indigenous and the colonial, a contest that could end only by the supercession of the *dai*, the repository of traditional, inherited 'female' knowledge by the 'scientific' male medical professionals.[57] Such arguments resonate with feminist analyses about the medicalisation of childbirth in Western countries, where, it is argued, women lost control of an autonomous domain presided over by the midwife. The male–female contest in the Indian context is overlaid by a colonial–indigenous conflict. Doubtless, various groups conjoined in their condemnation and denigration of the *dai*. Neither the colonial state nor Indian men had been particularly interested in the process of birthing, but the activities of women missionaries and wives of British officials brought the issue into the public arena. The indigenous *dai* as the traditional birth attendant became enmeshed in 'modernising' discourses, held responsible for high infant and maternal mortality rates. In the process, her role in childbirth was fundamentally reconstrued. The *dais* were primarily low-caste women with a ritual role in

[56] Nurgez J. Sethna, 'Nutritional Problems Among Infants of Low Income Group Families', *AIIH*, 12, 23, 1961.
[57] Forbes, 'Managing Midwifery'. For the conflict between 'indigenous' and 'colonial' medicine see Roger Jeffery, *The Politics of Health in India*, Berkeley, 1987; D. Arnold (ed.), *Imperial Medicine and Indigenous Societies*, Delhi, 1989; D. Arnold, *Colonizing the Body: State Medicine and Epidemic Diseases in Nineteenth Century India*, Berkeley, 1993.

cleansing the polluting afterbirth. The elder women in the household supplemented the *dai*'s expertise with their own experiences during the actual process of birthing. In the literature of infamy that grew around the *dai* from the late nineteenth century, she was transformed into the sole denizen of the accouchement chamber, either as the repository of traditional knowledge or as the dirty hag whose obstinate adherence to unhygienic superstitious practices led to death and morbidity.

Increasingly, from the nineteenth century, the medical profession was pressing for increasing restriction of practice through licensing legislation. Such professionalisation was quickly granted to doctors, and more gradually to nurses. The first demand for licensing nurses came from Bombay in 1908 and was followed by the formation of the Trained Nurses Association of India. The Health Visitors League came much later in 1922 and the Midwives Union in 1925. However, unlike doctors and nurses, midwives were never subjected to mandatory licensing. There were demands for such legislation from various quarters:

Provincial health authorities are awakening to the fact that since the health and life of a large proportion of women and children in India lies in the hand of the indigenous dai and will continue to rest there for many years to come, it is necessary to adopt towards her a more defined and consistent policy. Persuasion and bribery have failed to bring the dai under control and if progress is to be made some measure of compulsion is desirable.[58]

Others like Natarajan called for immediate 'legislation restricting the practice of midwifery only to those who are trained and registered'.[59] Middle-class women's organisations began to take issue against the state's neglect of a matter of such vital 'national' importance.[60] Even if they felt that continued reliance on the inefficient *dai* endangered women's lives, their demands were raised within the 'nationalist' concern for reducing infant and maternal mortality.

Official and public condemnation converged on the *dai* and her 'primitive', 'dirty' and 'unhygienic' methods. The low-caste *dais* practised their hereditary occupation on the basis of accumulated knowledge of generations passed on from mother to daughter. Elder women of the household, the community or the village were often summoned to assist difficult deliveries. Experience gave *dais* a certain ease in handling normal deliveries. It was in the case of abnormal deliveries or emergencies that they were ill-equipped, both in terms of knowledge and in

[58] Jean M. Orkney, 'Legislation and the Indigenous Dai', *JAMWI*, 31, 1943.
[59] B. Natarajan in S. K. Nehru (ed.), *Our Cause: A symposium by Indian Women*, Allahabad, 1937, p. 68.
[60] Forbes, 'Managing Midwifery'.

terms of tools to deal with the situation. Almost 70 per cent of maternal deaths were due to haemorrhage, sepsis and antenatal diseases.[61] In the village it was customary for *dais* to use a sharp reed (with healing properties) to cut the umbilical cord. In urban slum conditions, they used the usual kitchen knife or a sickle, increasing the dangers of infection. In fact, tetanus became a major maternal killer due to the 'country midwives not regarding aseptic methods'.[62]

One solution to these problems could have been an expansion of health services. The reality was a woefully inadequate medical service with very limited access for the poor. In the case of women, the cause averred was their unwillingness to submit to male medical treatment especially in gynaecological matters.[63] The Dufferin Fund's *zenana* hospitals were meant to address this difficulty by providing female medical personnel in secluded environments, but they deliberately excluded poor women, who were considered not 'truly' in *purdah* since they were willing 'to appear before men'. Factory women, of course, 'worked alongside men' and could hardly qualify as 'true' *purdah* women. What then was to be the solution for women who did not follow *purdah* in the 'true' sense as understood by colonial officials but were nevertheless chary of male doctors? Colonial officials themselves explained the lack of medical care received by factory women in terms of their unwillingness to consult male doctors to rebut the charge that medical facilities were not available. Government officers, while appreciating the medical services organised in jute mills, admitted that these were not extended to women: 'Indian women are not keen on male medical attendants, especially at childbirth'.[64] Similar arguments were offered to explain why poorer women did not attend the few district and *sadar* hospitals provided by the government.[65] However, such cultural constraints may not have been the only reason why poor women eschewed hospitals and health clinics. The hospitals maintained open wards and there were no provisions for nursing or protection of women patients.[66] And these were in any case very thin on the ground.

In Bengal, in 1930, there were 217 hospitals with 6,189 beds and 1,214 dispensaries staffed by 460 medical officers and 1,819 sub-

[61] In 1924, the Calcutta Corporation midwives (trained) reported only 2 deaths per 1,000 births, while the Calcutta Corporation Health Officer's report reported a rate of 18 per 1,000, and the Bengal Enquiry reported 12.2 per 1,000. *Health Bulletin No. 15*, 1928.
[62] *Modern Review*, January–June 1931, p. 187.
[63] Mukhta Sen, 'Child Welfare Work', *JAMWI*, 32, 1944; Orkney, 'The Health of Indian Women and Children', p. 6.
[64] D. B. Meek, WBSA, Comm. Comm., December 1924, A40–54.
[65] G. M. Broughton, *Labour in Indian Industries*, London, 1924, p. 125; Matheson, *Indian Industries*, p. 155.
[66] Curjel Report, Main Report, pp. 17–18.

assistant surgeons. The hospitals were usually supported by district or union boards.[67] Though the *sadar* hospitals in headquarters of districts had, as a rule, women's hospitals attached to them, maternity or gynaecological cases were rare. As often as not, the women's hospital was simply a female ward for ordinary medical and surgical cases. Very little nursing was available or even attempted. Only forty-three nurses and fifty-six midwives were trained annually.[68] And the Government was even less generous, it was felt, in industrial areas. The two baby shows held there received no Government support.[69] Maternity services were almost non-existent.[70] The mills themselves provided some rudimentary medical services. In 1930, there were only 5,778 medical men registered in Bengal of whom about 2,046 were employed in mills, tea gardens, collieries, factories. But only very rarely did these industrial schemes include special facilities for women.[71]

The annual number of births in British India in 1941 was approximately 10 million and there were 10,856 registered midwives, 622 assistant midwives and 522 registered *dais*.[72] The paucity of medical personnel made it impossible to do completely without the indigenous (unregistered) *dais*. At best some of them could be 'trained' in modern methods. Several hundreds attended classes and took certificates in the Barrackpore district, where lay the largest concentration of jute mills. Some mills, like Titagarh, employed their own trained *dais*. '[They were] persuaded to live in different parts of the Mill area so as to bring all bustees within the field of service. Of the present dhais one lives in the lines and the other three live in one bustee thus leaving a large area unsupplied.'[73] The Bengal Government helped by giving special grants to run these classes.[74] But it was a drop in the ocean.

The *dai* training schemes proliferated. There were voluntary agencies and most welfare centres had some sort of scheme to secure the services of 'properly trained midwives' who would persuade 'women to abandon the practice of calling in the usual ignorant low caste dai or midwife'.[75]

[67] J. B. Grant, *The Health of India*, Oxford Pamphlets of Indian Affairs, No. 12, Bombay, 1943. p. 16.
[68] Major-General G. Tate, IMS, Surgeon General with the Government of Bengal, *RCLI*, V, 2.
[69] Certifying Surgeon, *RCLI*, V, 1, p. 204.
[70] In 1921 a Medical Mission from England threatened to derecognise Indian medical degrees because of insufficient training in gynaecology and obstetrics. See Kanji Dwarkadas, *45 Years with Indian Labour*, London, 1962.
[71] D. B. Meek, WBSA, Comm. Comm., December 1924, A40–54.
[72] Certifying Surgeon, *RCLI*, V, 1, p. 345.
[73] DUL, TDP, Dr Jean Orkney, 'Report on the Titagarh Health Centre', May 1932.
[74] *RCLI*, V, 1, p. 204.
[75] M. Brooks, The Angus Jute Mill Company Limited, *RCLI*, V, 1, p. 394.

The most successful scheme was undertaken by the Kankinara clinic.[76] The Kulti Iron Works had a training scheme and gave *dais* Rs. 2 for every case reported. The Titagarh Welfare Centre held classes every Friday afternoon on the use of modern and scientific methods of delivery of children. The management insisted, 'it was a fight against prejudice and superstition', and that it was only after three years of perseverance, that the 'prejudice has been overcome' and 'dais attend willingly and appreciate the advantages gained by hygienic methods over the old dirty and primitive arrangements which have ... caused deaths of many children'.[77] Angus formed a maternity benefit fund in 1921–23 and it failed partly because

the payment of money ... was of less benefit to the women than obtaining ... (their) submission to proper medical supervision ... (and) persuading women to abandon the practice of calling in the usual ignorant low caste dai or midwife whose insanitary administration often caused the death of both mother and child.[78]

In the absence of supervision and facilities, most 'trained' midwives lapsed into their old methods very quickly.[79] Given the conditions of confinement, it is doubtful whether *dai*-training would have been effective without hospital back-up. Barnes's description of six expecting mothers in a single room with five *chullahs* became well known.[80] Curjel also reported that the usual practice of women was to collect the dirty jute waste for their confinement. Usually they erected an enclosure just outside their ordinary living room by means of bamboo poles and jute sacking used as *purdahs*.[81] Textbook procedures made little sense in these conditions. Two women, who were involved in a child welfare centre in a Chetla slum, found that poor women did in fact prefer hospital confinement, not only because it was free, but because it relieved them, for a few days, of domestic responsibility. The lack of space at home made confinement at home both difficult and undesirable.[82]

[76] They held special classes for local *dais* and paid them 4 annas. After an initial hesitation, the *dais* responded. WBSA, Comm. Comm., December 1924, A40–54.

[77] Ibid.   [78] M. Brooks, *RCLI*, V, 1, p. 394.

[79] The Director of Public Health offered a still easier solution, 'To bear a child is a normal physiological function ... (our) object should not be to push every pregnant woman into a hospital or maternity home' but 'train our womanhood in such a way that they would be able to perform this normal physiological function with as little assistance as possible'. Director of Public Health, Bengal, Lt. Col. A. C. Chatterjee, on the occasion of opening the Burdwan Municipal Maternity and Child Welfare Clinic, reported in *Amrita Bazar Patrika*, 21 July 1939.

[80] *Chullahs* are open fires, usually consisting of coal heaped in mud buckets. Barnes, 'Final Report of the Lady Doctor'.

[81] Curjel Report, Appendix B, Sl, No. 15.

[82] Sengupta and Bagchi, 'Dietary Habits of Bengali Pregnant and Lactating Women'.

Welfare centres and the Maternity Benefit Act

The jute mill owners' enthusiasm for *dai* training, welfare centres, baby shows and health exhibitions were dictated by several expediencies. Maternity benefit legislation had been in the air since 1919. Joshi's Bill in 1924 had given substance to the threat. Bombay already had an Act. IJMA realised that the Government of Bengal would soon bow before concerted pressure. They also realised that benefit payment, when it came, would be squarely the individual employer's responsibility. In the meantime, a system of voluntary benefits in cash and kind would serve to delay more stringent legislation.

In health and maternity schemes, voluntary agencies – Red Cross Society, Women's Friendly Society and Infant Welfare Society – helped with money and personnel. They established a number of their own welfare centres. The Bengal Social Service League, founded on 26 January 1915, included maternity and child welfare in its programme. The Dufferin Fund had, of course, been working for many years. Its activities were augmented by another official initiative. Lady Chelmsford founded the All-India League for Maternity and Child Welfare in 1920.

The main focus of these centres was the new 'mothercraft'. Motherhood was to be both 'natural', rooted in the physiology and psychology of women, and at the same time a 'craft' that had to be learnt. The declared objective of child welfare centres was the reduction of mortality among infants but the means of achieving this were not uniform. Some emphasised 'education', instructing mothers in the care of their own health and that of their children, while others continued to undertake free distribution of milk and the organisation of 'baby shows'.[83] Gradually the former gained more importance.[84] In her report on the Titagarh Welfare Centre, Dr Orkney spelled out the main task of welfare centres:

stimulating ... greater interest in the special problems connected with women's health under industrial conditions ... and ... to devote more time through education and propaganda in health and *mothercraft*, those simple rules whose practice brings physical perfection and whose neglect leads to lifelong suffering and chronic ill-health.[85] (emphasis added)

Maternity facilities often became a means of extending the already existing invasive and intrusive systems of inspection in the *lines*. Mill owners used the ideology of motherhood to justify women's increasing marginalisation in factory employment. Also, Company-employed lady

[83] Natarajan in Nehru (ed.), *Our Cause*, p. 68.   [84] Sen, 'Child Welfare Work'.
[85] Orkney, 'Report on the Titagarh Health Centre'.

doctors, midwives and health visitors proved useful in gathering information. In the 1920s and 1930s, as managers grew more apprehensive of workers' protests, they encouraged welfare centres and, especially, 'home visiting'. The payment of maternity benefits involved elaborate supervision: the mill doctors had to issue certificates to pregnant women, clerks had to check the actual facts of birth and the *sardars* had to ensure that women did not work elsewhere. Thus, even as 'mill doctors' were inducted to deal with the Workmen's Compensation Act, the impending threat of a Maternity Benefit Act made welfare centres highly desirable.

Many arguments were advanced to increase 'home-visiting'. It was felt that the husband and the mother-in-law had to be especially wooed because they played crucial roles in family decision-making and were in any case more suspicious of the new-fangled notions advocated by the centres.[86] It was an additional service that reached women who were too busy or otherwise constrained from attending clinics and centres.[87] The importance of home-visiting can be gauged from Table 4.2.

Table 4.2. *Attendance at the Titagarh Health Clinic, 1923–8*

	(1) 1923 (Apr. –Nov.)	(2) 1924	(3) 1928
Total attendance	576	13,112	10,177
Daily average attendance		30	40
New patients		973	2,048
Midwifery case calls		43	6
Home-visiting for newborn babies		815	505
Total number of women employed was 1,000.[88]			

Sources:
(1) WBSA, Comm. Comm., December 1924, A40–54, 1F4. (Figures provided include mothers and babies.)
(2) Capital, 18 June 1925.
(3) Royal Commission of Labour in India, V, 1, p. 283.

Despite the stated preference for education and propaganda, one of the most typical expressions of maternity concerns were baby shows which subjected motherhood to public recognition and judgement. The idea was almost certainly borrowed from British practice. But it never achieved the same popularity in India, and baby shows never became part of a state policy. But they were not limited to voluntary efforts. The

[86] Sen, 'Child Welfare Work'.   [87] Natarajan in Nehru (ed.), *Our Cause*, p. 70.
[88] Matheson, *Indian Industries*, Appendix B.

local governments made small financial and administrative contributions.

In fact, this was convenient. Educating a few mothers in a few welfare centres and baby clinics was easier and cheaper than expanding social and health services and permitted at the same time a direct supervision of working-class homes. For almost two decades, these were accepted as a desirable alternative to compulsory maternity benefit. The same attitude was seen in respect of other welfare measures. The 'rural' links of jute mill labour were a useful solution to many problems: maternity benefit was not necessary because women went home to the village for their confinement; sickness insurance would be impossible to administer because workers usually returned to their village for succour; unemployment insurance was spurious because workers 'tied up their bundles' and went home if they lost their job. This was seen as an advantage of Indian labour and if it 'does militate against efficiency . . . social benefits offset this disadvantage'.[89] In fact, of course, for mill owners therein lay the 'efficiency' of Indian labour: welfare measures like maternity benefit, sickness insurance and unemployment insurance would militate against their efforts to maintain the flexible character of the workforce. Yet the mill owners could not entirely escape some of the welfare issues that captured public attention in the period, especially sickness insurance and maternity benefit. Their response was to adapt some of these to their own particular needs. They used the *dai*-training and welfare centres to create networks of surveillance. The ideology of motherhood and child welfare provided a justification for the dismissal of women and children in large numbers when the industry entered a period of crisis.

In the post-war period, the issue of maternal and infant mortality, the move towards redefinition of the social meaning of motherhood, the morality of women's work and the importance of teaching women mothercraft were brought together in the debate over maternity benefit which followed from the Washington Convention. The ILO accepted the official view that India was not ready for legislation but asked Government to investigate the situation.

In India, maternity leave had already been mooted in 1910.[90] The Washington Convention introduced a new dimension to the issue – the question of compensation. The Convention stated explicitly that compulsory maternity leave without adequate compensatory payment was unacceptable. In India, neither the state nor the employer was willing to accept the burden of compensation. Official interest was not particularly

[89] R. N. Gilchrist, *Labour and Land*, WBSA, Comm. Comm., July 1932, B322.
[90] IOL, L/P & J/5/83, Civil Surgeon, Belgaum to Secretary to the Government of Bombay, 1910, Judicial Department Proceedings, 1911.

engaged. When Dr Dagmar Curjel first applied to be seconded from the Women's Medical Service of India in order to carry out 'an enquiry into causes of infant mortality in India' under the Indian Research Fund Association, the proposal was thrown out by the Minister for Education with the alleged comment, 'What does it matter if a woman has one child or two?' It was later in 1920 when the ILO required it, that Curjel was deputed, along with F. D. Barnes and G. M. Broughton, to investigate conditions of childbirth among industrial workers in Bengal, Bombay and the North-Western provinces.[91]

In the meanwhile, N. M. Joshi, the labour delegate to the Washington Conference, protested against India's exclusion from the maternity benefit convention. In 1924, he introduced a bill. Though unwilling to rock the boat by introducing a Maternity Benefit Act too soon, the Government of India was aware of the growing concern for child welfare:

There is a growing and important movement in India for the promotion of child welfare and the protection of women during the critical stages in the period of maternity. The government of India is in full sympathy with the humanitarian motives underlying the Draft Convention (on maternity benefit) adopted at Washington.[92]

Both the Government and the employers rejected Joshi's Bill in 1924. Jute mill owners were willing to grant leave and 'agreed on principle' with the Bill, but they regarded the payment provision as 'improperly burdening the industry'. If there was to be any 'benefit' at all, the IJMA held, the only effective instrument was health facilities and childcare instructions. The payment of cash in lieu of loss of wages would be, according to them, of no practical benefit to a pregnant mother or a newborn child. To prove their point they cited instances of schemes that had failed precisely because they had relied on payment of cash alone. In contrast, the 'growing success' of the Titagarh scheme was attributed to the substitution of 'benefits in kind for benefits in money' and the 'general classes for women and girls in which they are taught mother-craft and sewing'.[93] Similar schemes were run in various mills with varying degrees of success. The smaller and newer mills, unwilling to extend their investments, opted for the cheapest solution, 'a practical scheme', and pooled their resources to open 'baby clinics'.[94]

The Government of Bengal accepted, to some extent at least, the principle of voluntary maternity benefit in kind.[95] This was evident in

[91] M. I. Balfour and R. Young, *The Work of Medical Women in India*, Oxford and London, 1929, pp. 179–80.
[92] Secretary to the Board of Industries and Munitions, 11 May 1920, IOL, L/E/3/222.
[93] Government of Bengal, *IJMAR*, 1925.   [94] IJMA, *RCLI*, V, 2, pp. 160–1.
[95] Government of Bengal, *IJMAR*, 1925.

the scheme outlined by the Director of Public Health to IJMA. The scheme involved both women workers and wives of male workers, providing antenatal care, crêches, home-visiting, a health centre and a baby clinic. These would have to be supervised by trained, preferably European, women doctors, nurses and midwives.[96]

The scheme was expensive. The IJMA felt itself unable to interfere in what was 'the concern of individual mills'. But the tide of public opinion was against them.[97] Many mills started welfare centres incorporating some of the Director's suggestions. The most popular and well known was the Titagarh scheme. Thomas Duff had hoped for a joint scheme but other mills in the district were unwilling to commit themselves to this relatively elaborate scheme. Thomas Duff went ahead alone when the Lady Chelmsford League approached the Chairman of the IJMA.[98]

This scheme, begun in April 1923, was certainly the most elaborate.[99] Its chief objectives were to be the 'instruction of local *dais*' in midwifery and hygiene and by so doing 'help combat the great child mortality that is so prevalent in India'.[100] This centre, more than others, concentrated on 'mothercraft'. Biweekly pre-natal and post-natal classes and baby clinics were held 'where they [mothers] are taught to live hygienically' and 'instruction in hygiene, childcare and simple diatetics' were dispensed. The health visitor's function was actually of an 'educational and preventive nature and aims at reducing maternal and infant mortality'. Soon after the birth of the baby, mothers were advised about the care of the baby and their own health. When able to walk about again they were encouraged to bring the babies to the clinic and were taught 'mothercraft'.[101]

As in the case of crêches, the unpopularity of some welfare centres probably had something to do with the way they were run. 'The workers

---

[96] The Director of Public Health to the IJMA, 14 October 1925, *IJMAR*, 1925.
[97] Matheson, *Indian Industries*. Kamala Chatterjee in Nehru (ed.), *Our Cause*.
[98] Thomas Duff and Co. to IJMA, 23 November, 1925, *IJMAR*, 1925.
[99] Curjel Report, Main Report, p. 15; Maternity Benefit Schemes, *Bulletin of Indian Industries and Labour*, 32, August 1925; *RCLI*, V, 1, p. 45; Chief Inspector of Factories, 22 September 1924, WBSA, Comm. Comm., December, 1924, A40–54.
[100] Thomas Duff and Co. to IJMA, 23 November 1925, *IJMAR*, 1925.
[101] Miss E. Oliver, a trained Anglo-Indian Health Visitor with certificates from training courses at both Delhi and Calcutta was deputed from the Lady Chelmsford League. Pictures and pamphlets on infant welfare and maternity subjects with texts in Hindi, Urdu and English were put up. Careful nursing and proper treatment were provided. Mothers were put on a diet to make the milk stronger and in occasional cases given glaxo and virol free of charge. Women had to be convinced to come to the clinic at the first sign of any irregularity rather than after every treatment known in the *bazaar* had failed. House-visiting was aimed at encouraging hygienic arrangements for the delivery. Babies were weighed, sewing and knitting taught to mothers. Chief Inspector of Factories, WBSA, Comm. Comm., December, 1924, A40–54.

in charge' were 'mostly not properly qualified', they were 'badly housed and poorly equipped' and there was no 'responsible officer in charge of welfare work'. The lack of women inspectors and welfare officers was also keenly felt.[102]

By the time the Royal Commission came to Calcutta, the Titagarh scheme was certainly not the only scheme, though it remained the most elaborate and was held up as the model. One was opened at Kankinara along the same lines in 1926 with a qualified European woman in charge. After an initial hesitation, the women workers found it useful.[103] In the Bhatpara Municipality, a regular Health Welfare Exhibition was financed by the jute mills and the Public Health Department. It began in a small way in 1929, and was repeated on a larger scale in 1930. A special day was reserved for women to enable women in *purdah* to attend. The programme included, among other things, 'mothercraft' and child welfare.[104]

In the 1930s, most jute mills had some sort of a scheme in operation. By the early 1940s there were forty Labour Welfare Centres under the supervision of the Labour Commissioner.[105] Notably all the schemes were restricted to baby clinics, health visitors, lady welfare officers, or at best, as in case of Kinnison, a woman doctor.

The underlying principle of benefit in kind rather than in cash remained. Kelvin Jute Mill actually started giving cash benefits but discontinued their scheme because they could not ensure that women did not take up jobs elsewhere in the benefit period.[106] Angus introduced a maternity benefit fund with provision for leave allowance in 1921 and received only two claims in two years. Yet when they acquired a woman doctor and trained midwife and reintroduced the scheme in

[102] *Plans for a Better Bengal*, Directorate of Public Instruction, Bengal, Calcutta, 1944.

[103] It was a 'well-built and cheery clinic' standing just outside the *lines*. Maternity leave and benefit payment were available for women working a year in the mill and promising to attend the clinic. The clinic instructed mothers in the use of nappies, sewing and other basic principles in the care of infants. Interview, Shanti Pasricha, Calcutta, January 1989.

[104] It opened for three days and was attended by 5,000 persons. There were other health exhibitions all over the province. Along with epidemic prevention, a magic lantern or cinema show on the 'care of the growing child' was usual. These supposedly stimulated workers' interest in health and sanitation. Other items related to dietary and vitaminology, leprosy, health charts and baby shows with prizes. *FA*, 1930.

[105] Two paper mills and some cotton mills had similar programmes. Among the jute mills, Kinnison, Howrah, Kamarhatty and Clive expanded their maternity services. CSAS, BP, Box XI, Letter to E. C. Benthall, 15 July 1937. Birla Brothers opened a baby clinic. *FA*, 1930 and 1931.

[106] One case appears to have discouraged them. A woman having received the benefit, was followed by two sisters. The sisters 'as motherhood approached came from outside and took her place in the mill and claimed the benefit'. Secretary to the Government of Bengal, WBSA, Comm. Comm., July 1925, A32–68.

Table 4.3. *Number of women workers receiving maternity benefit in four jute mills in 1934*

	Mill Number			
	1	2	3	4
% of benefit to wages covered	0. 83	0. 88	0. 44	0. 43
Amount of benefit per woman in Rs.	0. 97	1.06	0. 49	0. 52
Total amount paid as benefit in Rs.	490	371	104	136
Number of women employed	506	349	211	260
Scheme started on	23.11.22	23.11.22	6.9.29	1.1.25

Source: Appendix, IJMAR, 1935.

1929, with the payment of wages being conditional on attendance at the maternity clinic, they had eighteen claims in fourteen days. Similar cash benefit schemes failed in Baranagore Mill for no discernible reason. The success of the Titagarh scheme was thus more emphatically attributed to the fact that they 'substituted benefits in kind for benefits in money'.[107]

IJMA held up their voluntary maternity scheme in lieu of sickness insurance. By this time most jute mills had voluntary maternity benefit, paying about Rs. 2.13–2.25 per week for four to five weeks on a non-contributory basis. A closer look at the figures shows how exaggerated were IJMA's claims to the Government that the average mill with 175 women paid out Rs. 292 per annum (average Rs. 1.7 per woman per annum) in maternity allowances (see Table 4.3).

Sickness insurance was closely tied with public health and so became a bone of contention between IJMA and Government. IJMA felt that the maternity schemes, its contributions to the Indian School of Tropical Medicine, the All-India Institute of Hygiene and Public Health, and to the Health Welfare School, in addition to its own dispensaries were quite sufficient. In fact most mills had medical dispensaries employing doctors mainly for first aid and minor treatment. In many cases there was only one doctor, sometimes not even qualified, for a whole mill. It was impossible even for the more well-meaning doctors to cope with the problem of medical care with no facilities.[108] Angus alone was extremely well-staffed: for a workforce of 6,180, they had eight doctors, seven male and one female. It was customary there for a doctor to visit the workers at their homes if they were too ill to come to the dispensary. In most cases, however, the dispensaries provided no special facilities for women.[109]

[107] Government of Bengal, WBSA, Comm. Comm., December, 1925, A40–54.
[108] Curjel Report, Appendix B.
[109] *RCLI*, V, 2, pp. 150–1. Out of the 73 mills (from a total of 186 mills), 70 mills

Table 4.4. *Estimated cost of free health clinic for 2,725 workers*

	Male	Female	Total
No. of cases treated	4,236	716	4,952
Estimated no. of weeks' leave required	8,524	1,324	9,848
No. of workers employed	2,550	175	2,725
No. of weeks leave required per worker per annum	3.3	7.5	

Source: *IJMAR*, 1935.

The Government felt that since public health schemes in mill areas involved the efficiency of labour, the industry should contribute to the expenses. When a hospital for infectious diseases and accidents was proposed for the riparian mills, the Government refused to foot the entire bill for a scheme that would mainly benefit the industrial population. The jute mills of the area pleaded that it was a heavy burden (Rs. 41,000) to maintain their own dispensaries and their donations to various welfare institutions.[110] In fact, none of the mills was willing to make up the balance when the Magistrate of the 24 Parganas offered land and Rs. 8,000 for a new hospital in Bhatpara Municipality.[111]

The idea of a comprehensive scheme of sickness insurance for industrial labour was mooted in the wake of the ILO Conference 1927. The Government of India was quite clear that the 'introduction in India of any comprehensive scheme of sickness insurance on the lines of the Convention is not practical' but was willing to consider something less ambitious if the mills could be made to bear the lion's share of the expenses.[112] Bengal Chamber of Commerce agreed that a sickness insurance scheme on the Western model was impossible and reiterated that, 'an expansion of general health work in the direction of a government free health service' in which 'the whole community would pay and the whole community would benefit', was the only fair solution. The Chamber, moreover, saw all that needed to be done in the facilities already offered: free dispensary treatment (and, stretching the point, free treatment in local hospitals to which mills subscribed), and 'allowances to the sick person's dependants' at the manager's discretion. In the jute industry at least, it was felt, there was no need for a sickness insurance scheme.[113]

On the basis of their experience in running free clinics, the IJMA

maintained their own dispensaries at least, and 18 mills contributed to local dispensaries and hospitals as well. WBSA, Comm. Comm., May 1927, A1–6.
[110] *IJMAR*, 1925.   [111] The Magistrate, 24 Parganas, *IJMAR*, 1930.
[112] Government of India to Government of Bengal, *Annual Report of the Bengal Chamber of Commerce*, 1929, II.
[113] Bengal Chamber of Commerce to Government of Bengal, ibid.

estimated the cost of treatment of 2,725 workers as indicated in Table 4.4. IJMA estimated that a comprehensive sickness insurance scheme would cost Rs. 29,000, while the Government could maintain a free dispensary at the cost of Rs. 3,435.[114] Thus, the IJMA was unwilling to go into any sickness insurance scheme without official labour bureaux under a social services department. Otherwise, the industry would be 'blindly saddle[d] ... with ... [a] scheme which could only prove one of trial and error mainly at the expense of the general body of employers'.[115] Only one mill (not named) operated a scheme of sickness insurance for its permanent employees, 50 per cent of whom were housed in mill *lines*, the rest living within seven to eight miles of the precincts of the mill. It had been operating for three years and the cost amounted to Rs. 3,000 per annum.[116]

The Washington Convention had been followed by a spurt of investigative activity. The two major reports of Dr Dagmar Curjel in Bengal and Dr Francis Barnes in Bombay emphasised the need for maternity benefit legislation.[117] The Royal Commission recommended, among other things, an extension of the welfare work already under way in the mills.[118] The only response was the appointment, by the IJMA, of Dr Margaret Balfour with assistants from the Bengal Training School for Health Visitors to undertake a survey. None of her recommendations (or those of the Royal Commission) was ever implemented. By the 1930s it had become fairly clear that there was really no alternative to maternity benefit legislation (compulsory leave and cash allowance as in the Bombay and Central Provinces Acts). The age of 'protective' legislation directed exclusively towards the conditions of employment of women and children, and without compensation, was over. A tacit understanding and acceptance of the handicap of working-class mothers prompted the first effort formally to give an economic basis to motherhood, a major break away from a purely educative approach to poor mothers.

By far the most important stumbling block to a Maternity Benefit Act was felt to be the 'non-domestic' character of jute mill labour. Ironically,

---

[114] The average expenditure on women was disproportionately large because dependants were included. At a possible rate of benefit of Rs. 3/4 for men and Rs. 2/4 for women and allowing for twenty-six maternity allowances, the cost to the mill of the sickness insurance and the maternity benefit (at the rate of Rs. 2/4 per week for five weeks) would be Rs. 29,293. *IJMAR*, 1935.
[115] *IJMAR*, 1936.   [116] *IJMAR*, 1935.
[117] ILO, *Official Bulletin No. IV*, November 1921, pp. 13–15.
[118] Health centres and clinics were asked to employ women doctors and health visitors with recognised qualifications. Larger mill areas needed more than one centre with trained midwives and compulsory crèches. Local authorities were requested to introduce child welfare centres. *IJMAR*, 1931.

though Curjel was quite clear that there was an urgent necessity for some kind of a benefit scheme, it was she who 'discovered' and passed on to official and academic wisdom the 'non-domestic' character of jute mill women. Her discovery might have been influenced in some measure by the fact that she was investigating the possibilities of extending the ILO Maternity Benefit Convention to India. It is perhaps not surprising that a great deal of her evidence, culled from the management, clearly indicated the unsuitability of maternity benefit in cash. An employers' association laid the failure of maternity benefit schemes at the door of women workers themselves: 'The peculiar type of female labour in the jute mills ... does not conduce to the creation of schemes which presuppose normal family life.'[119] In fact, considering the 'type of labour' where 'normal family life was notoriously absent', nothing very much more than jute mills had already done in the direction of maternity benefits was felt to be possible. The old morality arguments appeared in many new forms. 'In civilised countries child motherhood is considered very undesirable and is discouraged by the law ... it is possible that this Bill will encourage early child-bearing ... [and] at best ... indiscriminate procreation'.[120] It was also pointed out that no distinction was made between married and unmarried women.[121] In this respect, India followed the ILO Convention. When questioned, Mrs Cottle and Miss Headwards of India Red Cross Society affirmed that women lived under the protection of men who were not their husbands, 'it is a condition that exists', but they rejected any suggestion that such women should be excluded from a Maternity Benefit Act: 'all women should receive maternity benefit'.[122]

Employers made much of the fact that women went home to their village for confinement. Managers argued that it was safer and more healthy for women to have their confinement in their village home where they had more access to nutritive food (more cereals and therefore more calories, if not proteins and vitamins), but this practice made the administration of a maternity benefit scheme more difficult. The proportion of women going home for confinement was calculated at 40–50 per cent.[123] It was argued that the usual customs and traditional rituals surrounding childbirth and the 'pollution' period prescribed for newly

[119] The Commissioner of Madras was not convinced that 'special arrangements should be directed to an insignificant fraction of the population'. IOL L/E/3/222. Also see Government of Bengal, RCLI, V, 1, p. 45; Bengal Mahajan Sabha, WBSA, Comm. Comm., December, 1924, A40–54.
[120] Narayanganj Chamber of Commerce, ibid.   [121] Ibid.
[122] Mrs Cottle and Miss Headwards, RCLI, V, 2, pp. 1–8.
[123] Certifying Surgeon and K. C. Roychoudhury, RCLI, V, 1, pp. 207 and 126. Dr Batra, RCLI, V, 2, p. 31.

delivered mothers would be violated by a statutory definition of the length of permitted absence: 'The chamber is of the opinion that labour would regard maternity benefit schemes in the light of interference.'[124] The interference with traditional practice was put at par with intervention in family privacy; maternity benefit schemes would be 'interfering in the private life of workers'.[125] This was of course a difficult argument to sustain in the face of the ongoing welfare activity with its emphasis on home visiting and instruction of mothers. But then home visitors were asked to use moral suasion and win over the trust and cooperation of mothers with 'tact', 'perseverance' and 'patience'.

None of these contentions supported Curjel's evidence. Some, but not many, women went home for their confinement. According to her, most women, however ill, did not return periodically to the village like the men. A number of them had to depend on the charity of neighbours in cases of extreme distress. The length of absence for confinement depended on the economic conditions of the household rather than on any superstitious or ritual beliefs.[126] Customs varied widely and there was no standard period of pollution. There was no ritual bar on pregnant women's work. Even some employers admitted that 'women ... continue to work in factories in an advanced state of pregnancy' as 'they continue to carry on their duties at the same state when engaged in other industrial occupations and being so accustomed, can make less interruption of their normal routine'.[127] In other areas of India, officials confirmed that there was no particular hard and fast ritual 'pollution' maintained by factory women.[128] Since the majority of women earned a bare living wage most of them had to rejoin work very soon after their confinement. It was only when given financial assistance by the father of the child or other relatives that women could take more time off, but in many cases such assistance was not available.[129] If at all possible, women preferred to take more time off work after their confinement than before, and many women continued to work till the last. Curjel shows that out of 338 children, 139 were born when the mother was actually working in the factory.[130]

[124] Narayanganj Chamber of Commerce, WBSA, Comm. Comm., December 1924, A40–54.
[125] S. G. Panandikar, *Industrial Labour in India*, Bombay, 1933, p. 248.
[126] The usual 'pollution' rituals were rare among the working classes. Interview, Dr Kamala Basu (formerly of Nuddea Mill), Naihati, 28 October 1989.
[127] Narayanganj Chamber of Commerce, WBSA, Comm. Comm., December 1924, A40–54.
[128] Government of Madras, 5 August, 1920, IOL L/E/3/222.
[129] Some women found assistance and support from women relatives. Mathialu was supported by her mother. *RCLI*, V, 2, p. 79.
[130] Curjel Report, Appendix G.

The first Maternity Benefit Bill was introduced in the Provincial Assembly in 1937. Employers, still very suspicious of legislation, insisted, 'that since all mills ... already pay maternity benefit ... there is no objection' but in the same breath demurred that individual mills with extant schemes should be exempt from the Act.[131] Other employers made trifling stipulations.[132] Unlike in 1924–25, in the mid-1930s there was a much larger body of opinion in favour of Maternity Benefit Act, including some employers' associations.[133] For the first time some Indian women's organisations also joined the fray. The Association of Medical Women in India (AMWI), Eastern Division, consulted by the Government, suggested many improvements to the Bill to safeguard the 'health of the woman and her unborn child during the critical last weeks of pregnancy' and for the first time recognised that given compensation for the loss of earnings, 'few women are likely to want to work in the mills during the last weeks of pregnancy'.[134] They were supported in this by the All India Women's Congress, Calcutta, and the Bengal Presidency Council of Women.

However, these women's organisations raised the old bogey of benefit in kind. According to them, at least some of the benefit should be in kind, though that should not exceed one-quarter of the total cash benefit payable. This would ensure that at least some of the benefit would be 'for the benefit of the mother and child and not be paid exclusively to other members of the family'.[135] Curjel had argued in an earlier period that cash usually found its way into the men's pockets, and benefit in cash did not fulfil the primary purpose of providing the few extras necessary for the expectant mother and the newborn child.[136] Shanti Pasricha, however, pointed out that women preferred cash benefit to compensate the loss of her earnings from the family kitty.

[131] IJMA, WBSA Comm. Comm., May 1939, A7–22.
[132] The 'amount of maternity benefit should be paid after the employee resumes work' or 'the maximum period of leave with benefit should be limited to 4 weeks (instead of 5)' and a maximum period of twelve weeks should be allowed but without allowance, said the Indian Chamber of Commerce. The Bengal National Chamber of Commerce opposed 'compulsory' benefit payment. Ibid.
[133] Marwari Chamber of Commerce and Muslim Chamber of Commerce agreed unreservedly. Others like Dr Pownes, Chief Certifying Surgeon, and the District Magistrate of Khulna considered the Act far too limited. Ibid. Four out of the eighteen Select Committee members dissented. All of them wanted six weeks' leave. One felt that 8 annas was too little; one wanted the Act to extend to 'nurses, teachers, clerks or scavengers' outside the ambit of organised industry. Bengal Legislative Assembly Debate, Bengal Maternity Benefit Bill (1937), *Report of the Select Committee*, 4 June 1938.
[134] Association of Medical Women in India, WBSA, Comm. Comm., June 1939, A7–21.
[135] Bengal Presidency Council of Women, ibid.
[136] Curjel Report, Main Report, pp. 13–14.

Otherwise there was less to go around for other family members like older children. Benefit in cash thus contributed to her mental peace and well-being without actually diminishing her share of the family resources. The payment of benefit in kind by excluding those dependent on her created other problems.[137]

Meanwhile IJMA had given up the battle for maternity benefit in kind but continued to hold up their voluntary schemes as an alternative to legislation.[138] Such schemes gave five weeks' benefit to women employed for at least six months along with medical supervision, medicines and clinical treatment free of charge.[139] Five weeks were inadequate and benefit paid after the birth did not benefit the expectant mother when she was in most need of special nourishment.[140] IJMA, though well aware that their system was by and large below the standard set by the Act, continued to insist that individual mills should be exempted.[141] They also cavilled at many minor details.[142] By then it was quite clear that nothing short of maternity benefit legislation on the lines of the Bombay and C.P. Acts would be acceptable. In 1929, the Bombay Government passed a bill for maternity benefit allowing eight weeks' leave with pay on the basis of an average wage or eight annas daily whichever was less, conditional upon nine months' unbroken service and the women not working anywhere else in that period. The Act did not come fully into operation till 1934, after an amendment was enacted. Bombay's example was followed by the Central Provinces in 1930, Madras in 1935, Delhi in 1937 and United Provinces in 1938. Bengal was one of the last to introduce the legislation (Act IV of 1939) which came into operation from 1940.

By the time the Maternity Benefit Act was finally passed, the proportion of women in the industry was declining steadily. The process was accelerated during the renewed efforts at 'rationalisation' in the 1950s – women's share in the jute workforce declined from 14

[137] Interview, Calcutta, March 1989.
[138] IJMA, February 1937, WBSA, Comm. Comm., May 1939, A7–22.
[139] The system was simple – the woman reported her condition to the departmental time-keeper, who then advised the assistant-in-charge. A form was completed and signed by the latter and countersigned by the manager. Her name was removed from the ordinary wage-book. After delivery, the form, presented weekly by the woman or a relative, recorded the payment. Report of birth was accepted from the *sardar* and in doubtful cases investigated by the mill doctor. The amount varied from Rs. 2/2 to Rs. 2/4 for four weeks and a fifth payment required separate sanction. The manager could extend the leave pay for another two weeks after which the leave could continue but the payment had to stop. Ibid.
[140] Dr H. C. Pownes, ibid.   [141] IJMA, ibid.
[142] They said that eight weeks was too long and that 8 annas per day was too high. IJMA wanted a fixed amount of payment per week (calculated per day, the payment came to Rs. 3 while jute mills were paying a maximum of Rs. 2/4). Ibid.

to 4 per cent.[143] Managers and trade union leaders shared the conviction that it was the Maternity Benefit Act and the compulsory crêche provisions which had led to this drastic reduction of female labour. The employers, in fact, had agreed to the legislation only when they were restricting production and it was easier to dispense with women workers if granting the concession proved too expensive.

[143] *IJMAR*, 1950 and 1960.

5 In temporary marriages: wives, widows and prostitutes

Any attempt to trace the sexual and marital history of Calcutta's jute workers is beset with problems. It is difficult to visualise these men and women as the subject of this history as they have left only the faintest whispers in the records. What we find is a clamour of other voices. The medical men feared the rampant spread of venereal diseases; the mill owners and their managers elaborated workers' irresponsible and subversive behaviour; and the government officials tried to mediate between various conflicting interests. Their moralistic temper was reinforced by nationalists, reformers, trade unionists, journalists and novelists. In these proliferating discourses, jute mill women became symbols of infamy and depravation. In the attempt to designate these women as 'prostitutes' who entered 'temporary' marriages, the lines between prostitution, concubinage and marriage were constantly blurred. The term 'temporary' marriage lumped together many kinds of relationships and was portrayed as an institution peculiar to Calcutta's working classes. Such elisions derived credibility from the kinds of information collected about the working class which obscured both the continuities in their marriage practices and the material circumstances in which they lived.

The purveyors of information were predominantly elite men. Some of them were sympathetic to the social and economic deprivation that, they believed, drove workers to sexually lax behaviour. They offer interesting insights into the sexual and marital behaviour of the working classes. But they must be read with enormous caution. They were writing at a time when women's chastity and sexual purity had become an obsessional preoccupation of the middle classes. From this ideological vantage, working-class men and women's readiness to dispense openly with such cherished ideals as sacramental marriage and monoandry appeared shocking. To less sympathetic observers, the poor were merely endemically immoral. Almost invariably they all agreed that disease, crime and prostitution were the scourge of the poorer quarters of the city. Along with 'tribals' and the 'low castes', the inhabitants of the city's tenements, who were, of course, often of such tribal or low-caste origins, were seen to be peculiarly deviant. And the women were especially so. Seen through the mists of this prolix discourse, clouded at least in part by the prurient fascination of elite men for the seemingly unbridled sexuality of plebeian women, poverty, manual work outside the home and sexual promiscuity appear intimately connected.

It would be a mistake, however, to assume that the elite discourses embodied one voice, similar concerns and common anxieties. The idealised opposition between the home and the public sphere in the nationalist discourse was defining a distance between the *bhadramahila* and the *magi*. The early nineteenth-century common term for widows and prostitutes, *rarh*, was increasingly substituted by the words *bidhaba* for widows and *beshya* for the prostitute. Any public activity – public performance, freedom of movement and participation in labour outside the home – pushed women from their accepted role of mother, daughter, sister and wife to that of the prostitute who was an outcast. The space outside the home was the space of the *beshya*.[1]

The earlier social reform debates on *suttee*, polygamy, widow remarriage and child marriage had, however, raised uncomfortable questions about the characterisation and control of women's sexuality. The high-caste middle-class reformers selectively addressed issues relating to Hindu women. The legal and institutional innovations of the colonial state empowered these elite men to speak on behalf of the 'Hindus' in the widest definition. As a result, the low-caste peasants and artisans, who made up the community of poor in the city, were co-opted as participants in upholding the putative Hindu ideal of womanhood. Yet it was clear from the beginning that the poor did not practise *suttee*, in many cases allowed widow remarriage, adult marriages, and even divorce and remarriage. One *bhadralok* response to these protean practices was to define marriage more rigidly in accord with high-caste norms and to attempt the containment of women's sexuality within it.

The gradual diffusion of *purdah*, child marriage and the ban on widow remarriage directed social change towards greater conformity with brahmanical values. Colonial legislation aided these processes.[2] Both legal and ritual brahmanisation of marriage sought to divest lower caste women of their customary rights. In the brahmanical view, marriage was

[1] R. Chatterjee, 'The Queens' Daughters: Prostitutes as an Outcast Group in Colonial India', Report, Chr. Michelsen Institute, 1992; Samita Sen, 'Honour and Resistance: Gender, Community and Class in Bengal, 1920–40', in S. Bandopaddhyay et al. (eds.), *Bengal: Communities, Development and State*, New Delhi, 1984.
[2] Lucy Carroll, 'Law, Custom and Statutory Social Reform: The Hindu Widows' Remarriage Act of 1856', in J. Krishnamurty (ed.), *Women in Colonial India: Essays on Survival, Work and the State*, Delhi, 1989.

a sacrament and therefore irrevocable. The marital arrangements that violated the principle of a life-long sacrament, that allowed divorce and remarriage, and did not prescribe strict monogamy for women began to be considered illegitimate and presumed 'deviant'.

The issue about the control of women's sexuality within prescribed norms of marriage was also tied up with an anxiety about the 'family'. Among the middle classes, migration, urbanisation and the changing pattern of conjugal relations had riven the idealised 'joint family' with tensions. And yet, nationalist sentiments hankered for the harmonious family that would be both a bulwark against the intrusive colonial state and the unit of a regenerated nation.[3] The promotion of marriage as the middle classes understood it and the placing of the husband and father at the undisputed head of the family were important nationalist enterprises. Colonial laws complied. The repeated efforts to reconstrue a 'Hindu' law, assumed to be already fully formed and 'out there', resulted in a new rigidity of gender hierarchies. The authority of the paterfamilias was raised, theoretically at least, to its desired unassailability.[4]

On all these counts the urban poor afforded a potent challenge. Working men and women refused to conform to the ideal family. Their sexual trangressions – prostitution, concubinage, extra-marital sexual relations, divorce, desertion, adultery and polygamy – warred with the expected image. It is possible, however, that these did not actually 'trangress' the specific moral code to which workers considered themselves subject. In this moral code, stable and monogamous sexual relationships, even when they fell outside the legal definition of marriage, were vastly removed from sexual commerce. Thus, the 'kept' mistress may have felt deeply outraged at being equated with a prostitute under the common label of 'temporary wife'. Equally, not all working men and women conformed to the norms current in their communities. Some transgressed, manipulated and on occasion subverted rules of moral behaviour. Women, who found themselves at the less equal end of marriages, did use the lack of legality imputed to their 'temporary' marriages to break free of them. And finding themselves subject to sexual and physical abuse in the *basti*, the street and the workplace, they might have bartered sexual favours for access to employment, housing or credit. Neither heroic suffering nor defiant deviancy alone can explain their lives.

[3] Uma Chakravarti, 'Social Pariahs and Domestic Drudges: Widowhood among Nineteenth Century Poona Brahmins', *Social Scientist*, 21–9–11, 1993; M. Borthwick, *The Changing Role of Women in Bengal, 1894–1905*, Princeton, 1984.

[4] M. R. Anderson, 'Work Construed: Ideological Origins of Labour Law in British India to 1918', in P. Robb (ed.), *Dalit Movements and the Meaning of Labour in India*, Delhi, 1993.

The concerned officials, capitalists, middle-class professionals and politicians felt impelled to name the problem and trace its causes: predominantly male migration, rapid urbanisation, industrialisation, and above all the breakdown of patterns of gender segregation must have destroyed stable and harmonious family structures. The 'natural' integrity of the 'family' having been thus undermined, poor men and women were lured into a damaging and dangerous promiscuity. The various elite discourses converged in their condemnation of the 'non-family' and, therefore, immoral character of the jute workers.

Widows – remarriage, migration and work

In the early years of the jute industry when labour was mainly of local origin, a large proportion of women working in the mills appear to have been widows. In 1875, a Magistrate said of Budge-Budge Jute Mills that the 'men and women are mostly single' while the children came from adjoining agricultural villages. Significantly, 'none of the women employed have children'. Mr Wells, the Magistrate of 24 Parganas, testified that the women working in Gourepur Jute Mills were mostly 'widows' or 'single'.[5] The oral evidence collected by the Indian Factory Labour Commission of 1891 corroborated this. All the women interviewed were widows. Rajoni, a widow, came from Nadia and worked for about twenty years in Beliaghata Jute Mill. Doorga, from Bankura, was 40 years old, had worked for fifteen years at Bally Jute Mill, lived with an 'adopted husband' and had never returned home. She informed the Commission, 'All the Bengali women who work here are widows.' Digambari Bairagi, a widow working in a cotton mill at Hooghly, also lived with an 'adopted husband' and she too insisted that 'all women working here are widows'. Jaggo Kaibarta became a widow when she was 9 years old and came to work in the mill. Sukni worked in Baranagore Jute Mill while her husband was in the village. Taroni Bagdi was a widow from Midnapur working in Baranagore Branch Jute Mill with her mother. She began to work when she was widowed at the age of 12 years and she said to the Commission, 'Bengali women never come to work in the mills unless they are widows in bad circumstances.'[6]

Taroni's comment is revealing. Jute mill work was not considered suitable for women. It was usually widows who found themselves forced to take up this demeaning occupation. What made widows so economically vulnerable? There was a mistaken assumption in the discussions around the Widow Remarriage Act that remarriage was generally

[5] WBSA, General Miscellaneous, September 1875, A6–27.   [6] IFC, pp. 86–8.

prohibited. Were Doorga and Digambari rare exceptions, able to conduct their illicit relationships only in the lax environment of the mill towns? It seems unlikely. Among the intermediate and low castes in Bengal and Bihar, widows were allowed to remarry. All the four sub-castes of the Ahirs accepted it. They were the largest cultivating and pastoral caste in Saran, Patna and Monghyr, from where came much of the jute mill labour. Many Hindu castes in Bihar, with the exception of Brahmins, Babhans, Kayasths and Rajputs allowed widow remarriage.[7] It was also quite common in Orissa, except among the Brahmins, Kurrans and Kandaets.[8] It is probable then that a widow entering into a second marriage would not be regarded as a deviant. However, while a great majority of castes in Bengal Presidency may have permitted widow remarriage, it is difficult to ascertain the extent to which such permission was actually availed. Indeed, in Bengal proper, though some widowed women remarried, a high proportion remained widows: they constituted almost a quarter of the total female population.[9]

The Hindu Widow Remarriage Act did not lead to any great increase in the incidence of high-caste widows remarrying. Rather, widows of various intermediate castes who could remarry and retain their interest in their former husband's property, were by this Act divested of that right.[10] This legal disability reinforced social processes already in motion towards increasing prohibition of widow remarriage. The prohibition or acceptance of widow remarriage was, many scholars have argued, related to caste and status. What is less recognised is its relation to general social and economic forces in Bengal. From the late nineteenth century, many intermediate castes were adopting new restrictions on widow remarriage. This can be related to the overall devaluation of labour, in particular that of women, which was also leading to the gradual transition from brideprice to dowry.[11] The brideprice was of no benefit to the bride: it was paid to her father in compensation for the loss of her labour. A daughter's work on the family farm and in a wide range of 'domestic' tasks like childcare, cooking and food processing was crucial in the procurement of subsistence. The conjugal family had an incentive to retain the labour of a woman for whom they had paid a brideprice. Many intermediate peasant and trading castes thus preferred to marry the widow to a younger brother in the family. This was not only

[7] *BODG*, Monghyr, 1926, p. 60; *BODG*, Patna, 1924, p. 46; *BODG*, Saran, 1930, p. 118.
[8] In 1921, widows constituted 18 per cent of the total female population. *BODG*, Puri, 1929, p. 71.
[9] There were 2,128 widows in every 10,000 women. *Report on the Census of the Town and Suburbs of Calcutta*, 1881, Vol. II, p. 50.
[10] Carroll, 'Law, Custom and Statutory Social Reform'.   [11] See chapter 2 above.

justified by the brideprice they had already paid, but also meant saving another expense for the second brother. The move towards dowry which reflected the devaluation of women's work made widow remarriage more difficult. If bride-takers stood to gain from the payment of dowry for virgin brides, then marrying a widow might seem a financial loss. The natal family certainly would not pay dowry twice.[12]

As widows became unmarriageable, their labour and status were further devalued. The conjugal or natal family could then retain their labour at a lower cost. And so they did. In the Dayabhaga school pertaining in Bengal, widows had the right to inherit a share in the ancestral property of their husbands by law; by custom they had, anyway, a right to maintenance. In practice both were often denied. Even when husbands willed their property to their wives, women, often ignorant of court procedures, failed to ensure probate and, therefore, their inheritance. The Widow Remarriage Act was not explicit about their rights even to their *stridhan*, customarily assured to her. In the event of a dispute over *stridhan*, widows were required to appear before a magistrate which they often failed to do. As a result, they depended on their kin for support. Customarily, a widow's right to maintenance was contingent on her chastity, in practice it was conditional on her performance of every menial domestic task. Her domestic labour enabled the withdrawal of other women in the family from manual and visible work. The high-caste widows, who were completely dependent on either the conjugal or the natal kin for survival, had often to labour unremittingly for food, clothing and shelter. Moreover, they were the ones fed the least, who wore the cheapest and coarsest clothes and provided with the minimal space. A Bengali Brahmin judge gave a graphic description of the trials and tribulations of high caste widows.

Their purse and *stridhan* which ought to be held sacred, are robbed by means, fair or foul ... They are objects of panegyric and adulation, so long as they have strength to attend to domestic duties and command of their wealth. They are turned out of family as beggars when the purse is emptied and their strength fails. Even maintenance, which the sisters' humanity ordains, is denied them.[13]

In the context of western India, Uma Chakravarti has shown how the reciprocity of material and cultural elements within the structure re-

---

[12] Bengali fiction abounds in poignant tales of fathers of daughters impoverished by increasing dowry demands. Some of the most well known of these are Rabindranath Tagore's *Dena Paona*, Saratchandra Chattopadhyay's *Parinita* and *Biraj Bau*. In 1901, the clerical employees of the government requested advances on their provident fund to be able to meet dowry demands for their daughters' marriages. WBSA General Miscellaneous February, 1901 B219–26.

[13] Babu Manulall Chatterjee, Subordinate Judge of Beerbhoom, WBSA, General, April 1886, A355–9.

inforced the deprivation of widows.[14] In Bengal too religion sanctified the calendar crowded with days on which they were supposed to starve and prescribed for them an ascetic mode of life.[15] These made it easier for the household to make the lowest resource allocation to the widow.

Like *purdah* therefore, enforced widowhood was a relatively inexpensive means of seeking upward caste mobility. The Kurmis, for example, who came in large numbers to jute mills, were primarily an agricultural caste. They were divided into the Anadhiya (higher – strictly agricultural) and the Jaiswar (lower – personal service). The former marked itself off from the latter by not allowing widow remarriage. In the nineteenth century, the Sheikhs, Kunjras and Jolahas adopted the prohibition on widow remarriage to the extent that 'those who transgress the custom are liable to be socially banned'.[16] *Sagai*, now denoting an engagement ceremony in Bihar and UP, was recorded in the 1891 Census as a form of widow remarriage. In Bengal, a more widely used word for a second marriage, either for widows or for divorced or deserted women, was *sanga* or *sangat*.[17] The lower castes like Bagdis and Bauris usually allowed widow remarriage. However, as the Bagdis became more 'Hinduised', the Tentulia (highest) sub-caste forbade marriage of widows.[18] The Rajus did not allow widow remarriage though the Bayans, an inferior sub-caste in Midnapore, Dinajpur and Orissa, did.[19]

Increasingly, then, fewer widows were able to remarry. Taroni's statement quoted earlier is an eloquent testimony of the economic vulnerability of these widows. Even amongst the lower castes, elderly women who could not hope to remarry were thrown upon the most menial occupations, like spinning and weaving jute, for meagre remuneration. Economically deprived, forced into drudgery and indignity, widows were also vulnerable to sexual abuse. The use of the word *rarh* to denote both widows and prostitutes indicates that widows were thought to be sexually available.[20] Presumably some sought relief in sexual relation-

[14] Chakravarti, 'Social Pariahs and Domestic Drudges'.

[15] A widow wrote to her sister, 'The widow does not suffer through fasting. Her sleep is not disturbed if she lies on the floor, she does not die of harsh abuses. If I will not be able to bear all this, why am I a widow?' *Dasi*, 6, 1, January 1897.

[16] *BDG*, Muzzaffarpur, 1907, p. 37.

[17] The Commissioner of Chittagong wrote, 'the lower orders in this and other districts are in advance of their betters in having a form of remarriage called sagai'. WBSA, General Proceedings, April 1886. Refer a popular couplet. Rarh holey sabai eshey sanga korte chay (When one becomes a widow, everybody comes to 'marry' her). Sumanto Banerjee, *The Parlour and the Streets: Elite and Popular Culture in the Nineteenth Century Calcutta*, Calcutta, 1989, p. 56.

[18] *BDG*, Bankura, 1908, pp. 44–59.   [19] *BDG*, Midnapore, 1911, pp. 65–6.

[20] Sen, 'Honour and Resistance', p. 45. Aslo see Mrs Marcus B. Fuller, *The Wrongs of Indian Womanhood* (London, 1900), reprint, Delhi, 1984, p. 54.

ships, or they became victims of seduction and rape. 'Oftentimes the relations of their deceased husband annoy them in various ways, turn out bitter enemies, and drive them to commit immoral acts.'[21] The loss of chastity usually deprived them of the last precarious foothold in the conjugal family. Some of them went to places of pilgrimage like Benares or Vrindavan. For others, migration to the city would have been the only recourse. Often married women too were deprived of familial resources because of marital infidelity, inchastity or barrenness. These women also migrated to the city to take up a range of petty trades and service occupations. The largest number of women migrants to Calcutta between 1858 and 1873 were widows or rejected wives of barbers, milkmen, Malis, Jugis, Kaibartas and Haris.[22]

It was her sexual vulnerability and not the extraction of the widow's labour on which the middle-class male reformists focused. Vidyasagar himself, despite the final appeal to the *shastras*, found illicit sexual affairs and consequent abortions the most compelling argument in favour of widow remarriage. Colonial officials, *bhadralok* novelists, politicians and philanthropists felt that Bengali Hindu widows, because they were unable to remarry, swelled the ranks of the prostitutes in Calcutta and in the places of pilgrimage like Mathura and Vrindavan. This was felt to be the most deleterious consequence of the widows', especially the child widows', repressed sexuality. The fears about rampant female sexuality were not quite damped down by the newly constituted pure and chaste 'angel of the hearth' imagery.[23] The widows' material, emotional and sexual deprivations were seen to lead them to prefer prostitution.[24] Even more sympathetic portrayals represented the widow as the unwilling victim of male debauchery.

A woman became a widow at the age of 16 ... [S]he was beautiful ... and tempted into sin ... No one protected her but there was no harm in abusing her ... she was swept into degradation and her neighbours drove her away from home ... [B]ut the man who was responsible for her downfall is happily ensconced ... What is most regretful is that these are the leaders of our society!!! This life is full of temptation, even educated men succumb to it. How will a poor uneducated girl pass the test?[25]

The depictions of the helpless widow descending to the depths of vice rested on a seemingly sound economic logic. The female trades were disappearing in the countryside and the cities offered very limited

21 Babu Manulall Chaterjee, WBSA, General, April 1886, A355–9.
22 U. Chakravarty, *Condition of Bengali Women around the Second Half of the Nineteenth Century*, Calcutta, 1963, pp. 24–8.
23 Sen, 'Honour and Resistance', pp. 225–8.
24 Mrs M. B. Fuller, *The Wrongs of Indian Womanhood*, London, 1900, p. 128.
25 *Antahpur*, 5, 10, 1902, p. 192.

opportunities for paid employment. Spinning, the widow's prop and mainstay, was no longer a viable livelihood. Most women were forced to enter domestic services; in the cities and towns some worked in petty trades and services and increasingly in the jute and rice mills. Many of these occupations were synonymous with prostitution because wages were low and the fear of seduction so great. Prostitution was thought to be leisured and lucrative, an irresistible temptation to women toiling for a pittance. The factories were the most dangerous; not only were women poorly paid, but men and women worked together. Their physical proximity was itself felt to be an invitation to licentiousness. Moreover such proximity violated the custom of spatial segregation of the sexes, and the nationalist opposition of the home and the world. Factory work was thus automatically suspect. 'Factories are being established in this country and are going to grow. Many women are driven by starvation to go and work there. Further, they are endangered by their proximity to bestial men and are destroyed for life. They might be saved by the formation of asramas.'[26] The solution was borrowed from Britain. The proliferation of homes and refuges for 'fallen' women prompted similar schemes for the 'miserable widows' of Bengal.[27] Influenced by Mary Carpenter, Sasipada Banerjee and his wife opened a shelter home for Hindu widows called the *Hindu Bidhabasrama*. *Bamabodhini Patrika* urged the foundation of shelter homes on the model of a home for poor women and girls founded in London in 1878.[28]

These anxieties were extended to other female occupations in the city. When 'retired' prostitutes took up factory jobs, shopkeeping, husking, general labour or domestic service, such convictions were strengthened. Part-time maid-servants were presumed to inevitably take to prostitution to supplement their poor income. They, especially, were vulnerable to sexual violence in the affluent homes in which they worked. Many destitute Muslim women who obtained a livelihood as unpaid maid-servants – *bandi* – in wealthy Muslim mansions were supposed to live in concubinage.[29] In the context of Victorian England, Françoise Barrett-Ducrocq has argued that since sexual relations often resulted in pregnancy and sometimes in death from childbirth, and since visiting prostitutes were a drain on the household's resources, 'the professional duties of maids sometimes extended, unofficially, to the sexual servicing of another class'.[30] It is tempting to make the same argument for

---

[26] *Bamabodhini Patrika*, August 1892, p. 81.   [27] *Antahpur*, 5, 2, 1902, p. 29
[28] *Bamabodhini Patrika*, August 1892, p. 81.
[29] WBSA, Judl. Judl., October 1872, B252–79.
[30] Françoise Barret-Ducrocq, *Love in the Time of Victoria: Sexuality, Class and Gender in the Nineteenth Century*, London, 1991, p. 49.

Bengal. There are flashes of corroborative evidence in fiction and in the records, but the maid-servants of Calcutta have not left their own stories.

The point at issue, however, is not whether widows and rejected wives in poorly paid occupations in the city supplemented their meagre income with prostitution. Some may have. Others may have entered relatively stable sexual relatonships, for economic or emotional reasons, which to the middle-class moralist was concubinage. Certainly, even in the 1920s and 1930s, widows working in jute mills remarried, and this did not appear to have been regarded as an aberration by the participants. Mangari from Mirzapur district who was married when she was 10 years old, came to the mill area with her husband. Both worked in the mill and when he died, she married her sister's husband because 'her sister was barren'. Their widowed mother also lived with them and they all worked in the same mill (Titagarh No. 2). Gobardan, a *coolie sardar* from Muzzaffarpur, fell in love with his brother-in-law's widow when his wife went to her parents' house to have her first child. He married the widow, got her a job in the same mill and they all worked and lived together.[31] Such 'evidence' were used in elite discourses to illustrate a concomitance, inevitable though deplorable, between widowhood, urban migration, waged employment and prostitution.

The 'non-family' jute mill women

From the early 1920s, attention focused particularly on the factories and the mill towns as the incunabula of vice, crime, disease and prostitution. The concerned moralists, officials, managers, trade union activists, professionals, and even novelists discovered that women working in the jute mills almost invariably practised prostitution or lived in concubinage. The first comprehensive statement of this 'non-family' character of jute labour was by Dr Dagmar Curjel.

Imported labour usually brings its womenfolk with them into jute and cotton mills, these women work in the mills but in the majority of cases are not the wives of the men with whom they live. It is not possible for a woman worker to live or in many cases work without male protection ... and practically all such Bengalees found in the mills are degraded women or prostitutes.[32]

As already mentioned, her enquiries were a response to the ILO's Maternity Benefit Convention. It is not surprising that she found, mainly from the evidence of mill managers, a very alarming picture of female promiscuity and a breakdown of the family. One manager

[31] *RCLI*, XI, 2, p. 355.   [32] Curjel Report, Main Report, pp. 1–2.

emphasising the 'non-family' character of female labour said, 'many women carry on as prostitutes as well as working in the mill', as an argument against any scheme of maternity benefit.[33] What was widely quoted from her report was not the formidable evidence about appalling work conditions or her recommendation that maternity benefit be paid irrespective of marital status, but her statement about the 'non-domestic' character of jute mill workers, the women 'who were not the wives' of the men with whom they lived and the degraded Bengali prostitues in jute mills.

Janet Kelman, visiting the mills about the same time, wrote that the Bengali women were 'usually drawn from less respectable classes on the outskirts of Calcutta ... whose presence in mill compounds is least desirable'.[34] The gradual replacement of 'local' labour by migrants had reduced the already low proportion of Bengali women. As mentioned before, the few Bengali women in the industry were mostly single women or widows. As Bengali men provided a smaller segment of better paid workers, their wives rarely worked in the mills. Even in the 1940s, the few Bengali women working in the mills were 'unattached widows', not from 'families'.[35]

Over time, the 'non-family' character of jute mill workers assumed the proportions of a legend, notwithstanding Curjel's own evidence that a majority of women 'lived with men', even if they were not the 'wives' of these men or that most single women lived with and supported their children. These households did not qualify as 'family'. Writers of fiction closely associated with jute labour have reinforced the images of sexual irregularity. Many of these writers had long and intimate experience of the jute industry: Samares Basu, a novelist and a trade union leader, lived in a jute mill *basti* for some time;[36] Mohanlal Gangopadhyay worked in a jute mill;[37] Ashim Ranjan Choudhury also worked in the industry for over thirty years;[38] Tarasankar Bandopadhyay and Satinath Bhaduri.[39] Their experience and knowledge of these conditions did not prevent them from voicing the truisms of *bhadralok* patter. Tarasankar Bandopadhyay, a leading Bengali novelist, traced in *Chaitali Ghurni* the tragic fate of a couple, Damini and Goshtha, who were squeezed out of

[33] Ibid., Appendix B, Sl, No. 10, Budge-Budge Jute Mill.
[34] J. H. Kelman, *Labour in India*, London, 1923, p. 89.
[35] K. P. Chattopadhyay, *A Socio-Economic Survey of Jute Labour*, Calcutta University, 1952. Also see Bengal Board of Economic Enquiry, Bengal Labour Enquiry, Draft Report – Jagaddal: First Sample, 1941, P. C. Mahalanobis, Statistical Laboratory, Calcutta, 1949.
[36] Samares Basu, *Jagaddal* and other short stories, *Galpasangraha*, Calcutta, 1975–8.
[37] Mohanlal Gangapadhyay, *Asamapta Chatabda*, Calcutta 1963.
[38] Interview, 16 November 1989, Calcutta.
[39] Satinath Bhaduri, *Chitragupter File*, Calcutta, n.d.

their tiny parcel of land in the village and forced into seeking work in a factory. In the city, Damini is constantly exposed to sexual temptations. Living in dire and desperate poverty, she is torn between the offerings of food and clothing by her relatively better off suitors and fidelity to her husband. As she rejects a gift from the lascivious *chhotomistri*, the author comments, '[S]he is uneducated ... but she is a woman and she instinctively sensed the humiliation to womanhood ... self-hatred had burned her in heart when she had been lured into clasping Subal's gifted clothing, the bestial and naked insult heaped on her just now shamed and humiliated her beyond endurance.'[40]

Damini's 'instinctive' sense of shame and determined efforts to preserve her chastity are depicted as a lone and heroic struggle against the sexual laxity pervading the working-class neighbourhood. Her neighbour, Khendi, received gifts from the pointsman in exchange of sexual favours, '[e]veryone knows about it, Khendi too makes no effort to hide it. She is not ashamed.' Dasi, another neighbour, whose sick husband was unable to earn, accepted money from a mill clerk. As for the low-caste women in the *chhotolokpara* (literally, low class/caste neighbourhood) such bargains were part of their *swabhava* (nature; habit).[41] The author introduces us to these women thus:

The women gather in groups beside the road, now [in the evening] wearing fine thin-bordered saris and their thinning hair stuffed into knots. Even in the dark, their eyes burn with a hunger. Their greedy gaze is trained on men, but they also seek the gleam of silver. Their eyes, searching and scorching, reflect not merely their hearts' desires. The fire in their bellies has kindled the lusts of the flesh.[42]

The women workers in jute mills became surrounded with an air of fascinating immorality. A direct relation was perceived between manual labour and the lack of gender segregation, poverty and promiscuity. The last line in Saratchandra Chattopadhyay's short story 'Mahesh', that in jute mills women have neither *izzat* (honour) nor *abru* (covering; *purdah*), is the most oft-quoted in this connection. The story is about a marginal peasant who loses his last bit of land, and then his last asset when the cow Mahesh dies. Thus deprived of all means of sustenance in the village, he is forced to migrate, with his only surviving relative, his daughter, Amina, to work in a jute mill.[43] The heightened poignancy of this last act of desperation derived from the immorality associated with the mills. In the jute mills women lost both honour and *purdah*.

These attitudes were not limited to writers of fiction. Nalinaksha

---

[40] Tarasankar Bandopadhyay, 'Chaitali Ghurni', *Tarasankar Rachanavali*, I, Calcutta, 1972, reprint, 1973, p. 44.
[41] Ibid., p. 53.   [42] Ibid., p. 72.
[43] Saratchandra Chattopadhyay, 'Mahesh', *Sulabh Sarat Samagra*, II, Calcutta, 1989.

Sanyal suspected that complaints about sexual transgressions were rare 'due to want of the sense of morality'.[44] R. K. Das felt that 'the error' of indiscriminate migration 'is more apparent in the case of women labour ... so full of opportunities of immoral life'.[45] Women in menial occupations were automatically suspect. J. N. Ghose wrote, 'the jute presses and mercantile firms of Calcutta used to employ women labourers known as *jharoonis* (sweepers) ... and they were often prostitutes at night'.[46] This kind of dual identity – worker by day and prostitute by night – was ascribed to jute mill women by many contemporary sources, including by Margaret Read, a member of the Royal Commission on Labour.[47]

The simple economic equation that had led Ghosh to infer from the gold and silver ornaments of *jharoonis* that they must have supplemented their income from prostitution, increasingly gave ground, from the 1920s onwards, to more sophisticated social explanations. The low sex ratio in the overcrowded slums of Calcutta and the mill towns were seen to engender sexual immorality. Indian sociologists argued that in the urban context, the heterogeneity of castes and classes eroded the effective communal enforcement of moral standards. Together, these translated into a perceived instability of the 'family'. The government feared that rapid urbanisation would generate acute social instability.[48] Radhakamal Mukherjee called the first Convocation Address for the Sir Dorabji Tata Graduate School of Social Work in Bombay in 1938, 'Social Disorganisation in India'.[49]

Calcutta and the jute towns had very few adult women. This 'unnatural' situation was perpetuated, it was felt, because men were chary of bringing their wives into the overwhelmingly male world of the *bastis*.[50]

[44] Nalinaksha Sanyal, 'Jute Mill Operatives at Sibpur', *Welfare*, 1, January 1923.
[45] R. K. Das, 'Women Labour in India', *International Review*, October–November 1931.
[46] J. N. Ghosh, *Social Evil in Calcutta and Method of Treatment*, Calcutta, 1923. Also see S. K. Mukherjee and J. N. Chakrabarty, *Prostitution in India*, Calcutta, c. 1945. 'The sexual morality of the girls who work in the mills are naturally not very strict ... In the rice mills most of the women have gold ornaments on their persons. Most of them lead a life of vice at night', p. 125.
[47] M. Read, *Indian Peasant Uprooted*, London, 1931. A section is subheaded 'Millworker by Day and Prostitute by Night', p. 59.
[48] C. Dewey, 'The Government of India's "New Industrial Policy", 1900–1925; Formation and Failure', in C. J. Dewey and K. N. Choudhuri (eds.), *Economy and Society*, Delhi, 1979.
[49] He discussed the 'disintegrative' impact of a too-rapid transition from a rural to an urban economy which did not allow a gradual adaptation of habits and attitudes. The result was the disruption of 'traditional joint family', 'caste control', and 'unsettlement of status and custom'. Radhakamal Mukherjee, *Social Disorganisation in India*, Convocation Address for the Sir D. Tata Graduate School of Social Work, Bombay, 1939.
[50] In 1930, Gupta calculated that the ratio of adult (15–40 years) men to women was 8:3

Read calculated that in Calcutta there were only thirty-seven married women for every 100 married men while only 47 per cent of the total female population was married. 'Hence it is clear ... [there is] sexual immorality and this in its turn tends to discourage men from bringing their wives with them', she concluded.[51] Public attention focused on criminal activities in mill towns – gambling dens, liquor shops, drug-peddling and prostitution – seen to be organised by gangs under *goondas* (local toughs). Sometimes these were more closely associated with jute mills, a *sardar* owning or financing these operations, or mill workers doubling as *goondas*.[52]

A paradigmatic preoccupation with working-class immorality influenced administrators and journalists. The assumption of an inextricable link between poverty, sexual promiscuity and criminality overlaid the kinds of information collected about the urban poor. Crime, disease and mortality had become the points of entry into the lives of working women and men. The instances of rape, murder, child molestation, incest and wife-battering reported by newspapers of the time concentrated on working-class tenements. The reportage, in implying a higher incidence of such crimes among the poor, reflects the assumptions of the concerned middle classes.

A high incidence of venereal diseases among the urban poor caught public attention. According to Das, 80 per cent of mill workers suffered from venereal diseases.[53] Mrs Mann, a nurse in Baranagore Jute Mill, testified that half the workers suffered from the disease.[54] The concern over venereal diseases reflected a wider concern over prostitution and crime. It was felt that prostitution had become 'a way of life' in the *basti*.[55] Gilchrist, the Labour Officer, reported that among jute mill women, 33 per cent from Midnapur and 25 per cent from Hooghly admitted to being prostitutes. The Director of Public Health insisted that there was 'practically open prostitution near the

---

in Calcutta city while in the mill towns it came down to an abysmal low of 11:4. B. P. Gupta, *Labour and Housing in India*, Calcutta, 1930, pp. 49–50.

[51] Read, *Indian Peasant Uprooted*, pp. 58–60.

[52] WBSA, Poll. Police, March 1923, A1–3; October 1928, B149–57; HPC 908/30; 554/31.

[53] R. K. Das, *Indian Working Class*, Bombay, 1948, p. 376.

[54] Curjel Report, Appendix B, Sl, No. 15; M. I. Balfour and R. Young, *The Work of Medical Women in India*, Oxford and London, 1929, pp. 59–61; Memorandum of the British Social Hygiene Council, *RCLI*, IX, pp. 147–52. Balfour pointed out that there was no systematic information. 'The idea seems to be that with so much immorality there is bound to be much VD'. Balfour Report. See also M. N. Rao and H. C. Ganguly, 'VD in the Industrial Worker', *Indian Journal of Social Work*, 2, 1950–51. They concluded, 'so long as the worker has to live alone and away from his family, the raison d'être of the visit to the brothel is not removed'.

[55] Mukherjee, *Social Disorganisation*.

workers' houses'.[56] Prostitution and crime were seen to go hand in hand. One police officer wrote, 'One of the worst types of crimes the police have to deal with in Calcutta is the murder of prostitutes for gain. These unfortunates are as a class both well to do and helpless owing to their intimate relations with men and are quickly marked down by violent criminals as easy victims.'[57]

Jute mill women were 'public' women, and as such were vulnerable to violence. Moreover, violence against them was more likely to be reported to the police and made 'public'. The police went a step further in identifying the victim of every petty 'public' crime as a prostitute. These prostitutes seem invariably to have lived near the *lines* and *bastis* of the jute mills. One Gopal Ghose, a mill hand of Baranagore Jute Mill 'terrorised local prostitutes into complying with his immoral demands'. When Bhaba Peshakar refused to serve him without payment he assaulted her and her 'paramour', Habu. He brutally murdered Bhabatarini Dasi and caused 'grievous hurt' to Nulan Dasi, both 'prostitutes'. The 'female tenants' of Krittibas Majhi were so persecuted that they left the house. The reports hinted that these women were 'prostitutes'.[58]

If in European official, managerial and professional discourses, the immoralities of the 'single' Bengali women looms the larger, the *bhadralok* reserved their most scathing contempt for the low-caste migrants, the Muslim 'up-countrymen' and the Bilaspuris who crowded into the mill towns from the beginning of the twentieth century. The dirt, the stench and the overcrowding in the mill *lines* and *bastis* were, by themselves, proof of the lax and promiscuous nature of the inhabitants. The poor dirt-ridden hovels were thought to breed vice and crime. However, to all these concerned middle classes, association of the low castes and classes with sexual immorality was of longer standing and extended beyond the urban context. Some pre-existing stereotypes informed their understanding and characterisation of jute mill men and women.

Prostitutes – the criminal and the victim

The colonial state's interest in prostitution dated back to the mid-nineteenth century. The regulation of prostitutes was felt to be the only means of checking the spread of venereal disease among European soldiers. A means was ready to hand – the Contagious Diseases Act, modelled on similar legislation in Britain, was passed in 1868. Simultaneously, in the wake of the famine of 1866, missionaries raised a storm

[56] *RCLI*, V, 1, pp. 8–10; 2, p. 5.   [57] WBSA, HPC, 365 (1–4) of 1925.
[58] WBSA, HPC, 199(1–5) of 1925.

about the sale of young daughters to prostitutes. Together, they provoked a series of legislative and administrative efforts to control and
regulate prostitution.[59] The prostitute was designated a criminal, requiring constant policing.

In pre-colonial India, a complex and multilateral hierarchy divided
prostitutes. The accomplished courtesan, educated, trained in music,
dance, poetry and etiquette, aesthetically represented the feudal society
of which she was part. She shared little with the peasant or low-caste
'common' prostitutes who lived in the *bazar* and catered to men of their
own class.[60] The Contagious Diseases Act cut through these divisions.
Its enforcement involved a vigorous surveillance of the prostitutes in the
city. The officials, warned after the lessons of 1857 to be careful of
'native sentiments', sought to collect information about the prostitutes
before over-zealous administrative personnel caused too great a discontent. British administrators, who had in the East India Company's era
attended nautch parties, indulged in liaisons with *Bibis*, were now self-
consciously distancing themselves from the uncivilised salacity of a
native society which recognised, accepted and even celebrated prostitution. The efforts of surveys and censuses resulted in the hardening of the
category, and the multiple identities of performers, concubines, religious
mendicants and destitutes were collapsed into a single term, the prostitute. Under British military imperatives thus, prostitution was torn from
its earlier aesthetic, ritual and social contexts to be defined increasingly
as a labour-oriented service – as sexual commerce.[61] The *murali*, the
devadasi, the *tawa'if*, the *baiji*, the Hindu widow, the Muslim divorcee
and the *kulin* wife were jumbled in the same heap. As Veena T. Oldenberg has shown, in Lucknow, the distinction between the *tawa'if* and
the *randi* narrowed. The courtesans, bereft of court patronage, expro-
priated from their *mahals*, lived with the latter in the *bazar*.[62] There
remained only two categories of prostitutes – the registered and the
unregistered.

In Calcutta, the enforcement of the Contagious Diseases Act did not
prove easy. The women stubbornly resisted registration, examination
and internment in the Lock Hospitals. Soon after the Act was in

[59] WBSA, Judl. Police, November 1867, No. 85–6. The issue was raised in earnest again
in 1903–4. Stringent legislation was contemplated, and then abandoned for lack of
support. Judl. Police, June 1904, A35–53. Finally, the Bengal's Children Act, 1922,
enabled the removal of minor girls from the custody of prostitutes.
[60] Ratnabali Chatterjee, 'Prostitutes in Nineteenth Century Bengal: Construction of Class
and Gender', *Social Scientist*, 21, 9–11, 1993, pp. 159–72.
[61] Kokila Dang, 'Prostitutes, Patrons and the State: Nineteenth Century Awadh', *Social
Scientist*, 21, 9–11, 1993, pp. 173–96
[62] Veena Talwar Oldenberg, *The Making of Colonial Lucknow, 1856–1877*, Princeton,
1984. pp. 124–44.

operation, 'a very large number of the public women left the city and sojourned in the suburbs and further away'.[63] However, as more poor women drifted into the city, the problem of unregistered and 'clandestine' prostitution grew intractable. The police mounted vigilance on all widows and destitutes in particular, and poor women in general. The categorisation of prostitutes into 'registered' and 'unregistered' was futile; it seemed impossible to spatially and geographically separate registered and unregistered women, since these apparently faceless women could with ease melt into the poorer quarters of the city.

When a woman is reported as an absentee from the periodical examination a warrant for her arrest in immediately ordered ... When the police proceed to the woman's place of abode they find that perhaps ten days or a week previously she has absconded and left the jurisdiction ... It is very certain that none of her friends or relatives will afford the slightest clue to her whereabout, it is possible that she is lurking within the jurisdiction.[64]

Colonial administrators, despite the evidence of their own records, refused to admit that these women were not set apart from the community in which they lived. Most prostitutes returned to their villages occasionally to visit their mothers. The Commissioner of Police estimated that about 600 prostitutes left Calcutta in this way each year.[65] The Hindu prostitutes maintained caste rituals and operated within codes of caste.[66] They would not accept Muslim or European clients. 'Out of 1888 women on the rolls ... 878 women ... preserve their caste ... These women never receive Europeans. Such as lose their caste and receive soldiers invariably become Mahomedans, as they are outcasted by the other Hindu women.'[67] These were hardly social outcasts.

In the end, the 'clandestine' prostitute defeated them. In Calcutta, where 'the Act was longest in force and has been worked more actively', at one time a daily average of twelve women were arrested by the police for infringements of the regulations.[68] Since a large variety of practices were bunched together under this blanket term, increasingly larger numbers of poor women came under its purview.[69] The registering authorities found it difficult to deal with married women, wives of itinerant traders, 'seafaring men' and *kulin* wives, who 'practised prostitution' with the 'connivance' of their husbands to augment the 'family

[63] NA, General Sanitation June 1888, A107.
[64] Commissioner of the Presidency Division, NA, General February, 1878.
[65] WBSA, Judl. Judl., October 1872, B252–279.   [66] *Mahila*, I, 16, 1924.
[67] NA, Municipal Department, May 1883, No. 1438, Colln. 6–8/9, p. 20.
[68] A. Mackenzie, Secretary to the Government of India, NA, Home Sanitary Department, 20 February 1883, Municipal Department, March 1883, No. 47, Colln. 2–3.
[69] The Census of 1881 assumed that all unmarried women over the age of 15 years must be prostitutes, since 'every member of the female population' is married by then. WBSA, General, April 1886.

income'.[70] Moreover, 'Muslim prostitutes may marry and relapse several times' and many Hindu 'prostitutes' converted to Islam in order to get married.[71] It thus seemed to colonial officials that compared to Brahmanical codes, Islam offered women greater flexibility. Since Muslim women were allowed divorce and remarriage, there was 'not so rigid a social code' which facilitated the 'rehabilitation' of prostitutes within their own community. In contrast, not only were Hindu women compelled to become prostitutes 'to pursue extra-marital relations', once they had done so they would not be readmitted into their communities. The Sanitary Commissioner felt that such extra-marital relations led to the spread of venereal diseases among the 'husbands', but felt unable to tackle such a widespread practice.[72] Despite their best efforts, the Secretary of the Bengal Municipal Department admitted that an accurate but effective definition of the 'common prostitute' had eluded the government:

We would have to define 'common prostitute' in such a way as to get rid of the objection which the Courts showed invariably to inferential proof, and, as direct proof is for obvious reasons unattainable, this could only be done by so loosely defining the term as necessarily to place a most dangerous power in the hands of evil disposed persons and the police.[73]

Very often, women who defaulted, absconded, or failed to register got off with light sentences. But they found the periodic examinations in the Lock Hospitals most offensive and devised various means of evading them. When the Lock Hospitals were made voluntary, many women left before they were cured. The Superintendent realised that a minimum compulsory period of treatment could not be enforced. The women are reported to have said, 'Arrest me, I shall only get a month in prison; but if I register, I may have six months in hospital.'[74]

The troublesome prostitutes – professional or clandestine – were not the Government's only difficulty. The repeal agitators, so successful in Britain, turned their attention to the colonies. The New Cantonment Acts, they argued, were merely the Contagious Diseases Act under another name. It legitimised prostitution and undermined the 'civilising mission' of the Raj. Government struggled to explain that their policy was not based on an immoral principle that 'vice is a necessity to man'.[75] In Britain, they argued, prostitutes were merely 'fallen' women and required rehabilitation. In Britain, since the distinction between the

---

[70] Sanitary Commissioner, WBSA, Judl. Judl., October 1872, B252–79.   [71] Ibid.
[72] Sanitary Commissioner, WBSA General Sanitation, August 1872.
[73] NA, General Sanitary, June 1888, B106.
[74] Superintendent of Lock Hospitals, Calcutta, NAI, General Sanitary, June 1888, A113.
[75] Memorial of the National Association for the repeal of the Acts, February 1886, ibid.

merely unchaste woman and the prostitute was problematic, the Contagious Diseases Act caused serious injury to innocent women. These were the moral and legal grounds for the repeal of the Act. In India, of course, things were different. Government held that prostitution was an integral part of Indian society and prostitutes comprised a 'hereditary caste'. It could, therefore, never be abolished without grave offence to 'native sentiments'. 'The Indian prostitute is a recognised caste, or rather it would be more correct to say that India abounds in castes or sects of prostitutes with whom the calling is hereditary, who are born in and bred to that profession ... These women are in no sense ashamed of their calling; nor do they practice it in secret.'[76] A group of Indian middle-class reformers sought to rebut the characterisation of Indian society as thus endemically immoral. They cast the question, borrowing from the reformist discourse in Britain, in terms of the moral degeneracy of the poor. In the 1890s they mounted anti-nautch agitations, petitioned the government for greater control of the brothels in the cities, and pointed out the need for the rehabilitation of the prostitutes and the minors under their care. The missionaries in India had already been asking for similar measures.[77] Government taxed and fined the prostitutes to finance their treatment in the Lock Hospitals and thereby made itself more vulnerable to accusations of legitimising prostitution. The argument that in India prostitution was already legitimate was rejected by the repealers, missionaries and educated Indian opinion. However, they all accepted the broadly co-optive definition of 'the prostitute' which drew under its umbrella a wide variety of social practices. What they merely did was to turn the Government's logic on its head. The prostitute was now to be a victim, not a criminal – a victim of the Government's double standards of morality, of the brutal police, of greedy husbands and lascivious men.[78]

[I]t [the Act] offends against the moral law by forcibly subjecting women to degrading ordeals ... qualifying them to continue a career of vice, for the gratification of immoral men ... The frequent and offensive interference with the liberty of innocent and respectable women ... has resulted ... In this disease

[76] NA, General Sanitary June 1888 A124. In June 1888 an article in the *Pioneer* written under the pseudonym 'Fair Play' asserted, 'prostitution in this country is a recognised trade of a caste who (however revolting it may seem to us) are individually proud of their calling and most conservative in their observance of its usages'.
[77] WBSA, General August 1870 A2–3; Judl. Judl., September 1873 A68–70, General Miscellaneous, June 1875 B9; Political Police, July 1888 B227; Judl. Police, October 1894, A13–14; Judl. Police, March 1902, A22–4. See K. Ballhatchet, *Race, Sex and Class under the Raj: Imperial Attitudes and Policies and their Critics, 1793–1905*, London, 1980; Fuller, *The Wrongs*, pp. 137–47.
[78] Chatterjee, 'Queens' Daughters'.

men are regarded as innocuous, while their victims are subjected to repulsive ordeals.[79]

Despite parliamentary pressure, the Indian military authorities managed to keep some of the regulations intact, but the fire had gone out of the Government's zeal. In Calcutta, the operation of the Act was gradually curtailed until, finally, the separate Lock Hospitals were abandoned in 1881, when it was found that the regulations were proving more expensive than effective.[80]

The issue of the control and rehabilitation of prostitutes was not altogether abandoned by missionaries and middle-class Indians, but the emphasis changed. It became associated with the need to enforce 'social purity'.[81] The 'purity' debates were reactivated when international attention focused on 'white slavery' and immoral trafficking in the 1920s.[82] The notion of the prostitute being a symbol of the moral degeneracy of the poor had by then taken firmer roots. Increasingly, the *bhadralok* in Calcutta sought to distance itself from the community of poor in the city. They emphasised the chaste and modest demeanour of wives and daughters as a requirement for middle-class respectability; and the nationalist rhetoric about the women's proper sphere in the home grew strident. Until the early nineteenth century, Calcutta's rich and poor had shared an amorphous culture. By the late nineteenth century, the professional and service gentry, the *bhadralok*, had adopted distinct modes of speech, dress and food habits to demonstrate their superior status. This was most evident in the locational separation of the rich and the poor within the city and in the increasingly closed and 'private' homes of the elite.[83] The women, whose place was defined in the interior of these homes, had also to be socialised into a refined literate culture. In Calcutta, the conduct of middle-class women became hedged with new and more stringent restrictions.[84]

In contrast, the large concentrated areas of poor working-class settlements offered the new middle-class eye a shocking variety and fluidity of sexual practices. The city's poor women who worked and socialised in the streets and *bazars* became the symbol of working-class immorality.

[79] The memorial of the Calcutta Missionary Conference, NA, General Sanitary, June 1888, A107.
[80] NA, Municipal Department, May 1883, Colln. 6–10.
[81] Various pressure groups continued to petition the government for greater control over prostitutes and the Government of Bengal opened a file title called 'Social Purity'. BSA, Monthly Bundles, Secretary to Commissioner, Patna Division, No. 476 (1872) and No. 89 (1873); WBSA, Judl. Police, December 1901, A74–6, August 1902, 4–8.
[82] The League of Nations Convention on Suppression of Traffic in Women and Children was given effect in India by the Immoral Traffics Act and the Indian Penal Code (Amendmment) Act in 1923. WBSA Political Police, June 1923, A28–36.
[83] Banerjee, *The Parlour and the Streets.*   [84] Borthwick, *The Changing Role of Women.*

The same ratiocinative economic logic that had linked widowhood, poverty and prostitution in the late nineteenth century was extended to all waged women. Official investigations established sexual laxity as an urban social problem. The contradictions between women's need to work for wages, their low status in the labour market and increasingly restricted notions of respectability grew sharper.

Thus, the problem of 'clandestine' prostitution became once again especially onerous. The earlier arguments that had stressed the injustice of targeting the prostitute and not the client were abandoned. The assumptions of a powerful female sexuality and the gradual evolution of a more rigidly differentiated definition of male and female sexuality accepted professional prostitution as a 'necessary social evil'.[85] According to J. N. Ghosh, the former was the 'more dangerous form of prostitution'.[86] Mukherjee provided a list of clandestine prostitutes covering almost the whole range of female occupations: 'Domestic servants, female cooks, needlewomen, panwallis, laundresses (dhopanis), and kaprawallis (hawkers of cloth), factory girls, shop girls, and even some of the nurses and midwives may be included in this class [of clandestine prostitutes].'[87]

In 1924 *Mahila*, a journal, published a series of articles by Narendra Deb. According to him, many women 'take to prostitution secretly for extra earnings ... The harm caused by the professional prostitutes can be checked, but it would be no exaggeration to say that there would be no easy way to counter the damage done by the latter.' He also identified maid-servants and *panwallis* as 'irregular prostitutes'.[88] The Census of 1911 provided the numerical evidence: the two occupations in which women outnumbered men were midwifery and prostitution. It went on

[85] 'It is now a recognised fact that in modern society prostitution is a necessary evil, and a certain percentage of women must always belong to that class', said Rai Moni Lall Banerjee of Kidderpore. A file which dealt with the removal of minor girls from prostitutes has several letters expressing such sentiments. Babu Bhowani Charan Dutt argued that the 'evil' of prostitution could not be altogether suppressed. Babu Chaturbhuj Sahay stressed the ceremonial role of professional prostitutes in 'marriages and celebration of national and religious festivals'. WBSA Judl. Police, June 1904, A 35–50.
[86] Ghosh, *Social Evil in Calcutta*, p. 9.
[87] Mukherjee and Chakrabarty, *Prostitution in India*, p. 123. Dr S. K. Mukherjee practised medicine in north Calcutta and claimed that he had first-hand knowledge of prostitution. Dr Radhakamal Mukherjee also agreed that midwives, dressmakers and maid-servants were a 'common cover' for prostitution and these women gave 50–90 per cent of their income to their keepers; R. Mukherjee, *Social Disorganisation*.
[88] Narendra Deb, *Shaharer Abarjana* (The Garbage of the City), *Mahila*, 1924, I, 10. The series included, *Shamajer Bishakta Kshata* (The Poisonous Sore of Society), I, 11, an anonymous unnamed article in I, 12, an anonymous article, *Nari Adarsher Ekdik* (An aspect of Ideal Womanhood), I, 13, an anonymous and unnamed article in I, 16, and Sararibala Basu, *Patita Samasya* (The Prostitute Problem), I, 22.

to say, 'not everybody calls herself a prostitute' and that 'maid-servants' were a 'common euphemism'.[89]

What is at issue here is not the empirical validity of such statements. It is quite possible that some women in a few or even all of these poorly rewarded occupations sought to supplement their meagre resources in exchange for sexual favours. Women were paid lower wages on the ground that their earnings were 'supplementary' and it was assumed that their maintenance would be subsidised by fathers, husbands and sons. It is hardly surprising that when such expected subsidies were not forthcoming, as was frequently the case, women sought other alternatives. But the more these alternatives narrowed to extra-marital sexual activities or even sexual commerce, these women abrogated their claim to a social identity as a worker. Thus, in asserting that 'maid-servants' were a 'common euphemism' for 'prostitutes', the Census Officer explicitly gave priority to women's participation in sexual exchange over the hiring out of their domestic services. In thus characterising women primarily through their 'aberrant' sexual behaviour and by stigmatising a wide and amorphous range of popular sexual activity as 'aberrant', official and middle-class discourses collapsed the multiple social identities of poor women into the singular image of the 'prostitute'.

Temporary wives – marriage and cohabitation

When the colonial state directed towards prostitutes its passion for categorising the subject population, officials had to grope through, what appeared to them, a bewildering range and variety of cohabitation practices. Many different terms, haphazardly translated and torn from their social contexts, were used in an attempt to distinguish among different kinds of 'clandestine' prostitution. The term 'temporary marriage' was one of these, originally supposed to describe the more stable but legally invalid cohabitation arrangements that had widespread currency. But applied with assiduous regularity, as it was, it soon began to include an equally bewildering range of practices. It was also habitually used to describe the marital arrangements of jute mill women and men. Used as a blanket expression, it obscured a diverse set of changing sexual relations.

The phrase 'temporary marriage' seems to have been coined for the relatively informal systems of separation, divorce, remarriage and poly-

---

[89] *Census of India*, 1911, VI, 1, Calcutta, p. 548. The tables indicate that of the total female population, prostitutes comprised 6 per cent of those over 10 years, and 8 per cent of those between 20 and 40 years. They represented 21 per cent of the 'occupied' women and came mostly from Hooghly, 24 Parganas, Midnapore and Burdwan.

andry current among low-caste Hindus and poor Muslims. It was easily extended to include the women who having come to the mill towns alone set up a home with one of many available single men, as also the women who came to the city with 'men who were not their husbands'. Thus, Curjel began her thesis of breakdown of morality and family with the statement that though some men brought women with them from their regions, especially the Biharis and the Bilaspuris, these 'women were in many cases not the wives of the men'.[90] It is likely that in the urban working-class context, migration, poverty and insecurity of employment caused more divorces, desertions and remarriages than were already current in these communities. Legally, a 'temporary' marriage, like a second marriage, was concubinage; morally, it seemed akin to 'prostitution'.

The colonial administration's attempts to understand, document and redefine marriage arrangements stemmed from the need to disentagle property rights and inheritance laws. But their concerns often confounded their understanding. The lower castes, especially the rural labouring groups, attached greater importance to the control of women's productive capacities than to their reproductive value. Thus marriages between the poor sometimes resembled forced labour arrangements, and these were not marked by the same emphasis on women's chastity that characterised higher caste Hindu and upper-class Muslim marriages. In some such cases, there was no strict enforcement of monogamy on women.[91] For men of course polygamy was accepted across the castes and religions and, despite periodic Victorian revulsions, the colonial administrators pragmatically accepted and legalised these.[92] But, seen through the prism of high-caste norms and textual prescriptions of Hinduism and Islam, women's participation in multiple sexual relationships appeared particularly deviant, approximating prostitution.

Amongst the lower orders of Indians chastity is practically unknown. The women who are employed ... such as the coolies working on the public

---

[90] Curjel Report, Main Report, pp. 1–3.

[91] Poor men were thought, either through indifference or for gain, to turn a blind eye to their wives' extra-marital affairs. Since, 'however unnatural, husbands have been known to connive at the defilement of their wives', indignant missionaries wanted persons other than the husband to be empowered to sue women for adultery. WBSA, Judl. Police, May 1894, Petition from R. C. Mitter and thirty-three others. Among some low castes (notably the Magahiya Dom) it seemed to have been commonplace to ignore the infidelities of wives, as long as 'she brings grist to the mill'. BODG, Champaran, Patna, 1938 quoting Geoffrey R. Clarke, Outcasts, 1903.

[92] The existence and legality of polygamy was admitted by the Indian legislature in the Native Converts' Marriage Dissolution Act. WBSA, General Miscellaneous, August 1866, A38–9. Also see WBSA, General Miscellaneous, January 1867, A3; WBSA, General Miscellaneous, April 1874, B1–15.

buildings, the wives or concubines of the horse keepers ... the women of the lower classes ... are always ready to solicit ... [In some hill districts] the custom of polyandry obtains, or perhaps it would be more correct to say that men and women live promiscuously together. The women of these classes are always seeking to be hired.[93]

Moreover, the formalisation of sexual relations varied enormously across social groups and regions. Official expectations were confused by the ease and lack of ceremony with which some 'marriages' were entered into and dissolved. The centralised legal-juridical system, unable to reconcile these protean practices within the textualised framework of 'Hindu' or 'Muslim' law, furnished the 'evidence' on which common-sense notions about low-caste promiscuity were constructed.

The allegedly promiscuous low castes predominated in jute mill labour. To government officials, mill managers and the middle-class intelligentsia this itself was sufficient ground for suspicion. R. C. Dutt, for example, stated, 'Industrial labouring women usually come from the low castes ... they do not maintain high standards of morality.'[94] Jute workers came in equal measures from artisans, intermediate and low cultivating castes. In the early years, local labour was drawn primarily from the Bagdis, Muchis and Kaibartas.[95] In 1896, there was a high percentage of low agricultural (Dosadh, Kurmi) and artisanal (Tatwa, Hajam, Malla) castes.[96] Most of the first generation workers (up to 1890) were originally agriculturalists, fishermen and displaced weavers and artisans.[97] Detailed data on caste over a period of time is unfortunately not available. However, till the 1920s, the 'untouchable' Chamars and Muchis and intermediate agricultural castes like the Kaibartas and Kahars were well represented in the workforce.[98]

Among those who testified to the 1891 Commission, Jaggo was a Kaivarta, Digambari was a Bairagi, Doorga and Taroni were Bagdi, and Rajoni was a Tanti. Digambari Bairagi lived with an 'adopted husband'.

---

[93] NA, General Sanitary, June 1888 A124.
[94] Dutt, 'The Aboriginal Element in the Population of Bengal'.   [95] *IFC*, pp. 77–87.
[96] There were 2,952 men and 1,103 women. Of these, 1,965 were local workers. For the 1,065 Muslims, no caste was given. There were Mallas, Chamars, Tatwas, Dosadhs, Kahars, Chatris, Kalwars, Dhanuks, Kurmis, Gours, Binds, and Hajams. They were mostly from Patna, Muzzaffarpur, Arrah, Ghazipur, Benares, Azamgarh, Mirzapur and Monghyr. There were only twenty Brahmins from Arrah who worked in the mill departments. The other fifty Brahmins from Mirzapur were employed as Gatekeepers. *LEC*, Appendix O.
[97] R. Dasgupta, 'Material Conditions and Behavioural Aspects of Calcutta Working Class 1875–1899', *Occasional Paper No. 22*, Calcutta, 1979, p. 7.
[98] The best source is the Census of 1911 which detailed seventy-one castes in jute mills. The Census of 1921 which offered only twenty-one castes was, by comparison, incomplete. Nevertheless, these reinforce the evidence from the 1896 Commission. *Census of India*, 1911, V, 2, Table XVI and *Census of India*, 1921, V, 2, Table XXII.

Jaggo Kaivarta, widowed at the age of 9 had a son from a 'temporary' relationship. This did not prevent her returning for a visit to her village during the *Pujas*. It was this apparent acceptance and legitimacy accorded to informal cohabitation arrangements which at times prompted officials to distinguish 'temporary' marriages from 'prostitution'. At other times, the putative immorality of the 'temporary' marriage led to its equation with concubinage or prostitution. Police officers and journalists when referring to poor women in the mill towns used the words wife, mistress and prostitute interchangeably. Madhu Mallick was the 'son of an old prostitute from Tindelbagan' who was 'kept' by his father Gaffar Mullick, a mill hand. His 'wife' Mayabibi was also a 'prostitute' from Tindelbagan.[99] Rambala Dasi, who had been abducted from her husband, was a 'prostitute' for some time until she was 'sold' to Nagen and they 'lived as man and wife' until she became pregnant.[100] Nanda's mother was a 'prostitute' in his father Srinath's 'keeping' when he was born. Now his sister Elokeshi and her daughter Khandi are both 'prostitutes' and Nanda himself 'keeps a mistress'.[101] Surja Prasad had a 'local prostitute', Ram Dulahia, as his 'mistress'.[102] The 'kept' women strongly objected to being classified as prostitutes. 'I am aware of the objections raised by many persons leading an immoral life to being classed as prostitutes ... [T]here are the large number of women who work as maid servants during the day and add to their income by prostitution .... [T]he class of kept women ... chiefly resented being classed as prostitutes.'[103]

Even when they were acknowledged as 'temporary' marriages, the divorce and remarriage practices of, say, Chamars, Bagdis and Bairagis appeared thoroughly immoral and arguably illegal. In fact, the designation of their marriages as 'temporary' did anything but solve the problem. On the one hand, these were recognised as customary; on the other, they were decreed illicit. Colonial records confused matters further by highlighting their deviations from high-caste norms, as though to demonstrate their invalidity. It is unlikely that the marital practices of working men and women were completely autonomous from the values of the dominant Hindu and Muslim culture, but their negative evaluation ignored the existing differences in codes of formalising sexual relations.

The Bagdis were a very numerous caste in Howrah, Hooghly and the 24 Parganas, up and down the River Hooghly where the jute mills were concentrated. Their social status improved from west to east, probably

[99] WBSA, HPC, 56 (1–2) of 1925.   [100] *Amrita Bazar Patrika*, 6 April 1928, p. 10.
[101] WBSA, HPC, 218 (1–2) of 1925.   [102] WBSA, HPC, 219 of 1925.
[103] WBSA, Judl. Police, June 1904, A35–53.

because they were more prosperous in the lower Gangetic plains than in the Chhotanagpur area where they were more dependent on daily labour. This coincided with an increasing emphasis on women's chastity eastwards. In Bankura, Manbhum and north Orissa, where the Bagdis were 'more semi-aboriginal', they accepted adult marriages and pre-marital sexual relations. East of Bhagirathi, however, the rule was infant marriage. Thus they were supposed more 'Hinduised'. They allowed divorce – it was easily obtained and divorced wives could marry again. One of the reasons why the Bholla claimed superiority over the Bagdi was because divorce was subject to greater restriction in their community. They allowed a widow to remarry according to the *sagai* rite. Her rights and privileges were precisely the same as those of a virgin wife.[104]

Digambari Bairagi, a widow, lived with an 'adopted' husband. The Bairagis were a sect of Vaishnavas who followed Nityananda's *akhara* at Kharda, which was situated at the centre of the Naihati-Jagaddal concentration of jute mills. Unlike the followers of the Santipur *Akhara* (Vaishnava centre), Bairagis were treated as a different caste with its own rules. Except widows, higher castes rarely sought conversion to this sect. Their reputation was tarnished because 'most of its new recruits joined owing to love intrigues, or because they had been turned out of their own castes or for some other sordid motive'.[105]

They were a reformist sect who repudiated caste and many of the rigorous Brahminic rituals of marriage. The emphasis on love in their faith allowed them to change partners when they wished. The *sahajiya* tradition glorified *parakiya* – love with another man's wife – drawing directly from the Radha-Krishna tradition.[106] The relative sexual freedom enjoyed by their women outraged Indian and British moralists. In the early nineteenth century, Vaishnavis had been the disseminators of popular culture through song and poetry; some of them had been erudite women who undertook the education of the *bhadramahila*.[107] From the end of the nineteenth century, they came under systematic attack from reformers. Their *akharas*, always a refuge for destitute women, became associated with prostitution. It was believed that Hindu prostitutes, when they grew older, became Vaishnavis 'because widow remarriage is allowed . . . polygamy exists and therefore they can marry'.

[104] *BDG*, Burdwan, 1910; Birbhum, 1910, p. 38; Hooghly, 1912, p. 123. Similar differentiations appeared to have obtained among other low castes like the Bauris. See, for example, R. K. Ray, 'The Kahar Chronicle', *Modern Asian Studies*, 21, 4, 1987, pp. 711–49.

[105] *BDG*, 24 Parganas, 1914, pp. 69–72. See, for example, Saratchandra Chattopadhyay's *Ekadashi Bairagi* and *Panditmashai*, *Sulabh Sarat Samagra*, 2, Calcutta, 1988.

[106] Sashibhusan Dasgupta, *Obscure Religious Cults of Bengal*, Calcutta, 1969.

[107] Chatterjee, 'Prostitutes in Nineteenth Century Bengal'.

It was asserted that the 'vairagi castes do practice hereditary prostitution'.[108] Bankim Chatterjee, the novelist, then the Deputy Magistrate of Murshidabad, noted that the *Baisnabis* were akin to prostitutes.[109] British officials concurred.[110] The Census of 1881 found Vaishnavas to have a larger proportion of women. The officer discovered a semantic confusion between Vaishnavis and prostitutes: '[I]t is a common practice among public women to assume the style of Baishnabs, while the similarity between that name and the word *Vaisya* [or, more commonly, *beshya* meaning prostitute] which denotes their profession is near enough to have led to some mistakes.'[111]

The distortions of lower caste marriage practices were most evident in the case of the Bilaspuris. Official and non-official sources targeted the Bilaspuris for lax sexual behaviour and the women were characterised as attractive and 'loose'. In a short story, 'Jalsha', Samares Basu wrote:

[In] the Bilaspuri lines ... [there were] preparations for the women's macquillage ... they have a particular way of wearing their sari that makes their strong and supple bodies specially attractive to men ... They are very generous with their bodies. Possibly their overflowing vitality has outstripped the men, and that is why they are so in demand and men fight over them so often.[112]

Many such allusions to Bilaspuri women focused on their divorce practices. For instance, it was commonly held that Bilaspuri men left their 'wives' with other men of the community when they returned home. This could involve a monetary exchange – a man would 'sell' his 'wife' to another man for a consideration, and if he returned to the mill area, he could 'buy' her back.[113] These 'Bilaspuris' were mostly Chamars from the Central Provinces. Apart from the ordinary *Bihao* or *Sadi* (arranged marriages) they had other, equally common and accepted, forms of marriages. *Churi* represented the right of the first husband's brother to claim the widow. But 'very often, she runs away with someone else'. Only rarely did such affairs end up in prosecution for adultery. *Paithoo* allowed a married woman to go 'away to the house of her seducer and [begin] to live with him as his wife, and [obtain] the privileges and rights of one ... her new husband might have to pay

[108] Kashi Kinkar Sen, Deputy Magistrate, Rajshahi, WBSA, Judl. Judl., October 1872, B252–79.

[109] B. C. Chatterjee, ibid.   [110] *BDG*, 24 Parganas, 1914, p. 78.

[111] The community recorded the largest proportion of women. There were 1,162 women to every 1,000 men, whereas the next largest proportion of women were in the Ghatwals – 1,091 women to every 1,000 men. *Report on the Census of the Town and Suburbs of Calcutta*, 1881, p. 139.

[112] Samares Basu, *Galpasangraha 1, Jalsha*, Calcutta, 1978, p. 331.

[113] Narayan Banerjee, Interview, Bally Jute Mill, 9 December 1989, Purnabrata Roychoudhury, Interview, Calcutta, 16 October 1989, Khsetromohan Chattopadhyay, Titagarh No. 2 Jute Mill, 12 December 1989.

compensation, generally measured by the marriage expense'. It was pointed out by the Census Commissioner that 'the children of both the latter classes of marriages succeed equally with those of the married wife and such succession is often recognised by our courts'.[114]

The monetary exchanges that were constructed as 'buying' and 'selling' may have been a hang-over of the custom of the 'new' husband paying the old a compensation for the marriage expenses. This was, moreover, quite consistent with prevailing practices of brideprice, since in poor agricultural communities much value attached to women's labour. Such 'aberrations' were the norm according to the Commissioner:

[I]f the Indian penal Code be strictly administered in Chhatisgarh, almost one-tenth of the Chamars might be amenable to one or the other sections relating to marriage, and a good many women would go to jail for bigamy. But laws which are above the working level of society can scarcely be effectively administered, and the law is almost a dead letter in the face of facts, which are held to be quite consistent with good sense and Chhatisgarh morality.[115]

The official mind still could dredge a degree of prurient sympathy or advocate a sanguine and pragmatic recognition of curious marital and divorce practices. Increasingly, however, from the late nineteenth century, officials and, more especially, Indian middle classes became harshly condemning. In case of men, Government rejected demands to restrict polygamy to narrower textual prescriptions of Hinduism or Islam on the grounds that it was too widely practised and too difficult to legislate. In case of women, British habits, judicial temper and Indian elite convictions converged to condemn and outlaw all polygamous practices. The Commissioner of Burdwan realised that such laws 'play havoc with the *nikka* marriages of the divorced women of the low castes in some parts'. Despite the widespread prevalence of *nikka* among low castes, it was held that it was 'a Muhammedan institution and when the lower class of Hindus get *nikka* wives, the word is but another name for concubinage'.[116] For Hindu women, a variety of second marriages were declared to be 'not marriage at all' and a 'woman contracting a second marriage would know ... that the Government did not recognise her condition as that of a wife living in marriage but in concubinage'.[117] This took no account of the fact that in labouring groups, where marriage was one means of ensuring the extraction of women's labour, access to divorce may have represented an escape for women. Certainly, a large number of women in the jute mill towns appear to have taken

---

[114] *Census of the Central Provinces*, 1881, II, pp. 38–45.   [115] Ibid., p. 45.
[115] Commissioner of Burdwan, WBSA, General Miscellaneous, April 1874, B1–15.
[117] The Moorshedabad Magistry, ibid.

recourse to flight. They ran away with other men, or went to other mills in neighbouring towns. The law of restitution of conjugal rights allowed husbands to use the courts to restrain and recover their runaway wives.[118] The women who went to live with other men became criminally liable under sections 494–5 and 498 of the Indian Penal Code relating to adultery and bigamy.

Many women found a way round these disabilities. Increasingly, the administration of these laws became fraught with difficulties. As the Commissioner of Chhatisgarh had so acutely noted, 'laws which are above the working level of society' were in danger of remaining 'dead letters'. In any case, the government was not quite clear as to how rigorously restitution of conjugal rights ought to be applied. A Deputy Magistrate noted that, even if the husband won a declaratory decree, 'the wife cannot be bodily *delivered* over to the husband'. She could at best be charged with contempt of court which was a tedious and expensive procedure.[119] In many cases, even a declaratory decree proved difficult to obtain. When Rambalak charged Dehri Routh with kidnapping his wife, Ramratia, from Kanchrapara and bringing her to Bhadreswar, the courts refused to grant a decree. Ramratia refused to return, and Rambalak could not countermand her decision.[120] Similarly, Saifulla of Naihati failed to persuade the magistrate to grant him leave to force his wife to return from Kankinara where she had gone to protect herself from his assaults.[121] The courts' inability or reluctance to grant restoration decrees resulted from a loophole in the law. Both civil and criminal suits hinged on the definition of 'marriage'. Especially in the case of bigamy and adultery, 'even when the fact of marriage is not disputed, the law requires strict legal proof of the performance of the first marriage'.[122] In many cases, women themselves could and did deny the fact of marriage. Kalidassi, for instance, disputed a case brought by a man claiming to be her husband on the grounds that she had a former husband living. This, of course, made her marriage with the complainant bigamous, and his case invalid.

The prosecution case is that the complainant's married wife, Kalidassi had been enticed away by the accused ... Kalidassi in her evidence said that she was quite willing to go back to her former [first] husband [Dasu Bauri] ... but her stepmother had been compelling her to live with the complainant as his mistress ... The magistrate said the girl ... [had left] of her own accord.[123]

[118] This law was first introduced by a judicial decision in 1867. It was later incorporated in the Code of Civil Procedure (1882), Section 260.
[119] NA, Home Judl., March 1873, 66–8.
[120] *Amrita Bazar Patrika*, 26 November 1932.
[121] *Amrita Bazar Patrika*, 14 July 1928, p. 6.
[122] NA Home Judl. March 1873, 66–8.   [123] *Amrita Bazar Patrika*, 22 June 1936.

Where women willingly admitted to bigamy and concubinage, the courts often found themselves unable to uphold the rights of the men who demanded restitution of their 'wives'. When Bhagabat Passi accused Kheloan Passi of enticing his wife, the 'wife' categorically denied that status. She owned to being a widow, living with her mother in Jaunpur, and to being 'enticed' by Bhagabat who brought her to Calcutta. Forced by his tortures to leave him, she ran away to Kamar-hati, secured a job in a jute mill and rented a room. She maintained that she had never even seen the accused before she was brought to court. However, it emerged that Kheloan lived in the same house that she did, with his parents.[124] Often, it proved very difficult to decide which marriage came first and complied with the legal requirements. Ramnandan Bhar came with a warrant from the court to reclaim 'his wife', living in Kharda with Mangaru Bhar. Mangaru, who was absent from the house, returned to find that 'his wife' had been taken away. So, Mangaru subsequently brought out another warrant from the court to reclaim the same woman from Kankinara where she was then living with Ramnandan.[125]

In case of Muslim women this had for a long time constituted a special problem. Muslim women's divorce and remarriage (*nikka*) were legally accepted. However, as in the case of the Hindu *nikka*, the Shia Muslim *mota* was recognised as customary, but considered concubinage rather than marriage. According to this custom, a man and a woman would agree to 'cohabit a specified time varying from a few months to several years for an agreed sum of money. At the end of the period, the woman is free to accept any other man as her protector. If, however, the man leaves the woman before the period, he will have to pay the whole stipulated amount.' Though the father took responsibility for children born of such marriages, '[a] *mota* or temporary wife is nothing but a legalised kept mistress'.[126] This was unacceptable because women could not be empowered to leave marriages. Even the *khula* divorce, which women could have initiated, was replaced with the unilateral male *talak*.[127] This meant that if a man wished to divorce a woman, 'he gets rid of her by simply informing his neighbours that she is at liberty to go where she pleases, and he refuses to support her any longer'.[128] However, if women left their husbands, they became liable to charges of bigamy and adultery, and their *nikka* husbands to charges of enticement or kidnapping. However, though the criminal liability of women and their second husbands was beyond doubt, the courts could exercise

[124] *Amrita Bazar Patrika*, 1 May 1936.   [125] *Ananda Bazar Patrika*, 29 July 1935.
[126] Mukherjee and Chakrabarty, *Prostitution in India*, pp. 73, 121.
[127] Anderson, 'Work Construed'.   [128] NA, Home Judl., March 1873, 66–8.

some discretion in cases that appeared palpably unjust. The following case reported in the *Amrita Bazar Patrika* in 1939 illustrates how the law had to be, at times, bent.

'It is simply shocking that a little girl of 14 should be sent to prison for 3 months on a charge of bigamy ...' observed Mr Justice Henderson ... The prosecution case was that Halema Khatun was married to Abdul Rashid first when both of them were minors. Later the girl was married to Fazal Karim when the previous marriage was subsisting and she had not been divorced ... [T]he offence really was a technical one. No harm whatever had been done to the complainant, the alleged first husband by the alleged bigamy ... The person injured ... was the other party to the second marriage. For, if Karim did not know of the first marriage he was obviously injured. He had spent money on the marriage and it had no legal effect. As a result he had been sentenced to 6 months imprisonment. If he really knew of the first marriage no serious harm had been done to anybody by this bigamy and a nominal sentence would have sufficed.[129]

The case then hinged over the issue of which husband, the first or the second, was deemed to have been more 'injured'. It is also notable that the court gave some attention to Halema's age. After the Sarda Act, when the issue of the legal age of marriage had received considerable attention, this was not surprising. But age was difficult to establish. This report appears singular in that the 'facts' of the case seemed to have been incontrovertibly established. In most cases, the legal proof of either 'marriage' or divorce could not be easily furnished in the absence of marriage records. The upper classes often registered their marriages along with the *dain mohur* (dower deed), but among poorer Muslims registration was rare.[130] The courts accepted that by Muslim law and practice, if a man and woman lived together before the village public they were presumed married unless the matter was disputed. They also averred that in cases of bigamy and adultery, their sympathy was usually with the injured husband unless his misconduct could be proved. However, the law required the fact of the marriage to be proved by at least three witnesses. In a migrant context such proof could be hard to obtain since the marriage probably took place in a distant village. In Howrah, a rapidly expanding town, 'the omission to register Mahomedan marriages or divorces has led to a very loose system of morality as regards marriages'.[131] Besides, a woman could bring equal numbers of witnesses to argue that she had been given *talak*. Thus, aggrieved 'husbands' often found it impossible to force reluctant wives to return.

On the complaint of Abdul Sovan of Manicktolla, Sheikh Hussani was ... prosecuted ... on a charge of enticing away Shamsul Bibi, wife of Sovan for immoral purposes when the latter was not at home. Azizur Rahman deposed

---

[129] *Amrita Bazar Patrika*, 13 May 1939.   [130] WBSA, Judl. Judl., May 1894 A6–12.
[131] NA, Home Judl., March 1873, 66–8.

that he was the son of the complainant. His mother Shamsul Bibi lived with his father. She at present was living with the accused ... like his wife in the same room. Abdul Sovan stated that about 5 months ago ... he could not find his wife ... traced her ... at the house of the accused. He asked his wife to come with him but she refused to do so.[132]

Sovan claimed his 'wife' was 'enticed' away, though there was no proof that they were ever married. The son did not say that his father and mother were married. His mother 'lived with his father', and now she was 'living with the accused ... like his wife'. The 'wife' *refused* to return to the 'husband'. There was little the court could do. Women sometimes ran away and claimed maintenance if their husbands married again. Hanifan Bibi and Jabbar Mea's first wife left their husbands when the men married a second time. Jabbar's wife appeared to have taken 'shelter' in another man's house.[133] Even when women were not living with other men, they could resist a restoration order. When Moniruddin complained that his wife had been enticed away and concealed in 'a House of ill-fame', the defence argued that the girl was in fact not legally married to him.[134]

Thus, a narrower definition of marriage turned the laws of restitution of conjugal rights, adultery and bigamy, which were meant to enhance men's control over women, into an instrument which women could use against men they wished to leave. To do so they had to admit to concubinage, bigamy or adultery in the first place. It has been argued elsewhere that such admissions were easier because these women had already lost 'honour' by the very fact of migration. When widows and married women left their village homes with 'men who were not their husbands', they forsook the possibility of ever returning. Some women, who came to the city because rural resources were exhausted, had nothing to which to return.[135] Moreover, as argued earlier, among the labouring groups who constituted the bulk of the jute mill labour, notions of 'honour' may not have been very closely related to chastity and life-long monogamy. For such women, the imperative to deny men an exclusive right to their labour, wages and sexuality may have been stronger. In any event, the communities in which they lived had protean marriage practices. Adult marriage, divorce and remarriage were informal and frequent, having wide acceptability. Thus, the legal imputations of 'concubinage', 'bigamy' and 'adultery', based on upper-class norms, may have been socially less effective in their case. So, some

---

[132] *Amrita Bazar Patrika*, 17 January 1940.
[133] *Amrita Bazar Patrika*, 10 April 1940.
[134] *Amrita Bazar Patrika*, 13 January, 1935.   [135] Sen, 'Honour and Resistance'.

women could manipulate the law to deny to men the rights these legal innovations were supposed to guarantee.

These examples, however, must be treated with some caution. For every case that went to court and found its way into newspaper reports, there must have been many that did neither. Men did not depend only on the courts to bend recalcitrant women to their will. Social pressure and socially sanctioned violence against women were used more frequently and with greater effect. When widowed Hanifan Bibi would not marry her neighbour, he stole her baby to force her to agree.[136] Bagit Kunjra tried similar tactics to force a widow to marry (*nikka*) him.[137] Such methods may not have been frowned upon. Shanti Pasricha, the Labour Welfare Officer in Jardine and Skinner Company, mentioned that it was usual for neighbours and friends to arrange a marriage for a young widow to avoid such complications.[138] In an extreme case, a reluctant widow was cruelly punished for her refusal to remarry.

Mungri Passi alleged that one Wednesday morning the accused Sundar Passi and six others forcibly took her away from her house and confined her in a room for the night in a house at Cossipore. The next day they forcibly cut her locks, blackened her face and put a garland of small snails, shoes and earthenpots round her neck and made her sit on a donkey which paraded the streets and bustis of Narkeldanga. The woman said that Sundar Passi wanted to marry her but she refused and preferred to lead a life of liberty as she is a widow. The enraged Passi . . . with the assistance of his fellows tortured her severely.[139]

Such coercion could all too often take a drastic form – murder. In one case a man killed a widow who was living with him when he suspected her of trying to leave him for another man.[140] Many incidents of murder and suicide were attributed to sexual jealousy. The 'scarcity' of women in the mill areas led, it was believed, to competition among the men, impelling them to destroy the woman, the object of their desire, when their possession of that object was contested. It is not clear why competition would, *per se*, result in the destruction of the 'scarce commodity', i.e., women, rather than of competitors, i.e., rival men. The attempt to explain the murder of women in these terms, by ignoring the wider context of gender relations, in effect reduces the women into mere objects of male sexual desire. It can hardly be argued that it was the paucity of women that caused these extreme forms of violence against 'disloyal' and 'deserting wives'. It is more plausible to argue that these extreme reprisals were invoked by the convergence of various factors which allowed women to challenge male control over their

---

[136] *Ananda Bazar Patrika*, 15 May 1935.   [137] WBSA, HPC, 376 (1–8) of 1925.
[138] Interview, Shanti Pasricha, Calcutta, March 1989.
[139] *Amrita Bazar Patrika*, 17 May 1936.   [140] *Ananda Bazar Patrika*, 30 July 1936.

labour and sexuality. Certainly, women's access to wages, however restricted, offered a possibility of survival outside the 'family'. This in turn prompted them to try and defeat the purposes of punitive marriage laws. It is in this context that the 'scarcity' of women gave them a greater bargaining edge in their dealings with men – to use the rivalries between men to confound their claims. Equally, for these very reasons, the men may have felt impelled to exercise more coercive control to restrain them. Apart from morally edged assertions by contemporary observers, there is very little evidence by which to judge the extent of such 'matrimonial anomie'.[141]

Even if the police and journalists were prone to highlighting cases of crime and violence among the working classes, their prolific reports do testify to women's vulnerability in the mills, the *bastis* and the streets. Young women, especially very young women, seem to have been targeted for rape and abduction. Older women too were subjected to physical harassment by the men with whom they lived, local toughs and the police in mill neighbourhoods and *bazars*. In the mills, managers, clerks, *durwans* and *sardars* often exacted sexual favours in return for access to and regularity of employment. The low wages and the acute uncertainty of employment enmeshed jute mill workers within an informal network of credit, housing and jobs. Women's wages were lower, employment opportunities were more restricted and they rarely had any rural resources on which to fall back. Their choices must have been severely limited. They may have sought physical and economic protection in relatively stable and long-term marriages. However, they remained at the unequal end of these relationships. The men in many cases had a wife and children in the village to whom they were committed to send regular remittances and to whom they were eventually to return. These men, torn between the family in the village and in the city, depended on the women for the sustenance of the children. The risk of unemployment made it more likely that they would desert pregnant women. The wives in the mill towns were thrown entirely on very meagre urban resources to bear, rear and maintain their children. Their extra-legal relationships then became more risky and their households less stable.[142]

It was the instability of their marital relationships that lent credence to official and elite labelling of their marriages as 'temporary' and contributed to the immoral imaging of mill neighbourhoods and the women

[141] The term was used in the context of Indian workers in Fiji plantations. See Brij V. Lal, 'Kunti's Cry: Indentured Women on Fiji Plantations', in J. Krishnamurty (ed.), *Women in Colonial India: Essays on Survival, Work and the State*, Delhi, 1989.

[142] These arguments have been set out in Sen, 'Honour and Resistance'.

who worked in jute mills. In so far as contemporary observers made a distinction between the 'temporary' wife and the 'prostitute', widows and deserted wives 'living in and around the mill lines' were supposed to enter into 'temporary liaisons with some men', while professional prostitutes were seen to congregate near the *lines*.[143] There were, in fact, in some of the mills, separate areas designated the 'prostitute *lines*'.[144] In Naihati, the red-light area was located beside the mill compound, a few yards away from the main mill *lines* of Lichubagan. In most cases, the area where 'prostitutes' were supposed to have lived was rarely separated from the *basti* where the working poor lived. They, like other workers, tended to congregate in the heart of the town – around the *bazars* and the *lines*. The attempt to set aside 'prostitutes' as a distinct category and to designate them as 'public' women denied, by implication, their 'private' domains where they interacted with men and women of their own class. They were, in fact, in no way set apart from the rest of the community of the labouring poor.[145] Like the maid-servants, cooks, *panwallis* and other women engaged in service, petty trading or casual labour, occupations which often provided only a partial livelihood, the women workers in mills were faced with limited opportunities of employment and the reality of very low wages in towns which were hostile to young women living alone. The 'temporary' marriages might have increased their security, even as they added to their vulnerability. The perception that such alliances were 'deviant' was more a function of the retention and imposition of orthodox standards of sexual behaviour than the moral views of the communities in which the marriages were taking place.

In a variety of elite discourses, in different contexts, poor women alternated between the image of the victim and that of the morally flawed poor. There was a ubiquitous assumption, whether in sympathy or in harsh condemnation, that poor women were forced to practise prostitution. If poverty alone was sufficient to drive women to prostitution, then of course all poor women were prostitutes. The logical absurdity of this argument was in line with the identification of spurious sub-categories of prostitutes. The widow, the 'temporary' wife, the professional and the clandestine prostitute were torn out of their social and cultural contexts to reinforce the commonplace of an immoral, low-caste, migrant and urban poor. The jute mill women, especially, stood accused of sexual irregularities and promiscuity. Their work in the mills,

[143] *RCLI*, V, 1, p. 31.
[144] Curjel Report, Appendix B, Sl, No. 1, Evidence of Manager, Kinnison Jute Mill.
[145] See J. R. Walkowitz, *Prostitution and Victorian Society: Women, Class and the State*, London, 1980.

their socialisation in the streets, and their militancy in strikes were stigmatised by the narrowing emphasis on women's 'private' concerns. In these 'private' concerns, jute mill women violated high-caste norms of women's chastity by their frequent divorces and remarriages. These women could not, and sometimes would not, accept the dominant definitions of respectability. But they lived in a society which could punish them for their deviations. Magistrates, constables, managers, mill clerks, *durwans*, *sardars*, *goondas* and male workers could unleash coercive violence against them. To be identified as a prostitute could sometimes have serious material consequences – it could threaten their livelihood and security. Such threats to working women often stemmed from the ideological trappings of a sedulous elite discourse. Working women, like the men, were forced to negotiate the atomising effects of poverty and struggle against the social and cultural alienation entailed in migration.

Women workers, some feminist scholars have argued, suffer in their family roles and responsibilities. In fact, the working-class 'family' has, in political and scholarly discourses, veered between adulation as the site of political and cultural resistance and condemnation as the primary locus of working-class women's oppression. Doubtless, there were elements of both oppression and resistance in the 'family' lives of working men and women. The women were far from being the passive victims of salacious men, either of their own class or of more privileged groups. Such men could subject them to grinding poverty and intense sexual exploitation. The women, however, also fought to retain control over their own lives. They entered into sexual and marital liaisons with men of their own classes, bargained in sexual currency with men who had the power to extend credit, provide housing and secure employment. Given their economic and physical insecurities, women often looked to men in their search for independence and self-improvement. The urban situation allowed them a limited opportunity to manipulate men for personal gain and material advancement. They could sometimes change partners to suit themselves. When the men sought the help of courts to restrain them, they disrupted the intentions of colonial legislation by admitting to 'inchastity', 'adultery' and 'bigamy'.

These contradictions caused gender relations to become more volatile and mating patterns tended to lose stability. This flux in gender relations may have given a new meaning and a greater militancy to women's struggles against economic and sexual oppression.

6   Working-class politics and women's militancy

In Marxist analyses the 'economic' strike was considered the classic form of solidaristic working-class protest. As a result, the investigations of origins, conduct and consequences of strikes usually focused on the 'common' issues of the working class as a whole, excluding other issues, such as those of gender, which might be potentially divisive of a 'solidary working class'. If issues of gender were considered at all, they were limited to questions of whether women contributed to the success of strikes or whether their different and separate interests led them to weaken working-class movements. By contrast, when Feminist scholars began first to address 'women's role' in strikes, they often concentrated on the conflict of interest between men and women workers. Marxist and Feminist scholars were, of course, divided on whether gender or class provided the primary basis of social cohesion and schism. In the 1970s, the Marxist-Feminists attempted to resolve this impasse through the 'dual systems' theory which constructed antinomies between class/ gender, capitalism/patriarchy or production/reproduction, aligning class with the first term in each pair and gender with the second. This intervention established the importance of examining gender and class in tandem – gender cannot be collapsed into class, and class is not the exclusive, or even the primary conceptual paradigm for strike analysis. However, the analytic separation of class and gender, which is the main focus of the dual systems theory, can be exaggerated to obscure their complex historical interaction. The relation between gender and class is not, after all, a mechanically aggregative one, as though a gender dimension can be added on to class or vice versa. Rather, gender and class relations are embedded in and constructed through one another, through both production and reproduction, work and family, and their interplay can be examined through the prism of working people's protests.

In Indian labour historiography, there is no gender-versus-class debate because gender has been marginal to studies of class. The Bengal case runs true to type in ignoring the role of women in labour movements. The silence is comprehensive – even trade union activists, then and now, figured that there were too few women in the industry to justify any special effort to mobilise them. For most of the period under study, women constituted about 15–16 per cent of the workforce. Their proportion has declined sharply from the 1960s' decade hovering around 2 per cent now. When trade unions began to take off in Calcutta's surrounding industrial area in the 1920s, however, women in jute mills numbered about 50,000. Yet, they were the smaller proportion of the workforce. And as such, they remained relatively unimportant to the unions. On the whole, the issue of mobilisation of women was peripheral to organised labour politics in Bengal. Contemporary official and union records of working-class activities reflected this unconcern. Descriptions of meetings, demonstrations, strikes, or even violent crowds, rarely mentioned women specifically. Public meetings, in which women participated, were habitually described as if they were composed entirely of men. Accounts of riots took it for granted that the only participants were men, unless women were extremely prominent and, therefore, commanded attention. Strikes too were described without any reference to women. The term 'men' was often presumed to include women, while other terms like 'hands' or 'workers', or even more commonly used notations like 'crowd' or 'mob' bypassed the question altogether. Addresses in leaflets, for instance, often presumed an entirely male readership.[1] Trade unions assumed the working class as a homogeneous solidaristic male population and women, when they were considered at all, were expected to play a negative role in the labour movement.

Historians of class have faithfully reproduced this silence. They have even relied on the same reasoning – that there were too few women to matter – to justify their silence. Their diverse stories have taken for granted that they were being told about men – adult men who, by their participation in wage-labour in 'modern' industry qualify for a contested 'class consciousness'. The 'hierarchical and inegalitarian' culture of Bengal which, according to one historian, vitiated the growth of a fully-fledged working class, does not include inequalities and hierarchies embodied by gender. In his explanation, 'Most of the jute labourers were adult males, women on the average forming about 16 per cent of the labour force between 1921 and 1930.'[2] Such a banishment of

---

[1] Two leaflets issued by the *Bengal Chatkal Mazdur Union*: one was addressed to *bhaisab* (all brothers), the other to 'Dear Labour Brethren'. WBSA, HPC 60 of 1937 and 86 of 1940. There are numerous such examples.

[2] Dipesh Chakrabarty, *Rethinking Working Class History, Bengal 1890–1940*, Princeton, 1989, p. 9.

women from histories of class results in part from an uncritical reading
of government and managerial documents which attempted to construe
women as 'docile' and tractable labour. To some extent, the trade
unions shared this comfortable legend. Consequently, even they left
women out of official union records and thereby contributed to the
misleading stereotype. And the historians' conclusion that women were,
and indeed are, irrelevant to the working-class struggle remains un-
shaken. In part, however, the exclusion of women workers from narratives of protest is indicative of their marginality in various organised
political movements of the time. Their integration into socialised production did not lead to their incorporation into the movements or the
histories of the growth of proletarian consciousness, nor did they play
any role in the predominantly middle-class 'women's movements' of the
period. On both counts, they appear to stand divested of agency in
social change.

How then to set about the task of reconstructing women workers'
political roles and 'recovering' their diverse concerns? First, sympathetic
accounts of labour disturbances emphasised women's leading roles as a
testimony of the oppression faced by the working class, such as to drive
'even women' to extreme action. Participation of women in violent acts,
seemingly uncharacteristic of their usual public roles, were upheld as
illustrations of the power and force of class solidarity. Second, women
were portrayed in graphic and moving terms as victims of police and
managerial brutality. These served both as illustrations of the oppressive
character of the state and the capitalists and as a strategy for mobilising
class anger. There was also a third set of characterisations of bellicose
jute mill women. Unsympathetic officials and managers and, on rare
occasions, trade union leaders and journalists offered glimpses of violent
women leading strikes. But such images also underlined female deviancy
and reinforced the notion of the factory woman as aggressive, aberrant
and undeserving of public sympathy. Thus in various fragments from
newspapers, fiction, reminiscences of managers, workers and union
leaders, we come across violent and disorderly women, instigating
destruction of property, leading and exhorting the crowd. Many jute
mill women are remembered for turning on managers and supervisors
with a stick or a broom or just verbal abuse for real or imagined wrongs.
These otherwise mute women thus come to brief but startling life in oral
accounts of strikes. Their active participation in protest actions earned
them a special reputation for militancy in the industry.

And indeed how could it be otherwise? Unions could not entirely
ignore women. Women's participation could at times be crucial for the
success of strikes and strike-breaking women could spell disaster. Jute

mill women have left behind enduring memories of both strike-breaking and strike militancy. This is important to emphasise not only to redress the male bias in the historical and historiographical records, but to examine the possibility of looking at strikes with a gendered eye: to ask how far women's strikes took the form they did because they were undertaken by workers who were also women. And in that process to also ask how gender provided a basis for solidarity and schism. This is crucial to a deeper understanding of the historical character of work-based collective action. Since the 'economic' strike is generally regarded as the quintessential manifestation of class consciousness, women's participation in strikes, or their abjuration of them, have been made the measure of their class identity. This takes no account of the fact that women's different experience of factory work and city life may have led them into distinctive forms and modes of protest; that in many cases we have to throw away the measure to understand the phenomenon. It may even be that strikes were the vehicle through which women explored and articulated a new gender identity.

Trade union movements – the absence of women

Women appear to have been ready participants in strikes. They displayed great elan and a ready resort to disorder. Their typical tactics often included surrounding the manager in his office and holding him hostage as a means of winning their argument, or chasing the supervisory staff within the mill or damaging the machinery and sheds. This kind of violence, expressive rather than instrumental, usually came at the beginning of strikes. And it continued to be characteristic of women's protests even in the 1950s and 1960s.

From the 1930s, women began to lose the initiative to the unions very soon after the beginning of a strike. The process of unionisation was not gender-neutral. Trade union leadership increased women's involvement in strikes, but they also attempted to control their impulsive acts of direct protests. Thus, the women who had a reputation for militancy and aggression were not those associated with unions. In 1929, in the Hooghly area when 'women workers caused willing men to be locked out', this second wave of strikes was not organised through unions.[3]

Increasingly, in the post-independence period, strikes were interwoven into a more complex web of organisation, collective bargaining, industrial dispute legislation (and its machinery) and fragmentation of trade unions on overtly political lines (with its concomitant of action for

---

[3] DIG CID IB, Weekly Reports, Secret, 1930.

political purposes). Trade unions had to deal with the pressures of the numbers game, political brinksmanship, legal squabbling and the employers' divisive industrial relations practice. They attempted to establish principles of rational calculation and plan for long-term trade union growth, though their arguments grew increasingly tortuous and ratiocinative. As the processes of trade unions and collective bargaining became increasingly formalised, the bulk of (male) trade unionism began to find women's unorganised protest activities wanting in long-term gains and politically inexpedient.

'Spontaneity' and violence were not, however, unique characteristics of women strikers. In the early years of the industry, all strikes tended to be unorganised, sectional and violent. Certainly, the mangers' inability to anticipate or prevent lightning strikes figured in some of the earliest records of the industry.[4] This labour violence, according to Dipesh Chakrabarty, was a response to the violent nature of authority operating in conjunction with colonial power.[5] The European managers allied with the municipal administration of the mill towns and were granted special magisterial powers to arm themselves.[6] The managers', state officials' and local inhabitants' fear of labour violence escalated from the 1890s, as migrant labour began to crowd into hitherto sparsely populated villages.[7] The police believed workers to be endemically prone to rioting and perhaps quite realistically feared the consequences of a violent confrontation between the workers and the management. Government drew up elaborate lines of defence involving the managers, the police and the army.[8]

Muslim 'up-countrymen' came to acquire a reputation for 'turbulence' and violent disorder.[9] Fears on all sides were confirmed when from the mid-1890s a spate of riots and strikes hit the jute belt

---

[4] WBSA, General Miscellaneous, September 1875, A6–27; IJMAR, 31 December 1887.
[5] Chakrabarty, *Rethinking Working Class History*, chapter 5.
[6] WBSA, Judicial Police, June 1896, A8–9. Also see Subho Basu, 'Workers' Politics in Bengal, 1890–1929: Mill-towns, Strikes and Nationalist Agitations', Ph.D thesis, Cambridge University, 1994.
[7] Local inhabitants in Titagarh petitioned the police that the mill hands were under no control on Sundays and they would go to the 'grogshops' and 'get unruly to the annoyance of quiet people.' The residents of Naihati had similar complaints. WBSA, Judicial Police, June 1896, A8–9.
[8] The introduction to the scheme states, 'This [is] ... for protecting the mill areas ... in case of looting or rioting, etc. These areas swarm with a vast floating population consisting of Muhammedan and Hindu up-countrymen of various castes, and it is not infrequent for the local bodies to be confronted suddenly with a very serious situation.' Police Defence Scheme for the Hooghly Mill Area, Calcutta, 1916.
[9] Parimal Ghosh, 'Emergence of an Industrial Labour Force in Bengal: A Study of the Conflicts of the Jute Mill Hands with the State 1880–1930', Ph.D thesis, Jadavpur University, 1984.

culminating in the Talla riots of Calcutta which have been characterised as communal.[10] There were many so-called 'communal' riots over issues like cow killing, the spraying of coloured water during Holi, the defilement of mosques by Hindus or that of temples by Muslims. Equally, there were many outbreaks of violence where any such discernibly neat categorisation of issues or contestants is not possible.[11] There were series of strikes over holidays for festivals and wages.[12]

From the Swadeshi period, the middle classes began to draw workers into broader political movements. The strikes around 1905–7 appear, however, to have been as disorganised and sectional as in the earlier period. In most cases, workers targeted individual managers and supervisors.[13] It was during the non-cooperation and Khilafat movements in 1920 that politicians made a more concerted attempt to mobilise the working 'masses'. The period 1920–23 witnessed a series of strikes over issues like wages, the abolition of *khoraki* payment, dismissal of workers with union connections and the venality of supervisors and *sardars*. Given the post-war economic distress, workers blamed the 'government or their employers, who in the case of the concerns employing large bodies of industrial labour are mainly European firms'.[14] This kind of linkage gave the Congress and the Khilafatists an additional political leverage as evinced in November 1921, when, on the occasion of the Prince of Wales's visit, the city was brought to a standstill with the co-operation of the 'lower orders'. But the Congress and the Khilafatists, fully alive to the limits of their own control over the workers, hastily withdrew a projected *hartal* on 19 March 1920.[15] In any case, the Congress's declared commitment to class harmony militated against a determined unionising effort. They concentrated on negotiation between workers and mill owners and ultimately a containment of workers' grievances.

In the early 1920s, however, serious efforts at unionisation had

[10] Chakrabarty, *Rethinking Working Class History*, pp. 187–90.
[11] The riots at Titagarh and Rishra in 1896 did indeed begin over cow killing. Ibid., pp. 191–4. But both seemed to have been directed more at the police than at Hindu workers. See WBSA, Judicial Police, August 1896, A1–15 and July 1896, A52–7. Managers felt that strikes and riots broke out over 'quite unforeseen causes' or even 'many little things'. There was some violence against 'Peshawaris' in the neighbourhood of Hastings Jute Mills in 1896. WBSA, Judicial Police, June 1896 A8–9. Ghosh argues that these cannot be called 'communal' riots because they were not sustained by any political notion of an oppositional community. Ghosh, 'Emergence of an Industrial Labour Force in Bengal'.
[12] WBSA, Judicial Police, June 1896, A8–9.
[13] NA, Home Public, June 1906, A169–86. NMML, A. C. Banerji private papers. Sumit Sarkar, *Swadeshi Movement in Bengal: 1903–1908*, New Delhi, 1973; Ghosh, 'Emergence of an Industrial Labour Force', pp. 225–9.
[14] WBSA, HPC 39 (1–2) of 1921.   [15] WBSA, HPC 395 (1–3) of 1924.

begun. Most of the unions were short-lived and we have little information about them. One proved relatively stable – the Gourepore Works Employees Association formed by Santoshkumari Devi with the help of Bankim Mukherjee and Kalidas Bhattacharya. The moderate Kankinara Labour Union was formed in 1921 by K. C. Roychowdhury. The Nuddea Mill Workers Union and the Reliance Labour Union started with Santoshkumari's help were amalgamated in 1925 into the Bengal Jute Workers' Association (later Union) which was to provide leadership to the first general strike (1929) in the jute industry.[16]

There was what has often been called a 'paradox' in the development of the Bengal trade union movement.[17] Since the owners and managers of jute mills were largely European, one would expect a relatively easy relationship of the labour movement with the anti-imperial nationalist movement. This was not the case. After brief and temporary alliances during the Swadeshi and the non-cooperation movements, the two tended to diverge sharply. Almost forty years after the first union was formed in 1895 the trade union movement was still referred to as being in its 'infancy'.[18] The lack of organisation was revealed in the meagre membership rolls.[19] There were only two general strikes in the industry in the whole period, in 1929 and 1937. No large-scale protest could be organised against the retrenchment of 60,000 workers in 1930–31 – the Bengal Jute Workers' Union, which had organised the general strike of 1929, crumbled when Prabhabati Dasgupta and Bankim Mukherjee fell out.[20] This provides a remarkable and inexplicable contrast with the Bombay textile industry. In Bombay the capitalist, managerial and supervisory classes were not European. And yet, trade unions had closer links with the nationalist movement. Under the leadership of the communist-led Girni Kamgar Union, the Bombay working class achieved a

---

[16] DIG CID IB, 35 f 1926.

[17] Tanika Sarkar, *Bengal, 1928–1934: The Politics of Protest*, Delhi, 1987, p. 66 and Chakrabarty, *Rethinking Working Class History*, chapter 4.

[18] The first organisation, called the Mahomedan Association, was formed in 1895 at Kankinara. See Chakrabarty, *Rethinking Working Class History*, pp. 116–17. Chandavarkar contests this in the Bombay case. R. S. Chandavarkar, 'Workers' Politics and the Mill Districts in Bombay between the Wars', *Modern Asian Studies*, 15, 1981. In Bengal, unions sometimes described themselves in these terms. Phillip Spratt wrote to K. L. Ghose in 1937, 'union is in its infancy and it is difficult to organise things really well now'. DIG CID IB, 303A of 1937.

[19] Indrajit Gupta, *Capital and Labour in the Jute Industry*, Bombay, 1953.

[20] WBSA, HPC 161 (29–67) of 1934. The Bengal Jute Workers' Union failed to organise a general strike. A general strike was 'foreshadowed' in February in Howrah due to the activities of 'labour agitators' like Abdul Momin and M. A. Zaman. However, 'the local police anticipate no serious trouble'. There were short strikes in Kamarhatty Jute Mills, Lawrence Jute Mills, Victoria Jute Mill and Clive Jute Mill. DIG CID IB, Secret Reports, January–March 1931.

remarkably organised and militant character in the 1920s.[21] There appears to be no simple explanation for the failure of Bengal communists to make a comparable headway. Despite the advantages of a highly localised industry, trade unions remained under *bhadralok* leadership and confined their role to negotiation between the management and the workers during strikes.[22] Bitter inter-union rivalries in the 1920s, which flowed partly from the institution of a nominated labour seat in the Legislative Assembly in 1919, gave way to a more competitive labour politics when the labour constituency became elective. It was in the 1930s that the communists began to make real inroads with trade unions as was reflected in the more sustained general strike of 1937.[23]

This brief and rather potted account of workers' politics nevertheless highlights two issues. First, prior to the growth of a strong trade union movement, for most of the period under study, jute workers protested over relatively short-term issues: ad hoc demands over wages, holidays, dismissals, or restoration of *khoraki* payment. Some strikes were reactive: in response to insults by managers or supervisors, wage cuts, perceived interference with 'customs' like religious holidays or public conduct of religious festivals. They remained disorganised, sectional and prone to individual or group violence targeted against the state, the police, the management, and in some cases against each other – Bengalis against 'up-countrymen' or Hindus against Muslims, or even in some cases, strikers versus 'loyal' workers. In this plethora, women's protests followed no distinctive pattern. Like other workers, they were apt to reach for the broom or the stick in extreme situations, chase the supervisor to avenge an insult, or to walk out of the mill if they were not granted their desired wage raise or a particular leave of absence. Second, the balance changed as unionisation began to make a headway. Male workers were progressively unionised, especially towards the general strike of 1937. Strikes had begun to be less violent, increasingly better organised, better led and often reached the negotiation table. More

---

[21] Chandavarkar, 'Workers' Politics and the Mill Districts in Bombay'.

[22] Kishorilal Ghose, Bengal Trades Union Federation, WBSA, Comm. Comm., February 1929, A1–34.

[23] Chakrabarty, *Rethinking Working Class History*. Employers were quite sure that this general strike was a 'communist plot'. CSAS, Benthall Papers, Box X, Correspondence between B. B. Morton and E. C. Benthall. The IJMA issued a statement during the general strike of 1937, 'the workers (are) being exploited for communistic and political purposes only'. *Amrita Bazar Patrika*, 29 April 1937. The government believed that 'the spirit of defiance' was caused by communist propaganda. WBSA, HPC 128 of 1937. The Magistrate of Howrah wrote, 'the communists have decided to have a really big show . . . a communist fomented mass-rising on a small-scale'. WBSA, HPC 60 of 1937. The Commissioner of Chinsurah wrote, 'This unrest is due almost entirely to communist propaganda.' WBSA, HPC 72 of 1937.

industry-wide wage and welfare demands made their way into the strike repertoire. The leaders were sincere in believing that this was in the better interests of the workers. Possibly, they were right. But women remained largely outside the organised union movements and continued in the earlier pattern.

For most of the 1920s and 1930s, unions remained at the margin of working-class politics, to be called in for negotiating, but with very little effective control over the outbreak of strikes or its day-to-day conduct.[24] This general apathy to unionism was especially marked in the case of women. Even when women played prominent and militant roles in strikes, they rarely became union members. In the 1920s, hardly any jute mill union registered women members. During the general strikes of 1929 and 1937 when trade union registers filled up, only the Kankinara Labour Union returned any significant number of women as members. In 1938, the Kankinara Labour Union reported eighty-nine women among its 560 members, the Garden Reach Labour Union had seven women out of a membership of 440, while the Rice Mill Workers Union had forty-eight women out of a total of 204 members. Other jute mill unions had no women members at all.[25] Even in the 1950s, out of the total 37,531 women in the jute industry, only 7,080 women were members of registered unions.[26] If women were chary of unions, their low proportion in the workforce ensured union indifference. Trade unions made some effort to organise women to ensure success of strikes, but none to accommodate women either organisationally, to enable them to join meetings and register as members, or to address their specific needs. Maternity benefit and crèche facilities were the only two gender-based demands routinely included in strike charters along with other social insurance measures. Neither the unions, nor the management paid these any attention at the negotiating table.

For unions, women's participation was often merely a means of augmenting numbers. Reports of the Hooghly Jute Mill Workers' Conference, 1938, with an audience of 20,000 workers, and Sarojini Naidu in the chair, made only one reference to women: '(F)emale folks ...

---

[24] In 1928, the Ludlow and Chengail workers, and in 1930, the Lothian workers invited the union to negotiate after the strike had begun. *Amrita Bazar Patrika*, 25 April 1928; DIG CID IB, Secret Reports, May 1928 and 1930. It is well known that Prabhabati Dasgupta, despite her influence, could not get a part of the workforce to accept the settlement after the general strike of 1929.

[25] WBSA, Comm. Comm., March 1938, A1–3.

[26] *Social and Economic Status of Women Workers in India*. Even in 1984, 57.9 per cent of women workers were unaware of the legal benefits due to them. Only 81 per cent of women, against 91 per cent of the men were members of trade unions. *Socio-Economic Conditions of Women Workers in Textile, Khandsari and Sugar Products Industries*, Labour Bureau, 1984.

lined the roadway, blew conch shells and strew fried rice and raised cheer as she passed . . . Inside the pandal guards of honour was furnished by girl volunteers . . . and woman labourers who enthusiastically waved red flags and displayed hammer and sickle badges.'[27] This kind of 'token' participation of women was very common. The Conference raised no issues specific to women. Sarojini Naidu addressed only one sentence to women – to mothers, not to wage-earners – 'women must not train their children to be *badshas* [emperors] but to earn their living by honest and hard labour'.[28]

During labour unrests women often found their ascribed gender role – as housewife and mother – conflicted with their idealised solidaristic 'class' role. In the short term, strikes threw the precariously balanced domestic economy into disarray. The rural housewife, whether independent of male migrant urban earnings or dependent in whatever degree on such earnings, was either unaffected by strikes or incapable of influencing strike decisions. There were too few urban housewives wholly dependent on male urban earnings to warrant consideration here. But the urban housewife 'supplementing' male wage earnings by her own wage earnings and the urban housewife wholly dependent on her own wage earnings faced an irresoluble dilemma: the performance of her 'privileged' role as housewife and mother needed the ensuring of an adequate cash flow; the prescriptive norms of 'working-class' solidarity needed a suspension of such cash flow from wages. No wonder then that many women including those earning wages gave priority to the cash flow needs and sufficiently so to break or cause the break of strikes. The price of trade union hostility had to be incurred.

Also, in times of strikes, canny employers hit the workers where it hurt most – supply of housing and water were essential for survival in poor urban neighbourhoods and in jute mill neighbourhoods employers often controlled both these. The manager's first reaction to strikes was to cut off the water supply to workers' quarters. In April 1928, for instance, women joined work 'breaking' the Ludlow strike. The water supply to the *lines* had been cut off and children, especially, suffered. With twenty adults and children living in a room of 10 sq ft the misery was intense.[29] From discontinuing water supply to evicting strikers from their quarters in the *lines* was a short step for managers. But, consequences of eviction could be more serious for women than for men. In the Ludlow strike, *durwans* evicted women bodily from the *lines*. Some took 'shelter outside with friends and relatives', but though the men could 'live in the open fields, they had to send their wives to the nearest

[27] *Amrita Bazar Patrika*, 17 July 1938.   [28] Ibid.; WBSA, HPC 136 of 1939.
[29] *Ananda Bazar Patrika*, 2 May 1928.

village for shelter'.[30] In Hooghly Jute Mill, in 1936, 'one *cooly* woman refused to vacate her room until the return of her husband'. At that the manager pulled her out by her *hasuli*. A violent confrontation between the workers and *durwans* ensued.[31] During the 1929 and 1937 general strike employers appear to have gone into the workers' *lines* and with police help forced women workers into the mill.[32]

Thus not only did women face more economic and physical distress from strikes because of the reduction in family income, but they could become on occasion the direct targets of managerial violence. It is not surprising, therefore, that they often opposed strikes and were the first to rejoin work.[33] In Budge-Budge during the strike waves of 1929, '[T]he womenfolk are willing workers and are quite willing to resume, even on existing terms and prevailing conditions.'[34] In 1928, in Gourepur Mill[35] and in 1939, in Union (North) Jute Mill[36] women refused to join strikes. In November that year, Bengal Chatkal Mazdoor Union launched a strike against the Bengal Jute Ordinance in the Hukumchand Mill. Ten thousand workers downed tools 'except 100 women'.[37]

Managers utilised women's disinclination to join unions and their reluctance to participate in strikes. A few women in a mill could be used to undercut union solidarity or break a strike. Earlier, in 1875, managers employed some girls and women 'to counteract the threat of strikes among the boys'.[38] Much later, the Foley Report mentioned that women were 'docile' and 'tractable' and 'less prone to striking'.[39] In the 1920s, as union influence grew, managers even discriminated in favour of a small number of women to deflect predominantly male union activities.[40] In September 1929, the bagsewers, 126 women, went on strike for a rise in wages. The manager accepted their demands and work was restored the same day. Encouraged, the men struck work on the same demand. Their demand was rejected and the strike failed.[41]

---

[30] *Amrita Bazar Patrika*, for 25 and 26 April, 1, 3, 5 and 11 May 1928; *Ananda Bazar Patrika*, 2 May 1928.

[31] *Amrita Bazar Patrika*, 11 May 1937.

[32] *Ananda Bazar Patrika*, 10 and 27 August 1929; *Amrita Bazar Patrika*, 29 July, 5 and 15 August 1937.

[33] This attitude has been called 'defensive militancy' in a different context. Jane Humphries, 'Class Struggle and Resistance of the Working Class Family', *Cambridge Journal of Economics*, 1, 3, September 1977.

[34] *Amrita Bazar Patrika*, 1 September 1929.

[35] *Amrita Bazar Patrika*, 23 June 1928.   [36] WBSA, HPC 381 of 1938.   [37] Ibid.

[38] Gourepur Mill Manager, WBSA, General Miscellaneous, September 1875, A6–27.

[39] Foley Report.

[40] Ranjan Dasgupta made this comment about Mr Johnstone of Bally Jute Mill. Interview, Calcutta, 9 November 1989. This may have been a part of a general tactic to reduce 'communist' elements in unions.

[41] Delta Jute Mill, 29 September 1939, WBSA, HPC 132 of 1939.

Paradoxically, these tactics strengthened the stereotype of women as 'docile' and 'tractable' workers.

Unions played into management hands by accepting the gender barriers set up by employers. When unable to win women's confidence, picketers intimidated them into compliance. During the general strike of 1929, in Kankinara, 'women especially were threatened with assault and general molestation if they continued to work'.[42] Women may have been 'especially' threatened because they were more vulnerable to violence or because they were seen to jeopardise strikes. Threats could rapidly turn into sexual harassment. During the 1937 general strike, in Titagarh, a newspaper noted, 'women workers were more willing to resume work than the general body of male workers but they were afraid to get back to work in case there might be intimidation ... (W)hen some women workers were going to work they were molested and one of them was pushed back by some of the strikers.'[43] Such intimidation was bound to have some success. The 100 women of Hukumchand Mill who had come to work on the morning of a strike, did not return after the midday recess due to 'intense picketing'.[44] After a reduction of staff in North-brook Mill in December 1937, workers began throwing bobbins at the 'female workers of the batching department'[45] and then 'became rowdy in the afternoon and frightened the female workers who left the mill'.[46] In 1940, in Gourepur Jute Mill, spinners 'forced' women of the preparing department to stop work. The men threw stones at the sewing department, and 'so forced this department to stop work'.[47]

Despite their induction into the organised workforce, women remained primarily associated with and responsible for housework and childrearing. The double burden of worker and homemaker often led to severe stress and alienation. The emphasis on familial roles for women impeded a fuller commitment to their workplace – factory work was seen as necessary only for family survival.[48] As shown before, most working women living in *lines* and *bastis* spent at least three to four hours at an average on housework. Add to that eight to ten hours in a factory and there can have been little time left for community activities or union meetings. Given the reality of poverty, the strain of housework

[42] Memorandum to Royal Commission of Labour by R. N. Gilchrist, *RCLI*, V, 1.
[43] *Amrita Bazar Patrika*, 20 April 1937.   [44] WBSA, HPC 381 of 1938.
[45] CSAS, Benthall Papers, Box XIV, Northbrook Jute Mill, Paul Benthall to Edward Benthall, 14 December 1937.
[46] WBSA, HPC 60 of 1939.   [47] WBSA, HPC W267 of 1940.
[48] This has been called an 'instrumental' attitude. Lydia Kung, *Factory Women in Taiwan*, Epping, 1983, pp. 171–9. A reflection of this attitude is seen in Durgabala's statement, 'Khatbo-khabo' (I work to eat), 'I come, work and go home.' In reply to a question on her union affiliation, she said, 'I do not bother with unions.' Durgabala Dasi, Fort Gloster North Mill, Interview, 2 December 1989.

in *basti* conditions, multiple pregnancies and the heavy toll on infant life, it is not surprising that women's role as homemaker and mother weighed heavily on them. Many women were rushing in and out of the factory to feed or care for babies.

Unions rarely took all this into account. The only articulation of their interests by unions was in occasional demands for maternity benefit and crêche facilities. The emphasis on meetings, rallies and gate-speeches, the modus operandi favoured by most unions, left out women who could not or would not attend these. Abani Choudhury wrote to Muzaffar Ahmed in 1932, 'We have abandoned the old tradition of holding meetings', but the new methods were equally useless for mobilising women, 'we are ... (having) soap-box lectures at the work-shop gates'.[49] The communist unions held night classes when women were busy with household duties. Such indifference spelled the failure of the Ludlow strike. K. L. Ghose realised, 'as union officials were prohibited from entering the coolie lines and as the women workers generally could not attend union meetings, they were easily prevailed upon to join work'.[50]

While male trade unionists remained indifferent to their interests, women found it difficult to organise themselves. In the period between 1928 and 1932, and more so in the late 1930s, unionised women workers from Bombay cotton textile mills led strikes against retrench-ment in the reeling and winding departments.[51] These exclusively (wo)manned departments found a basis for solidarity in job-segregation. Such action was rarer in the Bengal jute mills. And when they happened, as they did sporadically in the 1930s, they seldom won the full co-operation of the unions. The reconstruction of the Union (North) Mill prompted a demonstration by women, but the movement was not taken further and failed in its objectives. On 11 May 1939, a public meeting was held in Calcutta by 500 retrenched women.

A unique scene was witnessed in the streets of Calcutta yesterday when about 500 women workers, belonging to various communities, old and young, married and unmarried, marched in a procession, with placards in their hand containing their demands ... the dismissal is a matter of great concern to thousands of women workers ... because the same act may be repeated ... resulting in the unemployment of large numbers of women workers.[52]

Such collective action by women was 'unique' in the jute mills, because

[49] Translation of Bengali letter from Abani Choudhury to Muzaffar Ahmed, 5 May 1932, DIG CID IB 168 of 1920.
[50] *Amrita Bazar Patrika*, 10 June 1928.
[51] Radha Kumar, 'Family and Factory: Women in the Bombay Cotton Textile Industry 1919–1939', *Indian Economic and Social History Review*, 20, 1, 1983, pp. 103–9.
[52] *Amrita Bazar Patrika*, 12 May 1939, p. 8.

the possibilities of women's workplace-based solidarities were vitiated by the pattern of gender segregation. There was after all no job that was considered exclusively women's, though they predominated in one job – the lowest paid and considered the most unskilled – hand-sewing of bags. Apart from this women were scattered across the mill departments, concentrated in preparing and drawing. In these departments men and women worked together; usually there were more men than women.

The highest paid jobs were spinning and weaving – and women were thought physically incapable of spinning and weaving. The segregation of jobs by gender and skill worked to the advantage of weavers and spinners. It has been mentioned that weaving was the highest paid department closely followed by spinning.[53] In the early strikes, especially, weavers, and (to a lesser extent) spinners took leading roles. In the 1920s, weavers were the most prominent. Between July 1920 and March 1921, out of sixteen strikes, ten were initiated in the weaving department, and four in the spinning department.[54] In the troubled months of 1937, between January and March, six out of eleven strikes started in the weaving department. Some of the strikes by weavers were often the most sustained, as in case of Ganges or Budge-Budge.[55] Their higher wages may have given them greater staying power. Also they were less replaceable given their higher level of skill and longer period of 'training'. This gave them greater bargaining power with the management. Spinners too came to the forefront in the 1930s. The depression had prompted a rapid adoption of high-speed spinning machinery leading to retrenchments and higher workloads. As a result, Victoria, Angus, Shyamnagar and Titagarh Mills suffered series of strikes by the spinners.[56] In Angus and Shyamnagar, the spinners initiated the 1937 general strike. The 'weavers', according to the manager, 'remained loyal'.[57]

In case of women workers, vertical and horizontal segregation hindered the potential for occupational solidarities. They were not separated into separate jobs which may have encouraged collective action over issues affecting their departments. They predominated in lower

---

[53] See chapter 3 above.

[54] J. H. Kerr, *Report of the Committee on Industrial Unrest in Bengal*, Calcutta, 1921; DIG CID IB, Weekly Reports, 1921. In Champdany, Dalhousie, Titagarh, and Northbrook Mills in January, only the spinners went on strike. In February, in Hastings, Wellington, Shyamnagar, and later in the year, in Ganges, Agarpara, South Union Mills only the weavers went on strike for various demands ranging from raise of wages to protests against dismissals.

[55] Weekly Report of Strikes, WBSA, HPC 484 of 1937 and 128 of 1937.

[56] DUL, TDP, Titagarh Jute Mills (No. 2), MRD, 1930, 1933, 1937 and 1939.

[57] DUL, TDP, Angus Jute Works and Shyamnagar Jute Factory (South), MRD, 1937.

paid piece-work, associated with lower levels of skill requirement. Moreover, in most departments, they were a minority, the men holding the better paid jobs. Though women spent the major part of their day in the mills, the notion of an 'occupational community' may have been lacking.[58] This may have influenced expectations of benefits from collective action. In sharp contrast with the radical unionising efforts in Bombay, Calcutta jute mill unions' indifference to women's collective action may have derived from the lack of any obvious cohesion of women's interests. The unions, committed to operating at the level of workplace relations, found the occupational heterogeneity of women incompatible with the perception of a common gender interest.

It has been argued that women were more susceptible to casualisation, and more likely to be laid off during the periodic 'short time working agreements' of the IJMA. Moreover, it was women who found periodic unemployment or underemployment more taxing. Their bargaining power was lower because of the conditions in which they migrated. Women migrated to the city either when rural resources were completely exhausted or because they were marginalised in the family. They could neither ask for support during strikes, nor could they return home if they lost their jobs. For these women, confrontational action against the management might have seemed less viable than other kinds of individual defensive action. The high labour turnover in individual mills may indicate that workers found it easier and safer to leave their jobs than take collective action. Moreover, the high rate of absenteeism, coming to work late and the frequent unscheduled 'breaks' which managers complained so bitterly about, have been regarded as the workers' attempts at informal 'everyday' protests.[59] Women were particularly associated with these 'inefficiencies' which in the managers' parlance constituted an indulgence 'to come and go' in deference to their housewifely and motherly duties. At times, these too may have been vehicles of protest, which did indeed pay practical dividends in terms of allowing them to accommodate their household and childcare schedules. Besides, managers having acceded to the system and accepted the justification, found it increasingly difficult to prevent women's relatively erratic attendance. In one case when the management wanted to remove the system of gate-passes which allowed women to leave the mill to feed their children, they gheraoed the manager and refused to disperse. This was one of their few successes.[60]

[58] Kung, *Factory Women in Taiwan*, pp. 171–9.
[59] Ranajit Dasgupta, 'Material Conditions and Behavioural Aspects of Calcutta Working Class 1875–1899', *Occasional Paper No. 22*, Calcutta, 1979.
[60] Interview, Mathur Naskar, Bauria, 2 December 1989. A similar strike was sparked off

While women in jute mills did not derive the benefits of departmental segregation, the values attached to gender segregation imposed constraints on their political action. While the need for family survival might justify working in factories, such an extension of the familial role did not include non-essentials like union activity. An old trade union leader, Bejoy Hazra, held that women 'never actually joined unions' because 'they were shy'.[61] Durgabala Dasi working on the teaser machine in Fort Gloster North Mill said that 'in case of trouble ... [she was] more likely to seek help from friends in the line' than from the unions.[62] The Mahars and the Dhangars who provided the main bulk of sweepers (especially for the municipality), were to some extent exceptions to the general rule and yet the limits they set to women's activities are revealing. The older and single women gave the lead in times of strikes. Age here signified not merely more experience and knowledge, as in case of men, but a relative lack of domestic encumbrance and a relative immunity from sexual assaults and gossip.[63]

In Bengal, women were never seen as a direct threat to male employment as in England. Their interests were not seen (except, as mentioned, in a few specific instances) as separate from or inimical to general working-class issues. The demands for higher wages and welfare measures embraced women automatically, but there was no attempt to counter discrimination against women. Though unions presumed to speak for the whole of the working class, they said very little about women.

Women in the trade unions – leaders and activists

Despite the overall uninterest in mobilising women, trade unions could not ignore women altogether. Their participation and support in strikes were crucial; their perceived 'betrayal' could, as we have seen, provoke male vengeance. A few unions addressed this problem by enlisting middle-class women activists, but not with conspicuous success. The success and popularity of two *bhadramahila* leaders has become legendary in jute trade union movement. Santoshkumari Debi was active in the early years of the 1920s and Prabhabati Debi led the general strike

---

at Clive Jute Mills when the management tried to stop the system of women leaving the mill to feed their children – usually called *Jhara Laoa* – in 1929. *Gharer Katha*, 2, 2, 1929, p. 130.

[61] Interview, Bejoy Hazra, Radhanagar Colony, Bauria, 4 November 1989.

[62] Interview, Durgabala Dasi.

[63] M. Searle-Chatterjee, 'Reversible Sex Roles: The Special Case of Benares Sweepers', *Women in Development*, 2, 1981.

of 1929. However, neither of them emerged as spokesman of the women workers in particular.

Prabhabati Devi and Santoshkumari Devi had to develop, sustain and even justify their leadership in terms of a universal motherhood. They thus reinforced from above the traditional notions of motherhood. Workers actually hailed Santoshkumari and Prabhabati as *Maiji, Mairam, Mataji* (all meaning mother). Maitreyee Bose and Sudha Roy were more commonly addressed as *Bahinji* (sister). This has been explained as part of the *zamindari* style of leadership in jute trade unions.[64] It is necessary to delve into the significance of the use of the 'mother' imagery in more specific terms. Women's traditional role in India was two-fold and 'normatively ambiguous'.[65] While on the one hand she was the self-sacrificing wife, self-effacing and obedient, she also became, as a mother, more powerful and self-sufficient with age. The mother image associated with power, strength and endurance provided a means of seeking public activity as an extension of the familial role.[66]

Both Santoshkumari and Prabhabati repeatedly cast their involvement in the language of *seba* (care) for the suffering poor rather than in the language of class struggle invoked by their associate male unionists. They invested an enormous significance in their 'mother' image. In the nineteenth century, middle-class women, encouraged by liberal reformers, had extended their nurturing role to 'social work'. Such women were among the first to found women's organisations. From this, politics was a short step – the national movement providing a moral legitimacy for such an extension. The few women who did participate in labour movements sought to invoke a similar idiom through the use of the image of the 'mother'. Despite a great deal of obfuscation and mystification, their role in class movements remained severely restricted and this is as significant as the apparent ease with which their motherhood transcended the very real social barriers of caste, class, community and language.

The women's movement in Bengal, as indeed in India, was too entirely middle class in composition and too committed to the national movement to address itself seriously to working-class issues. Embedded firmly in the constitutional tradition of moderate politics and the social reform movement, these organisations, best illustrated by the All-India

---

[64] Chakrabarty, *Rethinking Working Class History*, p. 138.
[65] Gail Minault, 'The Extended Family as Metaphor and the Expansion of Women's Realm', in G. Minault (ed.), *The Extended Family: Women and Political Participation in India and Pakistan*, Delhi, 1981.
[66] Jasodhara Bagchi, 'Representing Nationalism: Ideology of Motherhood in Colonial Bengal', *EPW*, 20–27 October 1990.

Women's Conference (AIWC), and the National Council of Women in India (NCWI), sought to resolve the conflict between the national movement and women's interests by severely restricting their definition of women's emancipation.[67] It may have been that in the context of the anti-imperialist struggle, it was impossible to separate the women's question from the national question and it was through their alliance with the nationalist movement that women gained the necessary legal guarantees after Independence.[68] But the issue of liberation remained limited to legal and political rights. No mass participation of women in struggles for gender equality was contemplated. Gender antagonisms, as much as class and caste antagonisms, remained inimical to the extant style of nationalistic politics. The infant women's movement was crippled by the limiting moral framework of the national movement which emphasised gender harmony rather than a more confrontational mode of protest.

It is not surprising, therefore, that women's organisations rarely ventured into the uncertain terrain of working-class politics. This is not to say that they were completely unaware of the problems of poor women. The Royal Commission on Labour provoked a spurt of interest in the early 1930s. The NCWI's standing committee on labour made some public avowals of concern for the 'poor and labouring classes'.[69] In 1937, AIWC passed resolutions condemning unemployment, the absence of an All-India Maternity Benefit Act, and poor housing facilities.[70] Other professional women's organisations like the Association of Medical Women in India took some interest in maternity benefit and child welfare centres. These minimal involvements drew inspiration and legitimacy from the tradition of social work. It could then be seen as an extension of the maternal and nurturing role of women from the home to the public world, from kin to a larger suffering humanity.

Trade unions could not afford to be quite so cavalier. To ensure women's participation, some trade unions inducted women activists. As the male leadership was predominantly drawn from the middle-class intelligentsia, so were the women. Labour leaders often pressed their female relatives into service. Dr Maitreyee Bose was the wife of Dr Swadesh Bose and they worked together among dock and jute labour; Sudha Roy's brother inducted her into the labour movement; Dheera Dhar and Indira Roy, nieces of Bina Das, worked with Prabhasini Debi

[67] Minault, 'The Extended Family as Metaphor'.
[68] Joanna Liddle and Rama Joshi, *Daughters of Independence: Gender, Caste and Class in India*, New Delhi, 1986.
[69] *Amrita Bazar Patrika*, 31 February 1940.
[70] *Amrita Bazar Patrika*, 27 November 1930.

(wife of Sibnath Banerjee) in Howrah.[71] Alaka Majumdar, Secretary of the Bengal Provincial Students Federation Girl Students' Committee in the 1940s, opened schools in *bastis*.[72] There appear brief mentions of other names: Malina Sen, Anima Biswas, Susmita Majumdar.[73] Bimal-pratibha Devi, an ex-detenu, worked with Niranjan Sengupta (of a CPI group led by Muzzaffar Ahmed) and Santibrata Sen to collect money through armed dacoities and robberies.[74]

These women, usually young students or professionals, did not pose any threat as role models for working-class women, being completely external to their community. In fact, they were, for this reason, more acceptable to workers as mobilisers than young married women from within the community (even if the latter were the 'target' for mobilisa-tion). The example par excellence of this kind of female participation in trade union activity was Prabhasini Debi. She acknowledges that she had no independent role in the trade union movement. As women workers were not quite comfortable before the *swadeshibabus*, her task was to explain the need for strikes and unions to the women. She mentions that she would especially target wives of union members.[75]

Of the few working-class women who joined unions, most were wives of union activists inducted into unions as part of a deliberate strategy to mobilise other women. Ramdeo was responsible for organising the 'first real union' under the auspices of the CPI in the Nuddea Jute Mill. His wife was a strong and belligerent (*laraku*) woman who helped him considerably in his work.[76] Another woman, Sonabarshi Bhar, and her husband were closely associated with Sita Sett of the Bolshevik Party of India; she addressed some of BPI's public meetings in the 1950s.[77] In Chandernagore Jute Mill, where she worked, she was popularly known as Comrade Tilki. The one figure who appears as an exception is Dukhmat whose husband was not involved seriously in union activity but she went on to become a full-time party member of CPI and pursued a life-long commitment to the union and the party.[78]

None of these women leaders or activists addressed women's specific problems. Gender issues were subsumed within the broader economic issues. Only maternity benefit and demand for crêches were routinely

[71] Interview, Prabhasini Debi, Calcutta, 11 November 1989.
[72] DIG CID IB, 363C of 1936.   [73] DIG CID IB, 390 of 1931.
[74] DIG CID IB, 271 of 1921.
[75] Interview, Prabhasini Debi, Calcutta, 11 November 1989.
[76] Kamal Basu, interview by Manju Chattopadhyay, 3 September 1987, unpublished.
[77] The Bolshevik Party of India's meeting in Matkal Maidan at Titagarh on 5 September 1954. DIG CID IB, 427 of 1935.
[78] Manju Chattopadhyay, 'Dukhmat Didi – Ek Sangrami Charitra', *Kalantar, Saradiya*, 1988.

raised. Many of these women came to the working-class movement from the background of social reform movements or nationalist movements. Bimalpratibha Debi was a former 'terrorist', Prabhabati Debi's mother had been active in the Congress and her brother was a 'terrorist'.

Santoshkumari in particular was associated with all three movements – the national movement, social welfare for women and working-class movement. A prominent member of the Swarajya Party, she had close links with C. R. Das. She was also the Secretary of the Association for Protection of Hindu Women against rape and abduction and helped in their 'rehabilitation'. Closely associated with Congress politics, she firmly repudiated ideas of class or gender antagonism. Neither Prabhabati nor Santoshkumari were communists, though Prabhabati was more bitter about them. Santoshkumari welcomed and hosted Saklatvala, Johnston and Simes. She was also more closely associated with welfare work than Prabhabati. She said, 'most of my time was spent with the workers'.[79] She started a night school in Salkea in August 1924 with 150 workers.[80] She was concerned with issues like housing, health and hygiene.[81] During a three-month strike at the Gourepur Mill in 1921–22, the 3,000 dismissed workers were kept in Santoshkumari's mother's house and fed *khichuri*. Her interest in 'women's conditions' was, however, limited to discussions with managers about 'medical aid for pregnant women'.[82] The first issue of *Sramik*, a journal she edited, sold 600 copies among workers.[83] Its only available issue reports the International Committee for Women formed by the Trade Union Congress.

Santoshkumari believed that she had received divine ordinance to alleviate the sufferings of labourers. Her father was a barrister and a *zamindar* with land in Garifa, very near the main heartland of the industry. The Gourepur and Nuddea mills were close to her home. In this area in the 1920s, she played a significant role in trade union activities. She organised the Gourepur Employees Union which enrolled 4,000 members.[84] At the peak of her power in December 1924, the AITUC asked her for an affiliation of unions. She was the President of the Sir Stuart Hogg Market Employees' Association, she was associated with the postal union and she tried to organise a boatmen's union.[85]

[79] Manju Chattopadhyay, *Sramiknetri Santoshkumari*, Manisha, 1984.
[80] Then there were other schools in Naihati, Garifa, Halisahar, Bhatpara, and Sodepur. DIG CID IB, Secret, August 1924.
[81] Chattopadhyay, *Sramiknetri Santoshkumari*.   [82] Ibid.
[83] DIG CID IB, Secret, April 1924.
[84] Santoshkumari Debi, Memoirs, unpublished typescript, courtesy Manju Chattopadhyay.
[85] DIG CID IB, Secret, 1923–24.

Santoshkumari was hailed as 'mother'. She herself derived assurance of her power from her mother image; not from her organisational skills or her fluency in Hindi and Urdu. She recounts the Spence Murder Case when witnesses hailed her entrance into court with shouts of '*Mai Ramki Jai*'.[86] In fact, her conduct of the Spence Murder Case showed a remarkable familiarity with court procedure: she collected money, transferred the case from the District court where the judges were more likely to be biased, arranged a false testimony and explained the case to the judge in his chambers.[87] She showed remarkable courage when Tegart came to break up a meeting.[88] She reacted very strongly and courageously when the *Ananda Bazar Patrika* published gossip about her connection with C. R. Das.[89]

Prabhabati Dasgupta was also an extremely popular leader in the late 1920s. When the general strike of 1929 began, 'Miss Dasgupta was entirely unknown' to the 'average jute mill worker'. Soon after, her control over the workers was 'absolute'.[90] The workers called her *Maiji* or *Mataji* and she believed that she 'only has to lift her little finger and the workers would obey'. The Government, to whom this was said, had no doubt that it was true.[91] She herself recalls later that she was hailed with *Mataji ki jai*, 'and that was my reward'.[92] Her rival trade unionist K. C. Roy Chowdhury said, 'both male and female workers – at least those living in Kankinara, Titagarh and Champdany – looked upon Miss Dasgupta as their "*Maiji*". They would do anything to carry out her orders, and would not even listen to any other organiser of her union.'[93]

She was the fourth daughter of late Rai Tarruk Chandra Das Bahadur, a sub-judge. They were a well-known Brahmo family. She was familiar in police circles as the revolutionary sister of Khagen Dasgupta, a known 'terrorist'. The revolutionary Atul Sen of Bagnan fame taught

---

[86] Santoshkumari Debi, Memoirs.   [87] Ibid.
[88] Ibid. She writes, 'He came up with a revolver in his hands jumped up and put it to my face ... putting his leg on the table ... I took a slipper in hand and said, "Here is a weapon to fight an unarmed woman". I flung my slipper.'
[89] She writes, 'I took the whip from my blouse and smacked him (the Editor) three times and apologised that I had to give him a lesson – how degrading it is to speak against a woman and give her a bad name ... show disrespect to motherhood (*matrijati*)'. The news published was a false report of a birth of a son to '*swaraj samraggi*', C. R. Das being popularly known as *swarajsamrat*. Ibid. She had become vulnerable to gossip because she was separated from her husband, K. G. Gupta (brother of B. L. Gupta, ICS). The story runs thus: she left home in protest against the ill-treatment meted by her husband's brother to his wife. She never returned to her conjugal home and forbade all references to the connection. Courtesy Indira Dutta Ray, 1991.
[90] *RCLI*, V, 1, p. 144.   [91] Ibid., pp. 149, 276.
[92] Interview, Prabhabati Das Gupta by K. P. Rangachary, 24 April 1968, Delhi, NMML.
[93] Chakrabarty, *Rethinking Working Class History*, p. 141.

her younger sister Tarulata.[94] In the USA, in June 1921, she spoke about the barbarous treatment meted out to Indian women.[95] She joined trade union politics during the Scavenger Strike. She was made President of the Union and she proved extremely successful in establishing a direct relationship with the men and women, especially women, to all of whom she became the *mataji*. Her style was totally different from her contemporaries. She was unusually highly educated.[96] Her fellow Brahmos taunted her for her association with the labour movement – *Sanibarer Chithi* published scurrilous cartoons about her. In her time, she would share a *biri* with the sweepers she was organising. After the general strike and the following inter-union split she continued only half-heartedly in union politics for about two more years. Yet, in 1937, she was asked to help in an election campaign, even as Santoshkumari's popularity with workers had prompted C. R. Das to seek her help in the election campaign in 1923. With Santoshkumari's help, B. C. Roy had defeated the veteran leader Surendranath Banerjee in Barrackpore.[97] Niharendu Dutt Mazumdar who was standing from Titagarh asked Prabhabati to attend a meeting in his support. She had then not been to Titagarh for six years, where workers had once declared that they would join work only on her orders. When she did come, she received a standing ovation from 10,000 workers for ten minutes, who ignored other popular figures like Somnath Lahiri and shouted, '*Mataji aya*' (mother has come).[98]

Women's strikes – the victim and the adversary

In the 1930s, trade unions began to make a greater headway, especially among the weavers and spinners. Though the earlier 'spontaneous' strike, usually undertaken by a small group of workers, was not quite abandoned, the unions began to play an increasingly important role in initiating, sustaining and resolving strikes. In the process, however, the gap between mobilisation of women for general or male interest goals and the articulation of women's interests widened. Neither women activists nor the two remarkably influential women leaders made any serious effort to close this gap.

[94] Also known as Bhabini. Atul Sen called her *Ma* (mother) and Prabhabati *Mashima*, (mother's sister). DIG CID IB, 49 of 1921.
[95] Ibid.
[96] She got a BA in 1918, an MA in Experimental Psychology in 1920, a Barbour Scholarship to go to the University of Michigan (USA). After this she went to Germany and got a Doctoral degree.
[97] Chattopadhyay, *Sramiknetri Santoshkumari*.
[98] Courtesy Goutam Chattopadhyay, 17 March 1989.

Mill owners, having failed to thwart progressive unionisation, adopted a two-pronged strategy. On the one hand, they attempted to establish more direct control over the workers, bypassing the middlemen, clerks and *sardars* in the recruitment procedure. After the general strike of 1937, the manager of the Shyamnagar Mill wrote to the Directors, '[a] section of the workers were absolutely Bolshevik' and that 'the labour as it is now must be supervised with the greatest care'.[99] Hence, the establishment of the Labour Bureaux and the attempt to issue workers with photo-identity cards. On the other hand, compelled to recognise the utility of unions in regulating and containing working-class grievances, they began to encourage the formation of rival unions.[100] Their strategies succeeded somewhat but not in the way they had expected. Even as the 'white' unions set up by H. S. Suhrawardy, Labour Minister in the late 1930s, began to temper the operation of the more militant 'red flag' unions, the hitherto 'docile' women workers became increasingly troublesome. Staying away from regularising union organisations, they staged walkouts without notice either to the management or the unions. Indeed it was these non-unionised women who came to the forefront of the opposition against measures like the identity card which were aimed actually at clipping the unions' wings.[101] It may well be that women, being active in protests at this time were more easily persuaded of the dangers of identification procedures. But, in many strikes initiated by women, the unions' assumption of leadership over subsequent negotiations meant that industry-wise 'class' demands overshadowed the specific issue over which the women had protested. The gender bias of the unions was exposed most explicitly over the progressive replacement of women by men workers. The economic crisis and the threat of male unemployment reinforced both middle-class leaders' and workers' ambivalence to women's factory work. Women, too, often acquiesced to a son 'inheriting' their job. In many cases, when the pill was not thus sweetened, and the women attempted to resist their retrenchment, they failed to win union support for their cause.

Perhaps their propensity to act outside the unions contributed to the

[99] DUL, TDP, Shyamnagar Jute Factory (North), MRD, 1937.
[100] A growing 'communist' influence was feared from the Bhatpara Labour Union by Kalidas Bhattacharjee and the Trade Union Conference in Bhatpara in 1926. The Trade Unions Act, 1925, and the Trade Disputes Act, 1929, sought to redirect labour movement along 'constitutional' channels. 'Loyal' trade unions, like the Kankinara Labour Union of K. C. Roychoudhury in the 1920s and the 'white' labour unions of Suhrawardy in the 1930s were seen as desirable alternatives.
[101] The strikes against this measure were led in at least two instances by M. A. Zaman. In Shyamnagar, Victoria and Angus, the women in the Preparing Department took the initiative in the strikes and remained out longest. DUL, TDP, Shyamnagar, Victoria and Angus, MRD, 1939.

jute mill women's characterisation as highly combative and adversarial. There is a recurring image of the militant woman fighting for justice with unconventional weapons like heavy ornaments or broomsticks. Khsetromohan Chattopadhyay recalls with amusement women armed with brooms chasing the Head Clerk Bhabanibabu after a 'minor disagreement'.[102] Kamal Sarkar, a union activist, reminisces that women were very combative (*jangi*) especially when there was an attempt to abort strikes or attack the *bastis*. They would pick up anything that came to hand to beat up the agents (*dalals*).[103] Equally, they might turn against trade union organisers. D. Gupta, now Managing Director of New Central Jute Mill, remembers a woman chasing a trade union leader with a broom.[104] Kamala Basu, a doctor in the Nuddea Jute Mill, remembers that about 1,000 women demonstrated against her dismissal. These were women with great leadership potential, like Sunia and Parbatia, who were aggressive and effective, shouldering men aside to make their point.[105] Rampatia of the winding department of Titagarh No. 2 Mill was an aggressive woman (*Jandrel*), Chattopadhyay recalls, she 'shouted and screamed to get her way'. When a woman died in the maternity clinic of the mill, she led a strong contingent of women workers to beat up the staff and ransack the building.[106] Another woman involved in this fracas was Annapurna. She was a *badli* worker, given to *gheraoing* the labour officer when the *badlis* were not given work and would 'abuse the labour officer freely'.[107] Women in the Bauria-Chengail belt were also famed for their militancy, especially during the 1929 strikes.[108] The events following the dismissal of Bejoy Hazra have become legend in Bauria.[109] Women surrounded him when entering and leaving the mill and chased away police spies. One woman was injured in a scuffle, and the others *gheraoed* the manager for two hours. One day when the police entered the mill, some of the women smuggled him out. One woman, Mohini, actually challenged the police to fire at the women with Bejoy in their midst.[110]

[102] Interview, Khsetromohan Chattopadhyay, Titagarh No. 2 Mill, 12 December 1989. He was then a Turbine *mistri* in the Titagarh No. 1 Mill.
[103] Interview, by Manju Chattopadhyay, 3 September 1987, unpublished.
[104] Interview, D. Gupta, Calcutta, 30 October 1989.   [105] Interview, Kamala Basu.
[106] Interview, Kashinath Shau, Titagarh No. 2 Mill, 12 December 1989.
[107] Interview, Khsetramohan Chattopadhyay.
[108] Interview, Mathur Naskar. NA, Government of India, Home Poll. 1–2/28/1928; Sarkar, *Bengal, 1928–1934*, pp. 62–3.
[109] He worked as a half-time shifter in Fort Gloster Mill then at the Budge-Budge, Gagalbhai and Ludlow Jute Mills. Dismissed from these mills because of his union activities, he rejoined Fort Gloster in 1932. Interview, Bejoy Hazra.
[110] Ibid. The story has been told as he recounted it. Also see Renu Chakravarty, *Communists in India's Women's Movement 1940–1950*, New Delhi, 1980, p. 118.

Apart from this personal experience which he remembers with gratitude, Hazra mentions that Bilaspuri women were bold, especially courageous and joined any affray with their brooms.[111]

These images of the militant jute mill women are fragmentary and suffused with ambiguities. The narratives generated by the trade unions and the middle classes have by and large sought to brush these uncomfortable images under the academic carpet. Instead, managers, union activists, scholars and reseachers have amplified and justified the stereotype of the woman as a 'docile' and manageable worker; at best, she was the quintessential 'victim' of state and managerial violence. In the process, working-class women's protests have been divested of their autonomy. The preoccupations with trade unions and their leaders did not lead to an examination of how middle-class and union mediations displaced gender and class issues. Newspaper reports and union statements focused on the image of the 'wronged woman' to tap its mobilising potential. Frequent reference to atrocities on women and children by a 'brutal' manager or the police was an easy and quick way of gaining public credence and strengthening resistance. Such portrayals were double-edged. In one sense they were powerful images that personalised political resistance and often successfully harnessed working-class anger and public outrage to the support of strikes. Consequently, however, women workers were continually portrayed as passive, powerless and the ones on whose bodies class and race oppression inscribed its violent message. They were in the process denied agency in moments of protest.

The managers too had a stake in the imaging of the woman worker as a victim, albeit of union and working-class male violence. It has been argued that unions, by coercing women workers into joining strikes, reinforced management strategies. But such evidence must also be treated with caution. Doubtless, there were cases when the unions or male workers resorted to intimidation of women to ensure the success of strikes. Managerial and police records, however, often detailed these occurrences for precisely the same reasons that union records emphasised managerial and police violence against women. The managers sought to promote their stereotype of women as 'docile' workers unwillingly forced into strike actions. Moreover, the 'molestation' of women by strikers provided an opportunity to delegitimise and condemn strikes. One of the least-remembered aspects of the general strike of 1937 is the role women in preparing, batching and winding played in precipitating stoppages in Shyamnagar, Angus, Titagarh and Victoria Mills. In describing the events of April–May, the Shyamnagar

[111] Interview, Bejoy Hazra.

Mill manager wrote, 'the tension was evident mostly amongst the female labour'. But the manager was not willing to accede to the women any independent agency in refusing to work. '[I]t was very evident from conversation with them that they were being intimidated and in fear of molestation refused to return.' When workers from Victoria came around with news of stoppages, first the 'female labour left their jobs'. While other workers pleaded ignorance, the 'female workers said if they went to work they would be molested and maimed'.[112] The South Mill could not be reopened because the 'females, through fear, did not turn up in any department'.[113]

This tactic was sometimes used even against women's own strikes. Managers' descriptions of women's strikes rarely permitted them any agency – women went on strike because they were 'deluded' by union leaders or forced into action by male workers. Both arguments were used in the protracted Victoria Jute Mill strikes of 1939 which began in response to the management's attempts to issue workers with identity cards containing photographs. Quite obviously, this was adopted as a means of curtailing union activity. From the manager's own report it is quite clear that the strike against this measure began in the Preparing Department with women in the leading role. It spread quickly to the Spinning Department. Two days later the male workers were 'willing to resume work' and the weavers even came to work. The mill failed to reopen when it became 'obvious that no female workers were going to attend'. In fact, till the end it was the 'female workers who carried on under the leadership of Zaman'. After an uneasy settlement, the strike recurred a few weeks later, and it was a female sweeper, Sukowari, who took the leading role. Nevertheless, the strike is attributed to men from neighbouring mills who 'paraded throughout the Bazar intimidating female workers to prevent them from turning out to work'.[114] When Angus faced trouble over the same issue, the manager admitted that workers had been restive for some time but the 'climax' came when 'the women in the Preparing Department stopped work and left the mill'. At first, the Preparing Department was run with the help of the women in the batching house, but soon the batching women too failed to turn up. To the manager, however, though it appeared that 'the women were the chief offenders', 'the men were really behind them and only encouraged the women to keep at the forefront knowing that they would put the mill authorities at a disadvantage'.[115]

112 DUL, TDP, Shyamnagar Jute Factory (North), MRD, 1937.
113 DUL, TDP, Shyamnagar Jute Factory (South), MRD, 1937.
114 DUL, TDP, Victoria Jute Mill, MRD, 1939.
115 DUL, TDP, Angus Jute Works, MRD, 1939

If managers played down women's protests by attributing their actions to male intimidation, sympathetic portrayals of strikes sought to legitimise women's participation by emphasising their role as victims of managerial violence. Even when women initiated strikes, reportage focused on the brutalities perpetrated on them. In writing about women strikers, the image of the martyr, not of the heroine, came more readily to the journalist's pen. The fate of victimhood overshadowed the act of protest. Thus a popular daily reported of the Ludlow strike of 1928, 'after this the other women workers were beaten up ruthlessly. They were pulled by their hair and dragged up ... One 60-year-old woman was beaten to unconsciousness ... a one-year-old baby was torn from his mother's breast and flung to the ground'.[116] The 'Infant Torn from Mother's Arms'[117] moved the District Magistrate, Gurusaday Dutta, to investigate the case. The matter became grist for inter-union rivalry with K. C. Roychoudhury protesting against 'the exploitation of women in labour disputes' by the Bengal Chatkal Mazdoor Union.[118]

The imaging of women as victims of managerial violence became more effective when linked with the metaphor of sexual violation. This is not to argue that women working in jute mills were not frequently sexually molested, as indeed the earlier argument did not intend to suggest that women workers were not subjected to police or managerial brutality. There is a great deal of evidence to suggest that women workers were physically and sexually vulnerable in the mill, the *basti* and the streets. The point here is that marking out men in authority like managers and supervisors, or their agents like *durwans* and *sardars*, as sexual predators afforded a potent and personalised symbol of exploitation. Accusations of sexual abuse against European managers and supervisors provided the basis for collective action, sometimes by women alone, and often with the help and support of male workers.

In protesting against sexual abuse, women often invoked the notion of *izzat* which had enormous appeal to the working community – women and men. Invoking potential anger against sexual abuse to muster working-class solidarity, however, meant that women workers were acting in their capacity as workers to reinscribe their gender oppression. The notion of honour, embedded in a cultural discourse that privileged above all women's chastity and 'purity', was a particularly male con-

---

[116] *Ananda Bazar Patrika*, 11 June 1928. Another description ran along the same lines, 'the women were indiscriminately assaulted and forcibly dispersed, dragged by their hair .... The outrage has been so barbarous as to form an unprecedented chapter in the history of labour throughout the civilized world'. *Amrita Bazar Patrika*, 15 June 1928.

[117] Appeared as a news headline in *Ananda Bazar Patrika*, 13 June 1928.

[118] DIG CID IB, Weekly Reports, Secret, 1928.

struction. Therein lay its power to tap men's emotions and attract their support. Thus, women workers sought to negotiate the contradiction of gender and class within which they were situated *vis-à-vis* managers and working-class men. The gains were obvious – the support of fellow workers in their attempts at protest against sexual abuse. However, they were trapped in a contradiction they could not fully surmount. They were drawing on the notion of honour to mobilise men's support and to make their protests effective. Yet, in doing so, they were drawing precisely on that discourse which emphasised their incapacity to act and depicted them as passive and powerless. Thus, only working-class men could protect them from sexually threatening managers.

When women called upon the emotive image of the victim, they did so in order to strengthen and legitimise their protests. They invoked 'honour' as a paradigm of resistance. However, the male construction of honour from which they drew could also be used in battles between working-class men, with the women as passive sites on which conflictual imageries of 'violation' and 'protection' were played out. It has been argued elsewhere that in all these contexts the notion of 'honour' was extended from the corporate family to a wider community. The definition of this 'community' was perpetually in flux. Just as a 'community' could at times be coterminous with 'class', or in the jute mill context with 'race' since managers were primarily European, it could also cut across class and racial solidarity. The construction of a community identity, and a notion of honour flowing from it, could be defined by language, habitat or religion. The boundaries of community, shifting continually across the interstices of these definitions, were drawn and redrawn in moments of crisis and protest. At such moments, 'honour' of women was subsumed within a community and it could assume highly codified and symbolic forms in which communities traded insults.[119] In the 1920s, and more especially the 1930s, accusations of violations of 'honour' of women gave an added potency to the larger 'communal' question in Bengal politics. In the working-class context, however, such clashes were not restricted to Hindu–Muslim antagonism. There were conflicts between 'Bengalis' and 'up-countrymen', 'loyal' workers or 'blacklegs' and strikers.[120] In each case, reports of molestation of women, whether true or not, would spark off a riot.

[119] Chakrabarty, *Rethinking Working Class History*, pp. 215–16.
[120] During the Ludlow Jute Mill strike of 1928, 'loyal' workers came to the *lines* and assaulted the strikers' family. The strikers rushed back from their meeting with their leader Kalidas Bhattacharjee (Bengal Jute Workers' Association). They found that two women had already been severely injured. The report reads, 'Gurkha durwans were preparing to evict bodily some women workers, which angered workers into a clash with the police.' *Amrita Bazar Patrika*, 15 July 1937, p. 6.

The emphases on societal constructions of women's honour that were essentially male reinforce the passive and powerless image of the working-class woman. The role of the victim is extended, from subjection to state and managerial brutality in moments of class conflict to a more comprehensive vulnerability to physical force within and outside continually shifting categories of community.[121]

Yet, the jute mill women had a reputation for being violent and adversarial. Forms of protest, mentioned earlier, which avoided confrontation with the management cannot explain this reputation. The problem is, of course, that the evidence points in two opposite directions. Women were mentioned as victims, as 'tractable' labour or when they opposed or 'broke' strikes. Elsewhere, they appear in the records as chief instigators in crowds. Samares Basu when describing the initiation of a strike in a jute mill said, 'first it was Chhedi (a Bilaspuri woman) who hit the sahib on his forehead with her thick and heavy silver bangle' or, 'Apparao's wife Sarama suddenly attacked the *barababu* like a tigress ... Hiralal's *meheraru* (woman) gave him a hard kick on his face with her heavy anklet'.[122] In the trial against the 'rioteers' of the Shyamnagar Jute Mill strike of July 1939, a manager is reported to have said that 'workers streamed out shouting *maro maro* ... throwing bricks at the office ... Ulangini ... was gesticulating wildly and urging on the mob'. In the same case, A. Houston, Overseer of the Hessian Department deposed, 'about 20 women were trying to enter his department ... one woman was very excited and the rest started throwing bobbins'.[123]

Women's prominent role in direct confrontation with authority has been noted in other historical contexts.[124] To say this is not to suggest that there is an essentially 'feminine' mode of protest. There can be little doubt that women did sometimes play the lead both in strikes and in violent protest, within or outside trade unions. But media and official records may have dwelled more on women's adversarial roles to amplify female deviancy. Women workers were regarded as sexually deviant and managers, the police and even union officials were discomfited by rough and disorderly women in the public space. Factory women were seen as 'public women' not only because they were working in the public sphere of production, but because they were perceived as inextricably linked with prostitution. When women strikers violated gender norms by going out on the streets – a symbolically male space, but one also frequented

[121] These arguments have been detailed in an earlier article. Samita Sen, 'Honour and Resistance: Gender, Community, and Class in Bengal, 1920–40', in S. Bandopadhyay et al. (eds.), *Bengal: Communities, Development and States*, New Delhi, 1984.
[122] Translated from Samares Basu, 'Jalsha', *Galpasangraha*, I, p. 340, Calcutta, 1978.
[123] *Amrita Bazar Patrika*, 9 August 1939.
[124] Humphries, 'Class Struggle and Resistance'.

by prostitutes – women's labour militancy reinforced associations between waged work and sexual deviancy.

Yet for this very reason, women's explosive and violent actions must have been particularly significant. Such female aggression marked a radical departure from the conventional norms of feminine behaviour and the very 'public' nature of their action, both conducted in the public space and subjected to public comment as they were, must have served as a powerful testimony to extreme injustice. Their aggressive and forceful behaviour may indeed have reflected a new confidence to 'speak' on their own behalf. In the mill towns, gender relations were in flux and working-class men and women sought to work out new identities. Different forms of protest, especially strikes, provided the vehicle through which they explored and elaborated these identities. Despite the apparent paucity of gender-specific issues in working-class politics (like equal pay for equal work), the posing of common class demands may have meant different things for men and women. For women, the espousal of wage demands was more than a struggle to make ends meet; it was an assertion of their right to economic independence. As indeed their demand for maternity benefit sought for the first time to give an economic basis to motherhood.

There are not many well-recorded instances of what can be called 'women's strikes', either in terms of the demands made by the strikers or in terms of active and predominant participation of women. I shall take up the cases of two such strikes – the Ludlow Jute Mill strike of 1928 and the Shyamnagar Jute Mill strike of 1939. These reflect the working women's attempt to negotiate and contest their gender identities. Their need for economic independence and their role as the chief provider and mainstay of their children were the two important planks on which these strikes were nailed. In the mill towns, cohabitation patterns had become more fluid and households more unstable. Women had often to bear sole responsibility for their children, they were in more replaceable 'unskilled' jobs and, unlike most men, had no base in the village. These factors lent a greater desperation to women's struggles and influenced their response to class challenges. At the May Day rally of 1940 in Calcutta, Dukhmat's speech was a plea for children's welfare: their children were starving and had no protection from the rain and the sun.[125] Since they were responsible for feeding their children, women, especially those working for a pittance in the rice mills, responded readily to the food movement following the 1942 famine.[126]

[125] *Amrita Bazar Patrika*, 2 May 1940.
[126] Chakravarty, *Communists in India's Women's Movement*, pp. 21–6. The prominence of women in food riots, noted in many cultures, has been ascribed to similar reasons.

In case of the Ludlow Mill strike of 1928, women had broken an earlier strike organised by the union on the promise of a 25 per cent wage hike. When the management failed to come through, the women workers staged a strike on their own. The manager tried to get away with another promise,[127] but this time the women would not rejoin without a written undertaking,[128] and some 8,000 workers were locked out. Meanwhile six Telugu-speaking women of the preparing department and two men were arrested and taken to the mill.[129] Shortly afterwards 300 women and a number of men marched to the mill and demanded their release. One description notes that a 'large number of women sympathisers followed the prisoners into the office and demanded their release' and when the manager refused they started throwing stones.[130] A riot ensued in which several police officers, mill *durwans*, and seven women were injured.[131]

It appears that only the women had gone on strike, and there was pressure on them to rejoin, since the mill could not otherwise be opened. The company pleaded financial inability to raise wages, but by then the arrests had 'stiffened the women's attitude'.[132] Two oppressive *jamadars*, dismissed by the terms of the earlier settlement, were reappointed to pressurise the women and they were 'almost by force carrying on the affairs of the mill'.[133] Besides, the women were upset at being accused of *hat*-looting of which they claimed to be innocent. The harsh measures won the sympathy of workers in neighbouring mills. Yet, despite the efforts of Bengal Chatkal Mazdoor Union, on 20 June about half the workers, including 450 of the original women strikers, joined work. The final settlement was negotiated by K. C. Roychoudhury. The wage rise was not granted.[134]

Another such strike was the Shyamnagar Jute Mill strike in 1939. A widow with four small children to support wanted re-employment and '2,000 workers suddenly left their machines at the call of one woman employee'.[135] The woman, Tetri, had been in permanent employment in the batching department of Mill No. 1 for ten years.[136] 'A hungry woman mill worker with four children, who has recently become a

M. I. Thomas and Jennifer Grimmet, *Women in Protest, 1800–1850*, London, 1982. Women were often prominent in *hat* and *bazar* lootings during strikes and riots (Ludlow strike of 1928). *Amrita Bazar Patrika*, 23 August 1928.

[127] *Ananda Bazar Patrika*, 11 June 1928.   [128] Ibid.
[129] *Amrita Bazar Patrika*, 23 August 1928.   [130] Ibid.
[131] *Ananda Bazar Patrika*, 13 June 1928; *Amrita Bazar Patrika*, 9 August 1928.
[132] *Amrita Bazar Patrika*, 15 June 1928.   [133] *Ananda Bazar Patrika*, 25 June 1928.
[134] DIG CID IB, Weekly Reports, Secret, 1928.
[135] *The Statesman*, 4 July 1939; *Amrita Bazar Patrika*, 4 and 5 July 1939; *Ananda Bazar Patrika*, 12 July 1939.
[136] Ibid.

widow is reported to be the cause of the serious disturbances that took place in some of the jute mills near Calcutta.'[137] She wanted to return to her former post after the expiry of her six months' maternity leave. She was taken in as a *badli* and worked with occasional breaks for six months. Her earnings as *badli* were insufficient.[138] The manager had promised her a permanent job, the overseer asked her to await a vacancy, but 'this did not satisfy the woman'. A *durwan* (Mahabir Jamadar) tried to turn her out of the mill drawing her out by the hand. When she protested, Mahabir slapped her in a temper.[139] At that other women in the department stopped work and came out of the mill. They were attacked with *lathis* and some received injuries. Meanwhile other workers became aware of the incident and came out.[140] One report insisted, 'there is no doubt that the attempt to expel the woman worker led to a feeling of deep resentment among the workers in general'. A crowd, of whom, according to the management, 2,000 were women, surrounded the buildings and five Europeans were forced to retreat from room to room. It was when 'the mob was battering down the door of an inner room that an armed police force arrived and averted what might have proved to be serious consequences. Two European staff and a number of others were seriously injured.'[141] The police entered the *coolie* lines and arrested six women. Among the thirty-four ultimately brought to trial, seven were women.[142] As the women were being escorted by the police 'a crowd of about 800 men and women followed them to the *thana* carrying red flags ... shouting slogans and demanding (their) release'.[143]

These serious strikes were not felt to be the result of concerted action. The trouble at Shyamnagar was 'on the spur of the moment. It is not surprising that the sympathy of the fellow workers of the woman who had been stricken by a series of misfortunes was easily enlisted.'[144]

The Shyamnagar strike was soon followed by another in Victoria Jute Mill. Both these strikes came at the heels of a wave of strikes over identity cards. In Victoria, the earlier strikes had been precipitated by the 'women in preparing'. They had been the most difficult to get back to work even after the union had accepted the management's assurance that the identity card scheme had been abandoned.[145] A settlement was reached, but the batching, spinning, preparing and winding depart-

[137] *Amrita Bazar Patrika*, 6 July 1928.   [138] Ibid.
[139] *Ananda Bazar Patrika*, 12 July 1939.
[140] *Amrita Bazar Patrika*, 4 and 5 July 1939.   [141] *The Statesman*, 4 July 1939.
[142] They were Ulangini, Sumitra, Juina, Badlu, Sonekuar and Jasoda. *Amrita Bazar Patrika*, 9 August 1939.
[143] *Amrita Bazar Patrika*, 24 April 1940.   [144] *Amrita Bazar Patrika*, 6 July 1928.
[145] DUL, TDP, Victoria Jute Mills, MRD, 1939.

ments remained tense. When, after a few weeks, the women went out again, the strike was called, rather disingenuously, a 'lightning strike'. The 'trouble started over a woman worker again'. Sukowari was a temporary sweeper dismissed for bad work.[146] However, it was suspected that the management deprecated her popularity and suspected her of having played an active role in the earlier strike.[147] The workers wanted the dismissed women 'reinstated at once'.[148]

These instances of women's active involvement in initiating and sustaining violent confrontations with the management and police are especially notable for the specific articulation of their demands. In the case of the Ludlow Mill strike, women's discontent at an initial 'unjust' act on part of the management spiralled because of brutal reprisals. In case of the Shyamnagar strike, amidst the general and protracted violence the central issue remained the 'plight of a widowed mother'. The Victoria and Angus Mill strikes were over women's retrenchment, an issue becoming increasingly sensitive in the 1930s.

Women's active contribution to the 'epidemic' of strikes in the 1920s and especially the 1930s have been subsumed within the story of workers' progressive class consciousness. When women were considered at all in this narrative of class, they were relegated either to negative or to sacrificial roles. The focus was on the growing role and influence of the trade unions. Doubtless unions were playing an increasingly important role in workers' struggles and were partly responsible for the longer duration of strikes (as in the case of the Fort Gloster strike of 1928 which lasted six months to be followed soon by the general strike). Greater organisation, increasing staying power and unionisation by the communists discouraged the 'lightning' strikes of women, especially since they could rarely be brought to successful resolution. When these strikes did occur, unions often attempted to deflect the immediate and short-term demands raised by the women – wage rise or reinstatement – with more general industry-wide demands. In the settlements negotiated by the unions in the Ludlow, Shyamanagar and Victoria strikes the original issues were not mentioned. But the enhanced frequency of strikes was not so much due to unionisation as to a spiralling discontent. The Ludlow, Shyamnagar and Victoria strikes must be seen in that general context.

The militancy displayed by women may then be related to the IJMA's strategies of labour manipulation, cutting wages, increasing workloads

---

[146] WBSA, HPC 19 of 1939.   [147] *Amrita Bazar Patrika*, 6 July 1928.
[148] WBSA, HPC 19 of 1939. In July 1937, the Belvedere Jute Mill closed 'to enforce their demand that one female worker who has been dismissed be reinstated'. WBSA, HPC 60 of 1939.

and retrenching workers.[149] Such manipulation of labour was strongly
resisted, precipitating the general strike of 1929.[150] It would be a
mistake, however, to assume that the 1929 general strike marked an
irreversible progress towards class solidarity. In the next year, in
1930–31, mills changed from multiple to single shift – 60,000 workers,
about a fifth of the industry's workforce and about a ninth of the
factory labour in Bengal, lost their jobs. The government's fears of
labour unrest were, however, seen to be misplaced, because '[t]he
workers just quietly tied up their bundles and retreated to their base,
the village. Their disappearance was gradual, and almost unfelt.'[151] In
fact, in the change from multiple to single shift women's jobs were
more affected than men's. It was women who suffered more from
periodic unemployment and underemployment since they were concentrated in unskilled jobs where casual employment was more in
vogue. As managers played on the diversities of their interests, workers
found any simple expression of their collective interests highly elusive.
In many such cases, workers were unable to resist the mill owners'
manipulative strategies.

Men and women workers' interests diverged more sharply in the
1930s. Mechanisation, like labour manipulation, tended to affect
women more adversely. Apart from spinning, the jobs that were most
affected were those of women – in preparing and finishing. Women who
remained in employment suffered higher workloads and closer supervision. The attack on their jobs provoked many strikes and walk-outs by
the women. In Titagarh, Victoria, Angus and Shyamnagar Mills,
women in preparing and batching began to grow restive from the 1930s.
In all these mills, the 1937 general strike began either in these or the
spinning department. Even 'loyal *sirdars* ' failed to have any significant
influence on the militant women. And in all these cases the erstwhile
'turbulent' weavers 'remained loyal'. Managers attempted to break
women's solidarity by introducing young men into jobs like feeding

[149] WBSA, HPC 150 of 1931. WBSA, Comm. Comm., February 1933, A5–37 and June
1935, A35–48. The index of real wages fell from 60.2 in 1927 to 51 in 1930. A
recovery in 1931 was followed by steady decline in the next two years. Table 1.7. In
1935 when the IJMA was contemplating further reduction of hours of labour in the
jute mills, in a frank letter to the Government of Bengal, the Secretary admitted,
'restriction of production means restriction of employment. The numbers employed in
the jute mill industry have been greatly reduced in the last few years .... Further the
reduced numbers employed have been obliged to work reduced hours, and there is
little indication of their having appreciably benefited from the improvement in the
mills' position in the last two years.' IJMA, 12 August 1935, CSAS, Benthall Papers,
Box X.
[150] WBSA, HPC 150 of 1930.
[151] R. N. Gilchrist, *Labour and Land*, Calcutta, 1932,p. 23. The workers were given three
weeks' wages and dismissed in March, just before the normal exodus to Bihar and UP.

breakers which had previously been undertaken by women.[152] So women were not only losing their jobs to machines, but to men workers. Their proportion in the workforce began to decline steadily. All this made significant inroads into the resources available to women and contributed to their heightened sense of grievance.

Thus, women who were stereotyped as strike-breakers, may have found precisely in those roles which sometimes led them to break strikes, grounds for solidarity in moments of protest. Often, faced with the need to feed and care for children and dependants, women may have found that their role in the household militated against strikes which, in the short term, threatened household survival. However, women also shared with kin, caste and neighbouring women the task of housework and childcare in grinding poverty and without any help other than that which they could give each other. Doubtless, these networks played a role in strikes – to divide them along sectional lines of caste, region or community or to sustain common action. Shared antagonism to those who exploited them as workers – and as women – could quickly override everyday divisions, producing momentary or even tenacious unity. These solidarities were sometimes tenuous, no doubt, but were as significant as the spectacular expressions of dissensions. In such moments of unity and strength women workers explored new possibilities of what it meant to be women. And their idioms were far removed from traditional models based on subordination and dependency. Women's leadership in such confrontations reflected, at the very least, a will to challenge authority against both economic and sexual oppression – an attempt to explore a new gender identity through class-based struggles.

---

[152] DUL, TDP, MRD, Shyamnagar (North and South), Titagarh (1 and 2), Angus and Victoria, 1930–39.

Select bibliography

1. MANUSCRIPTS

CALCUTTA, WEST BENGAL STATE ARCHIVES, GOVERNMENT OF BENGAL
FILES

Commerce Department Commerce Branch files.
Commerce Department Emigration Branch files.
Commerce Department Labour Branch files.
Finance Department Commerce Branch files.
Finance Department Emigration Branch files.
General Department Education Branch files.
General Department Emigration Branch files.
General Department Miscellaneous Branch files.
General Department Sanitation Branch files.
General Proceedings.
Home Department Judicial Branch files.
Home Department Political Branch Confidential files.
Judicial Department Judicial Branch files.
Judicial Department Police Branch files.
Judicial Proceedings.
Political Department Police Branch files.
Revenue Department Agriculture Branch files.

CALCUTTA, PAPERS HELD IN THE OFFICE OF THE DEPUTY INSPECTOR
GENERAL OF POLICE, CRIMINAL INVESTIGATIONS DEPARTMENT,
INTELLIGENCE BUREAU

LONDON, GOVERNMENT OF INDIA FILES HELD AT THE INDIA OFFICE
LIBRARY AND RECORDS

Judicial Department.
Legislative Department.
Overseas and Industries Department.

NEW DELHI, NATIONAL ARCHIVES OF INDIA, GOVERNMENT OF INDIA
FILES

General Department files.
Home Department Judicial Branch files.
Home Department Sanitary Branch files.
Judicial Department Municipal Branch files.
Municipal Department files.

PATNA, BIHAR STATE ARCHIVES, GOVERNMENT OF BENGAL AND
GOVERNMENT OF BIHAR AND ORISSA FILES

General Department Emigration Branch files.
Monthly bundles of letters from the Secretary to the Commissioner, Patna
    Division.

2. UNPUBLISHED GOVERNMENT REPORTS

Curjel, D. F., 'Report of Dr Dagmar Curjel on the Conditions of Employment
    of Women Before and After Childbirth', 1923, West Bengal State Archives,
    Calcutta. Commerce Department Commerce Branch, April 1923, B77.
Balfour, M. I., 'Report of a Survey of Women Workers in Jute Mills, 1931–2',
    West Bengal State Archives, Commerce Department Commerce Branch,
    January 1932, A2–6.

3. PRIVATE PAPERS

CAMBRIDGE, CENTRE FOR SOUTH ASIAN STUDIES

Papers of Sir Edward Benthall.

DUNDEE, UNIVERSITY LIBRARY

Thomas Duff and Co. Papers – Shyamnagar Jute Mill Papers, Directors' Minute
    Books, Managers' Report to Directors.

4. PUBLISHED PAPERS OF ORGANISATIONS

Report of the Committee of Bengal Chamber of Commerce, Calcutta (Annual),
    1890–1930.
Report of the Committee of Indian Jute Mills' Association, Calcutta (Annual),
    1896–1940.

5. PUBLISHED GOVERNMENT REPORTS

*A Textbook of a Sanitary Science for the Use of Senior Students in English and Anglo-
    Vernacular Schools in India*, Simla Government 1890.
Annual Report on the Administration of the Bengal Presidency, 1879–80.

Annual Report of the Chief Inspector of Mines in India, Calcutta, 1905.

Annual Report on the Operation of the Factories' Act in Bengal, Calcutta, 1892–1939.

Annual Report of the Public Health Commissioner with the Government of India, 1920–5.

Bengal Unemployment Enquiry Committee, 1922–24, Calcutta, 1925.

Census of Bengal, H. Beverley, Calcutta, 1872.

Census of India, 1881, Central Provinces, 2 vols.

Census of India, 1891, Vol. III.

Census of India, 1901, Vols. V, VI and VII.

Census of India, 1911, Vols. V, VI, X.

Census of India, 1921, Vols. V, VI, XVI.

Census of India, 1931, Vol. I.

Deshpande, S. R., *Report on an Enquiry into the Family Budget of Industrial Workers in Howrah and Bally*, Delhi, 1946.

Directorate of Public Instruction, Bengal, *Plans for a Better Bengal*, Calcutta, 1944.

Dufferin, Lord, Report Submitted to the Viceroy, P. Nolan, *Report on the Condition of the Lower Classes of Population in Bengal*, Calcutta, 1888.

Final Report of the Survey and Settlement Operations in the Muzzaffarpur District, 1892–1899, C. J. Stevenson-Moore, Settlement Officer, North Bihar, Calcutta, 1901.

Final Report on the Survey and Settlement Operation in the District of Gaya, 1911–1918, E. L. Tanner, Settlement Officer, South Bihar, Patna, 1919.

Final Report on the Survey and Settlement Operations (under Chapter I of the Bengal Tenancy Act) in the District of Monghyr (south), 1905–1912, P. W. Murphy, Settlement Officer, South Bihar, Ranchi, 1914.

Final Report on the Survey and Settlement Operations in Saran District, 1893–1901, J. H. Kerr, Settlement Officer, Calcutta, 1903.

Foley, B., *Report on Labour in Bengal*, Calcutta, 1906.

General Administration Report, 1879–81, Chittagong, 1881–82.

General Administration Report for the year 1884, Calcutta, 1885.

Health Bulletin No. 15, 'Maternal Mortality in Childbirth in India: A Summary of the Investigation Conducted under the IRFA', 1925, Calcutta, 1928.

Health Bulletin No. 23, W. R. Aykroyd, 'The Nutritive Value of Indian Foods and the Planning of Satisfactory Diets', 1935–38, Calcutta, 1939.

In the Matter of Industrial Disputes in the Jute Textile Industry in West Bengal between the Employers of 9 specified Jute Mills and their Workmen: An Award, Government of West Bengal, Calcutta, 31 August 1948.

Indian Factories Act 1881

Indian Factories (Amendment) Act, 1891.

Indian Textile Factories Act, 1911.

Indian Factories (Amendment) Act, 1922.

Indian Factories (Amendment) Act, 1926.

Kennedy, Lt. Colonel W. M., *Report on the Working of the Assam Labour Board for the Year Ending 30 June 1916.*

Kerr, H. C., *Report of the Cultivation of and Trade in Jute in Bengal: The Bengal Jute Commission, 1873*, Calcutta, 1877.

Kerr, J. H, *Report of the Committee on Industrial Unrest in Bengal*, Calcutta, 1921.

Labour Enquiry Commission, Calcutta, 1896.

Labour Investigation Committee, A. Mukhtar, *Report on Rickshaw Pullers*, Government of India, Delhi, 1946.

S. R. Deshpande, *Report on an Enquiry into Conditions of Labour in the Jute Mill Industry in India*, Calcutta, 1946.

Miscellaneous Annual Report of the Presidency Division, 1902–03, WBSA, General Miscellaneous, November 1903, A19–22.

Offical Bulletin, No. IV, International Labour Organisation, November 1921.

Report of the Census of the Town and Suburbs of Calcutta, H. Beverley, Calcutta, 1881.

Report of the Commission to Enquire into the Working of the Factories in Bombay, Bombay, 1885.

Report of the Commissioners appointed under the Chairmanship of George Campbell to Enquire into the Famine in Bengal and Orissa in 1866.

Report of the Court of Enquiry appointed under Section 3 of the Trade Disputes Act, 1929 (Act VII of 1929), to investigate the Trade Dispute between Messrs. George Henderson & Co. Ltd., of 101/1, Clive Street, Calcutta, Managing Agents, Bally Jute Mill, Bally, district Howrah, and the workmen of the Weaving and Jute Departments of the said Mill, Government of Bengal, Calcutta, 1941.

Report of the Indian Factory Commision, Calcutta, 1891.

Report of the Indian Factory Labour Commission of 1908, 2 vols., London, 1909.

Report of the Indian Industrial Commission, 1916–18, Calcutta, 1917–18.

Report of the Inter-Departmental Conference held in London in 1917 to Consider Proposals for a New Assisted System of Emigration from India to British Guiana, Trinidad and Fiji, Calcutta, 1918.

Report of the Royal Commission on Labour in India, Vols. I, V and XI, London, 1931.

Report of the Textile Factories Labour Commission, London, 1907.

Report on the Emigration from the Port of Calcutta to British and Foreign Colonies, 1909–18.

Report on the Famine in Bengal, 1896–97, Calcutta, 1898.

Report on the Municipal Administration of Calcutta, 1920–21, Calcutta, 1921.

Report on the Working of the Inland Emigration Act in the Central Provinces for the Year Ending 30 June 1905, Calcutta, 1905.

Roychoudhury, A. C., *Report on an Enquiry into the Standard of Living of Jute Workers in Bengal*, 1930.

Rules Under the Act VI of 1901, Calcutta, 1903.

Shirres, L. P., *Memorandum on the Material Condition of the People of Bengal in the years 1892–93 to 1901–02.*

Sixth Half-yearly Report of the Indian Jute Mills Association, 1887.

Skrine, F. H. B., *Memorandum on the Material Condition of the Lower Orders in Bengal during the Ten Years from 1881–92*, Calcutta, 1892.

Smyth, Major Ralph, *Statistical and Geographical Report of the 24 Pergunnahs District*, Revenue Surveyor, Calcutta, John Gray, *Calcutta Gazette* office, 1857.

Social and Economic Status of Women Workers in India, Labour Bureau, Ministry of Labour, Government of India, 1953.

Socio-Economic Conditions of Women Workers in Textile, Khandsari and Sugar Products Industries, Labour Bureau, Ministry of Labour, Government of India, Delhi, 1984.

Stevenson-Moore, C. J., *Report on the Material Condition of Small Agriculturists and Labourers in Gaya*, Calcutta, 1898.

Working of the Act VI of 1901, Calcutta, 1904.

6. GAZETTEERS

Imperial Gazetteer, Oxford, 1908, Vols. VII, IX and XIII.

Middleton, A. P. and Mansfield, P. T. (revised ed.) *Bihar and Orissa District Gazetteers*, Saran, Patna, 1930.

Neville, H. R., *District Gazetteer of the United Province*, Ballia, Allahabad, 1907.

District Gazetteer of the United Province, Ghazipur, Allahabad, 1909.

District Gazetteer of the United Provinces, Jaunpur, Allahabad, 1908.

District Gazetteers of the United Provinces of Agra and Oudh, Benares, A Gazetteer, Allahabad, 1909.

O'Malley, L. S. S., *Bengal District Gazetteers*, Bankura, Calcutta, 1908.

Bengal District Gazetteers, Birbhum, Calcutta, 1910.

Bengal District Gazetteers, Burdwan, Calcutta, 1910.

and Monmohan Chakravarty, *Bengal District Gazetteers*, Hooghly, Calcutta, 1912.

Bengal District Gazetteers, Midnapore, Calcutta, 1911.

Bengal District Gazetteers, Monghyr, Calcutta, 1909.

Bengal District Gazetteers, 24 Parganas, Calcutta, 1914.

Bihar and Orissa District Gazetteer, Champaran (revised ed.) R. E. Swanzy, Patna, 1938.

Bihar and Orissa District Gazetteer, Cuttack (revised ed.) E. R. J. R. Cousins, Patna, 1933.

Bihar and Orissa District Gazetteer, Monghyr (revised ed.) Patna, 1926.

Bihar and Orissa District Gazetteer, Patna (revised ed.) J. F. W. James, Patna, 1924.

Bihar and Orissa District Gazetteer, Puri (revised ed.) P. T. Mansfield, Patna, 1929.

7. NEWSPAPERS AND JOURNALS

Abalabandhab, Calcutta.
Alumni Association Bulletin, All India Institute of Hygiene and Public Health.
Amrita Bazar Patrika, Calcutta.
Ananda Bazar Patrika, Calcutta.
Antahpur, Calcutta.
Bama Bodhini Patrika, Calcutta.
Bangalakshmi, Calcutta.
Baromas, Calcutta.
Bulletin of Indian Industies and Labour.
Calcutta Review, Calcutta.

Education Gazette, Uttarpara.
Ekshan, Saradiya, Calcutta.
Gharer Katha, Calcutta.
Grihastha Mangal, Calcutta.
Indian Journal of Medical Research.
Indian Journal of Social Work.
International Labour Review.
Jayasree, Calcutta.
Journal of the Association of Medical Women in India.
Journal of Royal Asiatic Society.
Journal of Tropical Paediatrics.
Labour Gazette.
Mahila, Calcutta.
Manushi, Delhi.
Mashik Basumati, Calcutta.
Modern Review, Calcutta.
Prabasi, Calcutta.
Saradiya Basumati, Calcutta.
The Statesman, Calcutta.
Welfare, Calcutta.

8. BOOKS, ARTICLES AND THESES

Anderson, Michael R., 'Work Construed: Ideological Origins of Labour Law in British India to 1918', in Peter Robb (ed.), *Dalit Movements and the Meaning of Labour in India*, Delhi, 1993, pp. 87–120.
Arnold, David (ed.), *Imperial Medicine and Indigenous Societies*, Delhi, 1989.
Arnold, David, *Colonizing the Body: State Medicine and Epidemic Diseases in Nineteenth Century India*, Berkeley, 1993.
Bagchi, A. K., *Private Investment in India, 1900–1939*, Cambridge, 1972.
'The Ambiguity of Progress: Indian Society in Transition', *Social Scientist*, 13, 3, March 1985, pp. 3–14.
Bagchi, Jasodhara, 'Representing Nationalism: Ideology of Motherhood in Colonial Bengal', *Economic and Political Weekly*, 20–27 October 1990, pp. WS65–71.
Balfour, M. I. and Young, R., *The Work of Medical Women in India*, Oxford and London, 1929.
Ballhatchet, K., *Race, Sex and Class under the Raj: Imperial Attitudes and Policies and their Critics, 1793–1905*, London, 1980
Bandopadhyay, Brajendranath (ed.), *Sambadpatre Shekaler Katha*, 2 vols., 4th edn. Calcutta, 1977.
Bandopadhyay, Tarasankar, 'Chaitali Ghurni', *Tarasankar Rachanavali*, I, Calcutta, 1972, reprint 1973, pp. 1–82.
Banerjee, Himani, 'Fashioning a Self: Educational Proposals for and by Women in Popular Magazines in Colonial Bengal', *EPW*, October 1991, pp. WS51–62.
Banerjee, N., 'Working Women in Colonial Bengal: Modernization and Margin-

alization', in K. Sangari and S. Vaid (eds.), *Recasting Women: Essays in Colonial History*, New Delhi, 1989, pp. 269–301.

Banerjee, S., *The Parlour and the Streets: Elite and Popular Culture in the Nineteenth Century Calcutta*, Calcutta, 1989.

Bardhan, Kalpana, 'Women's Work, Welfare and Status: Forces of Tradition and Change in India', *Economic and Political Weekly*, 20, 50–1, December 1985, pp. 2207–20, 2261–9.

Barnes, F. D., 'Final Report of the Lady Doctor, Maternity Benefits to the Industrial Workers', *Labour Gazette*, September 1922, pp. 31–8.

Barnet-Ducrocq, Françoise, *Love in the Time of Victoria: Sexuality, Class and Gender in the Nineteenth Century*, London, 1991.

Basu, Samares, 'Jalsha', *Galpasangraha*, I, Calcutta, 1978.

Basu, Subho, 'Workers' Politics in Bengal, 1890–1929: Mill-towns, Strikes and Nationalist Agitations', Ph.D thesis, Cambridge University, 1994.

Bayly, C. A., *Rulers, Townsmen and Bazaars: North Indian Society in the Age of British Expansion, 1770–1870*, Cambridge, 1983.

Beech, Mary Higdon, 'The Domestic Realm in the Lives of Hindu Women in Calcutta', in H. Papanek and G. Minault (eds.), *Separate Worlds: Studies of Purdah in South Asia*, Delhi, 1982, pp. 110–38.

Bhattacharya, N. and Chatterjee, A. K., *A Sample Survey of Jute Workers in Greater Calcutta* (mimeo), Calcutta, 1973.

Bhatter, B. D. and Nemenyi, L., *The Jute Crisis*, Calcutta and London, 1936.

Borthwick, Meredith, *The Changing Role of Women in Bengal, 1894–1905*, Princeton, 1984.

Bose, Sugata, *Agrarian Bengal: Economy, Social Structure, and Politics, 1919–1947*, Cambridge, 1986.

Peasant Labour and Colonial Capital. Rural Bengal since 1770, New Cambridge History of India, III-2, Cambridge, 1993.

Boserup, E., *Women's Role in Economic Development*, New York, 1970.

Broughton, G. M., *Labour in Indian Industries*, London, 1924.

Buchanan, D. H., *The Development of Capitalist Enterprise in India*, New York, 1934.

Buchanan, F. H., *An Account of the District of Bhagalpur in 1810–11*, Patna, 1939.

An Account of the District of Purnea in 1809–10, Patna, 1928.

An Account of the District of Shahabad in 1812–13, Patna, 1934.

An Account of the Districts of Bihar and Patna, 1811–12, 2 vols., Patna, 1928.

A Geographical, Statistical and Historical Description of the District or Zilla of Dinajpur in the Province or Soubah of Bengal, Calcutta, 1833

Carroll, Lucy, 'Law, Custom and Statutory Social Reform: The Hindu Widows' Remarriage Act of 1856', *Indian Economic and Social History Review*, 20, 4, 1983, pp. 363–88; repr. J. Krishnamurty (ed.), *Women in Colonial India: Essays on Survival Work and the State*, Delhi, 1989.

Chakrabarty, Dipesh, 'Communal Riots and Labour: Bengal's Jute Mill-Hands in the 1890s', *Past and Present*, 91, May 1981, pp. 140–69.

Rethinking Working Class History, Bengal 1890–1940, Princeton, 1989.

'Sasipada Banerjee: A Study in the Nature of the First Contact of the Bengali Bhadralok with the working Classes of Bengal', *Indian Historical Review*, January 1976, pp. 339–64.

Chakrabarty, Dipesh, and Ranajit Dasgupta, 'Some Aspects of Labour History in Bengal in the Nineteenth Century: Two Views', *Occasional Paper No. 40*, Centre for Studies in Social Sciences, Calcutta, October 1981.

Chakrabarty, Usha, *Condition of Bengali Women around the Second Half of the Nineteenth Century*, Calcutta, 1963.

Chakravarti, Uma, 'Social Pariahs and Domestic Drudges: Widowhood among Nineteenth Century Poona Brahmins', *Social Scientist*, 21, 9–11, 1993. pp. 130–58.

Chakravarty, Lalita, 'Emergence of an Industrial Labour Force in a Dual Economy – British India, 1880–1920', *Indian Economic and Social History Review*, 15, 3, 1978, pp. 249–327.

Chakravarty, Renu, *Communists in India's Women's Movement 1940–1950*, New Delhi, 1980.

The Women's Movement in India, Communist Today, Communism and Women No. 5, Communist Party Publication, 1973.

Chandavarkar, R. S., 'Industrialization in India before 1947: Conventional Approaches and Alternative Perspectives', *Modern Asian Studies*, 19, 3, 1985, pp. 623–68.

The Origins of Industrial Capitalism in India: Business Strategies and the Working Classes in Bombay, 1900–1940, Cambridge, 1994.

'Workers' Politics and the Mill Districts in Bombay between the Wars', *Modern Asian Studies*, 15, 3, 1981, pp. 603–47.

Chatterjee, P., 'Agrarian Structure in Pre-Partition Bengal', in Asok Sen et al., *Perspectives in Social Sciences 2: Three Studies on the Agrarian Structure in Bengal*, Calcutta, 1982.

'The Nationalist Resolution of the Women's Question', in K. Sangari and S. Vaid (eds.), *Recasting Women: Essays in Colonial History*, Delhi, 1989, pp. 233–53.

Chatterjee, Ratnabali, 'Prostitutes in Nineteenth Century Bengal: Construction of Class and Gender', *Social Scientist*, 21, 9–11, 1993, pp. 159–72.

'The Queens' Daughters: Prostitutes as an Outcast Group in Colonial India', Report, Chr. Michelsen Institute, 1992.

Chatterji, Joya, *Bengal Divided. Hindu Communalism and Partition, 1932–1947*, Cambridge, 1995.

Chattopadhaya, H. P., *Internal Migration in India: A Case Study of Bengal*, Calcutta, 1987.

Chattopadhyay, K. P., *A Socio-Economic Survey of Jute Labour*, Department of Social Work, Calcutta University, 1952.

Chattopadhyay, K. (ed.), *Bharat Shramajibi*, Calcutta, 1975.

Chattopadhyay, Manju, 'Dukhmat Didi – Ek Sangrami Charitra', *Kalantar, Saradiya*, 1988, pp. 147–52.

Sramiknetri Santoshkumari, Manisha, Calcutta, 1984.

Chattopadhyay, Saratchandra, 'Mahesh' (first published in *Bangabali*, 1922, reproduced in *Pallisri*, 1922) *Sulabh Sarat Samagra*, II, Calcutta, 1989, pp. 1728–32.

Chaturvedi, H. K. and Chattopadhyay, K. P. (eds.), 'How Jute Workers Live', *Science and Culture*, 12, 8, February 1947, pp. 376–9.

Chowdhry, Prem, *The Veiled Women. Shifting Gender Equations in Rural Haryana 1880–1990*, Delhi, 1994.

Clow, A. G., 'A Historical Survey', *Bulletin of Indian Industries and Labour*, 37, 1926.

'Indian Factory Law Administration', *Bulletin of Indian Industries and Labour*, 8, 1921.

Curjel, D. F. and Acton, H. W., 'Jute Dermatitis', *Indian Journal of Medical Research*, 12, 2, 1924–25, pp. 257–60.

Improvement of the Conditions of Childbirth in India, Calcutta, 1918.

'Report on the Conditions of Childbirth in India' (Countess of Dufferin Fund), *Indian Journal of Medical Research*, 8, 2, October 1920.

Dang, Kokila, 'Prostitutes, Patrons and the State: Nineteenth Century Awadh', *Social Scientist*, 21, 9–11, 1993, pp. 173–96.

Das, Bhupati Ranjan, 'Paribaric Kahinite Chatkaler Itihas' (The History of the Jute Industry in Family Stories), *Baromash*, *Saradiya*, 1988, pp. 70–85.

Das, R. K., *Factory Labour in India*, Berlin, 1923.

History of Indian Labour Legislation, Calcutta University, 1941.

Indian Working Class, Bombay, 1948.

Labour Movement in India, Berlin, 1923.

Plantation Labour in the Indian Tea Industry, Bombay, 1954.

'Women Labour in India', *International Labour Review*, October–November 1931, pp. 372–545.

Das, Sarat Chandra, *Satidharma*, Calcutta, 1911.

Dasgupta, Ranajit, 'Factory Labour in Eastern India – Sources of Supply, 1885–1946', *Indian Economic and Social History Review*, 8, 3, 1976, pp. 277–329.

'Indian Working Class and Some Recent Historiographical Issues, *Economic and Political Weekly*, 24 February 1996, L-27–31.

'Material Conditions and Behavioural Aspects of Calcutta Working Class 1875–1899', *Occasional Paper No. 22*, Centre for Studies in Social Sciences, Calcutta, 1979.

'Migrant Workers, Rural Connexions and Capitalism: The Calcutta Jute Industrial Labour, 1890s to 1940s', Indian Institute of Management (Calcutta) Working Paper Series, April 1987, Mimeograph.

Dasgupta, Sashibhusan, *Obscure Religious Cults of Bengal*, Calcutta, 1969.

Datta, K. L., *Report on the Enquiry into the Rise of Prices in India*, III, Calcutta, 1914.

Davin, Anna, 'Imperialism and Motherhood', *History Workshop*, 5, Spring 1978, pp. 9–67.

De Haan, Arjan, 'Towards a Single Male Earner: The Decline of Child and Female Employment in an Indian Industry', *Economic and Social History in the Netherlands*, 6, 1994, pp. 145–67.

Unsettled Settlers: Migrant Workers and Industrial Capitalism in Calcutta, Rotterdam, 1994.

Dewey, C., 'The Government of India's "New Industrial Policy", 1900–1925; Formation and Failure', in C. J. Dewey and K. N. Choudhuri (eds.), *Economy and Society*, Delhi, 1979, pp. 215–57.

Dwarkadas, Kanji, *45 Years with Indian Labour*, London, 1962.

Eddy, George Sherwood, *The New World of Labour*, London, 1924.

Eisenstein, H., *Contemporary Feminist Thought*, London, 1984.

Eisenstein, Z. (ed.), *Capitalist Patriarchy and the Case for Socialist Feminism*, New York and London, 1979.

Engels, Dagmar, *Beyond Purdah? Women in Bengal, 1890–1939*, Delhi, 1996.

'The Changing Role of Women in Bengal, c. 1890–c. 1930, With Special Reference to British and Bengali Discourse on Gender', Ph.D thesis, London University, 1987.

Engels, F., 'The Origin of the Family, Private Property and the State', E. Leacock (ed.), New York, 1972.

Forbes, Geraldine, 'Medical Careers and Health Care for Indian Women: Patterns of Control', *Women's History Review*, 3, 4, 1994, pp. 515–30.

'Managing Midwifery in India', in D. Engels and S. Marks (eds.) *Contesting Colonial Hegemony: State and Society in Africa and India*, London, 1994, pp. 152–72.

Fruzetti, L. M., *The Gift of a Virgin: Women, Marriage and Ritual in a Bengali Society*, New Brunswick, 1982.

Fuller, Mrs Marcus B., *The Wrongs of Indian Womanhood*, London, 1900, reprint, Delhi, 1984.

Gangopadhyay, Mohanlal, *Ashamapta Chatabda*, Calcutta, 1963.

Garnsey, E., 'Women's Work and Theories of Class and Stratification', in A. Giddens and D. Held (eds.) *Classes, Power and Conflict: Classical and Contemporary Debates*, Berkeley, 1982, pp. 425–45.

Garratt, G. T., 'The Indian Industrial Worker', *The Economic Journal*, 42, 167, 1932, pp. 394–402.

Ghosh, J. N., *Social Evil in Calcutta and Method of Treatment*, Calcutta, 1923.

Ghosh, Parimal, 'Colonial State and Colonial Working Conditions: Aspects of the Experience of Bengal Jute Mill Hands, 1881–1930', *Economic and Political Weekly*, 30 July 1994, pp. 2019–27

'Communalism and Colonial Labour: Experience of Calcutta Jute Mill Workers, 1880–1930', *Economic and Political Weekly*, 28 July 1990, pp. PE61–72.

'Emergence of an Industrial Labour Force in Bengal: A Study of the Conflicts of the Jute Mill Hands with the State 1880–1930', Ph.D thesis, Jadavpur University, 1984.

Gilchrist, R. N., *Labour and Land*, Calcutta, 1932.

Glenn, Evelyn Nakano, 'Racial Ethnic Women's Labour: The Intersection of Race, Gender and Class Oppression', in C. E. Bose, R. Feldberg and N. Sokoloff (eds.), *Hidden Aspects of Women's Work*, Women and Work Research Group, New York, 1987, pp. 46–73.

Goswami, O., 'Agriculture in Slump: The Peasant Economy of East and North Bengal in the 1930s', *Indian Economic and Social History Review*, 21, 3, pp. 335–64.

'Collaboration and Conflict: Indian and European Capitalists and the Jute Industry of Bengal, 1919–1939', *Indian Economic and Social History Review*, 19, 2, pp. 141–79.

Industry, Trade and Peasant Society: The Jute Economy of Eastern India, 1900–1947, Delhi, 1991.

'Multiple Images: Jute Mill Strikes of 1929 and 1937 Seen Through Other's Eyes', *Modern Asian Studies*, 21, 3, pp. 547–83.

'Sahibs, Babus and Banias: Changes in Industrial Control in Eastern India, 1918–50', *Journal of Asian Studies*, 48, 2, pp. 289–309.

Grant, J. B., *The Health of India*, Oxford Pamphlets of Indian Affairs No. 12, Bombay, 1943.

Grierson, G. A., *Bihar Peasant Life*, 1885, reprinted Delhi, 1975.

Notes on the District of Gaya, Calcutta, 1893.

Seven Grammars of the Dialects and Sub-dialects of the Bihari Language, Calcutta, 1883.

Guha, Ranajit, 'Dominance Without Hegemony and its Historiography', *Subaltern Studies VI*, Delhi, 1989.

Gupta, Indrajit, *Capital and Labour in the Jute Industry*, Bombay, 1953.

Gupta, P. S., 'Notes on the Origin and Structuring of the Industrial Labour Force in India, 1880 to 1920', in R. K. Sharma (ed.), *Indian Society – Historical Probings in Memory of D. D. Kosambi*, Delhi, 1974, pp. 421–41.

Gupta, Raj Bahadur, *Labour and Housing in India*, Calcutta, 1930.

Hershatter, Gail, *The Workers of Tianjin, 1900–1949*, California, 1986.

Honig, Emily, *Sisters and Strangers: Women in the Shanghai Cotton Mills, 1919–1949*, California, 1986.

Hassain, Hameeds, *The Company Weavers of Bengal: The East India Company and the Organization of Textile Production in Bengal, 1750–1813*, New Delhi, 1988.

Humphries, Jane, 'Class Struggle and Resistance of the Working Class Family', *Cambridge Journal of Economics*, 1, 3, 1977, pp. 241–58.

Hossain, Hameeda, *The Company Weavers of Bengal: The East India Company and the Organization of Textile Production in Bengal, 1750–1813*, New Delhi, 1988.

Hunter, W. W., *A Statistical Account of Bengal, 24 Parganas*, I, London, 1876.

IJMA, *Handbook and Directory of the Jute Industry*, Indian Jute Mills Asociation, Calcutta, 1967.

Inden, Ronald B. and Nicholas, Ralph W., *Kinship in Bengali Culture*, Chicago, 1977.

Irvine, W., 'Baiswari Folk-songs collected by J. N. Rae', *Journal of Royal Asiatic Society*, 53, 2, 1, 1884, pp. 232–59.

Jacobson, D., 'Purdah and the Hindu Family', in H. Papanek and G. Minault (eds.), *Separate Worlds: Studies of Purdah in South Asia*, Delhi, 1982, pp. 81–109.

Jeffery, Patricia, *Frogs in a Well: Indian Women in Purdah*, London, 1979.

Jeffery, Roger, *The Politics of Health in India*, Berkeley, 1987.

Johnstone, Thomas and Sime, John F., *Exploitation in India*, Dundee, 1926.

Kelman, Janet Harvey, *Labour in India*, London, 1923.

Kishwar, M, 'Daughters of Aryavarta', in J. Krishnamurty (ed.), *Women in Colonial India: Essays on Survival, Work and the State*, Delhi, 1989, pp. 78–113.

Kumar, D. (ed.), *The Cambridge Economic History of India*, II, Cambridge, 1983.

Kumar, Kapil, 'Rural Women in Oudh, 1917–1947: Baba Ramchandra and the Women's Question', in K. Sangari and S. Vaid (eds.), *Recasting Women: Essays in Colonial History*, New Delhi, 1989, pp. 337–69.

Kumar, Radha, 'Family and Factory: Women in the Bombay Cotton Textile Industry 1919–1939', *Indian Economic and Social History Review*, 20, 1, 1983, pp. 81–110.

Kung, Lydia, *Factory Women in Taiwan*, Studies in Cultural Anthropology, No. 5, Epping, 1983.

Lal, Brij V., 'Kunti's Cry: Indentured Women on Fiji Plantations', in J. Krishnamurty (ed.), *Women in Colonial India: Essays on Survival, Work and the State*, Delhi, 1989, pp. 163–79.

Liddle, Joanna and Joshi, Rama, *Daughters of Independence: Gender, Caste and Class in India*, New Delhi, 1986.

Lokanathan, P. S., *Industrial Welfare in India*, Madras, 1929.

Mahalonobis, P. C., *Bengal Board of Economic Enquiry, Draft Report – Jagaddal: First Sample*, Statistical Laboratory, Calcutta, 1941.

Mani, Lata, 'Contentious Traditions: The Debate on Sati in Colonial India', in K. Sangari and S. Vaid (eds.), *Recasting Women: Essays in Colonial History*, Delhi, 1989, pp. 88–126.

Marshall, P. J., 'The Company and the Coolies: Labour in Early Calcutta', in Pradip Sinha (ed.), *The Urban Experience: Calcutta, Essays in Honour of Professor Nitish R. Ray*, Calcutta, 1987.

Marshman, J. C., 'Notes on the Right Bank of Hooghly', *Calcutta Review*, 5, 1845.

Matheson, C. M., *Indian Industries – Yesterday, Today and Tomorrow*, Oxford, 1930.

Mazumdar, Vina and Sharma, Kumud, 'Sexual Division of Labor and the Subordination of Women: A Reappraisal from India', in Irene Tinker (ed.), *Persistent Inequalities. Women and World Development*, Oxford, 1990.

Meller, H. E., 'Urbanisation and the Introduction of Modern Town Planning Ideas in India, 1900–1925', in C. Dewey and K. N. Choudhuri (eds.), *Economy and Society*, Delhi, 1979, pp. 330–50.

Minault, Gail, 'The Extended Family as Metaphor and the Expansion of Women's Realm', in G. Minault (ed.), *The Extended Family: Women and Political Participation in India and Pakistan*, Delhi, 1981, pp. 3–18.

Misra, Baniprasanna, 'Industrialization: An Appraisal in the Light of the Indian Factory Commission', 1890, *Indian Economic and Social History Review*, 12, 3, 1975, pp. 203–28.

Moore, H. L., *Feminism and Anthropology*, Blackwell, 1988 (reprint, 1991).

Morris, Morris D., *The Emergence of the Industrial Labour Force in India: A Study of the Bomaby Cotton Mills, 1854–1957*, Los Angeles and Berkeley, 1965.

Mukherjee, K., 'Trend in Real Wages in the Jute Textile Industry from 1900 to 1951', *Artha Vijnana*, 2, 1, March 1960.

Mukherjee, M., 'Impact of Modernization on Women's Occupations: A Case Study of Rice Husking Industry of Bengal', *Economic and Social History Review*, 20, January–March 1983, pp. 27–45.

Mukherjee, Radhakamal, *Social Disorganisation in India*, Convocation Address for the Sir D. Tata Graduate School of Social Work, Bombay, 1939
Mukherjee, Radhakamal (ed.), *Fields and Farmers in Oudh*, Calcutta, 1929.
Mukherjee, S. K., *Indian Sex-Life and Prostitution*, Calcutta, c. 1943.
Mukherjee, S. K. and Chakrabarty, J. N., *Prostitution in India*, Calcutta, c. 1945.
Mukherjee, S. N., *Calcutta: Myths and History*, Calcutta, 1977.
Mukhopadhyay, Nandalal, *Swami-stri*, Calcutta, 1933.
Murshid, Ghulam, *Reluctant Debutante: Response of Bengali Women to Modernization, 1849–1905*, Rajshahi, 1983.
Naidu, Mohun C. R. D., *Mohun's Coming Man*, I, Calcutta, 1931.
Nehru, Jawaharlal, *An Autobiography* (first published in 1936) Centenary Edition, New Delhi, 1985.
Nehru, S. K. (ed.), *Our Cause: A Symposium by Indian Women*, Kitabistan, Allahabad, 1937.
Newton, J. L., Ryan, Mary P. and Walkowitz, J. R., *Sex and Class in Women's History*, History Workshop Series, London, 1983.
O'Hanlon, Rosalind, *Caste, Conflict and Ideology: Mahatma Jotirao Phule and Low Caste Protest in Nineteenth Century Western India*, Cambridge, 1985.
For the Honour of My Sister Countrywomen: Tarabai Shinde and the Critique of Gender Relations in Colonial India, Oxford, 1994.
'Issues of Widowhood, Gender and Resistance in Colonial Western India', in Douglas Haynes and Gyan Prakash (eds.), *Contesting Power, Resistance and Everyday Social Relations in South Asia*, Delhi, 1991, pp. 62–108.
Oldenberg, Veena Talwar, *The Making of Colonial Lucknow, 1856–1877*, Princeton, 1984.
Olsen, A. B. and Olsen, M. E., *Health for the Millions*, London, 1908.
Omvedt, Gail, 'Migration in Colonial India: The Articulation of Feudalism and Colonialism by the Colonial State', *Journal of Peasant Studies*, 7, 2, January 1980, pp. 185–212.
Orkney, J. M., 'Legislation and the Indigenous Dai', *Journal of the Association of Medical Women of India*, 31, 1943, pp. 114–17.
'The Health of Indian Women and Children', *Journal of the Association of Medical Women of India*, 32, 1944, pp. 5–16.
Panandikar, S. G., *Industrial Labour in India*, Bombay, 1933.
Pandey, Gyan, 'Peasant Revolt and Indian Nationalism: The Peasant Movement in Awadh, 1919–1922', in Ranajit Guha (ed.), *Subaltern Studies I*, Oxford, 1982.
Papanek, Hanna, 'Purdah: Separate Worlds and Symbolic Shelter', in H. Papanek and G. Minault (eds.), *Separate Worlds: Studies of Purdah in South Asia*, Delhi, 1982, pp. 3–53.
Patrick, H. and Meissner, Larry, *Japanese Industrialisation and its Social Consequences*, California, 1976.
Purcell and Hallsworth, *Report on Labour Conditions in India*, The Trade Union Congress, General Council, London 1928.
Rao, B. Shiva, *The Industrial Worker in India*, London, 1939.
Rao, M. N. and Ganguly, H. C., 'Women Labour in Jute Industry of Bengal – A Medico-Social Study', *Indian Journal of Social Work*, 2, 1950–51, pp. 181–91.

'VD in the Industrial Worker', *Indian Journal of Social Work*, 2, 1950–51, 122–34.

Ray, R. K., 'The Kahar Chronicle', *Modern Asian Studies*, 21, 4, 1987, pp. 711–49.

Read, M, *From Field to Factory*, Student Christian Movement, London, 1927.

Indian Peasant Uprooted, London, 1931.

Land and Life of India, London, 1934.

Roberts, Elizabeth, *A Woman's Place, An Oral History of Working Class Women 1890–1940*, Blackwell, 1984.

Ross, Ellen, 'Survival Networks: Women's Neighbourhood Sharing in London before World War I', *History Workshop Journal*, 15, Spring 1983, pp. 4–77.

Safa, H. I., 'Class Consciousness Among Working Class Women in Latin America: Puerto Rico', in June Nash and H. I. Safa (eds.), *Sex and Class in Latin America: Women's Perspectives on Politics Economics, and the Family in the Third World*, Massachussetts, 1980, pp. 69–85.

Saleeby, C. W., *The Eugenic Prospect*, London, 1921.

Sarkar, Sumit, *Swadeshi Movement in Bengal:1903–1908*, New Delhi, 1973.

Sarkar, Tanika, *Bengal, 1928–1934: The Politics of Protest*, Delhi, 1987.

'A Book of Her Own, A Life of Her Own: Autobiography of a Nineteenth Century Woman', *History Workshop Journal*, Autumn 1993, pp. 35–65.

'Hindu Conjugality and Nationalism in late Nineteenth Century Bengal', in Jasodhara Bagchi (ed.), *Indian Women: Myth and Reality*, Calcutta, 1995, pp. 98–116.

'Politics and Women in Bengal: The Conditions and Meaning of Participation', in J. Krishnamurty (ed.), *Women in Colonial India: Essays on Survival, Work and the State*, Delhi, 1989, pp. 231–41.

Searle-Chatterjee, M., 'Reversible Sex Roles: The Special Case of Benares Sweepers', *Women In Development*, 2, 1981.

Sen, A. K., *Employment, Technology and Development*, Delhi, 1975.

Sen, Dinesh Chandra, *Grihasri*, Calcutta, 1915.

Sen, Mukhta, 'Child Welfare Work', *Journal of the Association of Medical Women of India*, 32, 1944, pp. 17–9.

Sen, Samita, 'Class or Gender? Women and the Bengal Jute Industry', in Arjan de Haan and Samita Sen (eds.), *A Case for Labouristory. The Jute Industry in Eastern India*, Calcutta, forthcoming

'Gendered Exclusion: Domesticity and Dependence in Bengal', in Angelique Janssens (ed.), 'The Rise and Decline of the Male Breadwinner Family?', *International Review of Social History Supplement 5*, 42, 1997, pp. 65–86.

'Honour and Resistance: Gender, Community and Class in Bengal, 1920–40', in Sekhar Bandopadhyay et al. (eds.), *Bengal: Communities, Development and States*, New Delhi, 1984, pp. 209–54.

'Motherhood and Mothercraft: Gender and Nationalism in Bengal', *Gender and History*, 5, 2, 1993, pp. 231–43.

'Unsettling the Household: Act VI (of 1901) and the Regulation of Women Migrants in Colonial Bengal', in Shahid Amin and Marcel van der Linden (eds.), 'Peripheral Labour? Studies in the History of Partial Proletarianization', *International Review of Social History Supplement 4*, 41, 1996, pp. 135–56.

'Women Workers in the Bengal Jute Industry, 1890–1940: Migration, Motherhood and Militancy', Ph.D Thesis, Cambridge University, 1992.

Sengupta, Nibha and Bagchi, K., 'Dietary Habits of Bengali Pregnant and Lactating Women of Low Socio-Economic Groups in Calcutta', *Alumni Association Bulletin, All India India Institute of Hygiene and Public Health*, 10, 19, 1961, pp. 11–16.

Sethna, N. J., 'Nutritional Problems Among Infants of Low Income Group Families', *Alumni Association Bulletin, All India Institute of Hygiene and Public Health*, 12, 23, 1961, pp. 25–7.

Sharma, G. K., *Labour Movement in India*, Delhi, 1963

Sharma, Ursula, *Women's Work, Class and Urban Household: A Study of Shimla, North India*, London, 1986.

Women, Work and Property in North-Western India, London, 1980.

Siddiqui, M. K. A., 'Caste among the Muslims of Calcutta', in S. Sinha (ed.), *Cultural Profile of Calcutta*, The Indian Anthropological Society, Calcutta, 1972, pp. 26–49.

Singh, A. Menefee, 'Rural-to-Urban Migration of Women in India: Patterns and Implications', in J. T. Fawcett et al. (eds.), *Women in the Cities of Asia*, Essex, 1984, pp. 81–107.

Sinha, P., *Calcutta in Urban History*, Calcutta, 1978.

Sivasubramonian, S., 'Income from the Secondary Sector in India, 1900–1947', *Indian Eeconomic and Social History Review*, 14, 4, 1977, pp. 427–92.

Tarkalankar, Umakanta, *Bidhaba Bibaha Nishedhak*, Calcutta, 1877.

Thadani, Veena N. and Todaro, M. P., 'Female Migration: A Conceptual Framework', in J. T. Fawcett et al. (eds.), *Women in Cities of Asia: Migration and Urban Adoption*, Essex, 1984, pp. 36–59.

Thomas, M. I. and Grimmet, J., *Women in Protest, 1800–1850*, London, 1982.

Thorner, Daniel and Thorner, Alice, *Land and Labour in India*, Bombay, 1962.

Throner, A., 'Women's Work in Colonial India: 1881–1931', Seventh European Conference on Modern Asian Studies, London, July 1981.

Tomlinson, B. R., 'Colonial Firms and the Decline of Colonialism in Eastern India, 1914–47', *Modern Asian Studies*, 15, 1981, pp. 455–86.

Walkowitz, J. R., *Prostitution and Victorian Society: Women, Class and the State*, London, 1980.

Wallace, D. R., *The Romance of Jute*, Calcutta, 1909, 2nd edn., London, 1928.

Washbrook, David A., 'Progress and Problems: South Asian Economic and Social History c. 1720–1860', *Modern Asian Studies*, 22, 1, 1988, pp. 57–96.

Yang, Anand, *The Limited Raj: Agrarian Relations in Colonial India, Saran District, 1793–1920*, Delhi, 1989.

Young, K., Walkowitz, C. and McCullagh, R., *Of Marriage and the Market*, London, 1981.

Zachariah, K. C., *A Historical Study of Internal Migration in the Indian Subcontinent, 1901–1931*, London, 1964.

Zhao, Zhangwei, 'Demographic Influences and Household Formation in Chinese History – A Simulation Study', paper presented to the 6th International Conference of the Association for History and Computing, Denmark, 28–30 August 1991 (unpublished).

9. INTERVIEWS

Bandopadhyay, Narayan, November–December 1989, Bally.

Basu, Kamala, October 1989, Naihati.

Chakraborty, Purnabrata, October 1989, Calcutta.

Chattopadhyay, Gautam, 1988–1989, Calcutta.

Chattopadhyay, Kshetromohan, December 1989, Titagarh.

Chattopadhyay, Manju, 1988–89, Calcutta.

Dasgupta, Prabhabati, interview by K. P. Rangachary, 24 April 1968, Delhi, Nehru Memorial Museum and Library.

Dasgupta, Ranjan, November and December 1989, Calcutta.

Dasi, Durgabala, December 1989, Fort Gloster (North Mill).

Debi, Prabhasini, November 1989, Calcutta.

Gupta, D., October 1989, Calcutta.

Hazra, Bejoy, November 1989, Bauria.

Naskar, Mathur, November and December 1989, Bauria.

Pasricha, Shanti, 1988–89, Calcutta.

Shau, Kashinath, December 1989, Titagarh.

Shau, Lilabati, January 1989, Nuddea Jute Mill, Kankinara.

Sengupta, Dr P., March 1991, Patna.

Index

accidents in mill 106–8

badli 50, 126, 243–4

Chakrabarty, Dipesh 8, 89 n., 118 n.,
    214 n., 217–20 ff.
Chandavarka, R. S. 6, 47 n., 49 n., 51,
    65 n., 90 n., 220
child labour
    inspection of 95–6
    prohibition of 152–6
    regulation of 94, 96, 98
Contagious Diseases Act 191–2, 194–6
Curjel, Dagmar 100, 108, 114–15, 124,
    147, 139–40, 150, 154 n., 166,
    171–3, 186–7, 199

Dasgupta, Prabhabati 219, 228, 232–4
Dasgupta, Ranajit 49 n., 52
Devi, Santoshkumari 219, 228, 232–4
domesticity 8–10, 17–18, 64–5
    and the circumscription of women's
        space 61–4, 133–5, 137–41
    and the construction of womanhood
        56–8, 60–2, 147–8
    brahmanical ideology of 56–9
dowry 86–8, 141
Dufferin Report 67, 74 n., 82, 85–6

Factories Acts 11–12, 92–9, 113, 116, 142
    and labour legislation 95–9, 124
family
    and devaluation of women's labour
        54–6, 59–60, 83–6, 113–15, 181–3
    and notions about marriage and female
        sexuality 18–19, 178–80, 186–90
    and organisation of agricultural
        production 54–6
    role in deployment of labour 65, 74–81
    and social practices like dowry 86–8

household
    and women's paid work 137–40, 142–3

budget 74–5
migration decisions and strategy 7
organisation of labour 7, 54
reproduction 53
size and composition 67–9
women's work 75–6, 79, 224–5
housing 130–3
    and crime 190–1
    and housework 135–6
    privacy 130, 132
    and prostitution 211
    and strikes 222–3
    and women's dependence on men 132–3
    and women's migration 130

IJMA 6, 36–8, 42, 92, 103–4, 227
    and maternity benefits 166–76
    production control policies 39–41,
        116–19
    resistance to labour legislation 31, 94–9,
        152
    strategies to control labour 39–50,
        116–17, 119–24
ILO 49, 118, 142, 144
    and Conference of 1927 170
    and the Washington Convention 97–8,
        146, 148, 165, 171
Indian Factory Commission 33–4, 70, 180

jute industry
    handloom sector 13–14, 23
    importance in Bengal economy 13–16
    industrial strategies 6–7, 41–2, 91
    labour control strategies 24–6, 144–6,
        245–6
    location and origins 14–16, 22–4

Kelman, Janet 100, 103, 108, 135, 187

labour force
    and communalism 217–18, 240
    casualisation of 32–3, 53, 227
    condition of 51–3

264